EMBEDDED AUTONOMY

EMBEDDED AUTONOMY

STATES AND INDUSTRIAL TRANSFORMATION

Peter Evans

PRINCETON UNIVERSITY PRESS   PRINCETON, NEW JERSEY

Library of Congress Cataloging-in-Publication Data

Evans, Peter B., 1944–
Embedded autonomy : states and industrial transformation / Peter Evans.
  p. cm.
Includes bibliographical references and index.
ISBN 0-691-03737-X (CL) ISBN 0-691-03736-1 (PBK)
1. Computer industry—Government policy—Brazil.   2. Computer
industry—Government policy—India.   3. Computer industry—
Government policy—Korea (South)   4. Industries—Government policy—
Brazil.   5. Industries—Government policy—India.   6. Industries—
Government policy—Korea (South)   I. Title.
HD9696.C63B7345   1995
338.4'7004—dc20   94-31963

This book has been composed in Sabon

Printed in the United States of America

10   9   8   7   6   5   4   3   2   1

(Pbk.)
10   9   8   7   6

ISBN-13: 978-0-691-03736-3

ISBN-10: 0-691-03736-1

For Benjamin, Alexander, and Peter Bret,
A next generation looking for its own answers,
with love and hope

Contents

List of Tables	ix
Acknowledgments	xi
List of Abbreviations and Acronyms	xvii
1. States and Industrial Transformation	3
2. A Comparative Institutional Approach	21
3. States	43
4. Roles and Sectors	74
5. Promotion and Policing	99
6. State Firms and High-Tech Husbandry	128
7. The Rise of Local Firms	155
8. The New Internationalization	181
9. Lessons from Informatics	207
10. Rethinking Embedded Autonomy	227
Notes	251
References	287
Index	311

Tables

6.1 Cross-Country Comparisons of R&D Effort 148

7.1 Growth of Informatics Revenues in Brazil, 1980–1989 162

7.2 University-Trained Employment in the Brazilian
Informatics Industry, 1979–1989 162

7.3 Top Ten Brazilian Computer Firms, 1986 162

7.4 Major Brazilian Electronics Groups, 1987 164

7.5 Indian Computer and Software Production/Exports, 1984–1988 169

7.6 Top Ten Indian Informatics Firms, 1990 169

7.7 Sales by Korean Participants in the Computer Industry, 1986 175

7.8 Growth of Korean Computer and Semiconductor Production 175

7.9 Korean Exports of Televisions, Computers,
and Semiconductors, 1980–1989 176

8.1 Foreign Firms in the Korean Electronics Industry: Share of
Production by Type of Ownership and Subsector, 1980–1988 199

Acknowledgments

BOOKS ARE curious products. To begin with, they take too long to write, much too long if the final product is the only reward. If an author is lucky the process is sufficiently rewarding in itself to make up for the distant and eventual character of the product. I was among the lucky. By looking at information technology, I gave myself an impeccably serious excuse for exploring new milieus and acquiring arcane knowledge. I found computer companies fascinating; state bureaucracies were equally mysterious in their own way. Eventually I had to relinquish the process and make sure that there was a product, but it was still the process that made the project worthwhile.

Just as the assumption that research and writing are simply a means of producing a book misrepresents reality, the conventional equation of authorship and ownership is a convenient fiction at best. In my case, I relied throughout on the insights and generosity of people who understood both computers and states much better than I did. Ideally, they should be the "owners" of this book. Instead, like any book, this one illustrates the extent to which intellectual proprietorship is akin to theft. Most of those who contributed the ideas and insights had no control over the final shape of the manuscript. Many would disagree fundamentally with the way that I have interpreted their reality. Even acknowledging their help implicates them in an outcome for which I am the only responsible party.

Acknowledging collaborators who are part of the academic world is easier. The references and notes that pepper the text are a start, and I will try to complement them here. Nevertheless, the most careful set of acknowledgments would still fail to reflect the true etiology of the ideas that went into this book. Even if the question of origins is arbitrarily limited to the decade during which I was actually working on the book, many contributors would be missing from the best list I could construct: colleagues and students whose casual hallway conversations sparked a new way of tackling a problem, unknown questioners at seminars who raised points I had not thought of before, antagonists whose views reshaped my own without my realizing it.

Even a full list of contributors would not, of course, absolve me of responsibility. I was an idiosyncratic filter for the myriad ideas and observations that came together to form the final manuscript. I sifted different versions of the reality I was trying to capture, elevating some and relegating others. In that sense it is very much "my" book. But this is not the place to resolve the perplexing relationship between authorship and ownership. The best I can do here is to flesh out the footnotes and references with a brief record of some of the contributions, diffuse and specific, that stick in my mind.

Recording the contributions is complicated by the fact that this book is only the latest reincarnation of my efforts to look at states and industrial transformation. Many of the ideas it contains have been tried out before as articles and tempered by the critiques and comments that those articles generated. More specifically, chapters 2 and 3 draw on my 1989 and 1992 articles on the state (Evans 1989b, 1992b). I hope I have tightened and clarified these earlier formulations. Chapters 5 through 7 draw on a series of articles on the computer industries of Brazil, India, and Korea published from 1986 to 1992 (Evans 1986a, 1989a, 1989c, 1992a; Evans and Tigre, 1989a, 1989b). Some of the detail presented in the articles is condensed in this version and the argument is more focused, but the basic analysis is the same. The numerous editors and reviewers of those articles and the even more numerous colleagues and practitioners who read and commented on them all played a role in shaping this book.

Diffuse intellectual influences are the hardest to capture, but I can say that the Committee on States and Social Structures played an important role in the genesis of this book. Housed first in the Social Science Research Council and later in the Russell Sage Foundation, the committee incubated my ideas about how states connect to societies for several years before I thought of researching the information technology industry. While all of its members have influenced my thinking, Albert Hirschman deserves special mention. His elegant and insightful analysis of institutional factors in economic development has been a model for me since my days as an undergraduate.

A diffuse set of debts is also owed to colleagues at the various institutions that put up with my comings and goings during the time that I was working on this project. From Brown University to the Graduate School of International Relations and Pacific Studies (IRPS) at the University of California, San Diego, to the University of New Mexico to Berkeley, I never lacked intellectual stimulation or collegial support. These institutions provided concrete forms of support as well. The Center for the Comparative Study of Development at Brown provided early infrastructural assistance. Colleagues at San Diego were kind enough to include me in a Pacific Rim research grant that helped fund my fieldwork in Korea. The Latin American Institute at the University of New Mexico supported both research and writing while I was there. The International and Area Studies Program and the Center for Latin American Studies at Berkeley helped fund the final stages of the research and writing. I am also indebted to one institution where comings and goings are a strictly enforced rule rather than something to be tolerated. My ideas on variations in state structure were formulated during a very rewarding and enjoyable year at the Center for the Advanced Study in the Behavioral Sciences in Stanford. Financial support from National Science Foundation Grant BNS87–00864 and the John Simon Guggenheim Memorial Foundation made this year possible.

While institutions and colleagues in the United States played an essential role, the bulk of my debts are held abroad—in Brazil, India, and Korea. Like much of my intellectual life, this book began in Brazil. In 1984 a fellowship from the Centro Brasileiro de Análise e Planejamento (CEBRAP) gave me the chance to become fascinated with the informatics industry. It also gave me the chance to meet Paulo Tigre, who became my most important collaborator. The Tinker Foundation provided the resources that enabled Paulo and me to continue our collaboration. Antonio Botelho was an important contributor to this project. A later grant from the Tinker Foundation brought us together with Claudio Frischtak, whose astute analysis of high-technology industry is drawn on repeatedly in chapters 5 through 8. Over the course of the ten years that followed my stay at CEBRAP, I got to know actors on all sides of the drama that was the Brazilian informatics industry. Everyone, from the original *barbudinhos* to owners of local firms to executives in IBM and the other major multinationals to the hard-pressed staff of SEI to local politicians, spent time they did not have to spare explaining to a naïve North American what was going on in the complex world of the Brazilian informatics industry. Some did so repeatedly. Mario Dias Ripper not only allowed me to take advantage of his original thinking on how the information technology industry was evolving, but even read and commented on the manuscript. Ivan da Costa Marques kept reappearing in different roles: first as owner of a small private firm, then as president of COBRA, then as a historian of the Brazilian informatics experience. His willingness to share his insights was a constant. Many others, including Simón Schvartzman, whose story introduces chapter 7, were equally generous.

I owe my initial interest in the Korean case to two students who worked with me at Brown University—Eun Mee Kim and Myong Soo Kim. During my stay in Korea, the Institute for Far Eastern Studies at Kyungnam University in Seoul was my home, literally as well as intellectually while I did fieldwork. The researchers and staff of the institute not only made me feel welcome and comfortable but also tolerated my inept lack of Ping Pong skills. A special debt is owed to Lee Su-hoon, who made my stay in Korea possible.

Once again, executives and government officials were extraordinarily gracious and tolerant in helping an inquisitive, uninformed outsider find his way through the maze of local industrial development, but the fieldwork was possible only because of the skillful assistance of Kim (now

Park) Mi Kyoung and Lew Soek-jin. A number of Korean colleagues, including Choi Byung Sun, Choi Jang Jip, Kim Byung Kook, Kim Doo-sub, Lim Hyun-Chin, and Moon Chung-in, not only were generous hosts but helped shaped my understanding of state-society relations in Korea. I am particularly indebted to Kim Kwang Woong of Seoul National University, without whose aid the fieldwork could not have been successfully completed. After my return, excellent research by Kang Mungu, Sang In-jun, and Jon Hae-ja enabled me to analyze and update the material.

My fieldwork in India was made possible by a grant from the Indo-American Fellowship program of the Indo-U.S. Subcommission on Education and Culture. The American Institute for Indian Studies offered me invaluable support during my stay in Delhi. Indian colleagues Mrinal Datta-Chaudhuri, Ashok Desai, Vijay Kelkar, and Kuldeep Mathur were extremely helpful, not just in giving me a sense of the complexities of their country, but also in helping me connect these complexities to more general theoretical issues. In addition, I had the good fortune to make contact with researchers like Eswaran Sridharan and C. R. Subramanian, whose extensive work on the information technology industry already encompassed much of the research I had in mind. For a third time I was amazed at the willingness of busy entrepreneurs and equally dedicated state managers to share their time and expertise with me. I am also especially grateful to Ashok Parthasarathi for his thorough critique of my first write-up of the Indian material.

Once my work moved from the field to the word processor, an embarrassingly large number of readers critiqued and reshaped the manuscript. Dietrich Rueschemeyer's ever-sound judgment helped me avoid a number of obvious errors. The final manuscript also benefited from Theda Skocpol's perspicacious reading of an early draft. The advice of Evelyne Huber and John Stephens was crucial in reshaping successive drafts of the introduction and conclusion. Peter Katzenstein worked hard to get me to improve the arguments connecting states and computers. Barbara Stallings provided both encouragement throughout the project and a clear-headed critique of the results. Michael Burawoy went far beyond the call of collegial duty, reading successive drafts, providing extensive comments, and using all the skills he has acquired as a veteran thesis adviser to prod me into getting the job done.

Among the many other readers who provided comments and criticisms, a number stand out in my mind. Alice Amsden, Pranab Bardhan, Martin Carnoy, Chris Chase-Dunn, Wally Goldfrank, Mark Granovetter, Ron Herring, Chalmers Johnson, Atul Kohli, Joel Migdal, Michael Rogin, Robert Wade, John Waterbury, and John Zysman all added new ideas and helped make the manuscript more coherent and convincing.

Often I succeeded in resisting my friends' advice, but to the extent that they prevailed, readers of this book have every reason to be grateful.

Students as well as colleagues have played an important role in the evolution of this book. Berkeley's sociology students deserve special credit. While enduring neglect as I tried to make a series of continually postponed deadlines for preparation of the final manuscript, they remained a superb "test audience" and an endless source of new ideas. My use of Patrick Heller's Kerala case in chapter 10 is only the most obvious example. In addition, a number of them worked directly on the research and production of the final manuscript. Brian Folk did an excellent job pulling together material on information technology in Europe. Youngmin Yun made it possible for me to update my understanding of the Korean case. Shana Cohen performed innumerable tasks, including a very useful critical reading of chapters 5 through 8. Several versions of the manuscript benefited from the painstaking reading and corrections of John Talbot. Beth Bernstein worked unrelentingly to turn the final version of the manuscript into something with which a publisher could live.

Some debts go well beyond this book. Having Louise Lamphere as a partner was a central source of sanity during the years this book was under way. Despite her full engagement with a professional career more hectic than my own, I always knew that I could count on her love and support when I needed it. My three sons, Benjamin, Alexander, and Peter Bret, were also sources of love and sanity. They were sources of hope as well. Whenever I got discouraged about the dubious world that is my generation's legacy, their enthusiasm, resourcefulness, and capacity for inventing the unexpected made me feel that the future could not be so bad after all. That is why this book is dedicated to them.

Abbreviations and Acronyms

ABICOMP	Association of the Brazilian Computer and Peripherals Industries (Brazil)
ACER	Taiwanese computer manufacturer
APPD	Association of Data Processing Professionals (Brazil)
ASIC	application-specific integrated circuit
AT&T	American Telephone and Telegraph (United States)
BARC	Bhabha Atomic Research Center (India)
BEL	Bharat Electronics Ltd. (India)
BNDE	National Economic Development Bank (Brazil)
BNDES	National Bank for Economic and Social Development (Brazil) (same as BNDE except for name change)
CAD	computer-aided design
CAM	computer-aided manufacture
CAPRE	Commission for the Coordination of Electronic Processing Activities (Brazil)
C-DOT	Centre for the Development of Telematics (India)
CEPD	Council on Economic Planning and Development (Taiwan)
CMC	Computer Maintenance Corporation (India)
COBRA	Computadores e Sistemas Brasileiros SA (Brazil)
CONCEX	Foreign Trade Council (Brazil)
COSL	Citicorp Overseas Software Ltd. (India)
CPqD	Telebrás' Center of Research and Development (Brazil)
CSN	Compania Siderúgica Nacional (Brazil)
CTI	Centro Technológica para Informática (Brazil)
CVRD	Brazil's state-owned iron exporter
DACOM	Korean data communications company owned by KTA together with private stockholders
DASP	Department of Public Administration (Brazil)
DCM	Delhi Cloth Mills (India)
DEC	Digital Equipment Corporation, second largest U.S. computer firm
DEPIN	Departamento de Política de Informática e Automação (Brazil)
DG	Data General, U.S. computer firm
DISNET	NIC system for information on India's districts
DOE	Department of Electronics (India)
DOT	Department of Telecommunications (India)

DRAM   dynamic random access memory (semiconductor memory chip)
ECIL   Electronic Corporation of India Ltd.
EIAK   Electronics Industry Association of Korea
EPB   Economic Planning Board (Korea)
EPBAX   electronic private branch automatic exchange
ESPRIT   European Strategic Program for Research and Development in Information Technologies
ESS   electronic switching system
ETRI   Electronics and Telecommunications Research Institute (Korea)
FERA   Foreign Exchange Regulation Act (India)
FKI   Federation of Korean Industries
FKTU   Federation of Korean Trade Unions
GEIA   Grupo Executivo para Indústria Automobilística (Brazil)
GTE-111   Grupo de Trabalho Especial-111 (Brazil)
HCL   Hindustan Computers Ltd., largest local firm in India
HP   Hewlett-Packard (United States)
IAS   Indian Administrative Service
IC   integrated circuit
ICL   International Computers Limited (England)
ICS   Indian Civil Service
IDB   Industrial Development Bureau (Taiwan)
IDM   Indian computer company acquired by HCL
IISCO   Indian Iron and Steel Company
IIT   Indian Institutes of Technology
IMPRESS   Indian railway reservation system designed by CMC
INTEL   leading U.S. manufacturer of microprocessors
ISDN   integrated service digital network
ISI   import-substituting industrialization
IT   information technology
ITA   Air Force Institute of Technology (Brazil)
ITI   Indian Telephone Industries, state-owned telephone producer
KIST   Korean Institute of Science and Technology
KIT   Korea Institute of Technology
KMT   Kuomintang; Nationalist party (Taiwan)
KTA   Korean Telecommunications Authority
JDB   Japan Development Bank
JECC   Japan Electronic Computer Corporation
LDP   Liberal Democratic party (Japan)
MC&A   joint venture between SID and IBM (Brazil)

Minicom	Ministry of Telecommunications (Brazil)
MITI	Ministry of International Trade and Industry (Japan)
MOC	Ministry of Communications (Korea)
MOST	Ministry of Science and Technology (Korea)
MTI	Ministry of Trade and Industry (Korea)
NAIS	National Administrative Information System (Korea)
NAS	National Advanced Systems, manufacturer of mainframes (United States)
NCCC	National Computerization Coordination Committee (Korea)
NIC	National Informatics Centre (India)
NICs	newly industrializing countries
NICNET	NIC'satellite-based communications system (India)
NIIT	National Institute of Information Technology (India)
NRC	National Resources Commission (Taiwan)
NTT	Japan's state-owned telecommunications monopoly
OEM	original equipment manufacture; equipment made for another company to sell under its own brand name
ÖGB	Austrian Trade Union Federation
OLTP	on-line transaction processing
ONGC	Oil and Natural Gas Corporation (India)
ÖVP	People's party (Austria)
PC	personal computer
PNDII	Brazilian development plan by General Geisel
POSCO	Pohang Iron and Steel Company Ltd. (Korea)
POSDATA	subsidiary of POSCO providing value-added network services to other businesses
POSIX	standardized version of UNIX
POSTEC	Pohang Institute of Technology (Korea)
PROCOMP	Brazilian computer firm
PSI	Indian computer firm
RAX	rural automatic exchange designed by C-DOT (India)
SAILNET	communications network provided for Indian steel authority
SBC	Brazilian Computation Society
SCL	Semiconductor Complex Ltd. (India)
SCOPUS	Brazilian computer firm
SECOMU	Seminars on Computation at the University (Brazil)
SEI	Secretaria Especial de Informática (Brazil)
SID	Brazilian informatics firm
SIDERBRÁS	holding company in charge of Brazil's state-owned steel companies
SISNE	indigenous Brazilian version of MS-DOS

SOD	early Brazilian-designed operating system
SOE	state-owned enterprise
SOX	Brazilian clone of UNIX
SPARC	Sun brand name for chips and work stations (United States)
SPÖ	Socialist party (Austria)
SNI	National Intelligence Service (Brazil)
SUFRAMA	Superindencia for Amazonia (Brazil)
TCS	Tata Consultancy Systems (India)
TDX	ETRI's electronic switching system (Korea)
TICOM	Korean supermini
TITAN	Telecommunications, Instrumentation, and Telecontrol in an Automated Network; automated monitoring system for Indian oil and natural gas wells
TNC	transnational corporation
TUL	Tata Unisys Ltd. (India)
UNIX	software operating system designed and owned by AT&T
USX	U.S. Steel
VAN	value-added network
VAX	DEC minicomputer
VLSI	very large scale integrated circuits
VÖI	Federation of Austrian Industrialists
WIPRO	Indian business group; includes WIPRO Information Technology Ltd., a large local producers of computers, and WIPRO Systems Ltd., a software specialist
X-OPEN	consortium of American and European companies founded in 1986 to establish international UNIX standards
ZFM	Manaus free zone (Brazil)

EMBEDDED AUTONOMY

1

States and Industrial Transformation

A PERENNIALLY popular Brazilian joke about two lions evokes one way of seeing the state. Escapees from the zoo, the two lions take different paths. One goes to a wooded park and is apprehended as soon as he gets hungry and eats a passerby. The second remains at large for months. Finally captured, he returns to the zoo sleek and fat. His companion inquires with great interest, "Where did you find such a great hiding place?" "In one of the ministries" is the successful escapee's answer. "Every three days I ate a bureaucrat and no one noticed." "So how did you get caught?" "I ate the man who served coffee for the morning break," comes the sad reply.

The moral is clear: bureaucrats do nothing and are never missed; even other bureaucrats care more about their morning coffee than about anything their colleagues do. The joke is popular because it affirms the conviction that Third World states deliver little of value. It is also popular because it converts bureaucrats from predators to prey. Identifying with the lion, listeners reverse their usual self-perception as victims of the state.

For those with less sense of humor, the quotidian power of the state over their individual lives can take on disturbing proportions. As Anita Desai (1991, 3–4) puts it, "In the present time, in which the laws and whims of politicians and bureaucrats are as pervasive and powerful as those of the gods, not only must a minister be propitiated before he will issue a license, allot a house, or award a pension, but so must every clerk through whose hands the relevant file passes." This is not a lament about dictatorship or authoritarian repression, it is a complaint about how the Third World state conducts "business as usual" in relation to ordinary citizens.

Identification with the escaped lion is natural, but until less hierarchical ways of avoiding a Hobbesian world are discovered, the state lies at the center of solutions to the problem of order. Without the state, markets, the other master institution of modern society, cannot function. We do not spend our valuable time standing in lines in front of the counters of bureaucrats because we are masochists. We stand there because we need what the state provides. We need predictable rules, and these in turn must have a concrete organizational structure behind them. We need some organizational reflection, however imperfect, of general as opposed to individual interests. We need something beyond caveat emptor to sustain the process of exchange. We need "collective goods" like sewage systems, roads, and schools.

Attempts to dismantle the state or make it wither away risk perverse consequences. Communist revolutionaries who fought to install a system that would lead to the state's "withering away" ended up constructing state apparatuses more powerfully repressive than those of the age of absolutism. Fervent calls for the dismantling of the state by late-twentieth-century capitalist free-marketeers served to derail the state's ability to act as an instrument of distributive justice, but not to reduce its overall importance.

From the poorest countries of the Third World to the most advanced exemplars of welfare capitalism, one of the few universals in the history of the twentieth century is the increasingly pervasive influence of the state as an institution and social actor.[1] None of which is to say that the existing states give us what we need. Too often we stand in line in vain. The contradiction between the ineradicable necessity of the state in contemporary social life and the grating imperfection with which states perform is a fundamental source of frustration. Dreams of cannibalizing bureaucrats are one response. Analyzing what makes some states more effective than others offers less immediate satisfaction but should be more useful in the long run.

Since analyzing states entails almost as much hubris as pretending to run them, it is important to place some boundaries on the endeavor. My boundaries are narrow and clear. I have focused on only one of the state's tasks—promoting industrial growth. The empirical discussion is even more specific—the growth of local information technology (IT) industries. In addition, I am primarily concerned with a particular set of states—newly industrializing countries (NICs). Within this set, the empirical narrative draws primarily on the experiences of Brazil, India, and Korea during the 1970s and 1980s. Despite the boundaries, the hubris remains. The underlying aim is to understand state structures and roles, relations between state and society, and how states contribute to development.

In this chapter I will try to do four things. I will begin with a brief excursus on how responsibility for economic transformation has become increasingly central to the state's role. Then I will set economic transformation at a national level in the context of a global division of labor. The third section sets out a telegraphic sketch of the argument to be developed over the course of the chapters that follow. Finally, I will try to explain the conceptual approach and strategies of investigation that lie behind the analysis.

States and Economic Transformation

States remain, as Weber defined them, "compulsory associations claiming control over territories and the people within them,"[2] but Weber's definition does not reduce the complexities of analyzing what states do. The first step in making analysis manageable is separating out the different roles that states perform. Making war and ensuring internal order are the classic tasks. In the contemporary world, fostering economic transformation and guaranteeing minimal levels of welfare are not far behind.

"Realists" tell us that, as sovereign entities in an anarchic world, states must concern themselves above all with the conditions of military survival.[3] Gilpin (1987, 85) puts it succinctly: "The modern nation-state is first and foremost a war-making machine that is the product of the exigencies of group survival in the condition of international anarchy." Historical analysis makes it clear that the task of war making, more than any other, drove the construction of the modern state.[4] War making is also the task that allows the state most easily to portray itself as the universal agent of societal interests.

War making is one justification for the state's monopoly on violence; avoiding Hobbesian chaos internally is the other. Here again the state projects itself as an agent of the universal interests of society. What happens when a state disintegrates demonstrates that the claim is at least partially valid, as the citizens of contemporary Somalia can bitterly attest. Yet the claim also masks other aspects of the state's role.

When it defends sovereignty and internal order, the state is also, as Charles Tilly (1985) puts it, running a "protection racket" on its own behalf. Classic Marxist analysis reminds us that states are instruments for dominating the societies they serve. State actions reflect and enforce disparities of social power on behalf of the privileged. When the state exercises its monopoly on violence internally, its identification with the interests of the nation is no longer automatic. All states would like to portray themselves as carrying out a project that benefits society as a whole,[5] but sustaining this image requires continuous effort.[6]

Making war and enforcing internal order are classic roles, shared by ancient and modern states. In modern times, a third role has increasingly stolen the limelight. As political survival and internal peace are more often defined in economic terms, states have become responsible for economic transformation. There was always a connection between economic success and the ability to make war; economic failure meant eventual geopolitical decline. Now the state's economic role goes beyond being a means to military ends. It is a source of legitimacy in itself as well as a means to accomplishing the classic goals of military survival and internal order.

Being involved in economic transformation has two different facets. First of all, it means becoming implicated in the process of capital accumulation. Wealth creation is no longer considered just a function of nature and markets; effective statecraft is involved as well. Eliciting entrepreneurship and facilitating the creation of new productive capacities require a more complicated involvement in the affairs of the citizenry than simply eliciting loyalty and enforcing good behavior. The capacity required for what I will call the state's "transformative role" is correspondingly greater.

Once the state is implicated in the process of capital accumulation, responsibility for economic hardship is less easily shifted to nature or markets. If the inegalitarian outcomes of market relations cannot be dismissed as "natural," the state becomes responsible for deprivation as well as oppression. Its involvement in conflicts over distribution and welfare is more explicit.[7]

Welfare and growth easily become entangled. Fostering growth is often portrayed as a substitute for addressing distributional issues. Equating the overall accumulation of productive capacity with the national interest makes it easier to claim the role of universal agent. Better a smaller share of an expanding pie than a larger piece of a shrinking one, the argument goes. In reality, of course, pieces often shrink faster than pies grow, and losers ask whose interests transformation serves. Nonetheless, growth remains a prerequisite to delivering welfare in the long term. Finding new ways to generate growth is a preoccupation even for welfare states.

As they become increasingly involved in economic transformation, states increasingly look at the international system not just as a system of sovereign political entities but also as a division of labor.[8] The connection between internal accomplishment and external context becomes intimate and direct. The very possibilities and criteria of economic transformation depend on the international division of labor. Transformation is inescapably defined in global terms.

The Global Context

Modern nations must fit their economic aspirations and activities into a global division of labor. Some produce cotton, others weave cloth, others market high fashion. Some mine iron ore, others make automobiles, others sell insurance. As "world-system" theorists have hammered home, each nation's place in production for global markets has powerful implications for its politics and the welfare of its citizens.[9]

Like any kind of differentiation, the international division of labor can be seen as a basis of enhanced welfare or as a hierarchy. The arguments for enhanced welfare are enshrined in the theory of comparative advantage: all countries will be better off if each concentrates on what it does best.[10] Compatibility with resource and factor endowments defines the activity most rewarding for each country. Trying to produce goods that other countries can deliver more efficiently will only lower everybody's welfare.

Poorer countries have always been suspicious of this argument. From Alexander Hamilton[11] to Friedrich List[12] to Raul Prebisch,[13] there has been the suspicion that position in the international division of labor was a cause of development, not just a result.[14]

No one denies that an interdependent global economy is an improvement over a system of autarky, even for those that occupy less desirable niches. Nor does anyone deny that countries should do what they do best, just as the theory of comparative advantage argues. Yet contemporary theorizing offers support for persistent convictions that trying to get into more desirable niches is an important part of the struggle to develop.

Recent developments in trade theory suggest that profit rates can differ systematically and persistently across sectors. As Paul Krugman (1987, 230) puts it, "with imperfect competition sustained by economies of scale and entry barriers, some industries may be able to generate persistent excess returns." Differential profit rates are, however, only part of what is at stake.

As Albert Hirschman (1977) has argued persuasively, filling a particular niche in the international division of labor has dynamic implications as well as static ones. Some sectors create a "multidimensional conspiracy" in favor of development, inducing entrepreneurial energies, creating positive spillovers in the rest of the economy, and molding political interest groups into a developmental coalition (Hirschman 1977, 96). Niches in the international division of labor are desirable not just because they may entail higher profits and more rapid accumulation of capital, but also because they facilitate the achievement of the social and welfare goals associated with "development" in the broadest sense of the term.

Ability to generate a "multidimensional conspiracy" in favor of development is not inherent in a product itself. It depends on how the product fits into a global array of sectoral possibilities. As such theorists of the "product cycle" as Vernon and Wells have shown, products also have developmental trajectories.[15] The country that catches them on their up-swing will reap different rewards from one that inherits them on their downswing. Textiles offered eighteenth-century England a "multidimensional conspiracy," but they are unlikely to do the same for late-twentieth-century India. Autos and steel supported a "multidimensional conspiracy" in the United States during the first half of this century, but not in Brazil during the second half. One era's multidimensional conspiracy may become another's "lagging sector."

From this perspective, "development" is no longer just a local trajectory of transformation. It is also defined by the relation between local productive capacity and a changing global array of sectors. The countries that fill the most rewarding and dynamic sectoral niches are "developed." Being relegated to niches that are less rewarding or filling less desirable links in a "commodity chain" reduces the prospect of progressive change.[16] Insofar as the international division of labor is a hierarchy, worrying about development means worrying about your place in the hierarchy.

Accepting national development as enmeshed in a global economy in which some positions are more dynamic and rewarding than others forces us to ask another question: Are positions in the international division of labor structurally determined or is there room for agency? Put more simply, can countries deliberately change the position they fill in the international division of labor?

Traditional renditions of the theory of comparative advantage are adamantly on the side of structure. Countries that attempt activities other than those most compatible with their productive endowments simply saddle themselves with wasteful output and lose potential gains from trade. If you are sitting on copper deposits, you are stupid not to sell copper. If your climate allows you to grow superior coffee, you should take advantage of it. Whether these are privileged or disadvantaged sectors in the global economy is neither here nor there. Countries must do what they do best. To do otherwise is self-destructive. The international division of labor presents itself as a structural imperative.

Traditional renditions make most sense in a world where international trade consists of unprocessed raw materials. In a world where manufactures dominate global trade and even services are increasingly considered "tradables," choices about what to make and sell cannot be deduced from a simple reading of natural endowments. Constructing comparative advantage is no less plausible than taking it as given. In William Cline's formulation, "increasingly, trade in manufactures appears to reflect an exchange of goods in which one nation could be just as likely as another . . . to develop comparative advantage.."[17] In a globalized economy where most value is added at several removes from natural resources, the global division of labor presents itself as an opportunity for agency, not just an exogenous constraint.

The idea of constructing comparative advantage is, in some ways, a natural extension of traditional theory. The original Ricardian version emphasized given natural endowments. Hecksher and Ohlin's refinements emphasized relative domestic scarcities of labor and capital that were themselves products of development rather than inherent features of a given national territory. The idea of constructing comparative advantage brings in social and institutional factors that are even more clearly consequences of the developmental process. Cline does not really mean that "one nation could be just as likely as another" to develop comparative advantage in a particular good. He means that a simple assessment of natural resource endowments or the relative scarcity of different factors of production cannot tell us who will have a competitive advantage in chemicals or computers or designer jeans. Social and political institutions must be analyzed as well.

Michael Porter's work makes the point more explicitly. Why should Switzerland specialize in textile equipment while Italy gains comparative advantage in machinery for injection molding? Why should Denmark be a leader in pharmaceutical exports while Sweden has a comparative advantage in heavy trucks (Porter 1990, 1, 149, 162, 314)? With hindsight, these specializations might be traced back to historical differences in endowments, but emergence of advantage depends on a complex evolution of competitive and cooperative ties among local firms, on government policies, and on a host of other social and political institutions.

Sociologists and historians have long postulated such connections between social and institutional endowments and subsequent positions in the international division of labor. Robert Brenner's (1976) classic analysis of the divergent roles taken by Eastern and Western Europe in the early modern period is a case in point. For Brenner, Eastern Europe's specialization in the production of commodity grains depended on the inability of the Eastern European peasantry to defend itself against the imposition of repressive labor control, while the more politically powerful peasantry of Western Europe forced agriculture into products that lent themselves to productivity-enhancing technological change. Maurice Zeitlin (1984) focuses more on the state and politics to explain Chile's relegation to the role of a producer of raw materials over the course of the first third of the twentieth century, but the argument is similar.[18] Dieter Senghaas's (1985) analysis of the evolution of Denmark's position in the international division of labor over the course of the nineteenth and twentieth centuries stresses how social and political factors facilitate state strategies, which in turn allow reconstruction of the country's niche in the global system.

In a world of constructed comparative advantage, social and political institutions—the state among them—shape international specialization.[19]

State involvement must be taken as one of the sociopolitical determinants of what niche a country ends up occupying in the international division of labor.

States with transformative aspirations are, almost by definition, looking for ways to participate in "leading" sectors and shed "lagging" ones. Gilpin (1987, 99) argues that "every state, rightly or wrongly, wants to be as close as possible to the innovative end of 'the product cycle' where, it is believed, the highest 'value-added' is located." These states are not just hoping to generate domestic sectors with higher profit rates. They are also hoping to generate the occupational and social structures associated with "high-technology industry." They are hoping to generate a multidimensional conspiracy in favor of development.

Even if states are committed to changing their positions in the international division of labor as Gilpin suggests, desire and capability have to be sharply separated. Constructing new kinds of comparative advantage may be possible, but it is not likely to be easy. If not immutable, the structure of the global hierarchy is certainly obdurate.[20] Explicit attempts to move within it are likely to be ineffective or even counterproductive. Aspiration without the requisite state capacity can lead to bungling that undercuts even the existing bases of comparative advantage. Efforts to reshape participation in the global economy are interesting, not just because they might succeed, but also because they reveal the limits of what states can do.

If institutional endowments and the exercise of agency can reshape the kinds of products a country produces, and if producing different kinds of products has broad implications for development, arguments about how and whether states might facilitate the local emergence of new sectors become centrally important to understanding states, national development, and ultimately the international division of labor itself. Laying out one such argument is the purpose of this book.

The Argument

Sterile debates about "how much" states intervene have to be replaced with arguments about different kinds of involvement and their effects. Contrasts between "dirigiste" and "liberal" or "interventionist" and "noninterventionist" states focus attention on degrees of departure from ideal-typical competitive markets. They confuse the basic issue. In the contemporary world, withdrawal and involvement are not the alternatives. State involvement is a given. The appropriate question is not "how much" but "what kind."

Ideas about variations in state involvement have to be built on the historical examination of particular states. I chose the set of states for which the challenge of industrial transformation is most salient. This study focuses on "newly industrializing countries" (NICs), defined, not narrowly as the four East Asia tigers,[21] but broadly to include those developing countries large enough or advanced enough to support a full range of industrial production. NICs are particularly good cases because they are less thoroughly constrained than peripheral raw materials exporters and more desperate to achieve transformation than advanced industrial countries.

Within this group I focused on Brazil, India, and Korea. At first glance this is an unlikely threesome. At the beginning of the 1970s, Brazil was the archetype of "dependent development," a country whose rapid industrialization was propelled by a combination of investment by transnational corporations and the demand for consumer durables that depended on rising inequality. India was a "multinational subcontinent" of three-quarters of a billion people, the vast majority of whom still depended on peasant agriculture, renowned for its penchant for autarky. In Korea, peasants were no longer the majority, and export orientation was considered the only sound basis for industrial growth. Yet all three are countries where state involvement in industrial transformation is undeniable. For understanding why it is more important to ask "what kind" of state involvement rather than "how much," they are an excellent triplet.

Variations in state involvement must also be situated in specific arenas. I chose to look at the evolution of the information technology (IT) sector in each of these countries during the 1970s and 1980s.[22] The IT sector (also known as "informatics" or the computer industry) is of obvious interest because it is the sector most likely to spark a twenty-first-century conspiracy in favor of development. It is a particularly good case because it provides an exceptionally strong test of the proposition that state involvement can affect a country's place in the international division of labor.

The information technology sector is fascinating in itself, but the purpose of a sectoral lens is to allow the concrete investigation of general concepts. The aim of this project is not to theorize the IT sector but rather to sharpen general ideas about state structures, state-society relations, and how they shape possibilities for industrial transformation.

My starting premise is that variations in involvement depend on variations in the states themselves. States are not generic. They vary dramatically in their internal structures and relations to society. Different kinds of state structures create different capacities for action. Structures define the range of roles that the state is capable of playing. Outcomes depend both on whether the roles fit the context and on how well they are executed.

How should we characterize variations in state structure and state-society relations? My strategy was to start by constructing two historically grounded ideal types: predatory and developmental states. The basic characteristics of these two types are laid out in chapter 3. Predatory states extract at the expense of society, undercutting development even in the narrow sense of capital accumulation. Developmental states not only have presided over industrial transformation but can be plausibly argued to have played a role in making it happen.

Associating different kinds of states with different outcomes is a start, but if the two ideal types consisted only in attaching appropriate labels to divergent outcomes, they would not get us very far. The trick is to establish a connection between developmental impact and the structural characteristics of states—their internal organization and relation to society. Fortunately, there are clear structural differences between predatory and developmental states.

Predatory states lack the ability to prevent individual incumbents from pursuing their own goals. Personal ties are the only source of cohesion, and individual maximization takes precedence over pursuit of collective goals. Ties to society are ties to individual incumbents, not connections between constituencies and the state as an organization. Predatory states are, in short, characterized by a dearth of bureaucracy as Weber defined it.

The internal organization of developmental states comes much closer to approximating a Weberian bureaucracy. Highly selective meritocratic recruitment and long-term career rewards create commitment and a sense of corporate coherence. Corporate coherence gives these apparatuses a certain kind of "autonomy." They are not, however, insulated from society as Weber suggested they should be. To the contrary, they are embedded in a concrete set of social ties that binds the state to society and provides institutionalized channels for the continual negotiation and renegotiation of goals and policies. Either side of the combination by itself would not work. A state that was only autonomous would lack both sources of intelligence and the ability to rely on decentralized private implementation. Dense connecting networks without a robust internal structure would leave the state incapable of resolving "collective action" problems, of transcending the individual interests of its private counterparts. Only when embeddedness and autonomy are joined together can a state be called developmental.

This apparently contradictory combination of corporate coherence and connectedness, which I call "embedded autonomy," provides the underlying structural basis for successful state involvement in industrial transformation. Unfortunately, few states can boast structures that approximate the ideal type. Korea can legitimately be considered a version of embedded autonomy, but, as chapter 3 shows, Brazil and India are definitely intermediate cases, exhibiting partial and imperfect approximations of embedded autonomy. Their structures do not categorically preclude effective involvement, but they do not predict it either.

Structures confer potential for involvement, but potential has to be translated into action for states to have an effect. I talk about patterns of state involvement in terms of "roles." To convey what Brazil, Korea, and India were doing in the information technology industry, I needed some new terminology. Traditional ways of labeling the state roles make it too easy to slip back into the comfortable feeling that the parameters of state involvement are known and we need only worry about "how much." New words are flags, recurring reminders that the question should be "what kind." I ended up with four rubrics, which are explained in more detail in chapter 4. The first two, "custodian" and "demiurge," represent variations on the conventional roles of regulator and producer. The second pair, which I call "midwifery" and "husbandry," focus more on the relation between state agencies and private entrepreneurial groups.

The role of custodian highlights one aspect of the conventional role of regulator. All states formulate and enforce rules, but the thrust of rulemaking varies. Some rules are primarily promotional, aimed at providing stimulus and incentives. Other regulatory schemas take the opposite tack, aiming to prevent or restrict the initiatives of private actors. The rubric "custodial" identifies regulatory efforts that privilege policing over promotion.

Just as being a custodian is one way of playing out the more generic role of regulator, the demiurge[23] is a specific way of playing the more generic role of producer. All states play the role of producer, taking direct responsibility for delivering certain types of goods. At the very least, states assume this role in relation to infrastructural goods assumed to have a collective or public character, like roads, bridges, and communications nets. The role of demiurge is based on a stronger assumption about the limitations of private capital. It presumes that private capital is incapable of successfully sustaining the developmentally necessary gamut of commodity production. Consequently, the state becomes a "demiurge," establishing enterprises that compete in markets for normal "private" goods.

Taking on the role of midwife is also a response to doubts about the vitality of private capital, but it is a response of a different sort. The capacities of the local entrepreneurial class are taken as malleable, not as given. Instead of substituting itself for private producers, the state tries to assist in the emergence of new entrepreneurial groups or to induce existing groups to venture into more challenging kinds of production. A variety of techniques and policies may be utilized. Erecting a "greenhouse" of tariffs to protect infant sectors from external competition is one. Providing subsidies and incentives is another. Helping local entrepreneurs bargain with transnational capital or even just signaling that a particular sector is considered important are other possibilities. Regardless of the specific technique, promotion rather than policing is the dominant mode of relating to private capital.

Even if private entrepreneurial groups are induced to tackle promising sectors, global changes will continually challenge local firms. Husbandry consists of cajoling and assisting private entrepreneurial groups in hopes of meeting these challenges. Like midwifery, it can take a variety of forms, from simple signaling to something as complex as setting up state organizations to take over risky complementary tasks, such as research and development. The techniques of husbandry overlap with those of midwifery.

Most states combine several roles in the same sector. Sectoral outcomes depend on how roles are combined. My expectations for the informatics sector are obvious from the descriptions of the roles themselves. Neither trying to replace private capital nor fixating on preventing it from doing undesirable things should work as well as trying to create synergistic promotional relations with entrepreneurs or potential entrepreneurs. Combining midwifery and husbandry should work better than combinations that rely more heavily on custodian or demiurge.

The evolution of information technology sectors in Brazil, India, and Korea provides a nice illustrative confirmation of this basic contention. The blend of roles varied across countries. The variations grew, at least in part, out of differences in state structure and state-society relations. Different role combinations were associated with differential effectiveness in the expected way.

As chapters 5 and 6 show, the principal difference between Korea and the other two countries was that Korea was able to build on a base of firms with a broad range of related industrial prowess, fostered by prior midwifery. This allowed the state to shift easily to the combination of prodding and supporting that I have called husbandry. Brazil and India made less thorough-going use of midwifery, got bogged down in restrictive rule-making, and invested heavily in direct production of information technology goods by state-owned enterprises. Their efforts to play custodian and demiurge were politically costly and absorbed scarce state capacity, leaving them in a poor position to embark on a program of husbandry that would help sustain the local industries they had helped create.

The similarities among the three countries were as suggestive as the differences. In each, the vision of a local information technology sector began with individuals convinced of the value of local informatics production who managed to find positions of leverage within the state apparatus. Their ideas were eventually turned into policies and institutions designed to bring forth local production. Initial state policies in all three countries began with "greenhouses," which provided space for local entrepreneurs to experiment protected from transnational competition. The greenhouses were a fundamental part of playing the role of midwife. Midwifery bore fruits in all three. The local industrial panorama in the mid-to late 1980s represented an impressive transformation of the scenery that had been in place two decades earlier, as chapter 7 shows.

By the end of the 1980s, Korea's industry was the largest and most robust, but local producers could claim significant successes in all three countries. Brazil had put together a new set of diversified informatics corporations that were significant actors on the local industrial scene. They presided over what had become a multibillion-dollar local industry. Local entrepreneurs commanded experienced organizations that employed thousands of technically trained professionals. Local *técnicos*[24] had demonstrated their technological bravura and even managed to turn their talents into internationally competitive products in the financial automation sector. India could boast early design successes by local hardware firms and the prospect of growing participation in international markets for certain kinds of software engineering. In Korea, production of information technology products had become a cornerstone of the country's overall industrial strategy. The *chaebol*[25] were going head to head with the world's leading firms in memory chips and had succeeded, at least for a time, in becoming a force in the world personal computer (PC) market.

All three industries had serious weaknesses, but they did demonstrate that developing countries could be producers as well as consumers of information technology goods. Overall, it was an impressive set of accomplishments for three countries that conventional analysis at the end of the 1960s would have categorically excluded from a chance at real participation in the globe's leading sector.

If I had stopped following my three information technology sectors in 1986 or 1987, this would have been the story—complicated in its details, but still relatively straightforward in its overall lessons. Some states and some roles were definitely more effective than others, but states could make a difference, even in what was universally judged an extremely difficult sector to crack.

Trends in the latter part of the 1980s gave the story a different twist, which is related in chapter 8. If nationalist industrialization had been the leitmotif in the 1970s, a new internationalization was clearly taking hold at the end of the 1980s. The hallmark of this new internationalization was a new relation between transnational and local capital, epitomized by IBM's new joint venture in India.[26] This was accompanied by a new emphasis on connectedness to the global economy, in terms of both increased openness to imports and increased concern with exports.

The easy interpretation would have been that this was a case of "the empire strikes back,"[27] of maverick nationalist aspirations being brought back under the discipline of the global economy. In fact, the new internationalization was not simply the negation of earlier nationalist policies. In some ways it was a vindication. IBM provides the emblematic case. Its expansion in the 1990s was increasingly based on alliances with locally owned firms. This was in part because the nature of the industry had changed globally, but it was also because local greenhouses had produced Brazilian, Indian, and Korean firms whose organizational strength, human capital, and experience made them legitimate partners. The new internationalization was in part the product of successful midwifery.

What was most interesting about this change, from the point of view of my argument, was its contradictory implications for relations between the state and the industrial constituency it had helped create. Local entrepreneurial groups had been at first tempted entrants, then grateful clients, and eventually actors strong enough to attract transnational allies. It was the state's opposition to foreign entry that gave local capital its trump card in negotiating the initial alliances, but once alliances had been negotiated, relations between firms and states changed again. The state's leverage was undercut. Firms had, in effect, traded the rents associated with state protection of the local market for those associated with their transnational corporate allies' proprietary technology and global market power. The new alliance of local entrepreneurs and transnational corporations make it harder to sustain the old alliance between local capital and the state.

If shrinking political support for state action corresponded neatly to the increasing developmental irrelevance of state action, the equation would be balanced, but that is not what analysis of the new internationalization suggested. New alliances were prone to devolve back into de facto subsidiaries. New exports, like software from India or PC clones from Korea, opened avenues for mobility in the global division of labor, but they also had the potential to turn into low-return dead ends. Continued husbandry was crucial, but in a sector populated with firms more beholden to transnational alliances than to state support, the political viability of past patterns of state involvement was in doubt.

I began my investigation of informatics industries trying to understand how state initiative could reshape local industrial efforts. I ended up intrigued by the way in which the very success of state efforts could undercut the political possibilities for sustaining state involvement. The neo-utilitarian perspective prevalent in the 1980s predicted that state involvement would produce an economically stagnant, politically stable symbiosis between officials with the capacity to create rents and private actors anxious to take advantage of them. I had found the opposite. State involvement was associated with economic dynamism, and the result was political contestation, not symbiosis.

The argument at the sectoral level, which is summarized in chapter 9, ends up combining a vision of how state initiatives might produce industrial transformation with ideas about how state-induced industrial transformation redefines the political possibilities for future state action. This sectoral argument in turn raises obvious questions for my societal-level analysis of state structures and state-society relations. If successfully fostering new entrepreneurial groups in a particular sector generates a new political relation between the state and the constituency it has helped create, should not the same logic hold more generally?

Reexamination of the evolution of state-society relations in chapter 10 suggests that the same basic dynamic does apply more generally. There is evidence to suggest that the transformative project advanced under the aegis of embedded autonomy in Korea may have undercut its own political foundations. If this is true, future state involvement will require some sort of reconstruction of state-society relations.

In the original formulation, embedded autonomy implied dense links not with society in general but specifically with industrial capital. From the point of view of other social groups, it was an exclusionary arrangement. Could embeddedness be built around ties to multiple social groups? Comparative evidence suggests that sometimes it can be. One way of reconstructing state-society relations would be to include links with other social groups, like labor. Chapter 10 explores this possibility by looking at some quite different cases, namely, agrarian communism in Kerala and European social democracy in Austria. These cases suggest that a broadly defined embeddedness may offer a more robust basis for transformation in the long run. This suggestive evidence argues for further exploration of potential variations in embedded autonomy.

The essential outline of the argument can be recapitulated in three points. First, developmental outcomes depend on both the general character of state structures and the roles that states pursue. Second, state involvement can be associated with transformation even in a sector like information technology where conventional wisdom would suggest little chance of success. Finally, an analysis of states and industrial transformation cannot stop with the emergence of a new industrial landscape. Successful transformation changes the nature of the state's private counterparts, making effective future state involvement dependent on the reconstruction of state-society ties.

Of course, there is no reason to believe any of this argument right now.

Its eventual plausibility depends on how well it fits the details of the cases. The way the cases are depicted depends in turn on the way in which the research was conceived and conducted. An explicit discussion of how I went about my investigation is in order.

Research Strategy

This study uses what I call a "comparative institutional approach": institutional because it looks for explanations that go beyond the utilitarian calculations of individuals to the enduring pattern of relationships within with such calculations are immersed; comparative because it focuses on concrete variations across historical cases rather than on generic explanations.[28]

Taking a comparative institutional approach to the state entails rejecting reductionism. The state cannot be reduced to an aggregation of the interests of individual office holders, the vector sum of political forces, or the condensed expression of some logic of economic necessity. States are the historical products of their societies, but that does not make them pawns in the social games of other actors. They must be dealt with as institutions and social actors in their own right, influencing the course of economic and social change even as they are shaped by it.[29] In chapter 2 I try to set out the distinctive features of the comparative institutional approach by contrasting it to what I call the "neo-utilitarian" approach, which dominated new work on the state in the late 1970s and the 1980s but now seems on the wane.

In the comparative institutional approach, the state is seen as a historically rooted institution, not simply a collection of strategic individuals. The interaction of state and society is constrained by institutionalized sets of relations. Economic outcomes are the products of social and political institutions, not just responses to prevailing market conditions. Understanding diverse outcomes is the aim, not forcing cases into a generic mold or onto a one-dimensional scale.

Having become fashionable again, "institutionalism" has also become a term with many meanings,[30] but in the analysis of the state's role in the economic development the "comparative institutional approach" can be defined concretely. It is grounded in a long tradition of work that runs from Weber through economic historians like Polanyi (1944), Gerschenkron, (1962), and Hirschman (1958, 1973, 1977, 1981) to contemporary work by political economists like Johnson (1982), Bardhan (1984), Bates (1989), Amsden (1989), and Wade (1990)[31] and sociologists like Cardoso and Faletto (1979), Hamilton (1982), Zeitlin (1984), Gold (1986), Stephens and Stephens (1986), and Seidman (1994).[32]

A comparative institutional approach implies a strategy of gathering evidence. Obviously, one central aim is to collect evidence that will locate specific state policies and societal responses in the larger institutional context that produces them, showing how that context helps define interests, aspirations, and strategies. At the same time, demonstrating variation across cases requires delving into specifics. Whether the focus is on society or within the state, the central methodological precept of a comparative institutional approach is to ground assertions of institutional effects in the analysis of the actions of specific groups and organizations. Above all, a comparative institutional approach must avoid treating the state as a reified monolith.

This chapter is full of statements like "the state can" or "the state wants." Other chapters share the same language. Such formulations have to be taken as metaphorical shorthand. The purpose of doing research is to figure out what lies behind them. In practice "the state wants" because some group of individuals within the state apparatus has a project. This does not mean the project is merely a reflection of their personal biographies or individual maximizing strategies. It does mean that their project may well be opposed by others elsewhere in the state and that the definition of what the state "wants" is the result of internal political conflict and flux. An investigation of state policy involves probing specific sources and supports, not attributing results to some sort of unitary volition.

Taking the state seriously as an institution without reifying it requires putting together a variety of evidence. I began my research with "secondary evidence," scholarly accounts of state and society in Brazil, India, Korea, and other countries that offered comparative perspectives on these three. Analyses by researchers working for organizations like the World Bank were also valuable sources. The secondary literature was supplemented by a variety of government documents and statistical evidence. Most important, however, were what are known among specialists in sociological methodology as "key informant interviews."

On the ground, "state structures" and "state-society relations" become relations among state agencies and organizations, relations between these agencies and individual firms, historical patterns of ties among individuals—all things that can only be appreciated by talking to individual state managers and private executives.

Interviews with dozens of current and former government officials were the primary source of my understanding of what was going on inside these states and the starting point for the description of state roles that is offered in chapters 5 and 6. Obviously, participants offer accounts that are biased and self-interested, but the biases and self-interest are important evidence in themselves. In addition, higher-level officials offer more than accounts of the events in which they have participated. They offer theories as well. Juxtaposing the theories that emanate from one position in the bureaucracy with those proffered in another is one of the best ways to get a sense of how roles emerge and decline.

Avoiding reification is also important when looking at society. States are connected to "economic elites" or "the capitalist class" via ties to particular firms and individuals. The success or failure of transformative projects depends on how they jibe with the strategies of particular firms. An investigation of the consequences of state policy, especially one that focuses on a particular sector, must look at individual firms and how their strategies resonate with state actions.

Understanding the information technology sector meant beginning with the daunting literature on the global evolution of the sector as a whole. There is also, surprising as it may seem, a large scholarly literature that focuses specifically on the evolution of informatics policies in Brazil, India, and Korea. In addition, each country's regulatory agencies and industry associations collect and publish data on the sector's evolution. The specialized business press reports day-to-day changes in the fortunes of individual firms and products. The annual reports and occasional publications of individual firms provide further detail.

In understanding society, as in understanding the state, the most useful sources of information were discussions with individuals. Executives' descriptions of the competitive problems facing their firms and the way in which state policy affected their strategies were the crucial complement to the perspectives of state managers in constructing chapters 5 and 6 and the matrix for my interpretations in chapters 7 and 8. Like government officials, executives offer theories and interpretations of how state and industry work. While no less biased and self-interested, their theories provide valuable perspectives on the sector's evolution.

The overall result is a mosaic of concrete evidence melded by an argument that is abstract and general. If the combination convinces, it is not because each piece of evidence or each link in the argument is irrefutable. It is because the overall gestalt makes sense. I hope that the argument is persuasive, but, in the end, I am as interested in provoking as I am in convincing. If the chapters that follow incite readers to stop arguing about "more" versus "less" state intervention and to begin debating the relative efficacy of different structures and roles, I will have accomplished my purpose. If my work provokes others to embark on concrete investigations of the process through which states and societies shape each other, that would be even better.

2

A Comparative Institutional Approach

IN THE FALL of 1991, at the annual meeting of the World Bank/International Monetary Fund, Attila Karaosmanoglu, vice president and managing director of the World Bank, made a surprising statement. He said, "The East Asian NICs and their successful emulators are a powerful argument that a more activist, positive governmental role can be a decisive factor in rapid industrial growth. . . . What is replicable and transferable must be brought to light and shared with others."[1]

What was surprising about Karaosmanoglu's statement was not its content; the same point had been made before by a variety of social scientists and knowledgeable observers of East Asia. What was surprising was the institutional source of the opinion. For more than a decade the upper echelons of the World Bank had been one of the most influential promulgators of the idea that developing countries should "get their prices right," return to reliance on markets, and dismantle existing machinery of state intervention. Acknowledging that an "activist, positive governmental role" could be a "decisive factor in rapid industrial growth" was a surprising about face, an important signal that the bank was aware of a general shift in perspectives on the state's role in development.

Among practitioners and policymakers there was growing disillusionment with "getting prices right" as a developmental panacea. At the same time Karaosmanoglu was making his speech, one of the bank's "major partners" in development lending was suggesting that the bank was stressing market mechanisms too much. A memo from Japan's Overseas Economic Cooperation Fund (1991, 10) argued, "As there are inherent limits of the market mechanism itself, the market mechanism cannot handle various issues properly. Government intervention in these areas, as result, is indispensable."

The "neoliberal" attack on the state had passed its zenith. The political hegemony of "neoliberalism" and the theoretical hegemony of the "neo-utilitarian" vision, which provided its intellectual underpinnings, were on the wane. Together they had dominated the terms of debate from the end of the 1970s through most of the 1980s, but by the end of the 1980s it was clear that something new was needed.

As the attractiveness of simplistic, asocial versions of neo-utilitarianism dissipates, the task of filling the gap with an institutionalist alternative becomes more urgent. The aim of this chapter is to outline the elements of one such alternative. In my view, the work of Weber and institutional economists like Polanyi, Gerschenkron, and Hirschman is the place to start. Polanyi provides a keen sense of the degree to which markets depend on state action. Weber offers a powerful hypothesis as to what kind of internal organization is likely to give states the capacity to construct markets and promote growth. Gerschenkron and Hirschman make it clear that state-society relations, particularly those that link states and entrepreneurial elites, are as important as internal structures.

A variety of contemporary insights must be added to this recuperation of earlier traditions, including insights offered by revisionist offshoots of neo-utilitarian theorizing. Work stimulated by the extraordinary developmental success of the East Asian NICs has been particularly important in the contemporary revival of institutionalist perspectives. Amsden (1989) and Wade (1990) are excellent examples. A synthetic combination of recent research with the durable insights of earlier work can provide the basis for a comparative institutional approach of great heuristic promise.

Two things need underlining from the beginning. First, I want to explicitly disavow sympathy for "statism" in the sense of utopian faith in the generic beneficence and efficacy of the state. A revival of open-ended faith in the state as a solution to the problem of underdevelopment is neither possible nor desirable. Naive statism was, after all, a faith based on a number of dubious premises. The feats of allocative foresight that states would have needed to live up to this vision were implausible. The implied freedom from entanglements with parochial interests was no less so. States can sometimes act on behalf of developmental goals, but they are always imperfect instruments.

Second, it would be foolish to deny the contributions of the neo-utilitarian perspective to contemporary understanding of the state. Ironically, the neoliberal attack focused attention on the state as an actor and thereby helped stimulate a variety of work that would eventually provide the basis of a new approach. In retrospect, neo-utilitarian analytics may well have been a precondition for the resurgence of a comparative institutional political economy. By wiping out the possibility of naïve faith in a naturally competent and benevolent state with such elegance and vitriol, neo-utilitarians forced everyone to take a closer look at what states did and why. Analysis of the neo-utilitarian vision is, therefore, a good starting point for understanding the roots of the new comparative institutional synthesis.

The Neo-Utilitarian Vision

The disillusionment with the state that was endemic by the beginning of the 1970s is easy to understand. In Africa, even sympathetic observers could not ignore the cruel parody of postcolonial hopes being enacted by most states on the continent.[2] Bloated state apparatuses were equally obvious targets for Latin Americans trying to understand the roots of the crisis-ridden stagnation that confronted them.[3] Unfortunately, rather than trying to separate what states might be able to do from what they were unlikely to be able to do and then focusing on institutional changes that would improve state performance, critics simply demonized the state.

Rapacious politicians and bureaucrats were only by-products. The real culprit was the state itself. Government bureaucracies were either strangling entrepreneurship or diverting it into unproductive "rent-seeking" activities. Getting rid of them was the first step on the developmental agenda. Abandoning the state as a possible agent of development left unrelieved pessimism or "uncritical faith in the market" as the main alternatives. Not surprisingly, the market became the answer. The ideological doctrine that became popularly known as "neoliberalism" coalesced around a series of policies designed to place full reliance on market forces.

Neoliberalism was hardly an intellectual innovation. In part it was simply a return to older canons of faith in the market. The contemporary version, however, was supported by an analytical apparatus that represented a significant modernization of previous justifications for relying on the market.

Neoclassical economics had always recognized that "the existence of a state is essential for economic growth" (North 1981, 20), but the essential state was a minimal state. In its minimal neoclassical form, the state was treated as an exogenous "black box" whose internal functionings were not a proper or worthy subject for economic analysis. Neo-utilitarian political economists, however, became convinced that the negative economic consequences of state action were too important to leave the black box closed. To unravel its workings, they applied the "standard tools of individual optimization" to the analysis of the state itself (Srinivasan 1985, 41). Economists like James Buchanan turned their considerable analytic talents to developing a "neo-utilitarian" model of the state that made it seem illogical for incumbents to behave in ways that were consistent with the common good.[4]

The exchange relation between incumbents and supporters is the essence of state action. To survive, incumbents require political supporters, and these in turn must be provided with incentives sufficient to prevent their shifting support to other potential officeholders. Incumbents may either distribute resources directly to supporters—through subsidies, loans, jobs, contracts, or the provision of services—or use their rule-making authority to create rents for favored groups by restricting the ability of market forces to operate. Rationing foreign exchange, restricting entry through licensing producers, and instituting tariffs or quantitative restrictions on imports are all ways of creating rents. Incumbents may also exact a share of the rent for themselves. Indeed, it is hypothesized that "competition for entry into government service is, in part, a competition for rents" (Krueger 1974, 293). High returns from "directly unproductive profit-seeking" activities dominate productive activities; economic efficiency and dynamism decline.

To escape these deleterious effects, the state's sphere should be reduced to the minimum, and bureaucratic control should be replaced by market mechanisms wherever possible. The range of state functions considered susceptible to "marketization" varies, but some authors even speculate on the possibility of using "prizes" and other incentives to induce "privateers" and other private citizens to provide at least partially for the national defense (Auster and Silver 1979, 102).

The neo-utilitarian vision unquestionably captures a significant aspect of the functioning of most states and the dominant aspect for some. "Rent-seeking," conceptualized more primitively as "corruption," has always been a well-known facet of the operation of Third World states. There is no doubt that some states consume the surplus they extract, encourage private actors to shift from productive activities to unproductive rent-seeking, and fail to provide collective goods. Nor is there any doubt that all states are guilty of some of these sins some of the time. The unique contribution of the neo-utilitarians did not, however, lie primarily in drawing attention to the empirical realities of Third World states. Their virtue was in providing an analytical frame that made these realities explicable, demonstrating how they could be derived from a parsimonious set of assumptions about how states worked.

Neo-utilitarian polemics buried the neoclassical economists' vision of the state as a neutral arbiter. Indeed, the assumption that state policies "reflect vested interests in society" (Collander 1984, 2) partially recaptures some of Marx's original insights into the biases that characterize state policy. By questioning both the effective pursuit of common goals (collective action) and following orders (principal-agent relations), the neo-utilitarians turned the coherence of the state as a Weberian "compulsory association" into something that had to be taken as problematic rather than assumed. Neo-utilitarian preoccupations with the "capture" of parts of the state apparatus by interest groups forced a reexamination of the state's claim to being an agent of society as a whole and focused attention on state-society relations.

As an explanation of one pattern of behavior that may or may not dominate in a particular state apparatus, neo-utilitarianism was an invaluable stimulus to reevaluation of the institutional nature of the state. As a monocausal master theory applicable to states generically, which is what it tended to become in the hands of its more radical adherents, it obscured more than it illuminated. In addition, despite its elegance and apparent rigor, the neo-utilitarian vision itself suffered from serious theoretical flaws. Its overreaching ambition and its flaws combined to make its eventual retreat almost inevitable.

The Retreat from Neo-utilitarian Orthodoxy

Neo-utilitarian political economy is both cynical and utopian: cynical in denying the practical importance of "public spirit" (cf. Toye 1991b, 322) and utopian in assuming that the "invisible hand" offers an easy substitute. Its utopian side gave it charisma but also burdened it with positions that were hard to defend, logically or empirically. Its extreme view of the state, however elegant, was, in the end, logically untenable. Its utopian belief in the power of the market to reconstruct society was equally so.

The neo-utilitarian vision of the state as an aggregation of individual maximizers does more than impugn the possibility of serving the public good. It makes the kind of limited state that neo-utilitarian economics requires an impossibility. The neo-utilitarian vision of an efficient economy requires a traditional, neoclassical state, a "nightwatchman state" whose actions are "restricted largely, if not entirely, to protecting individual rights, persons and property, and enforcing voluntarily negotiated private contracts" (Buchanan, Tollison, and Tullock 1980, 9). How does such a state arise out of individual maximizers? It is hard to explain why, if officeholders are primarily interested in individual rents, they do not all "free-lance."

Neo-utilitarian logic provides little insight into what constrains individual incumbents to work together as a collectivity at all. If we skip over this logical dilemma and postulate that somehow the state solves its own collective action problem, there is an additional logical problem. Why should those who have a monopoly of violence rest content being nightwatchmen? Why not try to expand rental havens indefinitely? In short, strict adherence to a neo-utilitarian logic makes the existence of the state as a collective actor difficult to explain and the nightwatchman state a theoretical impossibility.

Neo-utilitarian conceptions of the market are equally problematic. To begin with, they tend to slip from the assertion of neoclassical economics that competitive markets will result in short-run allocative efficiency to the much stronger assertion that competitive markets are sufficient to produce the kind of structural transformation that lies at the heart of development. Neoclassical economic theory is much more agnostic on the likelihood that marginal maximization will move inexorably in the direction needed to achieve long-run optimization.

If new activities, new forms of production, and new kinds of entrepreneurship are required in order to achieve substantial improvements in well-being, maximization of marginal revenues may leave productive capacity stagnating at a "local maximum." Incremental changes in current practices may be less attractive than the status quo, making it very hard to get to a superior position that lies too far away from current practices to be made "visible" by incremental adjustment. As Srinivasan (1985, 39) points out, if a system is operating at some remove from a long-run equilibrium point, the theoretically attractive features of a competitive equilibrium in no way assure that "profit-maximizing behavior by producers and welfare-maximizing behavior by consumers, taking the prevailing prices as given, will somehow lead the economy to a competitive equilibrium."[5]

Even if markets could be assumed to deliver structural change as well as allocative efficiency, the theoretical foundations of neo-utilitarian faith in the market as an independent agent of change would still be problematic. Neo-utilitarians often go well beyond the assertions of classical political economy in denying the importance of cultural norms and other kinds of social relations in sustaining exchange (cf. Colclough 1991, 21). Adam Smith, after all, considered *The Theory of Moral Sentiments* a natural complement to *The Wealth of Nations*.

There is no reason to believe that exchange relations are ontologically prior to other kinds of social relationships. Detailed studies of real processes of exchange (as opposed to analytical summaries of their results) find that markets operate well only when they are supported by other kinds of social networks, networks composed of polyvalent individual ties. Indeed, Granovetter (1985) argues that "the anonymous market of neoclassical models is virtually nonexistent in economic life." Instead, the smooth operation of exchange over the long run requires the dense, deeply developed medium of trust and culturally shared understandings, summarized by Durkheim under the deceptively simple heading, "noncontractual elements of contract." Exchange may reinforce these other kinds of ties, but it cannot be sustained in their absence.

Formal organizations that "internalize" exchange relations, providing enforceable norms for the transmission of information and thus lowering "transaction costs," may provide a partial substitute for polyvalent informal ties. As Williamson (1975) and others have emphasized, the modern economy is characterized by encapsulation of exchange relations inside massive formal organizations as much as by arm's-length transactions among disconnected individual maximizers. Formal hierarchies are probably best seen not as eliminating the role of informal networks and norms, but rather as enabling the construction of a set of ties within which an internal culture can grow. Nonetheless, whether the emphasis is on formal organizational ties or informal networks, the conclusion that exchange relations must be immersed in the nutrient culture provided by other kinds social structures is hard to escape.

Seeing markets as necessarily dependent on other kinds of social ties has serious implications for neo-utilitarian prescriptions. Efforts to "liberate" exchange relations from the encumbrances of other social structures are "unnatural" and therefore likely to be resisted by everyone involved. Insofar as liberation occurs anyway, it runs a strong risk of destroying the institutional underpinnings that allowed exchange to operate efficiently in its natural environment.

The contradictions involved in trying to implement neoliberal policies in practice were as serious as those confronting neo-utilitarian theories. First, there was the question of how to deal with the absence of efficient markets in many crucial areas of developing economies. As Michael Lipton (1991, 27) put it, analyzing the problems of agricultural markets, "Just as there is no free lunch, so there is no free market; markets are expensive. Agricultural risk and information are so structured that growing state involvement is a prerequisite [to freer markets]." If markets had to be socially constructed, who would construct them? States could not do it by fiat, but states were still likely to be essential. The search for markets led back to the state.

Analysts like Kahler (1990) have pointed out the "orthodox paradox" of neoliberal policy prescriptions. Imposing neoliberal orthodoxy implied the imposition of radical changes in existing business practices. Who would institute such changes? According to neo-utilitarian theory, rational politicians should be unalterably opposed to changing the rules that allow them to create rental havens. Yet, when formulating policy neoliberals had no choice but to assume that the state would somehow become willing and able to implement policies that eliminated its ability to provide rental havens. If incumbents behaved the way that they were supposed to according to neo-utilitarian theory, there was no way that this should happen. In short, if the policies proposed by neo-utilitarian theorists had a chance of being implemented, their theory of the state was wrong.

Neoliberal policy prescriptions did, of course, become increasingly hegemonic in the 1980s, but being put into practice was a mixed blessing as far as maintaining the charisma of the theoretical perspective was concerned. First of all, it made the "orthodox paradox" harder to ignore. When liberalization, privatization, and other policies associated with neoliberalism were implemented, it was in fact state managers who formed the core of the "change teams" that made change possible (see Waterbury 1992), making the neo-utilitarian theory of the state all the harder to sustain. In addition, it became clear that implementation of neoliberal policies was hardly a "magic bullet" as far as the ogres of stagnation and inefficiency were concerned. Looking back from the end of the 1980s at the developing world as a whole, the "statist" 1950s and 1960s hardly seemed the disaster they should have been according to neo-utilitarian theories. The orthodox reformers of the 1980s could claim successes, but, overall, the changes in performance were ambiguous rather than dramatically positive. It was still possible to argue that increasing the sway of market exchange was necessary to growth, but it was much harder to argue that it was sufficient.[6]

Practical results reinforced theoretical reflection in suggesting that the neo-utilitarian analysis was at best incomplete. Talk about "governance" and "institution building" became more fashionable as even the World Bank began to focus on the possibility that its clients' problems arose not just from bad policies, but from institutional deficiencies correctable only in the long term.[7] World Bank Vice President Karaosmanoglu's speech was not, then, the aberration that it might have seemed on first reading. It was part of the general and, one could argue, inevitable retreat of neo-utilitarian orthodoxy.

"Retreat" is a relative term. Neoliberalism was still a powerful political agenda at the end of the 1980s. The state remained discredited. Utopian faith in markets remained an attractive foundation for optimistic political rhetoric. Absent a compelling intellectual successor to neo-utilitarian theorizing, neoliberal policy prescriptions retained legitimacy and charisma despite their obvious problems. What was needed was a coherent, systematic response that filled the lacunae in the neo-utilitarian paradigm. How to produce such a response was less obvious, but the strands of a solution were beginning to come together.

Recapturing the Comparative Institutional Tradition

Neo-utilitarianism's inability to come up with a logically tenable portrayal of the state was inevitable given its failure to temper "methodological individualism" with an appreciation of institutional effects.[8] The neo-utilitarians' assumption that the behavior of states could be conceptualized in terms of the simple aggregation of individual motivations stood firmly in the way of their developing a realistic picture of the state. State managers do not engage in disembodied maximization. Their decisions depend on an institutional context composed of complex, historically emergent patterns of interaction that are embodied in social structures and taken for granted by the individuals that work within them[9]. These patterns have a reality that is prior to "individual interests." They define the priorities of competing individual goals and the range of means that will be considered to pursue them.

Lack of a comparative perspective was also a natural consequence of fascination with the asocial logic of individual decisions. As long as individual choices could be predicted from a simple set of universalistic motivational assumptions, and as long as the aggregation of individual choices was sufficient to predict organizational outcomes, a generic theory of how state managers behaved would suffice. If historically derived institutional patterns define individual interests and constrain the way they are pursued, then "one size fits all" diagnoses will not work. Both state actions and their consequences for development become contingent on the context in which they are immersed. A comparative analysis that starts with contextual differences and then looks for underlying regularities is the only way to proceed.

For anyone searching for a successor to the neo-utilitarian model of the state, one logical place to look is the long tradition of work analyzing the state in comparative historical terms. Methodologically, it is a tradition that takes institutions seriously. Theoretically, it comes closer to the spirit of classic political economy than does the "economic theory of politics" offered by the neo-utilitarians (Toye 1991b, 324). It is also a tradition that offers contrasting substantive assumptions regarding the state's nature and role. It has always been critical of the proposition that exchange was a "natural" activity that required only the most minimal institutional underpinnings, and it has seen a wide range of state action as fundamental to the initiation and sustenance of market exchange.

Fifty years ago Karl Polanyi (1957 [1944], 140) argued that "The road to the free market was opened and kept open by an enormous increase in continuous, centrally organized and controlled interventionism." From the beginning, according to Polanyi, the life of the market has been intertwined not just with other kinds of social ties, but with the forms and policies of the state. An effective state was not simply an adjunct to the market, it was an essential prerequisite of the formation of market relations.

Starting from Polanyi's perspective opens the door to recuperating even earlier Weberian insights. Looking at established market societies, Weber argued that the operation of large-scale capitalist enterprise depended on the availability of the kind of order that only a modern bureaucratic state could provide. As Weber stated (1968 [1904–1911], 1395, n. 14), "capitalism and bureaucracy have found each other and belong intimately together." Weber's assumption of the intimate relation was based on a conception of the bureaucratic state apparatus that was the mirror image of the neo-utilitarian view. Weber's bureaucrats saw their interests as fulfilled by executing their assignments and contributing to the realization of the goals of the apparatus as a whole. Using the prerogatives of office to pursue private interests was the archetypal char-

acteristic of prebureaucratic forms. The superiority of the modern bureaucratic state lay in its ability to supersede an individualistic logic.

For Weber, the state was useful to those operating in markets precisely
because the actions of its incumbents obeyed a logic quite different from
that of utilitarian exchange. In Weber's vision, the state's ability to support markets and capitalist accumulation depends on the bureaucracy
being a corporately coherent entity in which individuals see pursuing corporate goals as the best way to maximize their individual self-interest.
Corporate coherence requires that individual incumbents be to some degree insulated from the demands of the surrounding society. Insulation,
in turn, is enhanced by conferring a distinctive and rewarding status on
bureaucrats. The concentration of expertise in the bureaucracy through
meritocratic recruitment and the provision of opportunities for long-term
career rewards is also central to the bureaucracy's effectiveness.

The usefulness of the Weberian perspective is that it goes beyond a
discussion of what policies are likely to support markets and broaches the
issue of what kind of institutional structure the state must have in order
to be an effective counterpart to private entrepreneurial groups. Successful policies have structural foundations. Bureaucratic structures create a
set of incentives for state officials. They create an affinity between the
incentives facing state managers and the policies required for capitalist
growth.

If Weber is right, imposing different policies on a state apparatus without changing the structure of the state itself will not work. Real changes
in policies and behavior depend on the possibility of erecting new state
structures. At the same time, the Weberian perspective generates a powerful comparative hypothesis: differences in the structure of the state apparatus should predict differences in developmental efficacy. It should,
therefore, be possible to go beyond the tautological identification of developmental states as those that induce development and ground differences in developmental performance in enduring structural contrasts.

While Weber is clear on what kind of state structure best complements
the growth of the market, he takes the robustness and dynamism of capitalist accumulation largely for granted. As long as the state provides a
stable frame of rules so that the returns from investment are predictable,
private agents will do the rest. He does not address the question of how
the state might go beyond reinforcing the natural propensities of investors, or how it might respond to a situation in which private entrepreneurial forces fail to emerge. Weber's state is an essential adjunct to private capital, but not a transformative agent in its own right.

Thinking about how states might go beyond simply providing a stable
environment for private capital means looking more closely at state-society relations, particularly those that connect the state to entrepreneurial
groups. The work of institutional economists like Gerschenkron and

Hirschman provides a vision of state-society relations that is a nice complement to Weber.

Gerschenkron's (1962) work on late developers in Europe takes entrepreneurial capacities less for granted and focuses attention more directly on the relations between the state and capital.[10] In his view, late capitalist development was characterized by a disjunction between the scale of economic activity required for development and the effective scope of private economic networks. Competing with already industrialized states meant mastering production technologies with capital requirements in excess of what local entrepreneurs were capable of amassing. To resolve this contradiction, the state had to go beyond providing a suitable environment and become actively involved in organizing financial markets.

In Gerschenkron's argument, the state is still addressing the problem of risk-taking, but the provision of a generally predictable environment is no longer sufficient. Lacking both individual capitalists able to assume risks at the scale required by modern technology and private institutions that will allow large risks to be spread across a wide network of capital holders, the state must serve as investment banker, bringing together the necessary funds and encouraging their application in transformative activities.

Hirschman, who focuses on the "late late" developers of the Third World, carries Gerschenkron's emphasis on the state action as a potential stimulant to new activities a step further. He argues that capital is not the principal missing ingredient. What stands in the way of industrial transformation is a dearth of entrepreneurship in the simple sense of "the perception of investment opportunities and their transformation into actual investments (Hirschman 1958, 35)." Those with resources to invest have a hard time making the decisions necessary to turn their wealth into new productive activities. "Maximizing induced decision-making" becomes the key to economic progress (44).

Among the institutions that might stimulate decision making, the state is an obvious candidate. To play this role, the state must do more than provide a predictable environment or gather available capital together into larger lumps. Hirschman sees the state as a potential source of "disequilibrating" incentives that make decisions harder to avoid and thereby induce private capital to become more entrepreneurial.

Gerschenkron and Hirschman suggest that the state's repertoire must go well beyond the one envisioned by Weber. Do their ideas also have implications for Weber's vision of the state structures? Nothing in them negates the importance of a competent, coherent bureaucratic structure, but they do suggest that the aloof detachment suggested by Weber may not suffice. The surrogate entrepreneurship that Gerschenkron talks about and the subtle triggering of private initiative that Hirschman emphasizes demand more than predictable, impersonal rule making. In a "Gerschenkronian" or "Hirschmanian" process of transformation, the shape of a project of accumulation must be discovered, almost invented, and the state must be a participant in its invention.[11] It is not enough to lower perceived risk. Entrepreneurship must be selectively stimulated, complemented, and reinforced. This in turn demands more intimate connections to private economic agents, a state that is more "embedded" in society than insulated from it.[12]

Gerschenkron and Hirschman do not explore the forms of state-society relations that their models of state action imply, but their work points to the necessity of complementing the Weberian internal structure hypothesis with an analysis of state-society relations. How are the ties between the state and the entrepreneurial groups it is trying to stimulate structured? This is a challenge that Gerschenkron and Hirschman leave for future practitioners of the comparative institutional approach.

Gerschenkron and Hirschman are also less sanguine than Weber that the state will be able to play the roles they see as necessary. The bequest of this tradition was not some "statist" mirror-image of the neo-utilitarians' utopian faith in the market. Whether any given state will be able to compensate for the shortcomings of private economic agents and push a process of transformation remains an open question. Hirschman (1958, 65) is particularly adamant on this point, arguing explicitly that "The fact that private entrepreneurs will be unable or unwilling to do certain jobs which we would like to see done does not in itself ensure that the government can handle them."

What the comparative institutional tradition offers is a spelling out of some roles that the state might be called on to fulfill if the process of economic transformation is to move forward, and some suggestions as to what kind of institutional characteristics might be necessary for the state to have a chance of playing these roles. The questions for the successors to this tradition become: Can we identify more clearly the internal organizational features and patterns of external ties associated with effective state action? Can we find concrete historical examples that illustrate their variations? Curiously, by the end of the 1980s there were a variety of "institutionalist revisions" of the neo-utilitarian frame that thoroughly supported this agenda.

Institutionalist Revisions of the Neo-Utilitarian Model

The neo-utilitarian model of the state was only one part of a larger tradition of "strategic actor" or "rational choice" models, which continued to evolve during the 1970s and 1980s. As this evolution proceeded, a number of ideas quite subversive to the ideological precepts of the neoliberal policy revolution began to emerge.

In areas where rational choice models of some precision could be confronted with clear-cut empirical data, it soon became obvious that the logic of atomistic individual motivation was inadequate without complementary institutional arguments. Students of American politics like Kenneth Shepsle (1987) and Terry Moe (1987) realized that something stood between the chaos that majority voting rules should produce in theory and the stability (not to say ossification) that characterized the practice of American politics. "Institutions" in the sense of historically accreted practices and structures that were taken for granted had to be the answer.[13] A parallel evolution can be seen among economic historians interested in development, with the work of Douglass North being one prominent example.

Because it focused on property rights, North's earlier work (e.g., North and Thomas 1973) was taken as vindicating the neo-utilitarian focus on free markets as the key to development. The "new institutional economics" (North 1986) was therefore taken to be an adjunct to the neo-utilitarian perspective rather than an alternative. By the end of the 1980s, however, it was quite clear that North was up to something quite at odds with the neo-utilitarian project.

In North's later work, institutional analysis, very broadly defined, moves to center stage. Sounding more like a sociologist than an economist, North emphasizes the "pervasiveness of informal constraints," noting that "In our daily interaction with others, whether within the family, in external social relations, or in business activities, the governing structure is overwhelmingly defined by codes of conduct, norms of behavior, and conventions" (1990, 36). He then goes on to argue that "institutional frameworks" are "the critical key to the relative success of economies" (69) and to lament that "we have paid a big price for the uncritical acceptance of neoclassical theory" because "allocation was assumed to occur in a frictionless world, that is, one in which institutions either did not exist or did not matter" (131).

Such iconoclasm on the part of a Nobel laureate whose work had been seen as reinforcing the neo-utilitarian perspective was an important indicator that the tide was turning. Unfortunately, however, North provides only the vaguest of building blocks for the construction of an alternative approach. His discussion of "institutional frameworks" is grounded in only a few illustrative examples, most of which have to do with property rights.[14] Furthermore, since he sees cultural norms as primary and organizational forms as derivative, he is not inclined to focus on how organizational structures make a difference. North rejects the neo-utilitarian vision of the state as leviathan as "clearly not the whole story," but he offers little concrete analysis of how variations in state structure can have consequences for industrial change.

North's work offers moral support for a comparative institutional political economy without providing a clear empirical exemplar of how to go about it. Fortunately, others were constructing a more grounded revisionism. As a model of how an analysis can leave neo-utilitarian assumptions behind, replace them with a more institutionally sophisticated perspective, and still retain its analytical bite, there are few better exemplars than the evolution of Robert Bates's work on African agriculture.

In 1981 Bates published *Markets and States in Tropical Africa*, which soon became a classic statement of the perils of state intervention in developing countries. Bates's book provided considerable grist for the neo-utilitarian mill, but it was genuine political economy, not simply an application of economic logic to political institutions. Bates made it clear that the results he observed were produced by a specific, historically grounded institutional context, not an ineluctable generic logic of how states work. Nonetheless, the portrayal of the consequences of state action was quite consistent with a neo-utilitarian perspective.

In Bates's view, state officials in newly independent African countries, vested with powerful instruments of economic control inherited from colonial regimes, used these instruments to benefit urban elites, including themselves. Their policies destroyed farmers' incentives to increase agricultural output and thereby sabotaged the process of development. Seeking to combine political survival with self-enrichment, they created rental havens, erected bureaucratic obstacles to the efficient allocation of resources, and ended up debilitating peasant agriculture— the only economic sector capable of propelling future development. Dismantling state power and leaving the peasantry free to take advantage of market opportunities seemed to be the answer, just as a simpler neo-utilitarian model would have suggested.

Returning to African agriculture in a 1989 study of Kenya called *Beyond the Miracle of the Market*, Bates explores similar themes, but with a different leitmotif. He begins by criticizing what he calls "the neo-classic revival" for its "failure adequately to deal with institutions" and its "failure to analyze politics" (3), and he goes on to offer a very different analysis of the consequences of bureaucratic intervention in agricultural markets. He argues that only with "an intensive infusion of bureaucratic regulation" was it possible to secure the capital inputs necessary for the reconstruction of peasant agriculture. Bureaucratic monitoring and control of production inputs turn out to be the best way of insuring export crop quality, and administratively imposed restrictions the best way of capturing economies of scale in processing (75–81). Instead of being the enemy of agrarian production, state intervention enables its development.

This is not to say that the state has become the primary engine of development in Bates's later work. To the contrary, the crux of his argument revolves around the interaction of the state and its private counterparts. Initially, institutional endowments, predominantly those associated with the state, "shape the way in which economic interests are formed" while simultaneously shaping the political conditions that determine whether interests are realized or frustrated (152). Later, effective interest groups facilitate some state strategies and inhibit others.

Looking at the evolution of Kenyan agriculture, Bates notes, for example, that while state economic intervention dictated the emergence of large-scale facilities to process agricultural produce, the political institutions developed at the same time left processors "subject to economic predation" by small-scale producers working through their political representatives (86–87).[15] The argument is not simply that states help create classes. Societal interests once congealed become in turn crucial to shaping the state's future developmental strategies. In the Kenyan case, the "prosperous producers of cash crops" (147) were the crucial private counterparts. Their political clout was critical to the construction of supportive forms of state involvement. The key to Kenya's agrarian development was the fact that its leaders "allied the state with the fortunes of the incipient gentry" (39).

The key features of what we might call "the mature, comparative institutional Bates" are worth reiterating. First, the state is analyzed not as a generic entity whose economic impact can be deduced from the inherent predilections of bureaucrats, but as a historically contingent creation whose properties depend on specific institutional endowments and the character of the surrounding social structure. Second, under certain historical circumstances, state involvement in the process of accumulation may be an essential ingredient in the promotion of growth and transformation. As Bates puts it in his conclusion (1989, 150), "Bureaucracies and organizations do not necessarily stand in opposition to markets. Rather they are often put in place in an effort to underpin and to unleash market forces." Third, states and societies are mutually constitutive. Interests and classes are not logically prior to the state and its policies. States help define private interests and play a crucial role in the growth of classes and interest groups. Once classes and interest groups have coalesced, they constitute powerful constraints on subsequent state strategies.

Bates's work suggests the promise of a happy synthesis that would institutionalize work in the rational choice tradition, revitalize the comparative institutional tradition, and relegate the simplistic, asocial versions of the neo-utilitarian vision of the state to history's copious dustbin. In fact, things were not so simple. While revisionism was undercutting early neo-utilitarian thinking, the comparative institutionalist tradition was confronting the issue of the state in a variety of new ways, complicating the definition of a "comparative institutional approach."

Comparative Institutional Variations

The neo-utilitarian vision of the state, however flawed, was part of a whole set of diverse reactions to earlier failures to confront the question of the state. Development policy of the 1950s and 1960s may have been based on an implicit assumption of a benevolent and capable state, but this assumption was quite resolutely *not* explicitly theorized.[16] Theoretical debates between pluralists and Marxists during the 1960s and 1970s focused mainly on how the state was controlled by society, rather than on the state as an actor in its own right.[17] The 1980s saw a proliferation of work attempting to "bring the state back in.[18]"

By the end of the 1980s, it was no longer possible to allow the state to go unanalyzed, regardless of one's position on its benevolence, capability, or culpability, but there was still strong divergence even among those who adopted an institutional approach. Some were focused on extending the classic models of Weber, Gerschenkron, and Hirschman to account for contemporary developmental successes.[19] Others were more concerned with understanding how state initiatives were undercut by the social structures that surrounded them. One thing that united them was that both put state-society relations at the center of their analyses.

Joel Migdal's *Strong Societies and Weak States* is one of the best examples of the latter approach, in which state-society relations are seen as an undercutting counterpoint to state involvement. For Migdal (1988, 39), Third World states remain "weak" even though they have "become formidable presences even in the far reaches of their societies" and "greatly affected the course of social and economic change." They are weak because "diffused fragments of society have stayed strong" (137), retaining at the local level the ability to frustrate state actions. Egypt's Nasser, whose land reforms transformed Egyptian society, is one of Migdal's prime examples. Even though Nasser's "success in bringing about the demise of the powerful class of large landlords through the reform was resounding" (189), and even though "the state, in effect, transformed society" (195), Nasser could not replace the local power of rich and middle peasants and the local "strongmen" who represented their interests politically.

Migdal is obviously not a neo-utilitarian. He certainly makes no assumption that the state is simply an aggregation of individual maximizers. Like the neo-utilitarians, he sees the logic of the state's agenda as fundamentally in tension with the logic of social relations outside the state, but he poses his polarity in totally different terms and comes to correspondingly different conclusions. Instead of state versus market, Migdal's polarity is state versus society. For the neo-utilitarians, the ability of state incumbents to collaborate with private elites around projects of "rent seeking" makes the state a dangerously powerful threat to the market. For Migdal, the same behavior indicates the state's weakness vis-à-vis society. For the neo-utilitarians, increases in the scope of the state's action signify a reduction in the power of market forces. For Migdal, the social power of local elites signifies, almost by definition, a diminution in the power of the state. Because he focuses on social control, Migdal sees the basic project of local power holders as inherently in opposition to the basic project of the state. Local elites want to preserve their sphere of control; the state wants to expand its sphere. Both cannot win.

This zero-sum approach to state-society relations stands in contrast with the classic comparative institutional political economy that was outlined earlier. The underlying assumption of Weber, Gerschenkron, or Hirschman is that a shared project underlies the interactions of state and society. Both industrial elites and the state are interested in transformation, neither can implement this project on their own, and each brings something to the task.

Why is the idea of shared projects missing from Migdal's vision of state-society relations? His focus on social control rather than economic transformation is one reason. Shared projects require positive-sum outcomes, like increased output. Migdal is only tangentially interested in such outcomes. He has little to say about industrialists—the implicit counterparts for Gerschenkron and Hirschman—or even about accumulation-oriented rural elites—like Bates's "incipient gentry." The "local strongmen" and traditional rural elites that are his focus are much less likely to be interested in shared projects.

By focusing on societal groups whose primary interests are parochial and conservative, and by emphasizing social control as an outcome, Migdal highlights the zero-sum aspects of state-society relations. Nonetheless, even in Migdal's cases there are clearly times when joint projects predominate. The account of relations between Nasser and the "rich and middle peasants" is the best example. Nasser's antilandlord policies gave such peasants room to consolidate themselves as a powerful rural class. At the same time, this group made an important contribution to Nasser's economic agenda. According to Migdal (1988, 204–5), after the agrarian reform, under the rich and middle peasants' leadership, agricultural output and productivity exceeded Egypt's rapid population growth. This trend reversed the fall in output and productivity under the old regime.

This joint project may have eventually devolved into a struggle between the state and peasant "strongmen" over whether there would be further transformation of agriculture, but initially it was a mutually reinforcing relation. The state helped create a social group whose economic project in turn contributed to the state's own developmental agenda.[20]

The salience of shared projects depends on the historical moment, but it also depends on the analyst's agenda. For Migdal, African agriculture epitomizes state-society struggles over social control, but Bates manages to discover possibilities for shared projects.[21] Comparing Migdal's take on state-society relations in East Asia with other recent examples of comparative institutional analysis of East Asian development provides an even better illustration of the importance of the analyst's point of view. When Migdal turns to East Asia, he sees "massive societal dislocations" resulting in "strong states." States cannot be "strong," in Migdal's view (1988, 262), "without exogenous factors first creating catastrophic conditions." "Massive societal dislocation, which severely weakens social control," is a "necessary condition" for the emergence of a strong state (269).

Without denying that "societal dislocations" helped set postwar parameters in East Asia, other analysts focus on the nature of the shared project that emerged subsequently. Two country studies, one by Alice Amsden (1989) on Korea and one by Robert Wade (1990) on Taiwan, are among the numerous studies that illustrate this point.[22] Both authors consider the construction and execution of projects based on a symbiotic relation between the state and nascent industrial groups. The state's contribution to such shared projects is crucial, but they also require developmentally engaged partners on the societal side.

Amsden argues that "late industrialization" East Asian style[23] requires state intrusions beyond Gerschenkron's "state as investment banker" or Hirschman's "disequilibrating investments."[24] In Amsden's view (1989, 143), "The first industrial revolution was built on laissez-faire, the second on infant industry protection. In late industrialization the foundation is subsidy—which includes both protection and financial incentives. The allocation of subsidies has rendered the government not merely a banker, as Gerschenkron (1962) conceived it, but an entrepreneur, using the subsidy to decide what, when and how much to produce." In addition, the state must "impose performance standards on the interest groups receiving public support. . . . [I]n direct exchange for subsidies, the state exacts certain performance standards from firms" (145–46). The combination of incentives and performance does not just shape the behavior of existing industrial operations; it enables the state to coax into being a set of entrepreneurial groups that can serve as the societal side of a joint project of industrial transformation.

Wade's portrayal of the aggressiveness of the state's role is more restrained but fundamentally similar. He argues (1990, 26–27) that Taiwan's industrial success lay in the "governed market," a series of policies that "enabled the government to guide—or govern—market processes of resource allocation so as to produce different production and investment outcomes than would have occurred with either free market or simulated free market policies." He goes on to specify periods of "state leadership" in particular sectors, during which state initiatives were crucial to the transformation of key sectors (111). Again, state policies do not just change the behavior of existing actors, they also help bring into being the societal actors without whom industrial development would be impossible.

Looking at East Asia through the eyes of Amsden and Wade takes us full circle from the neo-utilitarians back to the iconoclastic endorsement of "activist government" by World Bank Vice President Karaosmanoglu with which the chapter started. It is precisely analyses like those of Amsden and Wade that provide the empirical grounding for Karaosmanoglu's conviction that "a more activist positive governmental role can be a decisive factor in rapid industrial growth."

Indeed, by the beginning of the 1990s, the World Bank as an institution felt it had to take the comparative institutionalist perspective seriously. Its major report on the "East Asian miracle" tried to locate the bank somewhere between a neoclassical view and the "revisionist" Amsden/Wade view. The report conceded (1993, vi) that "in some economies, mainly those in Northeast Asia, some selective interventions contributed to growth." It also adamantly affirmed the value of Weberian bureaucracies (157–89).[25]

Does this mean that the comparative institutional agenda has already been completed? Hardly. Despite neo-utilitarianism's theoretical difficulties in dealing with the state, no alternative frame can claim the encompassing elegance that gives the neo-utilitarian model its charisma. Recent contributions to the comparative institutional tradition validate the pursuit of such an alternative, but they also highlight the challenges that must be confronted along the way.

A Comparative Institutional Agenda

Any comparative institutional political economy of the state must offer a clear vision of both the state's internal structure and the character of state-society relations. Weber's "bureaucracy hypothesis" remains the point of departure for analyses of internal structure. The problem of state-society relations must be recast in a more dynamic form, along the lines suggested by Bates's analysis, one that makes state policy an endogenous factor in the changing character of the state's societal counterparts.

Weber's original assertion that bureaucratic state structures confer advantage is consistently supported by contemporary analysts. On this, Migdal concurs with Amsden and Wade. While stressing "dislocations" as the necessary condition of a "strong state," Migdal is careful to point out (1988, 274) that an "independent bureaucracy" is one of the sufficient conditions. Amsden and Wade both identify state bureaucrats as playing crucial roles in industrial transformation. Even the World Bank concurs.

There is, however, one important caveat. Weber tended to see the growing sway of bureaucracy as inevitable. Analyses like Midgal's make bureaucratic forms look harder to attain and more vulnerable. Getting effective bureaucratic organization to take hold in most Third World states is a daunting task. If and when real administrative machinery is established, dissolution and decay are as likely as expansion and reinforcement. If transformation demands an effective bureaucracy, there is no guarantee that supply will match demand. A comparative institutional approach turns the neo-utilitarian image of the state on its head. It is the scarcity of bureaucracy that undermines development, not its prevalence.

Unfortunately, this consensus still finds little reflection in policy debates and popular accounts (such as those invoked in chapter 1). "Bureaucracy" is still a pejorative term for citizens and policymakers alike. It is the moribund, ineffectual antithesis of entrepreneurial initiative and effective governance. Or it is the self-serving collection of privileged incumbents postulated by the neo-utilitarian image of the state. Or it may be thought of as a malignant combination of the two. Rarely, if ever, is it seen as the competence-enhancing set of structures and norms postulated by Weber. "Bureaucracy" is used as a generic term, equivalent to "the organizational apparatus of the state." States are not seen as varying substantially in the degree to which they are "bureaucratic." Underlying this conceptual problem is the surprising dearth of systematic comparative evidence regarding variations in the degree to which existing state structures approximate the Weberian ideal-type "bureaucracy."

To fulfill the potential of a comparative institutional approach, the Weberian hypothesis must be explored across agencies and countries. Looking at the state agencies involved in particular industrial sectors, as this study does, is one way of putting more empirical meat on the idea that it is scarcity rather than surfeit of bureaucracy that impedes development. The key is to identify differences in the way states are organized and then connect these differences to variations in developmental outcomes. Proving the connection empirically is not easy, but at least the logic of the argument is clear.

The question of state-society relations is more complicated. Two apparently conflicting positions coexist. On the one hand there is the "insulation" position. For Weber, insulation from society was a necessary precondition for a functioning bureaucracy.[26] Migdal agrees, seeing the ties between local "implementors" within the state apparatus and "strongmen" outside it as undercutting the state's ability to carry out its developmental projects. Bates (in his first book) and the neo-utilitarians go further, equating the development of state-society ties with "capture" of the state apparatus by rent seekers.

Logically the emphasis on insulation makes sense. Unless loyalty to the rest of the state apparatus takes some kind of precedence over ties with other social groups, the state will not function. The kind of coherent, cohesive bureaucracy that is postulated in the Weberian hypothesis must have a certain degree of autonomy vis-à-vis society. The problem is separating the benefits of insulation from the costs of isolation.

The whole idea of "joint projects," which is central to the visions of Gerschenkron, Hirschman, Amsden, and Wade, makes close ties to key social groups fundamental to developmental efficacy. This view also makes intuitive sense. We are, after all, talking about capitalist societies in which neither investment nor production can be implemented without the cooperation of private actors. The idea that states operate most effectively when their connections to society are minimized is no more plausible than the idea that markets operate in isolation from other social ties. Just as in reality markets work only if they are "embedded" in other forms of social relations, it seems likely that states must be "embedded" in order to be effective.

The question of how autonomy and embeddedness might be effectively combined is further complicated by the fact that states and social structures shape each other. The presence of organized social groups with something to gain from transformation enhances the prospect sustaining a transformative bureaucratic state; effective bureaucracies enhance the prospects that would-be industrialists or "incipient gentry" will become organized social groups. Conversely, a society dominated by loose-knit webs of local power holders with a vested interested in the status quo will make it harder for coherent, cohesive state apparatuses to survive, but the absence of a coherent state apparatus makes it less likely that civil society will organize itself beyond a loose web of local loyalties.

There are various ways to cut into this knot of reciprocal relations. In this study I have started with state structures and state-society relations and looked at their impact on subsequent changes in society, more specifically at their impact on industrial organization. Others may choose to start with social structures, then try to explain the emergence of particular forms of state organization and state-society ties.

Whatever tack is taken, the ultimate aim is the same. Capturing the dynamics of state-society relations and putting them together with the "Weberian hypothesis" on internal organization is the basic challenge facing the comparative institutional approach. Analytic generalizations must be grounded in the analysis of specific historical evidence. We need to look at the covariation of state structure, state-society relations, and developmental outcomes. What separates states that embody the neo-utilitarian nightmare from states that can legitimately claim to be developmental? How do shared projects of transformation work? What kind of state roles are involved? How do successful shared projects change relations between the state and its private collaborators? Using comparative historical evidence to answer these questions will exploit the opportunity opened up by neo-utilitarianism's retreat and forge a more satisfying vision of the state's place in the process of development.

3

States

IN LATE 1978, a government tax collector was killed in Bandundu Province, Zaire. That people's resentment against tax collection in Zaire should reach lethal levels is hardly surprising. The rapaciousness of the Zairian officialdom is legendary, and the state's most visible representative, the army, "lives on the backs of the ordinary people" since "for some unknown reasons, the Mobutu regime has always been unable regularly to pay its forces" (Kabwit 1979, 394, 399).

Once Joseph Mobutu Sese Seko gained control over Zaire in 1965, he and his coterie within the Zairian state apparatus systematically looted Zaire's vast deposits of copper, cobalt, and diamonds, extracting vast personal fortunes visibly manifested not only in luxuriant life-styles at home but also in multiple European mansions and Swiss bank accounts of undetermined magnitudes. In return for their taxes, Zairians could not even count on their government to provide minimal infrastructure. After fifteen years of Mobutu's rule, the road net, for example, had "simply disintegrated" (Kabwit 1979, 402)—by one estimate there were only six thousand miles left out of what was once a ninety-thousand-mile net (*New York Times*, November 11, 1979). In the first twenty-five years under Mobutu, Zaire's GNP per capita declined at a rate of 2 percent per year (World Bank 1991, 204), gradually moving this resource-rich country toward the very bottom of the world hierarchy of nations and leaving the country's population in misery as bad or worse than that which they suffered under the Belgian colonial regime.

Unfortunately for the citizens of Bandundu Province, the government's effectiveness at repression substantially exceeded its effectiveness at road building. State response to the death of the tax collector took the form of two detachments of soldiers who killed seven hundred of the local people. Later fourteen men were hanged as "ringleaders" in the tax collector's death (*New York Times*, June 3, 1978, 3).

The Zairian state represents a challenge, not just to its citizens, but also to theories connecting variations in the structure and behavior of state apparatuses to trajectories of national development. We need to understand what kind of a state this is. Does its internal structure warrant being called a bureaucracy? How should one characterize its relation to society?

Any general understanding of variation in the role of the state must take into account this predatory polar type.

Understanding the other pole is equally important. While states like Mobutu's were providing practical demonstrations of the perversions predicted by neo-utilitarian models of the state, the "East Asian NICs" offered empirical foundations for extending the comparative institutional arguments of Weber, Gerschenkron, and Hirschman and gave analysts like Amsden and Wade a chance to offer institutional descriptions of the "developmental state."[1]

Juxtaposing "predatory" and "developmental" states focuses attention on variation defined in terms of developmental outcomes. Some states extract such large amounts of otherwise investable surplus while providing so little in the way of "collective goods" in return that they do indeed impede economic transformation. Those who control these states plunder without any more regard for the welfare of the citizenry than a predator has for the welfare of its prey. Other states foster long-term entrepreneurial perspectives among private elites by increasing incentives to engage in transformative investments and lowering the risks. These states may not be immune to using social surplus for the ends of incumbents and their friends rather than those of the citizenry as a whole, but on balance the consequences of their actions promote rather than impede transformation.

No one would contest the fact of such variation. The challenge is to link obvious variations in outcome to underlying differences in state structure and state-society relations. Success in connecting performance and structure in these extreme cases offers in turn a start toward making similar connections in other, more ambiguous cases—intermediate states like Brazil and India that have enjoyed inconsistent but occasionally striking success in promoting industrial transformation.

Comparing concrete historical cases offers opportunity for fresh attack on the conceptual issues confronted in chapter 2. Is predatory behavior associated with an excess of bureaucracy, as neo-utilitarians argue, or with a scarcity, as a comparative institutional approach would suggest? Do developmental states reconfirm Weber's contention that bureaucracy and capitalism "belong intimately together"? How is the character of interaction between the state and dominant elites different in predatory and developmental states? Are developmental bureaucracies more or less insulated than predatory ones? Does the possibility of "joint projects" define developmental states? If so, how does the internal organization of the state interact with social structural opportunities to make joint projects possible?

A quick look at Zaire, an almost purely "predatory state," begins the discussion. Next, I will look at the three countries most often used as models of the "developmental state"—Japan, Korea, and Taiwan. Using the analytical leverage provided by these polar types, I will then analyze the intermediate cases—India and Brazil. My aim is *not* to explain the origins of predatory, developmental, and intermediate states, a task for historical scholarship that goes well beyond the ambitions of this study.[2] Instead, the idea is to take existing structural types as starting points, using them to show how internal organization and relations to society produce a distinctive developmental impact.

Zaire as the Archetype of the Predatory State

Without question, Zaire is a textbook case of a "predatory state" in the simple, commonsense definition of the term. It preys on its citizenry, terrorizing them, despoiling their common patrimony, and providing little in the way of services in return.[3] Condemning the Zairian state is easy. The challenge is to integrate this perverse case into a more general understanding of Third World states. Beyond its obvious penchant for predation, how would one characterize the internal structure of the Zairian state or its relations with society?

Conventional dichotomies like "strong" versus "weak" mislabel this state. By some definitions, it is a "strong" state. It certainly has what Michael Mann (1984, 188) would call "despotic power." It can undertake any action it chooses without "institutionalized negotiation with civil society groups." It also has a considerable amount of what Mann (189) calls "infrastructural power," the ability to penetrate society and implement its decisions. It has at least proven itself able to extract and appropriate resources. Yet it has little capability of transforming the economy and social structure over which it presides. In this sense, Migdal (1988) would call it a "weak" state.

Is Zaire's state "autonomous"? If "autonomous" means not having its goals shaped by societal forces, then it is very autonomous. No class or organized civil society constituency can be said to control it. If, on the other hand, "autonomy" implies the ability to formulate collective goals instead of allowing officeholders to pursue their individual interests, then Zaire fails the test. Instead, it embodies the neo-utilitarian nightmare of a state in which all incumbents are out for themselves. Certainly it bears no resemblance to the "relatively autonomous" state of structural Marxism, which fosters the accumulation of capital with greater effectiveness than private capitalists themselves (cf. Poulantzas 1973).

Callaghy (1984, 32–79) emphasizes the Mobutu regime's patrimonial qualities—the mixture of traditionalism and arbitrariness that Weber argued was characteristic of precapitalist but not capitalist states. True to the patrimonial tradition, control of the state apparatus is vested in a small group of personalistically interconnected individuals. At the pinnacle of power is the "presidential clique," which consists of "50-odd of the president's most trusted kinsmen, occupying the most sensitive and lucrative positions such as head of the Judiciary Council, Secret Police, Interior Ministry, President's office, and so on" (Gould 1979, 93). Next there is the "Presidential Brotherhood," who are not kin, but whose positions still depend on their personal ties with the president, his clique, and each other.

One of the most striking aspects of the Zairian state is the extent to which the "invisible hand of the market" dominates administrative behavior, creating a caricature of the neo-utilitarian image of how state officials act. In Zaire, repressive violence and market relations are joined to form the ultimate expression of neo-utilitarian rent-seeking.[4] A Zairian archbishop (quoted in Callaghy 1984, 420) described it as follows: "Why in our courts do people only obtain their rights by paying the judge liberally? Why do the prisoners live forgotten in prisons? They do not have anyone who can pay the judge who has their dossiers at hand. Why in our offices of administration, like public services, are people required to return day after day to be able to obtain their due? If they do not pay the clerk, they will not be served." President Mobutu himself characterized the system in much the same way: "Everything is for sale, everything is bought in our country. In this traffic, holding any slice of public power constitutes a veritable exchange instrument, convertible into illicit acquisition of money or other goods" (Lemarchand 1979, 248).

The prevalence of such a thorough-going market ethic might at first seem inconsistent with what Callaghy (1984) characterizes as an "early modern absolutist state," but it is in fact quite consistent. Personalism and plundering at the top destroys any possibility of rule governed behavior in the lower levels of the bureaucracy, giving individual maximization free rein.

Even a quick look at Zaire suggests that it is not a surfeit of bureaucracy but its absence that is central to Zaire's problems. Rule-governed behavior immersed in a larger structure of careers that creates commitments to corporate goals is notable by its absence. The only semblance of corporate cohesion centers on the state's repressive capacity and even that totters at the edge of incoherence, leaving even the regime's survival as a predator dependent on the sufferance of its powerful European and American allies.[5]

In fact, the Zairian case extends Weber's assertion of the "intimate connection" between bureaucracy and capitalism. Looking at Zaire, it is clear that the usefulness of bureaucracy lies not just in transforming pre-capitalist "traditional" social forms. Bureaucracy becomes even more crucial in a context where the market has so thoroughly penetrated the social consciousness that "everything is for sale." When "marketization" and personalism dominate instead of predictable, rule-governed bureaucratic behavior, the development of a bourgeoisie oriented toward long-term productive investment is almost an impossibility. With a bureaucracy whose maxim is "make the quest for wealth and money an obsession,"[6] anyone risking a long-term investment must be considered more a fool than an entrepreneur.

In addition to supporting basic Weberian contentions regarding the virtues of bureaucratic state structures, the Zairian case sheds interesting light on state-society relations. While the Zairian state's ability to penetrate and reshape civil society is certainly imperfect, the Mobutu regime has been quite effective at *disorganizing* civil society. It has systematically worked at weakening the cohesion of traditional collectivities. At the same time, it has made sure that coherent interest groups organized at the national level, which might be competitors for power, are disrupted before they emerge. Lacking its own program of social and economic transformation, the predatory state is threatened by the potential agendas of civil society. It deliberately tries to produce the kind of loose-knit society that, according to Migdal, undercuts a transformative agenda. The stagnation and disarray that follow from the state's active disorganization of civil society is not a disadvantage from the point of view of the predatory state; it is an advantage. Transformation might give rise to organized social groups. "Departicipation" is the goal politically (cf. Callaghy 1984, 41), and there is no possibility of joint projects.

Zaire confirms our initial suspicion that it is not bureaucracy but its absence that makes the state rapacious. At the same time, Zaire suggests that is it not so much "weakness" in relation to civil society that prevents the state from fostering transformation. Instead the state's energies are directed toward preventing the emergence of social groups that might have an interest in transformation. It is not just poor developmental performance that defines the predatory state. Internal organization and the structure of its ties to society mark it just as clearly. On both of these dimensions, the predatory state can be sharply distinguished from states whose performance has earned them the label "developmental."

The Archetype of the Developmental State

In 1982, with little theoretical fanfare, Chalmers Johnson introduced what was to become a focal point in future debates over the role of the state in industrialization. He argued that Japan's "developmental state" was a central element in explaining the country's post–World War II "economic miracle." At the same time, Wade and his colleagues at the Institute of Development Studies at Sussex University were describing Taiwan and Korea as "developmental states."[7] In both cases, a comparative institutional perspective made it easier for the figure of the developmental state to emerge out of the background of startling economic growth, although even observers with a neoclassical bent had a hard time ignoring the state's salience.[8]

Johnson's (1982) account of the golden years of Japan's Ministry of International Trade and Industry (MITI) provides the best starting point for trying to understand the structural features of the developmental state. His description is particularly fascinating because it corresponds so neatly to what a sophisticated implementation of ideas from Gerschenkron and Hirschman might look like in practice. In the capital-scarce years following World War II, the Japanese state acted as a surrogate for a missing capital market while at the same time helping to "induce" transformative investment decisions. State institutions from the postal saving system to the Japan Development Bank were crucial in getting the needed investment capital to industry. The willingness of state financial institutions to back industrial debt/equity ratios at levels unheard of in the West was a critical ingredient in the expansion of new industries.

The state's centrality to the provision of new capital also allowed it to implement "industrial rationalization" and "industrial structure policy" (Johnson 1982, 27–28). MITI was the "pilot agency" that oversaw this process. Given its role in the approval of investment loans from the Japan Development Bank, its authority over foreign currency allocations for industrial purposes and licenses to import foreign technology, its ability to provide tax breaks, and its capacity to articulate "administrative guidance cartels" that would regulate competition in an industry, MITI was in a perfect position to "maximize induced decision-making."[9]

Some might consider Johnson's characterization of MITI as "without doubt the greatest concentration of brainpower in Japan" (26) an exaggeration, but few would deny the fact that Japan's startling postwar economic growth occurred in the presence of " a powerful, talented, and prestige-laden economic bureaucracy." Nor was it controversial to assert that, at least in the period Johnson was describing, "official agencies attract the most talented graduates of the best universities in the country and the positions of higher-level officials in these ministries have been and still are the most prestigious in the society" (20). The ability of the higher civil service exam to weed out all but the top graduates of the top universities is apparent in the failure rate. As few as 2 or 3 percent of those who take the exam in a given year pass.[10]

The success of the Japanese developmental state is clearly consistent with the "Weberian hypothesis." Officials have the special status that

Weber felt was essential to a true bureaucracy. They follow long-term career paths within the bureaucracy and operate generally in accordance with rules and established norms. In general, individual maximization must take place via conformity to bureaucratic rules rather than via exploitation of individual opportunities presented by the invisible hand. Furthermore, these characteristics vary across the Japanese bureaucracy. It is the less bureaucratic, more clientelistic agencies like the Ministry of Agriculture that are likely to be associated with "pockets of conspicuous inefficiency" (Okimoto 1989, 4).

Weberian pronouncements regarding the necessity of a coherent, meritocratic bureaucracy are confirmed, but the Japanese case also indicates the necessity of going beyond such prescriptions. All descriptions of the Japanese state emphasize the indispensability of informal networks, both internal and external, to the state's functioning. Internal networks are crucial to the bureaucracy's coherence. Johnson (1982, 57–59) emphasizes the centrality of the *gakubatsu*, ties among classmates at the elite universities from which officials are recruited, and particularly the "*batsu* of all *batsu*," which brings together the alumni of Tokyo University Law School.[11]

Informal networks give the bureaucracy an internal coherence and corporate identity that meritocracy alone could not provide, but the character and consequences of these networks depend fundamentally on the strict selection process through which civil servants are chosen. The fact that formal competence, rather than clientelistic ties or traditional loyalties, is the prime requirement for entry into the network makes it much more likely that effective performance will be a valued attribute among loyal members of the various batsu. The overall result is a kind of "reinforced Weberianism," in which the "nonbureaucratic elements of bureaucracy" reinforce the formal organizational structure in the same way that Durkheim's "noncontractual elements of contract" reinforce the market (cf. Rueschemeyer and Evans 1985).

External networks connecting the state and civil society are even more important. As Chie Nakane puts it, "the administrative web is woven more thoroughly into Japanese society than perhaps any other in the world" (cited in Okimoto 1989, 170). Japanese industrial policy depends fundamentally on the maze of ties that connect ministries and major industrialists. "Deliberation councils," which join bureaucrats and businesspeople in rounds of data gathering and policy formation around an ongoing series of specific issues, are only one example of the "administrative web" (World Bank 1993, 181–82). Okimoto (1989, 157) estimates that deputy directors of MITI sectoral bureaus may spend the majority of their time with key corporate personnel.

Ties between the bureaucracy and private powerholders are reinforced by the pervasive role of MITI alumni, who through *amakudari* (the "descent from heaven" of early retirement) end up in key positions not only in individual corporations but also in the industry associations and quasi-governmental organizations that comprise "the maze of intermediate organizations and informal policy networks, where much of the time-consuming work of consensus formation takes place " (Okimoto 1989, 155). *Amakudari*, like other aspects of embeddedness, is carefully institutionalized. According to the World Bank (1993, 178–79), "retiring bureaucrats in Japan do not choose their sinecures, but are assigned them by a committee within their ministry."

The centrality of external ties has led some to argue that the state's effectiveness emerges "not from its own inherent capacity but from the complexity and stability of its interactions with market players" (Samuels 1987, 262).[12] This perspective is a necessary complement to descriptions, like Johnson's, that stress MITI's ability to act authoritatively rather than emphasizing its ability to facilitate the exchange of information and build consensus. The danger in this view is that it sets external networks and internal corporate coherence against each other, as opposing alternative explanations. Instead, internal bureaucratic coherence should be seen as an essential precondition for the state's effective participation in external networks.

If MITI were not an exceptionally competent, cohesive organization, it could not participate in external networks in the way that it does. If MITI were not "autonomous" in the sense of being capable of independently formulating its own goals and able to count on those who work within it to see implementing these goals as important to their individual careers, then it would have little to offer the private sector. MITI's "relative autonomy" is what allows it to address the "collective action" problems of private capital, helping capital as a whole to reach solutions that would be hard to attain otherwise, even given the highly organized Japanese industrial system.

This "embedded autonomy," which is precisely the mirror image of the incoherent despotism of the predatory state, is the key to the developmental state's effectiveness. "Embedded autonomy" combines Weberian bureaucratic insulation with intense connection to the surrounding social structure, offering a concrete resolution to the theoretical debate over state-society relations that was raised in chapter 2. Given a sufficiently coherent, cohesive state apparatus, isolation is not necessary to preserve state capacity. Connectedness means increased competence instead of capture. How autonomy and embeddedness are combined depends, of course, on both the historically determined character of the state apparatus and the nature of the social structure, as comparisons of Korea and Taiwan will illustrate nicely.

Variations on the Developmental State

The state's ability to facilitate industrial transformation in Korea and Taiwan, like its ability in Japan, has been fundamentally rooted in coherent, competent bureaucratic organization. In each case, however, the nonbureaucratic bases of internal solidarity and the nature of ties to the surrounding social structure are distinct. The state in both of the East Asian NICs looks more autonomous than the Japanese version, but Korea and Taiwan diverge in the way their states are embedded.

Korea

In comparing the Korean bureaucracy to Mexico's, Kim Byung Kook (1987, 100–102) points out that while Mexico has yet to institutionalize exam-based civil service recruitment, meritocratic civil service examinations have been used for recruiting incumbents into the Korean state for over a thousand years (since A.D. 788). This tradition is vital in providing both legitimacy for state initiatives and nonmaterial incentives for the "best and the brightest" to consider bureaucratic careers. Despite Korea's chaotic twentieth-century political history, the bureaucracy has managed to preserve itself as an elite corps.

In Korea, as in Japan, it is fair to say that the state has traditionally been able to pick its staff from among the most talented members of the most prestigious universities. Data on the selectivity of the *Haengsi* (higher civil service exams) are almost identical to the data offered by Johnson for Japan. Despite a sevenfold increase in the annual number of recruitees to the higher civil service between 1949 and 1980, only about 2 percent of those who take the exam are accepted (B. K. Kim 1987, 101).

Along with similar recruitment patterns comes a similar "corporate culture." Choi's (1987) discussion of the Economic Planning Board, for example, notes the same kind of confidence and esprit de corps that characterize MITI in Johnson's description. Finally, as in Japan, meritocratic recruitment via elite universities creates the potential for constructing batsu-like solidary interpersonal networks within the bureaucracy. Looking at passees in 1972, B. K. Kim (1987, 101) found that 55 percent were graduates of Seoul National University, and of these, 40 percent were graduates of two prestigious Seoul high schools.

Korea demonstrates the importance of bureaucratic traditions, but it also confirms post-Weberian concern with the vulnerability of bureaucracy. Under Rhee Syngman, the civil service exam was largely bypassed. Only about 4 percent of those filling higher entry-level positions came in via the civil service exam. Nor were those who entered the higher civil service able to count on making their way up through the ranks via a standard process of internal promotion. Instead, higher ranks were filled primarily on the basis of "special appointments" (B. K. Kim 1987, 101–2). The character of bureaucratic appointment and promotion under Rhee was, of course, quite consistent with the character of his regime. While it presided over a certain amount of import-substituting industrialization, Rhee's regime was more predatory than developmental. Despite massive U.S. aid, government deficits constituted a major drain on domestic savings (see Stallings 1992). Rhee's dependence on private-sector donations to finance his political dominance made him dependent on clientelistic ties with individual businesspeople; not surprisingly, "rent-seeking activities were rampant and systematic" (Cheng 1987, 200).

Only the ascension to power of a group with strong ideological convictions and close personal and organizational ties "enabled the state to regain its autonomy" (Cheng 1987, 203). The junior officers involved in the coup led by Park Chung Hee were united by both reformist convictions and close interpersonal ties based on service experience and close batsu-like network ties originating in the military academy.[13] The superimposition of this new brand of organizational solidarity sometimes undercut the civilian state bureaucracy as military men were put in top posts, but in general the military used the leverage provided by their own corporate solidarity to strengthen that of the bureaucracy rather than to weaken it. Under Park, the proportion of higher entry-level positions filled with Haengsi examinees quintupled, and internal promotion became the principal means of filling the ranks above them (B. K. Kim 1987, 101–8).[14]

One of the features of the revitalized state bureaucracy was the relatively privileged position held by a single "pilot agency," the Economic Planning Board (EPB). Headed by a deputy prime minister, the EPB was chosen by Park to be a "superagency" in the economic area (B. K. Kim 1987, 115). Its power to coordinate economic policy through control of the budgetary process is enhanced by mechanisms like the Economic Ministers Consultation Committee and by the fact that its managers are often promoted into leadership positions in other ministries.[15] As in the Japanese case, the existence of a "pilot agency" does not mean that policies are uncontested within the bureaucracy. The EPB and the Ministry of Trade and Industry (MTI) are often at loggerheads over industrial policy.[16] Nonetheless, the existence of a given agency with generally acknowledged leadership in the economic area allows for the concentration of talent and expertise and gives economic policy a coherence that it lacks in a less clearly organized state apparatus.

Without a deep, thoroughly elaborated, bureaucratic tradition, neither the Park regime's reconstruction of bureaucratic career paths nor its reorganization of the economic policy-making apparatus would have been possible. Without some powerful additional basis for cohesion in the upper ranks of the state, the bureaucratic tradition would have remained ineffectual. Without both in combination, it would have been impossible to transform the state's relationship to private capital.

When the Park regime took power, its goal seemed to go beyond insulation to include dominance over private capital. Criminal trials and confiscation were threatened, and the leaders of industry were marched through the street in ignominy. This soon changed as Park realized that autonomy without embeddedness was not going to produce transformation. He needed to harness private entrepreneurship and managerial expertise in order to achieve his economic goals (see E. M. Kim 1987; M. S. Kim 1987). The ties between the regime and the largest conglomerate business groups (*chaebol*) became so tight that visiting economists concluded that "Korea Inc." was "undoubtedly a more apt description of the situation in Korea than is 'Japan, Inc.'" (Mason et al., cited in Cumings 1987, 73).

As in the case of Japan, the symbiotic relationship between the state and the chaebol was founded on the fact that the state had access to capital in a capital scarce environment.[17] Through its ability to allocate capital, the state promoted the concentration of economic power in the hands of the chaebol. It "aggressively orchestrated" their activities (Wade 1990, 320), sometimes assigning them specific projects to carry out, as when Park told Daewoo to take over a state-owned heavy machinery company that was in trouble (Cheng 1987, 239–40). At the same time, the Park regime was dependent on the chaebol to implement industrial transformation, which constituted the basis for its legitimacy.

Embeddedness under Park was a much more "top down" affair than the Japanese prototype, lacking the well-developed intermediary associations and focused on a small number of very large firms. The size and diversification of the largest chaebol did give them interests that were relatively "encompassing" (cf. Olson 1982) in sectoral terms so that the small number of actors did not limit the sectoral scope of industrial growth. Still, the Korean state could not claim the same generalized institutional relation with the private sector that the MITI system provided, and it never fully escaped the danger that the particularistic interests of individual firms might lead back in the direction of unproductive rent-seeking.

Korea pushed the limit to which embeddedness could be concentrated in a few ties without degenerating into particularistic predation. The opposite kind of divergence from the Japanese model can be found in the region's second prominent pupil of the Japanese model—Taiwan. In this case, the relative absence of links to private capital might seem to threaten the state's ability to secure full information and count on the private sector for effective implementation.

Taiwan

The state has been just as central to the process of industrial accumulation in Taiwan as it has in Korea, channeling capital into transformative risky investments, inducing entrepreneurial decisions, and enhancing the capacity of private firms to confront international markets. In Taiwan, as in Korea, the ability of the state to play this role depended on a classic, meritocratically recruited, Weberian bureaucracy, crucially reinforced by extrabureaucratic organizational forms. As in the case of the Korean state, the Kuomintang (KMT) regime is built on a combination of long-standing tradition and dramatic transformation, but differences in the historical experience of the two states led to very different patterns of relations with the private sector and, in consequence, very different patterns of state entrepreneurship.

The transformation of the Kuomintang state subsequent to its arrival on Taiwan is more striking than the changes in Korea between the 1950s and 1960s. On the mainland the KMT regime had been largely predatory, riddled with rent-seeking and unable to prevent the particular interests of private speculators from undermining its economic projects. On the island it was able to remake itself. Not only was the power of the regime's problematic landlord constituency wiped out, but ties with the private capitalists that had been most powerful on the mainland were severed as well. As Gold states (1986, 59), "the most egregiously corrupt and harmful persons by and large did not go to Taiwan at all."

Using this space, the KMT transformed its corrupt and faction-ridden party organization into more of an approximation of the Leninist party-state that it had aspired to be from the beginning (Cheng 1987, 97), thus providing the state bureaucracy with a reinforcing source of organizational cohesion and coherence. Internal discipline and the application of sanctions against the pursuit of individual interests at the expense of corporate goals certainly reached levels that had never been achieved on the mainland. For example, K. Y. Yin, characterized by Gold (1986, 68) as the "one man [who] dominated and forged the broad lines of Taiwan's economic path in the 1950s," was actually forced from office for a year on grounds of his involvement with a dubious loan to a private firm.[18]

Within the reinforced governmental apparatus, the KMT was able to put together a small set of elite economic policy organizations roughly similar in scope and expertise to Japan's MITI or Korea's EPB.[19] The Council on Economic Planning and Development (CEPD) is the current incarnation of the planning side of the "economic general staff." It is not an executive agency but "in Japanese terms it is somewhere between MITI and the Economic Planning Agency" (Wade 1990, 198). The Industrial Development Bureau of the Ministry of Economic Affairs (IDB) is staffed primarily by engineers and takes a more direct role in sectoral policies. Both of these agencies, like their counterparts in Korea and Japan, have traditionally been successful in attracting the "best and the brightest." The staff tend to be KMT members and graduates of Taiwan National, the country's most elite university (Wade 1990, 217).

Without negating the fundamental transformation in the character of the Kuomintang apparatus, it is also important to keep in mind that, as in the case of Korea, the existence of a long bureaucratic tradition gave the regime a foundation on which to build. Not only was there a party organization that could be reformed, but there were also some economic bureaucracies with considerable managerial experience. For example, the National Resources Commission (NRC), founded in 1932, had a staff of twelve thousand by 1944 and managed over one hundred public enterprises whose combined capital accounted for half of the paid-up capital of all Chinese enterprises. It was an island of relatively meritocratic recruitment within the mainland regime, and its alumni eventually came to play a major role in managing industrial policy on Taiwan.[20]

The punishing experience of being undercut by the particularistic interests of private speculators on the mainland led the political leadership of the KMT as well as the alumni of the NRC to harbor a fundamental distrust of private capital and to take seriously the anticapitalist elements of Sun Yat-sen's ideological pronouncements. These predilections were reinforced by the pragmatic fact that strengthening private capitalists on Taiwan involved increasing the power of an ethnically distinct, politically hostile private elite. It is therefore hardly surprising that instead of turning Japanese properties over to the private sector as its American advisers recommended, the KMT retained control, generating one of the largest state-owned sectors in the non-Communist world (see Cheng 1987, 107; Wade 1990, 302).

Instead of eschewing direct state ownership like the postwar Japanese did, the KMT has used state-owned enterprises (SOEs) as key instruments of industrial development. In addition to the banking sector, which was state-owned as in post-Rhee Korea, the state controlled a formidable set of industrial corporations. Taiwan's state-owned enterprises accounted for over half of all fixed industrial production in the 1950s, and, after falling off a bit in the 1960s, their share expanded again in the 1970s

(Wade 1990, 78, 97).[21] SOEs are particularly important in basic and intermediary industries. China Steel, for example, has enabled Taiwan successfully to outcompete all Organization for Economic Cooperation and Development (OECD) steel exporters in the Japanese market (Wade 1990, 99). The state enterprise sector not only makes a direct entrepreneurial contribution but is also a training ground for economic leadership in the central state bureaucracy.[22]

What is striking to observers whose implicit basis of comparison is Korea and Japan is the extent to which the Taiwanese private sector has been absent from economic policy networks. Even though the current trend is to "expand and institutionalize decision-making inputs from industrialists, financiers, and others" (Wade 1990, 293) relations between the KMT state and private (mainly Taiwanese) entrepreneurs are distant compared to the tight "Korea Inc." ties that bind the state and the chaebol together in Korea.

The Taiwanese state unquestionably operates with a less dense set of public-private network ties than the Korean or Japanese versions of the developmental state. Nonetheless, its lack of embeddedness should not be exaggerated. It is hardly isolated from the private sector. The World Bank (1993, 184–85) suggests that Taiwan's extensive set of state-owned enterprises, each of which has its own set of relations with private firms, helps compensate for less-developed ties between the central state apparatus and the private sector. Networks may be less apparent, but economic policy formation in Taiwan still grows out of "a little understood but apparently vigorous policy network [that] links the central economic bureaus with public enterprises [and] public banks" (Wade 1990, 295).

Wade notes, for example, that IDB officials spend a substantial portion of their time visiting firms and are engaged in something very much like MITI's "administrative guidance" (1990, 284). He provides (281) a revealing example of the state's close interaction with private capital in his discussion of negotiations between raw materials producers and textile companies in the synthetic fiber industry. While the formal negotiations involved the downstream industry association (Man-made Fibers Association) and the upstream domestic monopolist (a state-TNC joint venture), state managers were continuously involved, making sure that neither the country's efforts at backward integration into intermediary products nor the export competitiveness of its textile producers was threatened by the outcome. Informal public-private networks may be less dense than in the other two cases, but they are clearly essential to Taiwan's industrial policy.

Despite the greater distance between private capital and the state, Taiwan not only offers useful examples of embeddedness, it also demonstrates how autonomy can enhance the effects of embeddedness. The early evolution of the textile industry offers the best illustration (cf. Evans and Pang 1987). In the early 1950s K. Y. Yin, going against the wisdom of the American-trained economists advising his government, decided that Taiwan should develop a textile industry. Yin's conviction that there was a developmentally valuable, potential comparative advantage in local textile production came well before local entrepreneurs were willing to take the risk of initiating production. Instead of setting up a state-owned enterprise to fill the gap,[23] Yin's textile "entrustment scheme" provided a set of supports and incentives that made textiles too attractive to ignore. Wade (1990, 79) sums up the state's role under the scheme as follows: "It supplied raw cotton directly to the spinning mills, advanced all working capital requirements, and bought up all production." In addition, it restricted local entry and restricted imports, both quantitatively and by means of tariffs. The result was a spectacular growth of local production, 200 percent in three years according to Wade (1990, 79).[24] By providing an assured market and raw materials, it minimized the entrepreneurial risk involved in entering the industry and successfully induced the entry of private capital. In this initial phase, the state was supportive in a classic Hirschmanian way, inducing investment decisions and stimulating the supply of entrepreneurship.

The "entrustment" scheme was unusual in the lengths to which the state was willing to go in order to ensure that entrepreneurship was forthcoming; otherwise it was very similar to the policies of most Latin American countries in the initial phases of industrialization. What distinguishes K. Y. Yin's program from typical Latin American support for import-substituting industrialization (ISI) is that it was not captured by the entrepreneurs it had created. Instead, the KMT regime progressively exposed its "greenhouse capitalists" to the rigors of the market, making export quotas dependent on the quality and price of goods and diminishing protection over time.[25] Thus, the state was able to enforce the emergence of a "free market" rather than allowing the creation of "rental havens." Without the autonomy made possible by a powerful bureaucratic apparatus, it would have been impossible to impose the unpleasantness of free competition on such a comfortable set of entrepreneurs.

The example reinforces the point made earlier in relation to embeddedness and autonomy in Japan. Private capital, especially private capital organized into tight oligopolistic networks, is unlikely to provide itself with a competitive market. Nor can a state that is a passive register of these oligopolistic interests give them what they are unwilling to provide for themselves. Only a state that is capable of acting autonomously can provide this essential "collective good." Embeddedness is necessary for information and implementation, but without autonomy, embeddedness will degenerate into a super-cartel, aimed, like all cartels, at protecting its members from changes in the status quo.

A final, equally important characteristic of the developmental state is also well illustrated by the Taiwanese case. While it has been deeply involved in a range of sectors, the Taiwanese state is very selective in its interventions. The bureaucracy operates, in Wade's (1990, 226) words, as a "filtering mechanism," focusing the attention of policymakers (and the private sector) on sectors, products, and processes crucial to future industrial growth. Like most of the KMT's Taiwan strategy, selectivity was in part a response to previous experience on the mainland. Having experienced the disasters of an overextended state apparatus, the KMT was determined to conserve its bureaucratic capacity in its new environment.

Selectivity is not unique to Taiwan. It seems a general feature of developmental states. While benefiting from extraordinary administrative capacities, these states have restricted their interventions to strategic necessities. Johnson (1982) describes how the Japanese state, having experimented with direct and detailed intervention in the pre–World War II period, limited itself to strategically selected economic involvement after the war. Okimoto (1989, 2) notes that in terms of its overall size the Japanese state could be considered a "minimalist state." Obviously, selectivity reduces the demands on the state bureaucracy and makes efficacious performance easier.

Looking at Korea and Taiwan makes it clear that the historical embodiments of the developmental state are likely to display a range of variation,[26] but the fundamental features of "embedded autonomy" are visible underneath the variation.

Corporate coherence gives these states the ability to resist incursions by the invisible hand of individual maximization. Internally, Weberian characteristics predominate. Highly selective meritocratic recruitment and long-term career rewards create commitment and a sense of corporate coherence. The sharp contrast between the Weberian character of the developmental state and the prebureaucratic, patrimonial character of the predatory state reinforces the proposition that scarcity, not surfeit, of bureaucracy underlies ineffectiveness.

By the beginning of the 1990s even the World Bank acknowledged the importance of having a well-trained, well-paid state bureaucracy. The Bank's *East Asian Miracle* report (1993, 176–77) points out that "high-performing" East Asian economies (in contrast to the Philippines, for example) have all made conscious efforts to provide their bureaucrats with wages comparable to those in the private sector, noting the contrast between Singapore (where bureaucratic salaries are 110 percent of wages in comparable private-sector positions) and Somalia (where they are 11 percent). The report also notes that the efforts of developmental states to gain the cooperation of big business would be "hamstrung without an efficient and reputable civil service" (187).

At the same time, descriptions of developmental states support "neo-Weberian" arguments that the "nonbureaucratic elements of bureaucracy" may be just as important as the "noncontractual elements of contract" (cf. Rueschemeyer and Evans 1985). Informal networks or tight-knit party organizations enhance the coherence of the bureaucracy. Whether these ties are based on commitment to a parallel corporate institution or performance in the educational system, they reinforce the binding character of participation in the formal organization structure rather than undercutting it in the way that informal networks based on kinship or parochial geographic loyalties would.

Having successfully bound the behavior of incumbents to its pursuit of collective ends, the state can act with some independence in relation to particularistic societal pressures. The "autonomy" of the developmental state is, however, of a completely different character from the incoherent despotism of the predatory state. It is not just "relative autonomy" in the structural Marxist sense of being constrained by the generic requirements of capital accumulation. It is an autonomy embedded in a concrete set of social ties that bind the state to society and provide institutionalized channels for the continual negotiation and renegotiation of goals and policies.[27]

"Embeddedness" is as important as autonomy. The embeddedness of the developmental state represents something more specific than the fact that the state grows out of its social milieu. It is also more specific than the organic interpenetration of state and society that Gramsci called hegemony.[28] Embeddedness, as it is used here, implies a concrete set of connections that link the state intimately and aggressively to particular social groups with whom the state shares a joint project of transformation.

Finally, it is worth underlining that either autonomy or embeddedness may produce perverse results without the other. Without autonomy, the distinction between embeddedness and capture disappears. Autonomy by itself does not necessarily predict an interest in development, either in the narrow sense of economic growth or in the broader sense of improved welfare. The secret of the developmental state lies in the amalgam.[29]

The appearance of this peculiarly effective amalgam in the developmental states of East Asia depended, of course, on a very unusual set of historical circumstances, but this does not detract from the usefulness of the concept of embedded autonomy as an analytical point of reference.

Having seen how the amalgam works in archetypal cases makes it easier to spot the partial appearance of its features in other states and to appreciate their implications. The analytical features of developmental states provide benchmarks for assessing the confused and contradictory reality of intermediate states.

Intermediate States

Most developing states offer combinations of Zairian predation and East Asian "embedded autonomy." The balance varies over time and from organization to organization within the state. Brazil and India are good examples. Neither can be simply dismissed as predatory. There is no record of decades of consistently declining GNP as in Mobutu's case. India amassed a remarkable record of industrial growth in the 1950s and early 1960s while Brazil was considered a state-led "economic miracle" in the late 1960s and early 1970s. Their internal structures and relations to society are, like their performance, hard to describe in unambiguous terms. They have been described as "strong" and as "weak." Depending on the analyst's prism, they may appear as "autonomous" or "captured."

After looking at the internal structures and state-society relations that characterize predatory and developmental states, what would we expect to find in Brazil and India? Presumably, there should be some semblance of bureaucratic organization, but not the degree of corporate coherence enjoyed by developmental states. Consequently, the contradictory balance of embedded autonomy will be hard to maintain. Imbalance could take the form of either excessive clientelism or an inability to construct joint projects with potential industrial elites. Inconsistency is another possibility. Joint projects may be possible in certain sectors or certain periods but degenerate into clientelism or isolated autonomy in other sectors or other periods. Analyzing internal organization and state-society relations in these cases will almost certainly require a more complicated diagnosis, one whose contours will have to be constructed from the historical specifics of the two countries.

Brazil

Brazil's state apparatus has been described in a series of detailed field studies and telling interpretive analyses, both historical and contemporary.[30] The differences between the apparatus that they describe and the ideal typical "developmental state" begin with the simple question of how people get state jobs. Barbara Geddes (1986) chronicles the difficulty

that Brazil has experienced in instituting meritocratic recruitment procedures. Unusually extensive powers of political appointment complement
lack of meritocratic recruitment. Extending Johnson's (1982, 52) comparison of Japan and the United States, Ben Schneider (1987a, 5, 212,
644) points out that while Japanese prime ministers appoint only dozens
of officials and U.S. presidents appoint hundreds, Brazilian presidents appoint thousands (15,000 to 100,000 by Schneider's estimate). It is little
wonder that the Brazilian state is known as a massive source of jobs (ca-
bide de emprego) populated on the basis of connection rather than competence and correspondingly inept in its developmental efforts.

Unable to transform the bureaucracy as a whole, political leaders try to
create "pockets of efficiency" (bolsões de eficiência) within the bureaucracy (Geddes 1986, 105), thus modernizing the state apparatus by addition rather than transformation (see Schmitter 1971; Schneider 1987a,
45). The National Economic Development Bank (BNDE), favored especially by Kubitschek as an instrument of his developmentalism in the
1950s, was, at least until recently, a good example of a pocket of efficiency.[31] Unlike most of Brazil's bureaucracy, the BNDE offered "a clear
career path, developmental duties, and an ethic of public service" (Schneider 1987a, 633). Early in its institutional life (1956), the BNDE started a
system of public examinations for recruitment. Norms grew up against
arbitrary reversal of the judgments of the bank's technical personnel
(opinião do técnico) by higher-ups. A solid majority of the directors were
recruited internally, and a clear esprit de corps developed within the bank
(Willis 1986, 96–126).

Agencies like the BNDE[32] were, not surprisingly, more developmentally effective than the more traditional parts of the Brazilian bureaucracy. According to Geddes (1986, 116) those projects in Kubitschek's
Target Plan that were both under the jurisdiction of Executive Groups or
Work Groups and under the financial wing of the BNDE fulfilled 102
percent of their targets, whereas those projects that were the responsibility of the traditional bureaucracy achieved only 32 percent. Because the
BNDE was a major source of long-term investment loans,[33] its profes-
sionalism was an impetus to better performance in other sectors. Tendler
(1968) notes, for example, that the necessity of competing for loan funds
was an important stimulus to the improvement of proposals by Brazil's
electrical power generating companies (see Schneider 1987a, 143).

Unfortunately, the pockets of efficiency strategy has a number of disadvantages. As long as pockets of efficiency are surrounded by a sea of
traditional clientelistic norms, they are dependent on the personal protection of individual presidents. Geddes (1986, 97) looks at the way in
which the Department of Public Administration (DASP)[34] (created by
Getúlio Vargas to oversee professionalization of the civil service) declined

once Vargas's presidential protection was gone. Willis (1986) emphasizes the dependence of the BNDE on presidential support, both in terms of the definition of its mission and in terms of its ability to maintain its institutional integrity.

Reform by addition makes strategic selectivity harder. Uncoordinated expansion is the more likely result. Having entered power in 1964 with the hope of shrinking the state by as much as 200,000 positions,[35] the Brazilian military ended up creating "hundreds of new, often redundant, agencies and enterprises" and watching the federal bureaucracy grow from 700,000 to 1.6 million (Schneider 1987a, 44, 109, 575). Trying to modernize by piecemeal addition also undercuts the organizational coherence of the state apparatus as a whole. As the pieces are added, an ever more baroque structure emerges. The resulting apparatus has been characterized as "segmented" (Barzelay 1986), "divided" (Abranches 1978), or "fragmented" (Schneider 1987a). It is a structure that makes policy coordination difficult and encourages resort to personalistic solutions. As Schneider (1987a, 27) puts it, "personalism . . . is now made indispensable by bureaucratic fragmentation."

The fragmentation of the structure is complemented by the character of the careers that take place within it. Instead of being tuned to long-term gains via a series of promotions based on organizationally relevant performance, Brazilian bureaucrats face staccato careers, punctuated by the rhythms of changing political leadership and periodic spawning of new organizations. Every four or five years they shift agencies.[36] Since the top four or five layers of most organizations are appointed from outside the agency itself, long-term commitment to agency-relevant expertise has only a limited return. Construction of an ethos that can act effectively to restrain strategies oriented toward individual gain is correspondingly difficult.[37]

Just as the internal structure of the Brazilian state apparatus limits its capacity to replicate the performance of the East Asian developmental states, the character of its "embeddedness" makes it harder to construct a project of industrial transformation jointly with industrial elites. As in the case of the East Asian developmental states, embeddedness must be understood in historical terms.

While the Brazilian state has been an uninterruptedly powerful presence in the country's social and economic development since colonial times, it is important to keep in mind what Fernando Uricoechea (1980), Jose Murilo de Carvalho (1974), and others have emphasized: "The efficiency of government . . . was dependent . . . on the cooperation of the landed oligarchy" (Uricoechea 1980, 52). Reactionary rural elites were never dramatically swept from the stage as in the East Asian cases. To the contrary, the traditional symbiosis that connected traditional oligarchs to the state has been reinforced by a perverse "modernization."

As Hagopian (1986, 1994) has carefully documented for the state of Minas Gerais, the traditional exchange in which landowning families delivered political support in return for the fruits of state patronage has become tighter rather than looser over time. As the state expanded its role, descendants of Minas's old "governing families" moved into direct control of leading political positions and came to rely more and more on access to state resources as their principal source of power and wealth.[38]

The fusion of traditional oligarchic power with the modern state apparatus distorts any possible joint project between the state and industrial capital. Projects of industrial transformation become additional opportunities for the traditional oligarchy, now encapsulated within the state, to pursue its own clientelistic agenda. At the same time, relations with industrial capital have been complicated by the early and massive presence of transnational manufacturing capital in the domestic market.[39] Disciplining domestic capital, as K. Y. Yin did in the Taiwanese textile industry or as Amsden sees the Korean state as doing, becomes very difficult when transnational capital is the probable beneficiary of any "gale of creative destruction."

Problems of internal organization and problems of state-society relations are mutually reinforcing. The lack of a stable bureaucratic structure makes it harder to establish regularized ties with the private sector of the "administrative guidance" sort and pushes public-private interaction into individualized channels. The persistent political power of the traditional oligarchy not only distorts attempts at transformation but also undercuts attempts at internal reform. Both internal and state-society problems have proven remarkably invariant across changes in political regimes.

The military regime, which had, at least initially, greater internal corporate coherence,[40] proved unable to construct an "administrative guidance" kind of relationship with the local industrial elite. The regime was "highly legitimate in the eyes of the local bourgeoisie, yet unconnected to it by any well-institutionalized system of linkages" (Evans 1982, 221). Instead of becoming institutionalized, relationships became individualized, taking the form of what Cardoso (1975) called "bureaucratic rings," that is, small sets of individual industrialists connected to individual bureaucrats. As Schneider (1987b, 230–31) points out, the ad hoc, personalized character of these linkages makes them both undependable from the point of view of industrialists and arbitrary in terms of their outcomes. They are, in short, quite the opposite of the sort of state-society ties that are described by Samuels (1987) and others in their discussions of the developmental state.

The Collor regime, democratically elected at the end of the 1980s, is perhaps the best single monument to the obdurate internal and external problems that plague the Brazilian state. Hailed by Washington and the Brazilian media as a representative of "modernity," Collor was in fact an archetypal representative of the kind of symbiosis of traditional oligarchic privilege and state power that is described by Hagopian. Scion of a leading landowning family in one of Brazil's most backward states, Collor adeptly combined a "typical oligarchic career" (Schneider 1991, 323) with media flair and convincing neoliberal affectations.

Collor's program provided a brilliant, if brief, demonstration of how the neoliberal attack on the state could be combined with the preservation of traditional oligarchic rule. Schneider (1991, 329) sums up his impact on internal state structures as follows:

> Collor's across-the-board cuts were indiscriminate, affecting the best and the worst of agencies alike. Consequently, Collor alienated productive bureaucrats—many of whom are responsible for implementing other modernizing policies—without visibly improving efficiency. By the end of 1990, although the government had eliminated less than a third of the 360,000 jobs it promised to cut, it had nonetheless managed to lower morale, motivation, and productivity throughout the executive branch.

At the same time, the Collor regime disdained the other side of embedded autonomy, evincing "a liberal aversion to organized capitalism" and taking pride in "verbal abuse of business leaders" (Schneider 1991, 332). Finally, of course, Collor's apparent passion for neoliberal reform was combined with a level of corruption unprecedented even in Brazil, thus undercutting the state's legitimacy along with its effectiveness.[41]

Overall, it is easy to understand Schneider's (1987a, 4) lament that "the structure and operation of the Brazilian state should prevent it from fulfilling even minimal government functions." What is surprising is that, despite its manifold problems, the Brazilian state has managed historically to play a major role in fostering both growth and industrialization. From its aggressive provisions of financing for railways and other infrastructure at the end of the nineteenth century[42] through its direct involvement in high-technology ventures like aircraft manufacture in the postwar period, the Brazilian state has played a central role in what has overall been an impressive record of industrialization.[43] How is this possible given the problems I have just finished describing?

First of all, Brazil's experience is testimony to the fact that it takes only a very rough approximation of the Weberian ideal type to confer advantage. Even developmental states are only approximations of the ideal type, but intermediate states show that the basic bureaucratic model can be stretched further and still deliver. Despite pervasive flaws and distortions, bureaucracy in the Weberian sense can still be found in a wide spectrum of state agencies. Brazil is not Mobutu's Zaire.

Second, it must be remembered that while pockets of efficiency have failed as seeds for a more general renovation of the state apparatus, they have still provided the basis for a number of successful projects of sectoral transformation. In certain sectors during certain periods something close to embedded autonomy has been achieved. Each of these cases has to be understood by looking at the characteristics of the sector and the specific role that the state tried to play within it, a task better left for the next chapter. Nonetheless, it is worth noting here that the elements that come together in these sectoral scenarios evoke strong echoes of the patterns found in developmental states.

A few illustrations will suffice. The creation of electricity-generating capacity in the 1950s and 1960s was a state project that spoke to the needs of a burgeoning industrial sector whose growth was being choked by lack of reliable electric power. Tendler (1968) shows how this "joint project" of the state and industrialists was accomplished by surprisingly efficient state organizations.[44] The implantation of the auto industry, which eventually became one of Brazil's major exporters, was a joint project of the state and the TNCs. Shapiro (1988, 1994) describes how the interagency organization set up to oversee the industry's implantation, the Grupo Executivo para Indústria Automobilística (GEIA), served as a sectorally specific "mini pilot agency," providing the predictability and coordination necessary to reassure risk-shy TNCs. In the 1970s construction of a local petrochemical industry was also made possible by a sectorally specific version of embedded autonomy. Petrobrás, the state-owned oil company universally acknowledged as one of the most competent and coherent organizations within the ambit of the state sector, provided the anchoring point for a dense network of ties that bound local capital and TNCs together around a remarkable joint project of sectoral transformation (see Evans 1979, 1981, 1982, 1987).

None of these sectoral successes should be taken as an excuse for playing Pollyanna. In a changing global division of labor, temporary successes in a selected set of modern sectors are not laurels on which to rest. Built primarily around the goal of replacing imports, Brazil's industrial successes are not necessarily competitive in the current global context. At the same time, the decay and dismantling of state institutions insures that examples of embedded autonomy will be harder to find in the future.

The public passion with which Brazil rejected Collor's corruption in 1993 was a strong signal that Brazilians will fight to avoid becoming a replica of Zaire, but the four years of Collor's combination of neoliberal attack and traditional corruption left deep wounds in the already problematic Brazilian state. If a coherent, effective state apparatus is a necessary element in responding to the challenge of the global economy, Brazilians have little cause to be sanguine. At the same time, Brazil's deeply divided social structure makes the pursuit of any collective agenda extremely difficult. Still, Brazilian state managers can be grateful that they do not face the level of social structural complexity and contentiousness that their counterparts in India have confronted since independence.

India

The vast and sprawling state apparatus of India is even more ambiguously situated in the space between predatory and developmental states than is Brazil. The Indian state's harsher critics (e.g., Lal 1988) see it as clearly predatory and view its expansion as perhaps the single most important cause of India's stagnation. Others, like Pranab Bardhan (1984), take almost the reverse point of view, arguing that state investment was essential to India's industrial growth in the 1950s and early 1960s and that the state's retreat from a more aggressively developmental posture has been an important factor in India's relatively slow growth in the 1960s and 1970s. Still others, like Rudolph and Rudolph (1987), talk of the "weak-strong" Indian state and argue that economic policies have ceased to be oriented around a project of transformation, becoming instead simply responses to pressure from mobilized "demand groups."

No one denies that India has a venerable bureaucratic tradition. At the time of independence, the Indian Civil Service (ICS) represented the culmination of a tradition that stretched back at least to the Mughal empire (see Rudolph and Rudolph 1987). Its 1,100 members formed a prestigious elite, and it was considered "the best possible career for a nice middle class Brahman boy" (Taub 1969, 11). For two hundred years it had provided "the steel frame of empire," serving as a model not just for other colonial administrations but for England's own civil service as well (Taub 1969, 3). Its successor, the IAS (Indian Administrative Service), carried on the tradition. Entry is primarily via a nationwide examination that is at least as competitive as its East Asian counterparts. Of twelve thousand candidates who take the exam, only eighty will be given places in the IAS.[45] While educational training is not concentrated in a single national university in the way that it is in East Asia, solidary networks are enhanced by the fact that each class of recruits spends a year together at the National Academy of Administration.[46]

This is not to say that India's bureaucracy is without defects. First, the British traditions that the IAS inherited were by no means unambiguous assets. Assimilation of the culture of the imperial power was an important criteria of acceptance into the ICS. Even after the English had departed,

IAS exams still had three parts: English, English essay, and general knowledge, and even the last was slanted toward knowledge of "Western civilization" rather than Indian political economy or relevant technical skills.[47] Thus, the exam has traditionally been very attractive to humanistically oriented members of the "literary castes" (Lal 1988, 314).

Unfortunately, there is a discrepancy between the kind of generalist education rewarded by the exams and the technical jobs that passees are increasingly expected to do. An intelligent generalist might perform well, if career patterns provided the opportunity for the gradual acquisition of relevant skills on the job. Careers seem, however, to be characterized by the same kind of rapid rotation that characterizes the Brazilian bureaucracy. Rudolph and Rudolph (1987, 34) report, for example, that chief executive officers in the petrochemical industry have an average tenure in office of about fifteen months.[48]

In addition to problems of the IAS tradition itself, the Indian state, like Brazil's, has experienced difficulty in sustaining its institutional integrity. While none of the advocates of neoliberal dismantling has had the charisma of Brazil's Collor, the IAS can no longer claim to be the preeminent institution that it once was. Rudolph and Rudolph (1987, chap. 2) argue that there has been an "erosion of state institutions" at least since the death of Nehru. The cultural stigma attached to private-sector jobs has dissipated, making it harder for the state to count on attracting the "best and brightest." Contemporary field studies, like Wade's (1985) study of irrigation, have found corruption endemic. The "steel frame" has definitely corroded over the course of the last thirty years. As one former member of the IAS put it, "There was a time when we were proud to say that there is corruption in the country but the IAS is incorruptible. You can't say that any more" (Gargan 1993).

Despite all this, India's bureaucratic apparatus still seems a better rough approximation of the Weberian ideal type than Brazil's, and not a qualitatively worse one than the bureaucracies of the developmental states. If a historically deep tradition of solid state bureaucracy is an important element in producing a developmental state, why is the Indian state so often characterized as predatory and so rarely as developmental? The principal answers to this conundrum lie in state-society relations. They begin with the recalcitrant challenges of India's social structure and are exacerbated by the way the bureaucracy has defined its relation to society.

In India, problems internal to the bureaucracy are dwarfed by those generated by the societal context. In a "subcontinental, multinational state" (Rudolph and Rudolph 1987), state-society relations are qualitatively more complex than in the East Asian cases. Ethnic, religious, and regional divisions add to the administrative nightmare of trying to govern (say nothing of develop) a country of eight hundred million people. Given the diseconomies of scale inherent in administrative organizations, it would take a bureaucratic apparatus of truly heroic proportions to produce results comparable to those achieved on an island of twenty million people or a peninsula of forty million.

From the time of independence, the political survival of Indian regimes has required simultaneously pleasing a persistently powerful rural landowning class and a highly concentrated set of industrial capitalists. The shared interests of larger landowners and the millions of "bullock capitalists" in the countryside give agrarian elites daunting political weight (see Rudolph and Rudolph 1987). The role of rural powerholders may not be quite as overwhelming as it was for the KMT on the mainland, but, even more than in contemporary Brazil, it complicates any attempt to construct a project of industrial transformation. At the same time, the large business houses like the Tatas and Birlas must be kept on board. They are dependent on the state in many ways, but they are also the largest contributors to both the Congress party and the opposition (Encarnation 1989, 136–38). Since business houses and landowners share no "encompassing" developmental project, the divided elite comes to the state in search of particularistic advantage. They comprise, in Bardhan's (1984, 70) terms, "a flabby and heterogeneous dominant coalition preoccupied in a spree of anarchical grabbing of public resources."[49]

Even leaving rural powerholders aside, the Indian state's relation with industrial capital was quite the reverse of the combination of support and discipline that Amsden (1989) postulates for Korea. The "license, permit, quota raj," as it has been pejoratively labeled (see Encarnation 1989), restricted private capital onerously in the abstract, but it was in practice the linchpin of a profitable "anti-Schumpeterian" bargain. With their "embassies" in Delhi and their hoarded licenses, the big business houses could rest assured that capacity restrictions would prevent Schumpeter's "gale of creative destruction" from threatening the lucrative "rental havens" that the custodial state had bestowed on them (see Encarnation 1989, 133–46).[50] What private capital lost in autonomy they gained in security, but their gain was at the expense of the overall dynamism of the industrial sector.

Traditionally, the micro politics of state-private interactions have further diminished the possibility of the state providing organizational coherence to a developmental project that would serve to induce private investment and focus it in strategic sectors. The stereotypical IAS veteran was an Anglophile Brahman of Fabian socialist ideological leanings. The private capitalists with whom he dealt were likely to be of lower caste, different cultural tastes, and opposing ideology. Lack of shared discourse and common vision on which to found a common project left the exchange of material favors as the only alternative to hostile stalemate.[51]

The kind of embeddedness that might allow state managers to provide information dissemination, consensus building, tutelage, and cajoling to potential entrepreneurs seems almost entirely absent from the Indian scene. Nor is it easy to find an example of a sectorally specific network comparable to the one that binds together the state and private capital in the Brazilian petrochemical industry. Unlike the developmental states, the Indian state cannot count on the private sector either as a source of information about what kind of industrial policy will "fly" or as an effective instrument for the implementation of industrial policy. Without a "policy network" that incorporates the expertise of private capital, civil servants are deprived of a crucial source of information that might compensate for their generalist backgrounds.

Lack of selectiveness in the state interventions further increases the burden on the bureaucracy. The "license, permit, quota raj" has attempted to enforce detailed control over the physical output of a broad range of manufactured goods. At the same time, the state is directly involved in production of a greater variety of goods than even relatively expansive states like Brazil have attempted. Indian SOEs produce not only computers but also televisions, not only steel but also automobiles.[52] Expansion of the state enterprise system has been sufficiently explosive to warrant being labeled "cancerlike" by its critics (Lal 1988, 256). The state-owned share of corporate assets moved from one-sixth to one-half between 1962 and 1982 (Encarnation 1989, 185) as the number of state enterprises grew from five in 1951 to 214 in 1984 (Lal 1988, 257). This unselective expansion has created an intense strain on state capacity and may well have contributed to the "erosion of state institutions" (see Rudolph and Rudolph 1987).

Despite all this, the Indian state has still made a developmental contribution. State investment in basic infrastructure and intermediary goods was a central element in maintaining a quite respectable rate of industrial growth in the 1950s and early 1960s. Even Deepak Lal (1988, 237) admits that infrastructural investments and the increase in the domestic savings rate, both of which depended largely on the behavior of the state, were "the two major achievements of post-Independence India." State investment in basic agricultural inputs (primarily irrigation and fertilizers) played an important role in increasing agricultural output. The state has also invested effectively (in the sense of increasing output), if not always efficiently (in the sense of getting maximum possible output per unit of input),[53] in basic and intermediate industries like steel and petrochemicals, and in certain cases in more technologically adventurous industries like electrical equipment manufacture (see Ramamurti 1987). The main difference between India's industrial efforts and those of Brazil is that India's initiatives are less likely to foster the emergence of new private-sector counterparts.

Overall, the Indian and Brazilian states share many of the same problems. Internally, they have bureaucracies that are not patrimonial caricatures but still lack the corporate coherence of the developmental ideal type. Organizationally consistent career ladders that bind individuals to corporate goals while simultaneously allowing them to acquire the expertise necessary to perform effectively are not well institutionalized. These intermediate apparatuses confront more complex and divided social structures with less well developed bureaucratic capacity and less well organized external ties. Yet both states were less selective in the tasks they undertook.

Less internal capacity, more difficult environments, and less carefully defined agendas of involvement combined to put embedded autonomy of the sort that characterizes the developmental state out of reach. Worse still, the resulting inability to deliver effective developmental performance created structural pressure in the direction of further decline. State managers in both countries experienced serious losses in their real standards of living during the 1970s and 1980s.[54] Maintenance of even existing levels of capacity and competence were in doubt as the 1990s got under way.

If the developmental states highlight the advantages of effective bureaucracy, these intermediate states underscore the fact that the reproduction of bureaucratic organizations cannot be taken for granted. Bureaucratic organization, once in place, does not necessarily reproduce itself. There is no inexorable tendency for the supply of bureaucracy to meet the demands that are put on it. State capacity is not only in scarce supply in intermediate states. It is a wasting resource.

Structural Types and Developmental Dynamics

Predatory, developmental, and intermediate states are not just associated with different degrees of developmental success. They are also characterized by different internal structure and external ties. Comparing them confirms the usefulness of the basic categories of institutional analysis that were introduced in chapter 2.

Basic Weberian ideas on the usefulness of the bureaucratic frame to capitalist development have been amply validated by these cases. Popular and scholarly identification of the problems of Third World states with "excessive bureaucracy" is a misspecification. Real bureaucracy is in scarcity, not excess. It is the absence of bureaucratic structures that leads to the utilitarian nightmare of the state as a collection of self-interested incumbents using their offices for purposes of individual maximization. Ineffective states are characterized precisely by the lack of predictable, rule-bound, bureaucratic norms and relations within the state apparatus. Most states, even more effective ones, must struggle to maintain bureaucratic norms and structures.

The comparative historical evidence also reaffirms the modifications of the Weberian frame suggested in chapter 2. Just as Smith overstated the "naturalness" of markets, Weber overstated the "inevitability" of bureaucratic rule. Long-run tendencies toward the growth of bureaucracy do not mean that supply and demand will be in equilibrium. Constructing an effective bureaucracy is an arduous task whose results appear only with a lag. Furthermore, permanence cannot be taken for granted even when construction seems successfully achieved.

In the absence of deeply rooted bureaucratic traditions, as in Zaire, construction is a task of generational dimensions. Even in the presence of such traditions, as in India, effective state bureaucracies are vulnerable institutions, much easier to undermine than to sustain. When inherited traditions are not as thoroughly articulated, as in the case of Brazil, successful bureaucracies are even more precarious. With centuries-old foundations and a propitious immediate conjuncture, as in Korea, bureaucratic traditions may be revitalized in relatively brief periods, but even then bureaucratic norms are subject to erosion.

Surprisingly, focusing on bureaucratic scarcity also reveals some common ground with those who see bureaucracy as the problem. Rejecting neo-utilitarian notions that states must be "shrunk" because market ties are the only effective form of large-scale social organization does not mean rejecting the idea that the modern state's reach exceeds its grasp. Plans for state involvement that assume that the supply of bureaucracy will naturally increase to meet demand are utopian. Without stringent attention to selectivity, overwhelmed bureaucracies deteriorate into developmental impediments or pools of patrimonial self-interest. Without the resources necessary to sustain rewarding career paths and build esprit de corps, eviscerated state apparatuses devolve into exactly the rapacious nightmares that neo-utilitarians fear. Developmental strategies must be concerned with conserving state capacity even more than with conserving fiscal or natural resources.

The traditional Weberian perspective takes bureaucracy too much for granted in another way as well. The "nonbureaucratic elements of bureaucracy" are as important to state apparatuses as Durkheim's "noncontractual elements of contract" are to markets. Solidary groups, like the Japanese batsu, built on an amalgam of meritocratic selection, intensive socialization, and quasi-primordial ties, play a central role in the internal cohesion of effective bureaucracies. Their presence provides critical reinforcement for the compliance to organizational norms and sanctions that Weber took for granted. Their absence makes it harder to prevent devolution into individual maximization and the "marketization" of state offices.

Just as it helps elucidate the role of variation in internal structures, comparing different types of states vindicates the idea that connectedness complements autonomy and that it is the balanced combination of the two that makes for efficacy. Simplistic notions of the virtues of insulating state from society must be rejected. Some degree of "insulation" is inherent in creating a cohesive collectivity, but real effectiveness requires combining internal loyalties with external ties.

Zero-sum visions in which the state's ability to behave as a coherent corporate actor varies inversely with its connectedness to civil society set us on the wrong track. Internal cohesiveness and dense external ties should be seen as complementary and mutually reinforcing. Efficacious states combine well-developed, bureaucratic internal organization with dense public-private ties. The recipe works only if both elements are present. Complementarity and mutual reinforcement are also clear at the other end of the spectrum. The incoherent despotism of the predatory state combines undisciplined internal structures with anarchic external ties ruled by the "invisible hand" of clientelistic exchange relations.

Embedded autonomy and its opposite both feed on compatible social structures and play a role in the emergence and preservation of their societal counterparts. Each kind of state helped foster the emergence of complementary social groupings or classes. Developmental states played a central role in producing the organized industrial classes they needed as counterparts. The Zairian state also helped produce the counterpart that it needed: a disorganized and divided civil society incapable of resisting predation.

The intermediate cases, Brazil and India, help flesh out the picture of how different blends of autonomy and embeddedness can play themselves out against disparate societal backgrounds. In each country the balance of embeddedness and autonomy was different, and in each case problems with one element of the combination made it harder to realize the benefits of the other.

Despite its pervasive presence, Brazil's state apparatus lacked the overall coherence and cohesiveness. Consequently, embeddedness was problematic. The tight symbiosis between the state and the traditional oligarchy turned modernizing projects into sustenance for traditional power. Yet if embeddedness was part of the problem for the Brazilian state on a societal level, it was often central to the solution in particular sectors.

Brazil's industrial successes involved dense ties, not insulation. Pockets of efficiency within the state apparatus sometimes had sufficient cohesion and coherence to draw industrialists into joint projects with impressive results.

In India the balance was different. The norms and ideology of the bureaucracy were designed to avoid the pitfalls of being too closely tied to a social structure full of contradictory demands. "Inventing" the private counterparts necessary for dynamic industrialization was correspondingly difficult. The state's apparent successes tended to come in areas where autonomous action could produce results, like constructing dams or building basic industrial capacity in the 1950s. When it came to building ties that would induce new industrial entrepreneurship from the private sector, India could boast nothing comparable to the "miraculous" Brazilian industrialization of the early 1970s.

As the 1980s drew to a close, there was a negative sort of convergence between the two cases. In Brazil, the Collor regime evidenced little interest in shared projects and even less in trying to spread the characteristics of the old pockets of efficiency more widely through the bureaucracy. In India, the coherence and cohesiveness of the bureaucracy were on the wane, and the possibility of constructing a more effective pattern of state-society ties seemed even more distant. In both cases, declines in the state's ability to perform as a coherent corporate actor and erosion of effective state-society ties went hand in hand, demonstrating once again that capacity depends on putting autonomy and embeddedness together.

One thing remains clear: variations in internal state organization and state-society relations create differential degrees of developmental capacity. Having become convinced of this, the next step is to explore in more depth how capacity (or its lack) is reflected in action. Developmental outcomes depend on what states do with the capabilities they have, what roles they play, and how their would-be counterparts respond. Looking at what states do, as opposed to what they are like, is easier when the focus is narrowed to particular sectors. Therefore, the next chapter builds on the comparative lessons of this one by shifting the focus from structures to roles and from societies to sectors.

4

Roles and Sectors

KWANGYANG BAY, on Korea's southeast coast, is not a traditional tourist attraction, but it does draw foreign visitors. They come to see a steel plant, acknowledged by industry experts to be unique in the world.[1] With 250 tons per charge BOF converters, a 2.7-million-ton continuous caster directly connected to the hot strip mill, and computerized process controls throughout, the Kwangyang plant is a steel engineer's dream (D'Costa 1989, 40–43). Kwangyang also fulfills Korea's aspirations to become a major power in the world steel industry, aspirations that took shape two decades earlier with the formation of the Pohang Iron and Steel Company Ltd. (POSCO).[2]

When President Park Chung Hee broached the idea of a large-scale integrated steel plant with the World Bank and Western corporate leaders in the 1960s, the experts said it made no sense for Korea to contemplate becoming a serious steel producer. Korea had no iron ore, it had no coking coal, it had no tradition of heavy industry (at least not in the south). Korea had better stick with its comparative advantage and work on making its cotton textile industry more competitive. Park Chung Hee was stubborn and eventually managed to leverage war reparations from the Japanese into a deal that included both financing for POSCO and technical assistance from Nippon Steel (generally considered the world's most efficient producer).

The risk of setting up such a giant venture, which at $3.6 billion was the largest single investment attempted in Korea at that time, was "assumed entirely by the state" (Amsden 1989, 292). Over the course of the 1970s and 1980s, POSCO proved not only that Korea had an unpredicted "comparative advantage" in steel, but also that the usual association between state ownership and high-cost, money-losing operations was not inevitable. POSCO was one of the world's biggest producers, surpassing all U.S. firms even before the Kwangyang plant came on line (D'Costa 1989, 4). More important, it was one of the world's lowest-cost producers, able to make a profit while selling hot-rolled coil in Korea for half the U.S. list price (Amsden 1989, 317) and able to capture more than half of the market for imported steel in one of the world's most competitive markets—Japan (D'Costa 1989, 129).

POSCO's eventual performance more than repaid the extensive state subsidies that had gotten it going (see Amsden 1989, 296–97). Its low-cost, high-quality steel was crucial to the emergence of key industries like shipbuilding and autos. It contributed to the growth of Korea's exports by exporting 30 percent of its output. Finally, it became an important source of innovative technological knowledge. When U.S. Steel (USX) wanted to modernize its Pittsburgh, California, plant in 1986, it formed a joint venture with POSCO to take advantage of POSCO's design expertise (Amsden 1989, 291–92). Within Korea, POSCO served as a model of a well-managed company. It also branched out, helping found in the late 1980s the Pohang Institute of Technology, which was touted, even in the academic bastions of Seoul, as having the potential to become "Korea's MIT." Finally, in 1989 POSCO decided to build on its extensive experience with computerization and form a new subsidiary, POSDATA, which will provide value-added network (VAN) services to other businesses (*Electronics Korea* 3, 5:57–58).

POSCO represents an extreme form of state involvement. Going against the apparent logic of the market, the state created the sector on its own, substituting its own entrepreneurial initiative for that of private capital, then managing the production directly through a state-owned enterprise. While enough POSCO stock has been distributed now to make it officially a "private" company, it still has no real private competitors within Korea, nor is it likely to.

POSCO demonstrates that the most intrusive forms of state involvement can sometimes be successful in promoting industrial transformation, but it hardly provides a basis for generalizing. To begin with, it is an undertaking by an archetypal developmental state. Equally important, it is an undertaking in a sector where the diffusion of process technology and the relatively stable character of product technology have allowed more space for the state to act as an entrepreneur.

If POSCO shows that "more" involvement is not necessarily correlated with less transformation, there are other examples that demonstrate that reliance on less intrusive forms of state involvement, like regulation, is no guarantee that less developmental damage will be done. The textile industry, the locus classicus of private entrepreneurship, provides some of the best examples of how even modest state involvement can go deeply awry.

In 1985 Delhi Cloth Mills (DCM), one of India's most venerable "big business houses," filed a petition to close down its Bara Hindu Rao textile mill in New Delhi (*Financial Express*, October 30, 1988, 1). The mill was a classic example of a "sick" firm, inefficient and making heavy losses. In addition, it was a nonconforming use according to the Delhi Master Plan and therefore would have had to be shut down anyway, barring amendment of the plan (*Economic Times*, November 13, 1988, 1). Finally, there were problems of "discharge of toxic effluents," which made its continued operation in the densely populated Delhi district undesirable to say the least.

The response of the Delhi administration was steadfast refusal to allow a shutdown. It seemed to define its primary role as protecting textile workers from the dislocation of industrial change. There was fear that "if the mill was allowed to close down . . . then the other mills in the Capital—like those of the Birlas and Swatantra Bharat Mill—would also demand permission for closure" (*Financial Express*, October 30. 1988, 1). Yet the state seemed to lack the capacity to facilitate better uses for the site, new job-creating investments by the company, or new opportunities for the workers.

Four years later the case was still unresolved. The plant should have been statutorily closed down according to the master plan, but the Delhi administration still refused to allow closure. By this time the textile workers themselves were irate. Afraid that further delay might cost them the "golden handshake package" (amounting to several thousand dollars per worker) that they had been promised if the plant were allowed to close, union leaders argued that "the administration's stand makes a mockery of the pro-worker philosophy of the Congress party" (*Economic Times*, March 2, 1989, 1). The Delhi administration remained steadfast in its refusal nonetheless. When the Delhi high court ruled that the plant should be allowed to close, the administration vowed to take the matter to the Supreme Court.

The Delhi administration and the Park Chung Hee regime both violated the "natural logic of the market" and were therefore practitioners of state intervention. By any reasonable measure, Park Chung Hee engaged in "more" intervention than the Delhi administration. Founding POSCO involved allocating billions of dollars to a particular industrial activity and retaining control over how those massive resources were used for a period of decades. By founding POSCO the state opted for the role of "demiurge," a creator and manager of capital in its own right, taking responsibility for the course of sectoral transformation into its own hands. The Delhi administration was simply trying to be a good custodian, enforcing rules intended to keep powerful private economic actors from doing damage to the less powerful.

Should we conclude that more intervention is better, at least in the sense of being more likely to foster industrial transformation? Obviously not. The consequences of state intervention depend on what kind of intervention is attempted by what kind of state in what context. Arguing about whether one state has intervened "more" than another misses the point. *How* do different states get involved? What roles do they play or adopt? What consequences do these choices have?

Focusing on "sectors," that is, complexes of productive activity that result in a related set of products, makes it easier to see differences among states. Comparing what Korea did in steel and what India did in textiles may tell us more about differences between steel and textiles than about differences between Korea and India. Looking at how two states become involved in the same sector makes it easier to compare roles and strategies.

By looking at roles and sectors across the board, this chapter sets the stage for the next three chapters, which compare what Brazil, India, and Korea did in a particular sector—information technology. I will begin by setting up some heuristic categories of state involvement, some roles that can then be used to characterize state involvement in different sectors. Then I will look at how roles vary across sectors. Finally, I will explain why the information technology sector is particularly pertinent if we want to understand state involvement in the contemporary global economy.

This chapter builds on the last chapter's discussion of state structures. Without a modicum of bureaucratic coherence no role will be played effectively. Predatory states have neither the will nor the capacity to effect industrial transformation, so they drop out of the discussion. Developmental and intermediary states may adopt similar roles, but which roles they adopt and how well they play them depends in large measure on their structural characteristics. Embedded autonomy makes it easier to play most roles and creates an affinity for particular kinds of roles. Lack of it creates problems in playing most roles. Looking at the implementation of roles is the best way to see structural capacities come into play. Structures create the potential for action; playing out roles translates the potential into real effects.

Roles

In developmental states and intermediate states alike, the tenure of individual incumbents and the legitimacy of the state as a whole depend on fostering the growth of new industrial capacity. What roles might achieve this goal? Regulating production is a classic option, and there are a variety of ways to play the role of regulator. Alternatively, the state can make and sell goods itself, taking on the role of producer. Or the state can focus on "maximizing induced decision making"[3] by trying to draw private entrepreneurial forces into a new sector, which I call playing the role of midwife. Having helped bring new entrepreneurial groups into a sector, the state can focus on nurturing them and promoting their further evolution. I call this process of cultivating, nurturing, and prodding the entrepreneurial forces that have been awakened "husbandry."[4] Together, midwifery and husbandry create the social foundations for new sectors. Nonetheless, the role of regulator remains the most universal and the best place to start.

All states formulate rules and try to enforce them. Barring thoroughly perverse content, any consistent, predictable set of rules is a collective good. Constructing and enforcing rules is a function that not even the mythical miminalist state can avoid. Usually, however, rules go beyond the minimalist prescription of eliminating force and fraud in exchange relations. The character of the collective good then depends on content. Some rules are primarily promotional, aimed at providing stimulus and incentives. Others take the opposite tack, aiming to prevent or restrict the initiatives of private actors.

Custodians are regulators. They provide caretaking in the sense of protection and policing. They prevent proscribed behavior. The mininimalist state plays the custodial role, but custodial behavior extends well beyond minimalist proscriptions. At the beginning of the 1970s the Indian state with its "license, permit, quota raj" was particularly renowned for playing the custodian.[5] It was preoccupied with preventing private capital from engaging in undesirable or inappropriate activities, not with stimulating capitalists to take new risks.

Custodial rules are not the only form of state regulation.[6] Rules can be spurs as well as reins. They can be used for promotion as well as policing. Rules can focus on signaling and encouraging private actors rather than constraining them. For example, fiscal regulations may be designed to compensate for the difficulty of appropriating returns from innovation or to encourage investment in risky "sunrise" sectors. Even regulations that are ostensibly custodial and proscriptive may have promotional facets. Creating a protectionist "greenhouse" restricts the behavior of importers and foreign investors but spurs local capital to take the risk of entry.

While promotional strategies usually include a regulatory component, the custodial role is not a promising transformational tool. When the state deals with a new sector by playing the role of custodian, preoccupation with policing overshadows the developmental potential of regulatory rules, and possibilities for transformation are lost.

Just as all states play the role of regulator, all states play the role of producer, taking direct responsibility for delivering certain types of goods. Like the role of regulator, the role of producer can be played in different ways. As long as the product is infrastructural goods or "social overhead capital,"[7] the state as producer is a traditional role. State provision of transportation, communication, power and water supplies, and other standard kinds of social overhead capital has almost as long a tradition behind it as state provision of regulation. All are goods assumed to have a sufficiently collective or public character so that they would be undersupplied by private producers.

The role of **demiurge** takes the role of producer further. When the state decides to play demiurge, it becomes involved in directly productive activities, not only in ways that complement private investments but also in ways that replace or compete with private producers. The label, which equates the state with a mythological creator of material things, is meant to capture the extraordinary faith in the state's productive capacity that is implied by replacing rather than complementing private capital.[8]

Playing the demiurge implies strong assumptions about the inadequacies of private capital. Local capital is presumed incapable of becoming a "transformative bourgeoisie," of initiating new industries and sectors. Transnational capital is presumed uninterested in local development. If local capital is indeed unable, and transnational capital is in fact unwilling, to develop a new sector, then taking the role of demiurge may be the only way to move industrial development forward. In hindsight, it made sense for Korea to build an integrated steel plant in the 1960s. Neither transnational nor local companies were likely to undertake the task, and its subsequent "linkage" effects were important in stimulating industrial growth in other sectors. The same scenario is plausible in other sectors. Nonetheless, becoming an independent agent of accumulation is a risky choice.

Once embraced, the role of demiurge has an expansionary logic. It is expansionary partly for ideological reasons. John Waterbury (1993, 260) lays out the utopian vision that made the role of the demiurge attractive to Third World state elites: "a dynamic, carefully and rationally planned, state enterprise sector could, as far-sighted helmsman of the economy, mobilize scarce resources, stimulate markets, adopt new technologies, and rapidly lift the entire economy to a level of self-sustaining industrial growth." However attractive, such visions encouraged expansion far beyond the state's real capacity to produce effectively.

The demiurge role is also expansionary for organizational reasons. State-owned enterprises (SOEs) are the concrete embodiments of the role of demiurge. Like private firms, SOEs tend to grow and diversify. A firm created to initiate endeavors apparently beyond the capacity of local capital may end up competing in sectors where no such rationale applies, or even producing commodities indistinguishable from those already offered on the market by the private sector, defending its market share at the expense of private entrepreneurs. From inside the state apparatus, temptations of institutional aggrandizement may be hard to distinguish from possibilities for promoting transformation. What are presented as requisites of further sectoral transformation may in fact be the organizational interests of the demiurge.

Expansion increases the risk of bringing state firms into sectors where they are unlikely to perform well. The annals of the demiurge are littered with massive and conspicuous enterprise failures. It is a politically risky role as well. If private capital sees state firms taking away profitable territory, the state pays a price in terms of its legitimacy with the very groups whose support is essential to the overall transformative project.

Both custodian and demiurge grow out of negative conceptions of the private entrepreneurial class: as primarily requiring restraint in the case of the custodian and as incapable of entrepreneurship in the case of the demiurge. More optimistic assumptions are also possible. Capacities of the local entrepreneurial class can be seen as malleable instead of given. Greater optimism about the vitality of private capital leads to different roles.

Instead of substituting itself for private producers, the state can try to assist in the emergence of new entrepreneurial groups and to induce existing entrepreneurs to take on more challenging endeavors. This puts the state in the position of being a kind of **midwife**. Hirschman's ideas of "maximizing induced decision making" are most closely embodied in this role. K. Y. Yin's "textile entrustment scheme" is a classic example.[9] Yin's midwifery lowered risks, increased anticipated returns, induced entrepreneurship from local capital otherwise unwilling to take the plunge, and thereby got Taiwan's formidable textile industry rolling.

If promoting a new sector is the goal, acting as a midwife is likely to be easier and less risky than creating state-owned productive capacity. Of course, playing the role of the midwife leaves the state dependent on private response. The more daunting the technical and economic requisites of production in a particular sector, the harder it will be to lure private actors into it. The less developed the local entrepreneurial class, the smaller the range of sectors they can be expected to enter. Midwives can make a difference, but they are, after all, auxiliaries.

A variety of techniques and policies can be utilized in playing the role of midwife. Most of them involve reducing the risk and uncertainty entailed in entering a new sector or a new kind of endeavor. Even ostensibly custodial behavior can be adapted to serve purposes of midwifery. Erecting a "greenhouse" of tariffs, import prohibitions, and investment restrictions in order to protect infant sectors from external competition is the most obvious example. Providing subsidies and incentives is likely to be part of the midwife role. More subtle strategies may also work. Signaling that the development of a particular sector is considered important can create a generalized expectation of support that has an effect well beyond specific incentives or protections.

In principle, midwifery can also involve inducing transnational capital to make deeper commitments to local development. In practice, most states have a strong preference for energizing local entrepreneurs. Transnational capital becomes part of the strategy when local capital cannot do the job on its own. Bargaining with transnational capital to ally itself with local capital is one possibility. A direct alliance between state enterprises and transnationals is another. If neither of these two suffice, creating conditions that will induce independent TNC entry still remains an alternative. Whatever the techniques and whatever the nature of the capital involved, the aim of midwifery remains the same: inducing private capital to play an entrepreneurial role that it would otherwise be reluctant to undertake, thereby creating organizational and institutional resources committed to new sectors or new kinds of endeavors.

Ensconcing new entrepreneurial groups in a promising sector is a good beginning, but not the full transformative job. Local firms must continually respond to global changes in technology and markets. New entrants can easily fall by the wayside. Once persuaded to enter a sector, firms need encouragement and assistance to move ahead as the sector changes. Otherwise the fruits of midwifery will be lost. New entrants are as vulnerable as seedlings or foundling stock. They require a modern version of the old agrarian skills and techniques associated with husbandry.

Husbandry, like midwifery, can take a variety of forms. It may be as simple as signaling the prospect of state support for firms that venture into the more technologically challenging areas of the sector. It may be as complex as setting up state enterprises to take over riskier complementary tasks, like research and development, without which private firms cannot move forward. Whatever the techniques, husbandry involves a combination of support and prodding.[10] In some respects it is less demanding than midwifery because there are already private counterparts in the sector to work with. It is more challenging for the same reason. The existence of a directly interested private sector increases the risk of "capture."

Taken together, these four roles provide a framework for labeling the involvement of particular states in particular sectors. They are not mutually exclusive. To the contrary, they often appear in combination. The state may act as custodian and demiurge in the same industry, or combine both with midwifery. The combinations and their consequences depend in turn on the sectoral contexts.

Sectoral Variations

Sectors[11] are more than just arenas for observing specific kinds of state involvement. Their techniques of production, forms of industrial organization, and "modes of governance" vary systematically.[12] Consequently, each sector presents distinctive constraints and opportunities for state involvement. Whether a role or combination of roles fosters the growth of a particular sector depends on the state's capacity to play the roles in question, but it also depends on whether the blend of roles fits the sector.

In a classic comparative analysis, Jones and Mason (1982) found systematic variations across sectors in the extent to which states took on the role of producer. They argued that these variations reflected the "revealed institutional advantage" of state-owned enterprises. Underlying "revealed institutional advantage" was the balance between "market failure" on the side of private enterprise and "organizational failure" on the side of the state.

Market failure was assumed to be associated with high barriers to entry and consequent lack of competition. Organizational failure was rooted in the necessity of decentralized decision making. Jones and Mason concluded (41) that several characteristics gave SOEs "institutional advantage": Firms in the sector are typically large relative to product and factor markets. Firms are capital intensive. The sector overall has high forward linkages, produces standardized commodities, or is based on high-rent natural-resource exports.

Jones and Mason's argument implies that we should expect common patterns of state involvement in the same sector, even across states with different characteristics. Looking at specific sectors makes it clear that this is indeed the case. From Austria and France to Jamaica and India, state enterprises play a more prominent role in steel and minerals than in textiles. Sectoral specializations obviously constrain state strategies, as Michael Shafer (1994) and other have argued persuasively,[13] but the aim here is to show how the state's capacities and choices interact with the characteristics of sectors.

The structures and traditions of a state and its historical experience in particular sectors create predilections for some kinds of involvement and a congenital ineptitude for others. Like any organization, the state apparatus will tend to do what it knows how to do, even if what it knows how to do is not what it ought to be doing.[14] Sectors congruent with the state's "talents" will be more likely to emerge and survive than others. Over time the state's affinity for certain combinations of roles will affect the country's productive profile.

This leads us back again to constructed comparative advantage and the international division of labor. I argued in the first chapter that certain sectors are globally privileged in the sense of providing higher returns and better opportunities for growth.[15] If we add to this the idea that the emergence and survival of any sector depends in part on the state's ability to assume a blend of roles congruent with the sector's needs, then the state's capacities and choice of roles help determine a country's ability to improve its position in the global economy. The success of "constructed comparative advantage" will depend on the state's willingness and ability to play roles that grow sectors offering "multidimensional conspiracies in favor of development." This possibility is precisely what makes looking at state involvement in the information technology (IT) industry so interesting and important.

To understand why some roles and not others are helpful in constructing comparative advantage in a particular epoch, it is first necessary to understand how roles vary across sectors. I have chosen to look at a small but diverse set of sectors: mineral extraction, steel, textiles, and autos. They illustrate the historical variation of roles across sectors. They also make it clearer how the institutional nature of the state and the changing character of the global economy interact with sectoral characteristics to favor certain roles and frustrate others.

Mineral extraction provides an important baseline. Extractive industries are the locus classicus of the state as demiurge. From the oil fields of the Middle East to the copper mines of Africa and Latin America, extractive industries have been sites in which the state has acted in the stead of a local entrepreneurial class, creating state-owned enterprises and taking the burden of development on itself. Minerals provide the most transparent cases of state involvement in sectoral transformation.

After establishing a baseline case in mineral extraction, I will look at variations in industries that have been important in Brazil, India, and Korea. As a basic industry, steel, like mineral extraction, is a site where state enterprises have proliferated. The production of basic inputs is not, however, an industrialized replica of the extractive pattern. Technology is already too important for the state to operate on its own. The more technologically challenging production becomes, the more the state comes to depend on its relations with transnational capital.

A look at consumer goods, specifically textiles and autos, increases the range of sectoral variation. In textiles, where Jones and Mason would predict the role of demiurge to be problematic, the state indeed eschews direct production in favor of a regulatory role, either in its custodial form or as a tool for midwifery. Autos also leave little space for the demiurge, but custodial regulation is not really an option either. Inducing the emergence of the sector is the task, not trying to control an existing entrepreneurial structure. The problem is that global control of technology and markets makes it almost impossible for local producers to survive on their own. Midwifery must focus on building alliances with transnational capital.

Taken together, these four sectoral vignettes offer concrete illustrations of the importance of sectoral differences. They also show that sectoral characteristics are not static. Each sector changes over time, and the forms of state involvement must change accordingly. Changes in the over-all characteristics of the global industrial order, reflected most concretely in the changing strategies of transnational capital, affect what roles work in a given sector. Finally, these vignettes show how the institutional character of the state affects the way a role is played. Playing the right role poorly is as bad as playing the wrong role.

Mineral Extraction

Mineral extraction has often been claimed as a traditional prerogative of the state, but for twentieth-century Third World states, initial involvement usually took the form of regulating the industry.[16] Regulation demanded less capacity than actually running the industry. At the same time it provided the basis for cultivating technocratic expertise within the state apparatus.

The organizational capacity acquired by playing a regulatory role paved the way for efforts to play the demiurge. In Chile, the Copper Department's twenty years of experience in monitoring copper TNCs was the foundation for taking over production (see Moran 1974, 123–25). In Jamaica, the accumulated experience of a small nucleus of talented technocrats in the Jamaica Bauxite Commission and the Jamaica Bauxite Institute enabled the state eventually to take an ownership role in the industry (see E. H. Stephens 1987; Stephens and Stephens 1986).

The growth of state capacity is only half the story. State initiatives depended on the absence of private initiative. The capital requirements for participation in international mineral exports were well beyond what local capital could muster. The global structure of incentives facing extractive TNCs did not point to maximizing local returns in Third World countries. TNCs were reluctant to expand output and resisted integrating vertically through the construction of local refining and processing capacity.

The result was an "empty space" in the sector. In David Becker's words (1983, 229), "there was 'empty economic space' in the mining sector which local private enterprise could not fill and which transnational enterprise, constrained by oligopolistic and market forces, did not wish to fill." This "empty space" plus the gradual accretion (and diffusion across states) of expertise and capacity combined to produce a proliferation of state-owned mining companies.[17]

In many cases, the demiurge delivered. Becker's analysis of Peru in the 1970s is a case in point. After Cerro del Pasco, Peru's oldest copper TNC, withdrew in 1974, Centromin, Cerro's state-owned successor, tripled production relative to the TNC's peak output. It modernized old mines, added new refining capacity, and managed Cerro's old operations with a skill that produced a substantial improvement in profits (156). At the same time, the new state-owned enterprises invested in expanded refining capacity, including a zinc refinery that answered the "long-term prayers" of the small-scale, private-owned mines that produced zinc (222).

Unfortunately, the beneficent cycle in which involvement enhances capacity, allowing adoption of a more active role, which in turn fosters transformation, is only one version of the mineral extraction story. Other work suggests that the cycle can be vicious instead of virtuous, especially in the absence of a minimal level of generalized state capacity.

Michael Shafer's (1983) analysis of Zaire and Zambia is the best example.[18] It shows how involvement attempted in the absence of adequate initial capacity may not only fail to produce sectoral transformation but end up undercutting the state's institutional integrity. According to Shafer, "the real variable is political—whether the state possesses the trained personnel to run such operations and the strength to deny the temptation to manipulate them for short-run economic and political gains" (119).

In Zaire and Zambia, which enjoyed neither "strong, autonomous state institutions nor sufficient cadres of trained managers and technicians" (97), the role of demiurge brought disaster. In both Zambia and Zaire, declining efficiency (along with a deteriorating international market) eventually turned the mines into a drain on the central treasury. The World Bank estimated the cost in the 1980s of required rehabilitation and expansion for African producers in general at $1 billion a year, a figure far larger than mining cash flow (Shafer 1983, 106).[19]

Karl's work (forthcoming) on petroleum exporters provides a complementary version of how the state's institutional capacity interacts with sectoral characteristics. In her analysis, the state may develop sectorally specific capacities in bargaining with oil TNCs and eventually managing their operations, but it does not develop "the skills and talents that arise from the penetration of public authority to the far corners of the land in search of revenue" (230). The fiscal linkage to petroleum encourages unlimited expansion of the state's role along with a "general relaxation of fiscal discipline" (155), while at the same time creating tremendous incentives to rent-seeking efforts that focus on the state. Overall, petroleum generates demands without building commensurate capacity, leaving the "petro-state" vulnerable to the consequences of shifts in the international market.

Extractive industries offer more than edifying illustrations of how sectoral and institutional factors interact. They also illustrate the constraining power of the global context. Even when Third World states control the mines, vertically integrated TNCs still control global markets. Once

TNCs have no more ownership stake in Third World mining operations, they have every incentive to develop alternative sources of supply over which they can exercise full control (even if these alternative sources have higher production costs).

In the early 1970s Moran (1973) raised the specter that state-owned firms might be marginalized by the dominant TNCs and forced to bear a disproportionate share of the burden of the risks of global trade. According to Shafer, this is exactly what happened to African copper producers. He points out that during the worldwide recession from 1974 to 1978, total Western copper production continued to rise by 4 percent a year while Zaire's and Zambia's output was falling by 6 and 8 percent annually.[20] In minerals, sectoral characteristics make a demiurge response natural at the local level, but transnational alliances are the prime requisite for success at the global level. Steel suggests a similar lesson.

Steel

Steel is the archetypical basic commodity, an archetypal home for state-owned enterprises, and another good site for understanding the attractions and pitfalls of the demiurge role.

As they moved toward industrialization in the 1960s and 1970s, developing countries found themselves exporting vast amounts of iron ore while importing vast amounts of iron and steel.[21] Yet by some estimates, Third World sites were likely to have a cost advantage in producing steel.[22] Third World planners also wanted to take advantage of steel's exceptional levels of backward and forward linkages (Hirschman 1958, 106). With strong arguments for local steel production and a weak response from both local and transnational capital, direct production by the state made sense.

Like most Third World countries, Brazil, India, and Korea responded to the obvious logic by initiating state-owned steel companies. Their shared success at becoming major steel producers demonstrated the potential of the demiurge strategy. The rise of state steel firms went together with rapid industrial growth. As time wore on, however, country differences began to overwhelm sectoral similarities. Differential success depended on both the relative efficiency of the state organizations involved and the state's ability to combine the demiurge role with midwifery in the form of alliance building.

Brazil was one of the first LDCs to set up state-owned production. The genesis of Brazil's Compania Siderúrgica Nacional (CSN) fit the "empty space" model. Local capital was unable and foreign capital unwilling to invest in steel. Belgo Mineira, the foreign subsidiary that was the country's largest pre–World War II private producer, was reluctant to expand its capacity on the eve of World War II (Baer 1969, 95), and U.S. Steel declined to invest (Wirth 1970, 112; Baer 1969, 111), so Getúlio Vargas used the threat of assistance from Germany to extract sufficient U.S. funds to found the CSN in 1941 (Evans 1979, 88–89).

In India some of the world's best-quality iron ore created a promise of comparative advantage (Kelkar 1990, 57). There was already a growing gap between the output of the private sector and the country's demands in the early 1950s. The private sector's penchant for expansion was, to be sure, dampened by the official designation of steel as a sector to be developed by the state,[23] but even in the absence of official discouragement it is doubtful that the private sector would have been able to expand fast enough to meet demand.[24]

Korea was the last of the three to take up the challenge of becoming a steel producer, but it epitomizes the success of state steel. As the description of POSCO that begins this chapter indicates, Pohang Steel has not only grown, but grown with impressive efficiency. Despite the high capital costs associated with more recently constructed plant, it is "on average still the world's lowest cost producer" (D'Costa 1989, 135). Korean prices range from 56 to 70 percent of U.S. costs, depending on the product (D'Costa 1989, 135, table 5-13). The company's low costs make it a formidable exporter to both Japan and the United States. Perhaps even more important, the local availability of low-cost, high-quality steel has allowed Korea to compete in downstream manufacturing industries in a way that it was never able to do before. Pohang Steel is a crucial element in Korea's ability to win shipbuilding contracts[25] as well as being an important element in the success of Korea's auto exports. All of this was, of course, accomplished by ignoring international experts' almost unanimous disapproval of the idea of implanting integrated steel capacity in Korea.[26]

Pohang demonstrates that the demiurge strategy can be a powerful instrument for industrial transformation, but it is not alone. During their initial periods of expansion, state-owned steel companies in India and Brazil were also relatively efficient contributors to their countries' overall industrial expansion.[27] Studies of the performance of these industries in the 1950s and 1960s indicate that they not only were providing a badly needed industrial input but were doing so relatively efficiently.[28]

By the end of the 1980s, Brazil and Korea were part of state-owned Third World steel's general thrust to become a force in the world market.[29] The central thrust of state steel's entrepreneurship was still in the classic linkage role of supplying downstream domestic producers whose demand was growing even more rapidly than production.[30] Nonetheless, the most impressive feature of state steel's expansion was its capacity to export. Exports from both Korea and Brazil mushroomed over the course of the 1970s and 1980s until each of them had surpassed the United States as a steel exporter, with most of their exports going back to the advanced industrial economies.

Unfortunately, while Brazil, India, and Korea share a common claim to success as far as the growth of output is concerned, the experience of state-owned steel in Brazil and India also shows how the organizational and institutional problems of the state can all too easily undercut the effectiveness of the demiurge, even in a site where the state has "institutional advantage."

Problems of efficiency in Indian steel reached mythic proportions over the course of the 1970s and 1980s, undercutting the industry's ability to satisfy domestic demand and putting export expansion of the kind achieved by Brazil and Korea out of reach.[31] Even a sympathetic observer like K. Krishna Moorthy (1984, 268), was forced to admit that "Despite the great promise it showed in the years of its infancy, Hindustan Steel Ltd. over the years became . . . the symbol of monstrous inefficiency in the public sector."[32] By the end of the 1980s, state steel was in such bad shape that the head of the Bureau of Industrial Costs and Prices, whose duty it was to keep track of the industry's progress, recommended increased private-sector entry into the industry as a way of stimulating better performance (Kelkar 1990, 57). The demiurge had had its day.

State steel's problems reflected the overall organizational problems of the Indian state. Just as the government bureaucracy in general suffered from a lack of effective embeddedness, steel's central bureaucracy was too far removed from day-to-day operations.[33] The same tendency for the general institutional problems of the state to be reflected in the specific maladies of the sector is evident in Brazil.

The fragmented character of the Brazilian state apparatus and the tendency of the state to sacrifice its own agenda to the interests of its private allies helped undercut the efficiency of state steel in Brazil. Fragmentation led to indecision and delay in the programming of capital investments.[34] This in turn led to exorbitant capital costs and financial charges.[35] As part of the fight against inflation, state regulators dictated prices that subsidized private users downstream (many of them TNCs) at the expense of the financial health of state-owned steel companies.[36] Brazilian steel did benefit from the state's general willingness to construct alliances with transnational capital. Like Pohang, Brazilian state steel managed to tap the production technology of efficient Japanese producers like Nippon and Kawasaki.[37] International alliances were not, however, enough to make up for the problems created by fragmentation and short-sightedness of the state apparatus as a whole. The financial hemorrhaging passed the critical point, and by the end of the 1980s Brazil was thinking about putting its steel companies onto the auction block in hopes of turning them over to the private sector.[38]

Steel shows three things. First, under certain historical conditions in certain sectors, the demiurge can indeed generate transformation. Second, even in a sector where production technology is well established, international ties are still crucial. Finally, and most important, operational problems of state actors in specific sectors are likely to reflect the general institutional problems of the state apparatus as a whole.[39]

Textiles

Textiles could hardly be more different than steel. While textile production has been critically shaped and sometimes even created by state involvement, the role of producer is not the source of transformative influence. Instead, the regulatory role is the key. Sometimes regulation is used for purposes of midwifery and husbandry, as in K. Y. Yin's entrustment scheme.[40] Sometimes it is used for purely custodial purposes, as in the case of the Bara Hindu Rao mill that opened this chapter.

Korea is a classic case of using regulatory mechanisms for purposes of midwifery and husbandry. State support and greenhouse protection played an important role in fostering the emergence of the industry in the period following the Korean War. During the 1960s the issue was whether local entrepreneurs would be able to transform themselves from domestic producers into internationally competitive exporters. Would the state be able to husband the fragile entrepreneurial resources that had emerged, or would local firms fall behind the curve of global technological change and stagnate?

When the industry's exports surged in the early 1960s, it became clear that the project of husbandry was succeeding. Export success depended critically on a "sharp rise in subsidies" provided by the state (Amsden 1989, 66). Export-promotion measures included preferential loans, tax and tariff exemptions, and social overhead and administrative supports (Y. B. Kim, cited in Amsden 1989, 68). Without such subsidies, Amsden argues, Korean textile manufacturers would not have been able to compete with the Japanese in export markets. Exports were not only subsidized, they were also used as the price of admission to the highly protected and lucrative domestic market.[41]

Given the extent of state intervention, long-run success depended on making sure that husbandry did not devolve into clientelism. A focus on export markets where competitive pressures were inescapable helped, but there was still the danger that the oligopolized domestic market would devolve into a stagnant, state-supported, price-fixing cartel. This possibility was dramatized in 1973. The Textile Industry Association was subjected to the largest audit and inspection of any private association in Korea's history, resulting in the dismissal of over one hundred government officials (on grounds of having accepted bribes from the association) and the resignations of most of the association's board of directors (E. M. Kim 1987, 185).

Once it was clear that a comfortable but stagnant clientelism would not be tolerated, the industry took a more Schumpeterian tack. Government-subsidized profits were invested in modernized plant and equipment, new synthetic fibers capacity,[42] and improved production techniques, gradually enabling the industry to wean itself from reliance on subsidies.

India's state has been no less involved in textiles than Korea's, again principally via regulation rather than direct production. The thrust of Indian regulatory policy has, however, been almost the mirror image of Korea's. The custodial role has dominated at the expense of midwifery and husbandry.

The opening vignette describing the plight of the Bara Hindu Rao mill is a typical case. The ostensible aim of custodial regulation was preserving jobs. Prohibitions on the dismissal of workers (World Bank 1987b, 52) were combined with measures designed to ensure that inefficient producers were not threatened by the expansion of more modern, competitive plants. To protect the small-scale sector, the total number of looms in the organized (large-scale) sector was frozen in the mid-1950s. Consequently, the organized sector's share of industry output plummeted.[43] At the same time, capacity licensing regulations ensured that more efficient producers could not absorb the capacity of less efficient ones (Lall 1987, 114). Strict limits were also imposed on the possibility of replacing old-fashioned spindles with modern open-ended rotors.

Custodial regulation was quite effective in slowing the pace of modernization in the industry.[44] It was also effective in increasing the local price of cotton textiles relative to world prices[45] and decreasing the domestic availability of woven cloth per capita.[46] Finally, it produced an almost complete stagnation of exports. The value of textile exports scarcely rose between the beginning of the 1950s and the beginning of the 1980s.[47] Thus, the country's share of world textile exports declined despite the fact that Indian wages by the end of the 1970s were a small fraction of Korean wages.

In the long run, the prevention of modernization and the stagnation of output undercut the goal of protecting textile workers' jobs. Furthermore, the perverse consequences of custodial regulation ended up pushing the state to play the role of demiurge in an industry whose characteristics in no way suggested "revealed institutional advantage." Indira Gandhi's government, for example, ended up nationalizing thirteen closed textile mills in Bombay in 1984 as a last-resort attempt to preserve jobs (Rudolph and Rudolph 1987, 90).

Brazil lies somewhere in between Korea and India. As in Korea and India, the historic emergence of the textile industry depended on the state's willingness to exercise it regulatory powers on the industry's behalf, principally in the form of erecting a "greenhouse" to protect it from external competition. In contrast to Korea, Brazil was unable to impose a weaning process on the infant industry it had helped create. It lacked the autonomy required to move from midwifery to husbandry. Instead, industrialists clung to their privileges, escaping the winds of Schumpeterian change, and remained relatively minor contributors to Brazil's manufactured exports.

Textiles make it clear that midwifery is not enough. Firmly established local capitalists can become entrenched opponents of change instead of allies in a transformative project. Established capital is much more likely to look to the state as a source of security than to welcome prods to move in new directions. Only a capable and determined state apparatus that retains autonomy in relation to the sector is likely to succeed at husbandry.

Automobiles

Automobiles share with textiles an affinity for regulatory strategies rather than direct involvement in production,[48] but building alliances with transnational capital is crucial to midwifery. TNCs are crucial because rapidly evolving product technology, tightly held by a few internationally dominant producers, is the key to participation. Midwifery revolves around bargaining with TNCs. They must be induced first to enter, then to increase local content, then to export, ideally all in alliance with local firms.

Alliances and greenhouses went together in autos. As in textiles, the erection of a greenhouse to protect local production was a universal feature of state policy toward autos throughout the 1970s and 1980s. Successful NIC exporters, like Korea's Hyundai, were beneficiaries of protection along with technologically antiquated domestic producers like India's Birla group.

Brazil was a Third World pioneer in establishing local auto production. Even though the industry that was implanted in the 1950s took the form of 100 percent foreign-owned TNC subsidiaries, the state's role was still crucial.[49] Without the state's ability to present organizationally convincing assurances of protection from external competition and further support when necessary, transnational auto companies would have found the prospect of investing in full-fledged local production somewhere between too risky and completely nonsensical.[50]

Having been induced to enter, the TNCs found life inside the Brazilian greenhouse very profitable during the 1960s and 1970s. The auto industry became a major contributor to Brazil's "economic miracle," eventually reaching an output of a million cars a year, spawning a large local parts industry with a substantial proportion of local ownership, and becoming one of the most important contributors to Brazil's manufactured exports.

India, like Brazil, was a pioneer in the local auto assembly, but it characteristically tried to minimize the participation of transnational capital. Ignoring the problem of technological obsolescence and eschewing any aspirations to participate in global markets, India was content to create a greenhouse and allow a locally owned, technologically stagnant industry to supply the domestic market based on licensing of technology rather than ongoing alliances with TNCs. Only much later, in the 1980s, did India begin to consider developing alliances, most prominently in the form of a state-TNC alliance between Maruti Udyog and Suzuki (see Chatterjee 1990; Venkataramani 1990).

As in other manufacturing industries, Korea started later than India or Brazil. By the 1970s and 1980s, however, it was "the developing world's automotive success story" (Doner 1992, 401).[51] Korea's exports of assembled autos dwarfed those of other NICs, and export success was being accomplished with an exceptionally high proportion of local content.[52]

The state's involvement in the creation of this industry took a variety of forms. To begin with, it helped to create the organizational foundations on which the industry is built by fostering the growth of major chaebol like Hyundai and Daewoo. Without this generalized midwifery, the specific trajectory of local auto production development would have been impossible. When the industry was getting started, the state used its regulatory power to push for "rationalization," limiting both the number of firms competing in the industry and the number of models being produced (Doner 1992, 410–12).[53] At the same time, it actively signaled that the industry was worth investing in.[54] Finally, the state was involved in bargaining with TNCs over technology transfer, prices for imported inputs, and equity participation.

The success of the state's ambitious automotive plans did not mean that it had made the industry as it chose. Embeddedness and autonomy went together and private response was as important as public initiative.[55] Likewise, it proved impossible for even the "developing world's success story" to avoid dependence on TNCs technology. There were no wholly owned foreign subsidiaries like those that dominated the industry in Brazil, but even Hyundai, the most successful and the most nationalist of the local chaebol, ended up closely tied to Mitsubishi,[56] while Daewoo, the second most successful firm, was 50 percent owned by General Motors and depended completely on GM for its export markets.

Looking at autos underlines the extent to which the consequences of state strategies are dependent on a global context. Korea's success in negotiating alliances, rather than having to rely on wholly owned subsidiaries as Brazil did earlier, depended on a global environment in which TNCs had become convinced that international alliances, even with Third World firms, made strategic sense. The kind of alliances that Korea built in the 1980s would have been impossible for Brazil to construct in the 1950s. At the same time, successful alliance building also depended on "adroit state interventions" (Doner 1992, 425). The prior midwifery that produced plausible partners was crucial. So was the state's ability to articulate and defend a cohesive position. The global context creates a changing array of opportunities, but taking advantage of them requires institutional capacity effectively implemented through a variety of roles.

Implications of Sectoral Variation

State involvement varies systematically across sectors. What roles states try to play depends on the technological and organizational characteristics of the sector. How well the roles are played and with what consequences depend on each state's institutional characteristics.

Jones and Mason were on the right track in suggesting that sectoral characteristics like economies of scale and the relative importance of technology help create "institutional advantage" for different kinds of state involvement. States are most likely to take the demiurge role when barriers to entry are large (making entrepreneurship by local capital problematic) and technology is not closely held by a few global firms (making independent entry by the state possible). Lower barriers to entry, as in textiles, make local capital a feasible source of entrepreneurship and midwifery a realistic possibility. Tightly held technology, as in autos, makes bargaining and alliances with TNCs a necessary part of both midwifery and husbandry.

Trying similar roles does not mean producing the same outcome. All states played the role of demiurge in steel. Korea's demiurge was far more efficient and effective. Brazil, India, and Korea all tried to direct the development of their textile industries through various kinds of regulatory strategies, but only Korea was able to master the sequence of midwifery and husbandry. Sectoral characteristics define what roles are likely to work; the nature of the state determines whether a role can be carried out.

State structures and capacities make a difference, but states are not the only actors involved. Sectoral transformation depends on the interaction of states and local firms. Both operate in an environment profoundly constrained by the prevailing strategies of transnational firms. Private capitalists are anything but passive clients of state policies. State policies may lure them into new sectors but they become protagonists in their own right, with their own interests and agendas. The textile industry is the best single illustration. Having provided the protected environment that nurtured the growth of local textile firms, both Brazil and India found the firms that populated the sector quite capable politically of preventing further transformation of the industry. Even Korea came close to having its textile policies undercut by the vested interests of firms that were historically its "clients." How roles play themselves out depends on the changing character of state-society relations.

Global constraints also place compelling limits on what sectoral roles are possible. From minerals to autos, local sectoral strategies must continually contend with limits imposed by the way production and markets are structured globally. As the organizers of global markets and proprietors of state-of-the-art technology, TNCs are the most obvious embodiment of global constraints. Their changing stance vis-à-vis local strategies offers a good indication of how limits are shifting over time. As seen most clearly in autos, one decade's impossible bargain may be another decade's dominant strategy.

Looking at minerals, steel, textiles, and autos generates an appreciation for how state involvement works in specific sectors. Extrapolating this appreciation to the information technology (IT) industry remains a challenge. As the late twentieth century's most likely source of "multidimensional conspiracies in favor of development," it was an obvious target for state initiatives. Yet it was an industry where formulas from other sectors seemed difficult to apply.

The Challenge of Information Technology

As long as basic industries like steel were considered most central to the Third World's developmental agenda, there was an analytically comfortable, if not always practically attainable, correspondence between state-building and industrial transformation. Development planners who had the ill luck to operate in the 1970s and 1980s, instead of the 1950s and 1960s, faced a global economy that frustrated easy prescriptions for state involvement. Diverse manufactured exports, not increasing capacity in basic industrial inputs, were the new locus of the "multidimensional conspiracy in favor of development." The increasing importance of services, not just as adjuncts to manufactures but as international commodities in their own right, further confused the picture. Small wonder that the neo-utilitarian formula—get the state out of the economy—had growing appeal. Right or wrong, it was a clear program of action.

The information technology sector was the quintessential crystallization of the contradictions of state involvement. The combination of computer hardware, software, components, and peripherals that constituted information technology had a strong claim to being the master industry of late-twentieth-century development. Informatics was permeating the production process in all sectors and accounted for a growing share of output in all advanced industrial economies. From the late 1950s to the early 1980s, the share of computer production in the U.S. GDP increased fourfold (Flamm 1987, 29). By the end of the 1980s, the top one hundred information systems producers had combined sales of over $250 billion, two and a half times larger than the figure at mid-decade (*Datamation* 36, 12: 22; 33, 12: 28).

Electronic data processing not only was a sector of exponentially increasing weight in the world economy, but also represented the late-twentieth-century embodiment of technological change. The real cost of computing power has declined at a rate of 20–25 percent per annum consistently over the last thirty years (Flamm 1988b). In comparison, the rate of technical change in cotton textiles during the original industrial revolution was tortoiselike.[57] Since IT products are primarily capital goods, not consumer goods like cotton textiles, the productivity increases they generate diffuse across other sectors.

Any vision of improved position in the international division of labor must include increased participation in information technology—if not as a producer, then certainly as a user. What does this mean for strategies of state involvement? When moving up in the international division of labor meant amassing workers for the mines, the state's role was clear. When it meant amassing capital to build a steel mill, there was still a case to be made. When moving up means fostering an industry that depends on agilely exploiting rapidly changing international technology and staying on top of a lightning-fast product cycle, what is the state's role? The most obvious answer is the neoliberal one: states lack the agility necessary to enter as direct producers and the perspicacity to act as effective midwives; regulation will drive away the TNCs around which an IT sector must be built and is the antithesis of what local entrepreneurs need anyway.

It is not necessary to be a neoliberal true believer to argue that the dawn of a global economy in which information technology is the leading sector means the sunset of state involvement. Anyone moderately skeptical of the efficacy of state involvement can see the logic of the argument. Regardless of whether state involvement has made a contribution to the development of earlier industries, the characteristics of the late twentieth century's new leading sector make it seem that the time has come for the state to get out of the business of trying to reshape industry.

However sound the logic, the conclusion was hard for aspiring NICs to accept at the beginning of the 1970s. Without intervention, even advanced Third World countries looked destined for exclusion from what was likely to be the master industry of the twenty-first century. What were the odds of private entrepreneurs entering the sector without some kind of state prodding and support? Accepting traditional versions of the theory of comparative advantage would leave the NICs with low-paying, foreign-controlled assembly operations on the lagging edges of the industry. Forswearing state involvement came uncomfortably close to forswearing a productive place in the world of information technology.

Becoming a good user was an alternative, but even this option was vexed. Information technology products were not commodities, like steel I-beams or bolts of cloth, that could be easily inserted into a wide variety of environments without adjustment. To be used well, informatics had to be incorporated into local cultural and organizational patterns. Unloaded at the dock and wheeled into local offices, informatics goods were likely to end up gathering dust as expensive desk ornaments. Countries with local producers, who understood local cultural and organizational patterns and had a strong incentive to make the technology fit, would have a big advantage in becoming good users. The problem of fit was only the beginning. With demand for information technology in advanced industrial markets growing faster than most firms could keep up with, it was unclear how a country with 1 or 2 percent or less of the global market was going to get any attention at all from global suppliers.

Looking at the behavior of industrialized states made it even harder for Third World technocrats to accept the idea that the state should wither away. States in developed countries had been deeply and continuously involved in the development of the sector since its inception. From Japan's fifth-generation project to Europe's ESPRIT to Sematech in the United States, the state was intimately involved in trying to shape the development of informatics in advanced industrial countries.[58] As Kenneth Flamm (1988b, 10) put it, "The bottom line is that government plays a central role in investments in computer technology around the world. . . . The practical significance of the ubiquitous role of government in technology investments is that such involvement is one of the rules of the game everywhere." Obviously, the obstacles to successful involvement by developed states were much fewer than those facing Third

World states, but their example still made it harder for Third World states to eschew the effort.

Forsaking explicit efforts to stimulate the growth of local IT industries was hard for noneconomic reasons as well. On the one hand, depending on foreign suppliers for essential electronic data-processing equipment was any general's nightmare. On the other hand, participation in the informatics sector had an appeal for social reformers. Given its growth and research intensity, informatics, broadly defined, is the most important worldwide generator of good jobs for those with technical training. Its absence stimulates "brain drain." Invigorating it is one of the best strategies for expanding technical employment. For countries that see the lack of a "modern middle class" as central to their political and social problems, informatics has an allure that goes beyond the economic.

All of this makes the IT industry a fascinating case for anyone interested in states and industrial transformation from a comparative institutionalist perspective. Since it is an arena apparently rigged in favor of neo-utilitarian presumptions, any evidence gathered here that the state can play a transformative role is particularly telling. Moreover, if most involvement in the information technology industry is not likely to work, but ambitious states are likely to get involved in any case, then IT is an ideal arena for focusing attention on variations in *how* states intervene. Given the lack of any obvious formula for success, the question of "how" is also likely to be answered in ways that reflect internal state structures and state-society relations. For anyone interested in showing how state structures affect roles, the IT industry is too good an opportunity to pass up.

What forms of state involvement should we expect to find in the IT industries of Brazil, India, and Korea? The general characteristics of the Brazilian, Indian, and Korean states presented in chapter 3 certainly have implications for what should happen in the IT industry. Likewise the affinities between sectoral characteristics and roles that have been discussed in this chapter are a source of expectations as to what might go on in information technology.

Based on the discussion in this chapter, playing the role of demiurge in information technology would seem to be almost ruled out, especially in countries like India and Brazil, which had trouble sustaining a directly productive role even in an industry like steel, where state enterprises were the rule rather than the exception. Custodial regulation would seem completely inappropriate, except as a minor theme in the context of an overall emphasis on midwifery. IT should demonstrate the relative efficacy of midwifery and husbandry, despite the obvious obstacles to playing those roles well. Midwifery, however, would have to involve a large component of alliance building with TNCs.

If these expectations are confirmed, Korea should have a clear advantage. The natural affinity between the structures of embedded autonomy and engaging in midwifery and husbandry works strongly in Korea's favor. The Indian state, whose ambivalent relations with the private sector make it hard to play the midwife or engage in husbandry, would seem at a serious disadvantage. Sticking to the roles it has preferred in other sectors—the custodian and the demiurge—would certainly be disastrous. The Brazilian state is hardest to predict. Its past record of working closely with TNCs and its generally closer relations with the private sector should make an alliance-oriented midwifery more natural, but its relative lack of overall bureaucratic coherence would still constitute a disadvantage.

As the twenty years of informatics policies described in the next three chapters will show, such expectations, generated from simple distinctions among structures and roles, are a surprisingly useful starting point for analyzing the IT sector. Some of them are wrong, but they are still useful. What the next three chapters will also show, however, is that the process of industrial transformation is much more dynamic than a simple framework of structures and roles suggests. State involvement is not a one-shot process. As surely as states shape the emergence of IT sectors, emerging IT sectors force a redefinition of state involvement.

5

Promotion and Policing

AT THE END of World War II, Britain, the home of Alan Turing and other pioneers of computer science, had a comparative advantage in the computer industry as great as that of any country in the world except for the United States. In fact, according to Kenneth Flamm (1987, 159), "In 1950 British computer technology matched or surpassed that of the United States in many respects."

Forty years later, at the beginning of the 1990s, the last major British computer company, International Computers Limited (ICL), was purchased by Fujitsu, a company that in 1950 had been a small supplier of communications equipment to Japan's state-owned telecommunications monopoly. The demise of ICL as an independent firm was only the most dramatic of a series of symptomatic events that signaled Britain's inability to sustain internationally competitive informatics firms. As the 1980s closed, the country's leading computer companies had gone bankrupt one by one or been bought out by foreign firms.[1] Somehow Britain's apparent advantage had been squandered.

Fujitsu's success was as emblematic of the changing position of the Japanese industry as ICL's failure was of the decline of British prowess. In 1990 three of the top five information technology firms in the world were Japanese (*Datamation* 37, 12: 11). Yet in 1950, when British prospects appeared so promising, no industry expert would have picked Japan as a future power in the world informatics industry. Even in the early 1960s, Japanese computer companies were considered "mosquitoes" relative to the American "elephant" (IBM).[2] Somehow, over the course of the ensuing thirty years, comparative advantage was constructed.

State involvement was only a piece of the story of Japan's rise and Britain's demise as informatics powers, but it was a piece nonetheless. The divergent paths of their IT sectors are linked to quite different forms of state involvement in the computer industry. Taken together, Britain and Japan provide an interesting backdrop against which to consider the attempts to foster information technology sectors in Brazil, India, and Korea.

Britain's approach had two primary features.[3] First, like the United States, Britain assumed that industrial policy should be an adjunct to defense policy (see Flamm 1988a, 29–79). Firms involved in defense-related production were treated well, but promotion of the industry stopped there. Unfortunately, postwar British defense expenditures were not of the same overwhelming magnitude as those provided by the U.S. state. To make matters worse, British recipients of defense funding, unlike their U.S. counterparts, restricted themselves to defense production rather than defining themselves primarily as commercial competitors. Thus, according to Flamm (1988a, 148), "business-oriented firms received no support from the British Government."

The failure of defense expenditures to preserve competitiveness led to the second thrust of state policy, promotion of a single "national champion," ICL, which was created in 1968 through a series of state-sponsored mergers (see Flamm 1988a, 149–50). Even though ICL was a private firm, the "national champion" strategy had some of the same defects as relying on a state-owned firm. It was no substitute for a dynamic set of competitive firms.[4]

State involvement in Japan was much more variegated.[5] It began with a classic "greenhouse" strategy of protecting fledgling local firms from the cold winds of the international market. When the industry was getting started in the 1960s, domestic manufacturers were aggressively protected from foreign competition. Tariffs were double or triple those in force in Britain.[6] More crucially, no computer could be imported without an import license from MITI, which imposed quotas and discouraged those who tried to buy foreign machines. Domestic users "complained bitterly" but to no avail about being forced to use "low quality, unreliable domestic computers" (Anchordoguy 1988, 513–14).

Foreign investment was controlled as tightly as imports, but policymakers recognized that local industry could not start from scratch without access to foreign technology. Tight control over the domestic market was used not as the starting point for an autarkic policy, but "as leverage for acquiring foreign technology cheaply and for pressuring foreign companies to make joint ventures with Japanese companies" (Anchordoguy 1988, 514). Most important, IBM was persuaded to license its basic technology to Japanese firms in return for the right to enter into local production.[7] The right to use IBM's patents was vested not in a state-owned demiurge or in a private "national champion," but in fifteen competing local firms (Anchordoguy 1988, 516).

At the same time that it was limiting foreign competition and insuring access to foreign technology, MITI was also working on developing the demand side of the industry. The traditional instrument of government procurement was used aggressively. In 1975, when foreign computers accounted for 44 percent of the value of all computers installed among Japanese users, they accounted for only 7 percent of total value in government offices (Flamm 1987, 144).[8] The specific relationships that tied the state-owned telecom giant, Nippon Telephone and Telegraph (NTT), to its "NTT family" of suppliers were an especially important part of the procurement stimulus. NTT offered a total market of $13.3 billion between 1965 and 1975 and financed a substantial amount of its suppliers' research (Anchordoguy 1988, 525).

The Japan Electronic Computer Corporation (JECC) was a second, more innovative contribution to solving the demand problem. JECC was set up by MITI in 1961 as a "quasi-private" company, owned jointly by the major computer producers[9] and managed by retired MITI officials (Anchordoguy 1988, 517; Flamm 1987, 145). By using funds borrowed at below-market rates from the Japan Development Bank (JDB), or private loans guaranteed by the JDB, JECC was able to purchase computers outright from the producers and then rent them to users. The JECC rental system both stimulated demand (by reducing the upfront expenditures of buyers) and improved the cash flow of the producers.[10] For the firms involved, the increased cash flow was almost equal to the total investment in plant, equipment, and R&D during the 1960s.[11] The flow of investable funds to the former "mosquitoes" was further enhanced by a plethora of tax breaks and fiscal incentives, including special depreciation rules for computers, deductions for computer personnel training, and tax deferment for software revenues (Flamm 1987, 148).

The combination of protection from foreign competition, government support of demand, and fiscal subsidies transformed what would have otherwise been an extremely risky, if not impossible, industry into an attractive proposition. Consequently, it generated intense domestic competition among a number of strong players. Managing the resultant competition was another part of the state's role. The number of players in the industry was continually winnowed. Fifteen were allowed to share the IBM patents; only six were co-owners of JECC. JECC itself acted as "manager of a price cartel," ensuring that competition would not take the form of cutthroat price-cutting.

The state also pushed technological change. In the 1950s, prior to commercial interest in computer development, government labs like MITI's Electrotechnical Laboratory and NTT's Electrical Communications Laboratory were the principal sources of local innovation (Flamm 1988a, 173–79). Once a domestic industry had been structured, a long series of MITI-sponsored research programs, from the Super High-Performance Computer Project in the 1960s through the VLSI project[12] in the 1970s, were critical to moving the major firms forward technologically (see Flamm 1987, 132–33). Through these projects MITI pioneered the notion of bringing major companies together to cooperate on "precompetitive" generic research, the results of which would then be transformed into competitive commercial products by individual companies (Flamm 1987, 171).

State sponsorship was more than just an additional source of R&D funds (though the financial contribution was far from trivial). MITI's co-operative projects focused and structured technological competition. For example, the 3.5 Generation Program, launched in the mid-1970s, not only provided important financial resources at a point when IBM's system 370 had just blown RCA and GE out of the water, it also divided up the major computer producers into three pairs, with each pair focusing on a different computer size range (Flamm 1987, 131,4–5; Anchordoguy 1988, 523–24).

MITI's projects signaled the parameters of future technological competition. For example, when the VLSI project was announced, computers based on very large-scale integrated circuits were still hypothetical. Yet the existence of a project in which most major competitors would participate meant that no firm dared ignore the challenge and risk missing out on gains that the rest of the field could then exploit. The very existence of the project helped induce firms to "take the risky step of committing themselves to VLSI" (Anchordoguy 1988, 529). The projects also provided disciplinary leverage. Companies that were not considered commercially competitive or that failed to take advantage of the fruits of previous projects ran the risk of being excluded in the next round.[13]

No single facet of the state's involvement was decisive. Yet its cumulative effect over twenty years was to change Japan's place in the international division of labor. State involvement ensured that Japanese entrepreneurial groups would take advantage of the opportunities inherent in the computer industry. By the end of the 1970s, the task of midwifery had been accomplished. Powerful firms were committed to becoming international players in information technology.

What are the lessons of this story? First, it shows clearly that the rise of informatics did not signal the twilight of the state's transformative role. The high-tech nature of the computer industry did not preclude effective state action. Japan's midwifery in information technology was no less successful than its efforts in steel or autos. Second, the comparison of Britain and Japan shows that it is not state involvement per se that counts (the involvement of the British state was in many ways just as great). What counts is finding the combination of roles or strategies that fits the industry.[14]

Japan proved that state action could help construct comparative advantage, even in the information technology industry. This does not, of course, prove that Brazil, India, or Korea could do the same thing. Japan started with a superior set of industrial resources, operating in a domestic market much larger than Brazil, India, or Korea could claim. Japan also started earlier. In the IT industry, decades are eons. The industry that the NICs' technocrats had to deal with in the 1970s and 1980s was quite different from the one that Japan started breaking into in the 1960s. NIC efforts at industrial transformation should be seen against the backdrop of a rapidly changing global industry.

The Changing IT Industry

The IT industry[15] that Japan confronted in the 1960s was essentially the industry that IBM built. In the mid-1960s it was still "the computer industry," "computer" still meant "mainframe," and IBM still controlled the vast majority of worldwide mainframe sales. Hardware was what firms sold; software came with the hardware. Systems were proprietary, not open. IBM machines ran IBM software and were hooked up to IBM peripheral equipment. Getting an integrated information technology system meant buying everything from the same company. The IBM system 360, launched in the mid-1960s, epitomized the era. For IBM it was an immensely profitable industry. Gross profit margins ran in the neighborhood of 70 percent (Ernst and O'Connor 1992, 38). It was also a very hard game to break into. Conventional wisdom said you had to have 7 percent of the global market to finance the R&D necessary to remain competitive. Since IBM already had 60–70 percent of the market, that implied room for only five or six other firms.

During the 1970s things began to change. New firms like Digital Equipment Corporation (DEC) began to focus on smaller machines, "minicomputers." The minicomputer market never got as large and concentrated as the mainframe market, but among minicomputers the DEC VAX was almost as successful as the IBM 360 was in the mainframe market. Newer entrants also moved in the direction of "openness" by making sure that their machines could be connected to peripheral equipment (printers, communications devices, etc.) made by other manufacturers. They were willing to sell their hardware to "systems integrators" who would add peripherals and specialized software and turn out systems for final users.

The 1970s also saw the advent of the "semiconductor revolution." As transistors turned into integrated circuits (ICs), more and more data processing took place on the surface of a single chip. Because chip manufacturers did not have proprietary hardware of their own, they were willing to sell to anyone on the "merchant market," so the semiconductor revolution made it easier for newcomers to get into the computer business. The growing importance of semiconductors gave Japanese firms leverage to challenge IBM. By focusing their manufacturing talents on chips, struggling Japanese firms were able to counter IBM's overwhelming command of computer architecture.

Despite these changes, the computer industry of the mid-1970s was still the recognizable descendant of the industry that had existed in the 1960s. The important customers were still "data-processing departments" in large or medium firms. The market, like the producers, was located primarily in the United States, but American firms sold all over the world. By the mid-1970s foreign markets, primarily Europe, accounted for 40–50 percent of their revenues. Large, vertically integrated producers trying to replicate the IBM model by providing whole systems were still the most important category of firms.

Between 1975 and 1990 the IT industry turned into something else entirely. Data processing became something that happened on very large-scale integrated circuits, chips etched with millions of transistor "gates." Chip design, not computer architecture, became the technological core of the industry. Once computing power was moved onto the chip, personal computers were a realistic possibility and the individual user could displace the data-processing manager as the king of the market. Computers became consumer goods as well as producer goods, and the difference between marketing computers and marketing televisions or VCRs began to blur. The IT industry was also on its way to becoming an industry in which value of software would be more important than value of hardware. By the beginning of the 1990s, customers spent a dollar on software for every dollar they spent on hardware, instead of twenty cents as they had in 1970 (cf. Ernst and O'Connor 1992, 75). Information technology was shifting from the world of IBM to the world of INTEL and Microsoft.

Old corporate strategies became obsolete along with old technology. R&D was still important, but "network transactions," which provided access to key components like microprocessor chips, replaced vertically integrated production as a source of strategic advantage.[16] Marketing and distribution networks were as important as the networks that provided key components. The IT industry had room for more firms—from assemblers like DELL and AST, to workstation specialists like SUN Microsystems, to a range of "niche" producers—but profit margins were a fraction of those that IBM had enjoyed.[17] For computer producers looking back from the 1990s, the old days of the mainframe would eventually look like a golden era.

As they formulated their plans in the 1970s, state technocrats in India, Brazil, and Korea had no way of knowing what the IT industry of the 1990s would look like. Like everyone else, they had to extrapolate from the world they knew. It was a world in which IBM's comfortable monopoly on profits was being challenged by corporations as different as DEC and Fujitsu, but it was also a world that held no promise of any space at all for Third World producers, unless they created the space themselves.

The Roots of State Involvement

At the beginning of the 1960s, no Third World country had policies or institutions aimed at developing informatics capacity. Over the course of the decades that followed, first India, then Brazil, and finally Korea decided that local production of advanced electronic data-processing equipment must be part of national development. Economic calculus, an abstract quest for national stature, and preoccupation with the techno-logical side of military strength all converged in the desire to create locally controlled informatics industries.

In each of these three countries, individuals convinced of the value of local informatics production managed to find positions of leverage within the state apparatus. Powerful allies in the executive branch and the mili-tary increased industry advocates' leverage. In each case their ideas were eventually turned into policies and institutions designed to bring forth local production. In each case, the policies brought forth new economic and political actors whose interests and capacities then shaped the direc-tion of the industry's growth.

Shared aspirations played themselves out on very different playing fields. Local entrepreneurial classes varied widely in capacity and ambi-tion. Equally important, the state apparatuses that were the initial agents of transformation had, as chapter 3 showed, quite different strengths and weaknesses. Each had distinctive traditions of intervention, distinctive relations with the private sector, and distinctive organizational capacities. India had a relatively coherent bureaucracy to work with, but a peculiarly ineffective kind of embeddedness. Brazil had had more success in formu-lating joint projects with the private sector but could count at best only on "pockets" of bureaucratic coherence. Neither Brazil nor India could draw on the kind of embedded autonomy that was already propelling industrial growth in Korea. Nonetheless, as the old Brazilian saying goes, "He who has no dog hunts with a cat." Each country pushed ahead with the institutional resources they had.

India

India's Bhabha Committee[18] was first to formulate a set of goals for local informatics development and most visionary in its assessment of what was possible. In 1966 the committee reported that it was "entirely feasible technically to become self-sufficient in the manufacture of computers of a wide variety of kinds within this period of ten years" (Grieco 1984, 22). The goals of the committee, like India's vision of its industrial future more generally, were autarkic. Satisfying domestic demands with minimal reliance on foreign inputs was the aim. Questions of comparative advantage or what role India might play in international markets were beside the point.

The men who pursued the Bhabha Committee's vision were technocrats. The best examples were the members of the Bhabha Atomic Research Center (BARC) group, which included Vikram Sarabhai, M.G.K. Menon, A. Parthasarathi, N. Seshagiri, A. S. Rao, and a number of others with impressive scientific credentials. Possessing technical aptitude and expertise on a par with their fellow graduates from elite English universities, they saw no reason why they had to rely on outsiders to design their country's computers.

Their vision jibed not only with the autarkic traditions of the country's economic planners, but also with the logic of geopolitics as seen by the military. Eswarhan Sridharan (1989, 376) puts it flatly: "The best explanation for indigenization in computers is the need for self-reliance in defense." Sridharan points out that the Bhabha Committee's 1966 report advocating self-sufficiency must be seen in the context of surrounding geopolitical events. Shocked by its defeat in the 1962 border war and China's 1964 entry into the "Nuclear Club," India was then confronted with a U.S. cutoff of electronics equipment during the 1965 Indo-Pakistan War.[19] Since the military already produced a variety of technically sophisticated goods through state-owned companies like Bharat Electronics Ltd. (BEL), extending its repertoire to computers seemed natural.

The relatively weak contribution of transnational capital to the development of local information technology made self-reliance more attractive. Even though IBM had been in India as a manufacturer since 1963, the closest it came to manufacturing computers was reconditioning antiquated model 1401s that had already been retired from more developed markets (Subramanian 1989, 174–75). IBM's import markups were huge[20] and its profits large, but its contribution to making India a producer of information technology was questionable. Britain's increasingly moribund ICL was the other major transnational corporate presence.

The initiators of India's informatics aspirations were doubly bold. They were convinced that local technical prowess could give India the IT goods it needed, and they believed that the state itself could muster the organizational and productive capacity necessary to deliver those goods. Acting as a midwife to bring local capital into the industry was not part of the agenda, much less mediating ties to transnational capital.

Brazil

Brazil's information technology agenda was less ambitious, and with good reason. The "frustrated nationalist *técnicos*"[21] who formulated the country's initial policy stance toward computers in the early 1970s were not as well placed in relation to the state as their Indian counterparts, though their backgrounds were not dissimilar.

Like the members of the BARC group, Mario Dias Ripper, Ivan da Costa Marques, Ricardo Saur, and the other frustrated nationalist técnicos were technological cosmopolitans, trained at places like Berkeley (Ripper, Costa Marques) and Stanford (Saur). Their American educations and familiarity with the "Silicon Valley" gave them a sense of participation in an international process of development and a sense of frustration with their local environment. Brazil's computer industry as it was structured at the beginning of the 1970s denied them the jobs they had been educated to do. In Brazil they could become salespeople for IBM or they could process data for the federal government. If they wanted to engage in technological entrepreneurship—designing products, producing them, and then seeing whether the market validated their ideas—they would have to forsake Brazil and return to the Silicon Valley. Unless, of course, they could do something to transform Brazil's informatics industry.

They saw the computer industry as part of a broader problem. The number of technically educated Brazilians was growing rapidly in the 1970s. Unless technically challenging jobs expanded just as fast, education would only increase the "brain drain" from Brazil to developed countries. Industrial organization implied social structure. Brazil's current place in the international division of labor fit all too well with its polarized social structure. Without the right jobs, the growth of an economically secure, politically active middle class would continue to be stunted, as it was in the rest of Latin America. Changing the social structure meant changing what Brazil produced. The *técnicos'* perception of a connection between local industrialization and ameliorating Brazil's shockingly inegalitarian society gave their project a "leftist" tinge. Their beards conveyed the same impression and earned them the nickname *barbudinhos* (young bearded ones).

Brazil's recent industrial past did offer some leverage for promoting a vision of a locally controlled information technology industry. By the early 1970s. when informatics became an issue, the "Brazilian miracle" had produced general confidence that industrial transformation was possible. General Geisel's second national development plan (PNDII), with its emphasis on "deepening" Brazil's industrial capacity and expanding the role of local capital, provided a precedent (Evans 1982). Despite the general dominance of free-market ideology among economic planners, technocrats sympathetic to nationalist industrial policy were scattered through the policy-making apparatus.

As in India, the military was a potential ally. Brazil's military had developed a formidable set of state-owned defense producers. In fact, the arms industry, led by state-owned enterprises, was a principal contributor to Brazil's export performance (cf. Gouveia 1988). Anyone who could get military inputs potentially subject to U.S. export controls produced by local firms was an ally in the eyes of the military. Since the military ruled Brazil throughout the period during which informatics policy was formulated, this was an important source of political leverage.

Many within the military, as in the rest of Brazilian society, identified with the tradition of heroic (though usually unsuccessful) struggle against the dominion of Yankee (or British) investors. The tradition went back at least to Delmiro Gouveia's ultimately quixotic but still admired fight against the international cotton-spinning cartel. The idea of a "national bourgeoisie" that would challenge the "neocolonialism" of transnational capital remained a potent ideological theme. Calls for "technological autonomy" tapped a reservoir of politically powerfully sentiments.

At the same time, the military's ideological convictions made its relations with the barbudinhos profoundly ambivalent. The military's fierce anticommunism made it suspicious of initiatives that did not privilege private capital, despite their penchant for taking such initiatives themselves. Even nationalist calls for autonomy raised suspicions of leftist sentiments, especially if they came from intellectuals. The idea of local technological development might be admired, but its carriers were still viewed as potential subversives.

The barbudinhos's equivocal position in relation to the rest of the state did have one positive by-product. It meant that Brazil's informatics pioneers needed local capital, not just as an instrument for generating products and productive capacity but also as political protection against adversaries within the state. The barbudinhos were thus doubly motivated to join their Korean counterparts in choosing a strategy of midwifery.

Unfortunately, possibilities for midwifery ran directly up against Brazil's prior internationalization. A powerful set of transnational corporations stood between the barbudinhos and the kind of industrial structure they needed to realize their professional ambitions. IBM and Burroughs dominated the local computer industry. Both had been in Brazil since before World War II. Both had well-established, 100-percent-owned subsidiaries manufacturing less technologically sophisticated products and doing some assembly of the computers sold in Brazil. The involvement of IBM do Brasil in local production and its consequent political clout were of a different order of magnitude than in the Indian case. IBM do Brasil was even an important exporter. Other multinational firms, like DEC and Sperry, were less well established but still presences. The internationalization of the Brazilian computer industry was well established long before the barbudinhos began wondering how to create locally controlled production.

The computer industry reflected the standard Brazilian division of labor in which technology-intensive industries were dominated by foreign capital. Experience in the post–World War II period, and especially in the early years of the military regime, suggested that such foreign dominance was only likely to expand and solidify. By the 1970s, most Brazilians took for granted inextricable entanglement in an international division of labor organized by others. In this context, the idea of implanting an autarkic, technology-intensive industry that would move toward self-sufficiency, along the lines envisioned by the Bhabha Committee, would have seemed completely fanciful. The idea of somehow creating space in which local firms could develop their own technologically sophisticated products was radical enough.

The problem was exacerbated by the specific inheritance in electronics. Having opted, for reasons of regional politics and geopolitical concern, to shift the brunt of consumer electronics development to the Manaus free zone in the middle of the Amazon basin, the Brazilian military had separated consumer electronics from the industrial heartland of São Paulo. Generous benefits such as import freedom and tax rebates were introduced in the late 1960s for Japanese and other firms wishing to set up electronics plants. The Manaus free zone developed into an "import platform" (Baptista 1987), flooding the Brazilian market with foreign goods assembled from imported parts and driving established Paulista manufacturers of televisions and other consumer electronics out of business. Consumer electronics became a caricature of internationalization, leaving Brazil without local industrial prowess that could serve as a springboard for informatics manufacture.

In short, Brazil's barbudinhos started with ambiguous relations to the rest of the state apparatus and a less than promising local private sector. A less determined and less creative group would have despaired of ever getting the leverage to make such an ambitious project happen.

Korea

Korean aspirations for participation in informatics emerged well after India and Brazil had begun trying to join the club of informatics producers, but its initiators had several advantages. They were technocrats but also political insiders. Prior state policy left them an inheritance of powerful local private firms well positioned to venture into informatics. Their version of technological nationalism lent itself to mediating between local firms and the international industry.

The technocrats pushing for informatics in Korea did not have to worry about ambivalent relations with military rulers. Those most intimately involved in projecting Korea's future as an "information society" centered around the presidential Blue House. Within the Blue House, Chung Hong Sik, secretary to the president for science and technology, and Hong Sung Won, assistant secretary for science and technology, were key participants. Connected to the Blue House was a group of individuals including a number of ex-military officers with advanced degrees in engineering. Some had been involved in early attempts to develop indigenous weapons technology in the Agency for Defense Development. Kim Sung Jin, a classmate of President Chun Doo Hwan and President Roh Tae Woo at the military academy, is a good example. After graduating first in his class, he went on to graduate training in the United States, served as president of the Agency for Defense Development, and later became head of both the National Computerization Agency and the National Computerization Coordinating Committee.

Unlike Brazil's barbudinhos, Korea's informatics advocates had an important bureaucratic base of support in the powerful Ministry of Communications (MOC), which attracted technocratic cadre quite similar to those surrounding the Blue House. MOC saw the development of indigenous information technology directly in its own interests. It also had an independent source of funds—operating revenues from the phone system—that could be used to bankroll projects that the less technologically nationalist economists in the EPB or Finance Ministry might oppose.

Secure relations to the state apparatus made life simpler, but other advantages were equally important in their eventual success. The results of past midwifery were the most critical resource. Park Chung Hee's push for heavy industrialization in the 1970s paralleled General Geisel's strategy of increasing the vertical integration of local capital in Brazil during the same period, but the corporate products of Park's efforts were more formidable and better endowed with expertise that could be harnessed to informatics production. Two of the four giant chaebol (Samsung and Goldstar) quickly became consumer electronics manufacturers of international stature, and the other two (Daewoo and Hyundai) were able to build on their general manufacturing prowess to move rapidly into electronics in the 1970s.

Conversely, transnational capital was not entrenched in the local computer sector the way it was in Brazil. The first transnational corporation, IBM, arrived in Korea in 1967, almost fifty years after it began its Brazilian operations. Even then it did not become involved in manufacturing.

Because international capital arrived late, after local corporate power had been constructed in an allied sector, confidence that TNCs could be controlled and channeled was greater.

A less entrenched foreign presence made it easier to adopt what Amsden (1989) calls the "learner" model of technological development. The ability to control and assimilate borrowed innovations, not "technological autonomy," was the name of the game. Constructing local technological capacity remained the primary goal but the relation between local technological development and foreign ties was seen as complementary. Instead of trying to restrict and discipline technological connections between local and international firms, the aim of policy was to proliferate international ties while mediating them in order to increase their positive impact on local capabilities.

Having local private firms available made it unnecessary to try to construct a state-owned demiurge. Worrying less about restricting technological ties to foreign firms simplified the custodial role. Focusing on assimilation rather than autonomy meant more modest technological aspirations. Approaching a more simply defined task from a more secure position within a more powerful bureaucracy, the promoters of Korea's IT aspirations were in an enviable position relative to their counterparts in India or Brazil.

While Brazil, Korea, and India each started with a different set of organizational and entrepreneurial resources, the parallels in the roots of state involvement across the three countries are striking. In each case, a small group of individuals with internationally recognized technical training decided to use some niche within the state apparatus as a point of leverage to get local informatics production going. In all three countries, everyone assumed that the state must take an active role if a local information technology industry was going to emerge. There were even some similarities in initial definitions of what role the state should play.

Greenhouse Construction and Custodial Institutions

Korea, India, and Brazil all began their informatics efforts by following the hallowed dictums of Alexander Hamilton and Friedrich List on growing "infant industries." All three relied on "protectionism." Like MITI in the 1960s, all three built "greenhouses," sets of rules that would protect seedling computer firms from the cold winds of international competition. All three limited the entry of imports, and they all restricted investments by foreign firms. It was underneath the generic greenhouse umbrella that crucial policy differences took shape.

Maintaining the greenhouse was more difficult in Brazil than in Korea or India because of the historically stronger presence of TNCs. From its inception, informatics policy stood in tension with the momentum of Brazil's dependent development. There was a long tradition of protecting local production, but foreign capital willing to produce locally had always been welcome. Often transnational subsidiaries were the principal beneficiaries of protectionism, as in the auto industry. There was precedent for setting conditions on new foreign investment, but excluding established TNC subsidiaries from the benefits of protection was a radical move. Brazil's emphasis on technological autonomy also complicated the greenhouse. It required careful policing to make sure that local firms did not abuse their privileges by forming illicit technological ties with the international industry.

In India as in Brazil, restrictive rules were central to policy implementation, but the reasons for supervision were somewhat different. The regulatory role was required in part by the fact that the state was trying to play a demiurge role. Initially at least, the privilege of operating within the greenhouse was the preserve of the state itself. Regulation was necessary, not just to make sure that domestic producers were not threatened by foreign capital, but also to make sure that private local capital did not poach in the state's preserve.

Because TNCs were less entrenched in Korea's domestic market (and less interested in it, at least initially), the task of maintaining the greenhouse was less difficult. Because its definition of technological nationalism stressed assimilation rather than autonomy, Korea had to worry less about policing ties with TNCs. The basic premise that applied to industrial development in general applied also to informatics. Firms that expected support from the state were expected in turn to perform effectively, expanding their production and markets, demonstrating international competitiveness (cf. Amsden 1989). Consequently, no regulatory organization specific to the informatics industry emerged in Korea, just as none had in Japan. The parts of the state apparatus most directly connected to informatics policy—the Ministry of Communications, the Ministry of Science and Technology, the Ministry of Trade and Industry, the Blue House, and the National Computerization Agency—had a promotional rather than a custodial relation to local entrepreneurial groups.

The experiences of Brazil and India, where greenhouse construction was inextricably bound up with the emergence and evolution of sectorally specific regulatory agencies, illuminate the contributions and contradictions of the role of custodian. The institutional histories of the Department of Electronics (DOE) in India and the Secretaria Especial de Informática (SEI) in Brazil demonstrate the limits of custodial policing. The particularly convoluted life of Brazil's SEI shows how the contradictions of policing are compounded when the architecture of the greenhouse goes beyond the prevailing local traditions of industrial policy.

India

In India, as would be expected given the status of the policy's initiators and the tradition within which they were operating, fitting a new regulatory organization into the bureaucracy was unproblematic. The Department of Electronics and a corresponding Electronics Commission were formed early (1970–71) and remained organizationally intact throughout the 1970s and 1980s. Would-be electronics firms were, of course, subject to a host of generic rules relating to investment and production and had to deal with a myriad of other agencies, from Customs to the Reserve Bank of India, but the DOE took pride of place in passing judgment on the advisability of informatics investments (see Grieco 1984; Sridharan 1989; Subramanian 1989). The DOE was supposed to approve not only a firm's entry into electronics, but any changes in product line or increased output for a product already approved.

The DOE was not just a policing entity. A variety of projects were funded through its budget, ranging from the CLASS program designed to increase computer literacy in the schools to the Society for Applied Microwave Electronics Engineering and Research (Subramanian 1989; DOE 1988, 1989). From the perspective of private firms, however, the agency's regulatory face overshadowed its promotional side. The department's tight ties to the sector's state-owned national champion were even more important in overshadowing whatever promotional effects it might have had vis-à-vis private entrepreneurs.

The Electronic Corporation of India Ltd. (ECIL) was chartered under the Atomic Energy Commission in 1967, even before the DOE was created. The DOE's leading cadres came largely from the Bhabha Committee/BARC group, which was in turn closely associated with ECIL.[22] The private sector naturally suspected that the restrictive tendencies of the custodial state were being exaggerated by efforts to ensure that ECIL had no competition. Thus, for example, the 1972 recommendation of a panel on minicomputers calling for licensing a dozen applicants to make minicomputers was ignored by the DOE and the Electronics Commission, leading the *Economic Times* eventually to accuse the custodial state of trying to "keep at bay the emergence of a vibrant nationally based minicomputer industry" (Grieco 1984, 133).

The DOE's problematic relation with local private capital was not simply a question of self-serving bureaucrats carving out a rental haven. Corruption was not the issue. Relative to other parts of India's increasingly corrupt regulatory apparatus, the DOE preserved a reputation for dedication and probity. Protecting ECIL was seen by the company's backers as the only way of implementing the Bhabha Committee's vision. ECIL was making strenuous efforts to follow the committee's exhortations to achieve maximal technological autonomy. The DOE was not convinced that private capital would do the same.

Whatever the DOE's intentions, conflating the state's custodial role with its role as demiurge impeded the emergence of local private firms and delayed India's exploitation of new microprocessor-based technologies. Nonetheless, the greenhouse still created and preserved space for local producers. The archetypical example of space creation is, of course, the departure of IBM from India in 1978 following its refusal to conform to the government's requirements for local capital participation in local manufacturing.[23] By indicating its willingness to operate without the world's hegemonic computer company, the state made it clear that local firms would have first crack at the local market.

What is remarkable about the DOE's role is not that it initially supported the demiurge option. That made perfect sense given the traditions of the state apparatus of which it was a part and the histories of the individuals involved. What is remarkable is that, despite being inserted into one of the world's most sclerotic administrative structures, the DOE changed its position radically over a relatively brief period of time. The end of the 1970s and the beginning of the 1980s saw the emergence of local firms. Belief in private IT firms' potential developmental contribution among India's political leadership reached its culmination in the prime ministership of Rajiv Gandhi, sometimes called the "computer kid." Having shaped the initial emergence of the sector, the DOE was itself gradually reshaped by the sector's own evolution.

As the master agency for the implementation of Indian informatics policy, the DOE might easily have been expected to resist the changes that were challenging the state's strategy in informatics. It was, after all, founded with a mission of protecting and expanding the turf of the principal informatics demiurge, ECIL, and staffed, even in the 1980s, by people who came out of the demiurge tradition.[24] The policies formulated in the 1970s gave DOE incumbents a great deal of power over the private sector. Licenses to engage in electronics production were narrowly defined. Firms wishing to expand their product lines as well as those trying to enter the industry were thoroughly dependent on DOE approvals.

From the perspective of a neoliberal or neo-utilitarian analysis, in which bureaucrats are self-seeking maximizers of power and privilege, the interests of the DOE technocrats should have been clear. If the primary source of job satisfaction in the state bureaucracy is the visible exercise of power, as symbolized by heads of large corporations waiting in the hallways of government office buildings as supplicants, then the DOE should have resisted new policies tooth and nail. If the less visible but more materially satisfying extraction of rents from the same supplicants is the primary goal, the same conclusion follows.

Surprisingly, at least from a neo-utilitarian perspective, a number of DOE incumbents promoted change rather than resisting it. When Rajiv Gandhi came to power in 1984 with an agenda of promoting computerization by liberalizing entry for local firms, imports, and even the formation of joint ventures, he had key supporters inside the regulatory apparatus. N. Seshagiri, a DOE veteran from the time of the department's formation, was a primary author of directives liberalizing the rules on investments and imports in 1984 and 1986. He was backed in this endeavor by S. R. Vijayaker, who, despite (or perhaps because of) his experience as managing director of ECIL, had become convinced that the custodian/demiurge combination could not deliver the informatics goods that India needed.[25] Other members of the department also greeted the changes with enthusiasm rather than opposition.

Why were the DOE's incumbents willing to abandon policies that maximized their bureaucratic power and privilege? To begin with, informatics was an unlikely post for someone whose principal interest was self-aggrandizement. The sector represented neither a nationally important political constituency (like agriculture) nor a major source of patronage jobs (like the railways). Consequently, the machinery of clientelistic politics was never as fully engaged as in other sectors. Equally important, the DOE had always been dominated by technically oriented managers with a strong substantive interest in the sector for which they were responsible. High-level DOE incumbents do not seem to have been significant beneficiaries of corruption. Private-sector managers who dealt with the agency generally agreed that, minor corruption aside, DOE standards were high. Like their counterparts in Brazil and Korea, DOE technocrats were immersed in a project of transformation that was of greater interest than minor individual perquisites.

Whatever their motivations, the DOE's top managers did not act as though preserving their regulatory power was a priority. As Rajiv's period in office drew to a close at the end of the 1980s, major actors in the DOE expressed themselves less in custodial terms and more in terms of midwifery or husbandry. Asked what he thought were appropriate criteria for judging the department's performance, one veteran said, "Industry reaction is the best gauge of the DOE's success. If you want to know if I am doing a good job, ask WIPRO, TUL, or TCS."[26] Another longtime DOE manager explained that in his view, "The DOE's function should not be setting out rules but promotion of the industry." He expressed the hope that the 1990s would see the department get completely away from licensing and become primarily promotional. N. Seshagiri took particular pride in the department's new orientation, saying, "We broke 26 separate rules to accommodate TI's [Texas Instruments] Bangalore subsidiary and are willing to break more"(*SIPA News* 2, 2; 2).[27]

The companies that dealt with the DOE at the end of the 1980s remained more impressed by the persistence of the regulatory restriction than by the emergence of a new approach, but most admitted that the DOE was easier to deal with than traditional Indian bureaucracies. One sophisticated entrepreneur with interests in a variety of sectors contrasted the behavior of the DOE with that of the Department of Civil Supplies, which regulates basic consumer goods. He argued that while Civil Supplies continued to have a "control mentality," taking pleasure in minute regulation for its own sake, the DOE has tried to market the electronics industry, behaving like a "product manager" for electronics, especially vis-à-vis other parts of the government.

The DOE's new approach seemed likely to endure. As a new government took office in 1990, the incoming secretary of the Department of Electronics described his role with an indigenous variation on the midwife theme drawn from Hindu mythology. He said that the DOE should play the role of Jabavan and the local entrepreneurial class the role of Hanuman, the monkey god. In the myth, Jabavan bolstered the courage of Hanuman, thereby helping him make a crucial leap to the Island of Lanka, but it was Hanuman who actually made the leap and became a hero (*Dataquest*, August 1990: 23).

The DOE's conversion to a focus on promotion rather than policing is a nice example of the way in which growing sectors reshape the parts of the state apparatus that deal with them. First the DOE presided over the emergence of the industry, then the industry became the catalyst for the reorientation of the DOE. The process can be seen even more vividly in Brazil.

Brazil

Brazil began with an agenda of midwifery, not policing. Its técnicos hoped that policing would be an instrument for promotion, not an end in itself. The trajectory of Brazil's regulatory institutions demonstrates how greenhouse policies can give a small number of visionaries within the state apparatus surprising transformative leverage.[28] It also shows how debilitating it can be to combine promotion and policing within a technologically defensive framework once the initial phase of midwifery has succeeded.

The Commission for the Coordination of Electronic Processing Activities (CAPRE) is an archetypal illustration of how unlikely niches in the state apparatus can become sites for far-reaching policy innovation. CAPRE began its life in 1972 as an innocuous bureau within the Planning Ministry, charged with rationalizing the government's utilization of electronic data processing (see Helena 1980; Adler 1986, 1987; Evans 1986a). The military regime's modernizing ambitions stimulated the government's appetite for data, especially in relation to increasing the take on federal income taxes. The regular bureaucracy was short on the required expertise, so creating a new nucleus of specialists made sense.

CAPRE became the home of the "frustrated nationalist técnicos" and their vision of what Brazil needed to become a participant in the world of informatics, a vision that went far beyond rationalization of government usage. In 1974, thanks to the oil crisis, CAPRE's técnicos got their chance. By then, Brazil's computer imports were one of the items most responsible for exacerbating Brazil's balance-of-payments problems (Piragibe 1983, 121). With the oil price revolution making things worse, the Foreign Trade Council (CONCEX) saw CAPRE as the obvious candidate to control computer imports. Soon, anyone who wanted to import computers or electronic components used in the assembly of computers had to have prior permission from CAPRE (Evans 1986a, 794).

In other hands, such regulatory power might have remained exactly what it was intended to be, a way of slowing the import of superfluous hardware, but it did not take CAPRE's frustrated nationalist técnicos long to realize that their regulatory power could be wielded in the interests of creating industrial policy. Since no one, including IBM, could manufacture a computer in Brazil without imported components, CAPRE had the power to decide not only what should be imported, but also what computers would be manufactured locally, and by whom.

The test of whether CAPRE could really turn the prerogative of regulating foreign trade into a tool of industrial policy came in 1976 when IBM decided to produce its System 32 minicomputer in Brazil. To IBM's surprise, their project was turned down. Instead, proposals were solicited from a range of local and foreign companies (including IBM), and in 1977 permission for the local production of minicomputers was granted to Brazilian firms using licensed foreign technology,[29] but not to IBM or the other foreign firms that had entered the competition without local partners. Since Brazil's half-century-old "law of similars" allowed imports of foreign products to be restricted whenever locally produced "similars" were available,[30] CAPRE's minicompetition created a "market reserve," a prohibition on foreign involvement in production or sale of small computers.[31]

CAPRE's victory was not simply the result of the will and skill of a few individuals. CAPRE's vision succeeded because it resonated with ideas coming from other parts of the state apparatus. Even before CAPRE came into existence, the National Economic Development Bank (BNDE) had formed a special working group to explore the possibility of creating a local computer industry (see Adler 1986, 627; Tigre 1984, 76). As result of the special working group's activities, the "First Basic Plan for Scientific and Technological Development (1973–74)" came out with the recommendation that the government should promote a *"tri-pé"*[32] company to produce minicomputers. The same ideas were reflected in General Geisel's second national development plan, which included the "basic electronic industry" among its proposals for the upstream investments in vertical integration known as "deepening" (Evans 1982; Helena 1980, 76).

Positive reverberations from inside the military were critical in keeping the process alive. The BNDE's Special Working Group was cochaired by Commander José Guaranys. Guaranys's presence reflected the growing concern of the navy, which was beginning to purchase ships that contained substantial amounts of electronic equipment and was leery of having to rely on foreign firms and technicians (Evans, 1986a, 793). The security apparatus had been quietly experimenting with computers for cryptographic reasons and was anxious to have their own machines to work with. All of this created an atmosphere in which the CAPRE técnicos were able to garner the crucial support of the military Ministers and win the day against the more market-oriented economic policymakers.

Without this diverse group of allies within the state apparatus, CAPRE could never have carried off the initiation of the greenhouse, but CAPRE still had more enemies than allies. Market-oriented economic planners had never liked the barbudinhos, and many within the military continued to suspect that their beards indicated leftist leanings. By 1979 their enemies had won. The barbudinhos' bastion had been extinguished and replaced by the Special Secretariat for Informatics (SEI). The old group of técnicos was out,[33] replaced by a new set of state officials, drawn primarily from the National Intelligence Service (SNI).[34]

More surprising than the political demise of the old técnicos was the fact that their agenda proved politically robust. CAPRE's ideological legacy lived on in two quite distinct but politically complementary forms. New cadres from the security apparatus turned out to support the proposition that creating a local computer industry was essential to national security. Equally important, CAPRE left behind a constituency in Brazil's emerging civil society. The original winners of the minicompetition had been joined by dozens of smaller PC manufacturers. These employed several thousand university-trained people,[35] who in turn swelled the ranks of the Seminars on Computation at the University (SECOMU), the Brazilian Computation Society (SBC), and the Association of Data Processing Professionals (APPD).

In 1980, when SEI's new head, Octávio Gennari, wavered over whether IBM would be allowed to produce a very small mainframe[36] that local firms felt would compete with their products, he found himself up against Didier Vianna, a former navy engineer, now head of a local firm producing computer peripherals and, more important, the president of the Association of the Brazilian Computer and Peripherals Industry (ABICOMP). ABICOMP, which brought together all locally owned computer firms (and only locally owned firms), had become an aggressive lobbyist on behalf of the técnicos' vision, a vision that had now become central to the industrialists' own interests.

As Brazil's political system opened up, the nationalist appeal of CAPRE's message was carried by newly elected representatives, such as Senator Severo Gomes and Congresswoman Christina Tavares. Finally, with the passage of the National Informatics Law in October 1984, the frustrated nationalist técnicos saw their ideas embodied, not just in the policies of a small "guerrilla" state agency, but in the law of the land.

In the ten years following 1974, the politics of informatics had changed completely. In 1974 there were no local entrepreneurial groups with an interest in local computer production. Clientelism was irrelevant because no entrepreneurial groups defined themselves as even a potential client of informatics policy. Rather than the policy being the product of interests as neo-utilitarian logic would predict, interests were the product of policy. Once the policy was in place, the local groups that had been drawn into production did have an interest in maintaining it. A political constituency for the policy grew in the wake of economic interests, and the policy's advocates within the state apparatus came to depend on this constituency to protect both the policy and the parts of the state apparatus that were associated with it. Actors whose interests were initially defined by state policy were now political protagonists in their own right.

Unfortunately for CAPRE's successors, the new politics of informatics did not take the form of a simple neo-utilitarian symbiosis in which the state set up rules to protect local capital and local capital provided political support for policymakers. The growth of the industry did more than call forth new, politically supportive producers. It also engaged the interests of computer users and raised the stakes in the conflict with international capital. Even more important, the producers themselves became a less homogeneous group. At the center of the new political controversies was the issue of technological autonomy, which seriously complicated the task of simultaneously promoting and policing the industry.

Had the five local winners of the 1977 minicompetition been able to use their licensed technology as a base for a follow-up generation of indigenously designed minicomputers, simultaneously promoting and policing the informatics industry might have been manageable. A technologically autonomous indigenous industry would have been created, and CAPRE's role would have been limited to making sure that foreign subsidiaries did not cross the line that had been drawn. Instead, the licensed technology, which was antiquated to begin with, did not provide an adequate base for a new generation of machines.[37]

Special Informatics Secretary Edison Dytz became convinced that only if the scale and financial strength of local informatics firms was increased could the technology problem be addressed (see Dytz 1986). To give large-scale capital more incentive to get into the industry, he initiated a new competition.[38] When the results were announced in 1984, it was clear that informatics was no longer going to be an industry of small entrepreneurs. Three major financial groups—Itaú by itself and Bradesco and Doca de Santos in combination—were persuaded to submit proposals. They in turn succeeded in licensing international technology from firms like DEC and Data General that had refused to consider licensing a few years earlier.[39] Getting into the Brazilian market had become a bigger prize for transnational capital as well as local capital.

Dytz's success notwithstanding, the incentive structure presented to local firms remained contradictory. The goal of Brazil's "informatics policy" was not just to stimulate the growth of local firms, but to stimulate the growth of local firms that would contribute to the growth of local technological capacity. Two different policies were combined to push local firms to invest in innovation. The carrot was having the lower end of the computer market "reserved" for them. Their "greenhouse" was protected from both imports and local production by TNCs and therefore much more profitable than it would otherwise have been. The stick was the prohibition on acquiring technology abroad without permission from the Special Secretariat for Informatics. The combination was supposed to create sufficient incentive so that local firms would develop new generations of products themselves rather than simply license and manufacture (or, worse still, just distribute) foreign products.

Unfortunately, the policy also created powerful incentives *not* to engage in local innovation. The market reserve was a collective good. Like all collective goods, it lent itself to abuse by free riding. Firms that pirated or surreptitiously licensed foreign products had all of the advantages of the greenhouse but none of the expense and uncertainty of doing their own research and development.

A surprising number of firms responded in the real spirit of the policy. Some made quite heroic efforts, produced impressive results, and managed to achieve profitable growth on the basis of indigenous designs.[40] Not surprisingly, other firms responded to the obvious advantages of free riding and reaped their rewards on the basis of technology that was either simply pirated or purchased without SEI's sanction.

Policing abuses was difficult for two reasons. First, and most obviously, it required substantial investigatory and administrative capacity on the part of SEI. With well over a hundred firms in the hardware market alone and hundreds of technologically complex products being introduced, timely certification of the authenticity of each purported local innovation would have required a staff many times the few dozen that struggled in SEI to perform the myriad functions demanded of them.

The political problems involved in trying to enforce the rules were more complex, but just as important. Local abusers of greenhouse privileges may have been outlaws, but they were still part of the policy's core political constituency. To expose them would have been to alienate key supporters and to discredit the greenhouse in the public eye. Nonetheless, tolerating firms that exploited the greenhouse without delivering the quid pro quo of real research and development efforts turned firms making genuine technological efforts into "suckers," whose "unnecessary" efforts were lowering the returns to their own shareholders.

Like local producers, SEI itself was caught by the contradictory requirements of the policy. Even though its primary constituency was producers, not users, it could not ignore user demands entirely. Since it was next to impossible for a few dozen local firms, tiny by international standards, operating several thousand miles from advanced informatics markets, to keep up with the evolution of global technology without relying on foreign ties, users grew increasingly restive. Some response was necessary. Yet every time SEI yielded to demands for expanded access, it undercut the returns accruing to prior efforts at autonomous technological development.

The 1984 licensing competition was a good example. Many local firms considered the fact that new technology was being licensed at all a betrayal on the part of SEI. Firms like SCOPUS felt they could produce competitive hardware without having to resort to licensing.[41] They saw the very existence of the competition as prejudicing the interests of firms more faithful to the goal of technological autonomy.

Variations on these complaints were repeated even by those involved in the competition. When Dytz announced the competition at the end of 1982, he specified that preference would be given to machines using commodity components and that technology transfer contracts should assure the "necessary technological autonomy" of the local enterprise.[42] The Itaú group took these provisions seriously, making a deal with a tiny New Jersey company called Formation, which was willing to open up its technology completely and used standard, not proprietary, components.[43]

Itaú's strategy fit the prescriptions of SEI's invitation perfectly, but when the results of the super-minicompetition were announced in 1984, Itautec (Itaú's computer subsidiary) found itself facing competition from the DEC VAX, which had been licensed by Elebra, a firm owned by Itaú's biggest financial competitor. The VAX was built out of proprietary components, and DEC was unlikely to open its technology the way Formation had, but it was an extremely popular technology with a vast amount of available software. Itaú mastered the Formation design and even built a much faster version of the machine, but by 1988 it had still only sold thirty machines, while Elebra had sold almost three times that number (Evans and Tigre 1989b, 22).

In short, firms that took the rules at face value were made "suckers" not only by the opportunistic free riding of other firms, but also by the agency's own pragmatic drift in the direction of greater reliance on licensed technology.

Given its problems with its own constituents, it is not surprising that SEI's position within the state apparatus remained problematic, despite its leadership's past connections with the security apparatus. SEI remained a favorite bête noire for the market-oriented technocrats and politicians. From the Planning Ministry through the Ministry of Commerce and Industry to the Treasury (Fazenda), these groups became increasingly vocal over the course of the 1980s. Beginning in 1985, when the Reagan administration began threatening retaliatory actions against Brazilian exporters because of Brazil's computer policy, SEI became even more of a target for market advocates (see Evans 1989b; Bastos 1992). Proposals to extinguish SEI, or to eviscerate it by eliminating the Ministry of Science and Technology and putting SEI under the essentially hostile Ministry of Commerce and Industry, remained ever popular.

Ministries with adjacent jurisdictions and more internationalist ideologies were equally hostile. The Ministry of Telecommunications (Minicom) is a good example. Minicom used its procurement leverage to force foreign equipment manufacturers to take on Brazilian partners, but it made no pretense that the resulting joint ventures were headed toward technological autonomy. From SEI's perspective, Minicom was enriching certain local entrepreneurs and developing its own clientelistic base without enhancing Brazil's technological autonomy vis-à-vis the international telecommunications industry. From Minicom's point of view, SEI was taking an unrealistically nationalist position that impeded the possibility of making use of globally competitive technology.

The Superintendencia for Amazonia (SUFRAMA), which had responsibility for production in the Manaus free zone (ZFM), was another obvious enemy (see Meyer-Stamer 1989, 17–18). For would-be assemblers of microcomputers, the free zone represented a potential bonanza of access to duty-free, internationally priced components. For SEI, allowing informatics to move into the free zone would have ended any pretense at local technological innovation. What was already done illicitly through smuggling, pirating foreign technology, and "under-the-table" technology deals not only would become legitimate but would receive government incentives for aiding the development of the Amazon region.

All of these problems were further compounded by SEI's internal "capacity gap," the gap between the demands placed on it and any reasonable assessment of its capacity to respond. Even at its height, SEI never employed more than a few dozen professionals.[44] Yet in theory SEI's staff was supposed to review the technology of all new products offered by local firms to make sure that it was original. This might have been a real possibility in an industry consisting of six firms making minicomputers. It was almost impossible for an industry with hundreds of firms producing everything from software operating systems to point-of-sale accounting devices.

In addition to policing local firms, SEI was supposed to police TNCs, making sure that TNC products did not stray into the market reserve. At the same time, it was responsible for making sure that Brazil was not completely cut off from new technology by approving the import of products that no one was capable of making in Brazil. Finally, the agency was supposed to be monitoring the industry's progress and helping plan its future growth.

The increasing diffusion of information technology across industrial sectors made matters worse. When CAPRE got its original assignment, the electronic processing of information was concentrated in what was in retrospect a relatively simple computer industry. By the mid-1980s, SEI's mandate had spread to numerically controlled machine tools, instruments, computer-aided design (CAD), and industrial robots (see Meyer-Stamer 1989, 7). In addition, silicon-managed information flows had spread from spark plugs to vacuum cleaners. The old charge of controlling inflows of electronic components now affected the inputs used by manufacturers of products like automobile and household appliances, for whom SEI was not supplying any protection to compensate for its restrictions.

Given the inevitable magnitude of the capacity gap, it is not surprising that SEI's constituents found it maddeningly slow and sometimes arbitrary in its decisions. Nor is it surprising that they began to see the agency less as a protector and more as a bureaucratic impediment to the growth of their enterprises. Thus, when SEI was attacked at the end of the 1980s as an authoritarian holdover from the military epoch that was standing in the way of Brazil's participation in the information society, even some of its core constituents were sympathetic to the charge.

One thing, however, should be underlined. Through it all, from the heady days of the first mini competition to the end of the informatics policy in the beginning of the 1990s, neither CAPRE nor SEI degenerated into clientelistic corruption. The privilege of producing a given machine was unquestionably a source of rents, yet SEI's personnel remained remarkably aloof from the temptations of making individual bargains with rent-seekers. Meyer-Stamer (1989, 24) asserts that SEI is "one of the very few Brazilian authorities that has never had to contend with accusations of corruption." Entrepreneurs that dealt with the agency generally shared Meyer-Stamer's view. To reduce SEI's problems to a study of self-serving bureaucrats and rent seeking clients would miss the point entirely.

The point is that while SEI was not a collection of self-seeking rent generators, it was also not an example of embedded autonomy. Hobbled by its custodial duties, it could not negotiate the sustained adherence of its industrial constituency to a trajectory of industrial growth, disciplining noncontributors and selectively promoting the successful. Its political vulnerability robbed it of any prospect of really exerting discipline on local firms. If it did not feel it had sufficient autonomy even to expose violators of its technology policy, the kind of "winnowing" of local firms that was practiced by MITI was clearly beyond its reach.

The problems of the Brazilian midwife/custodian should not, of course, obscure CAPRE/SEI's accomplishments. CAPRE especially is a perfect illustration of how the terrain of the state apparatus—even a state apparatus as hidebound, hierarchical, and conservative as Brazil's—may serve as fertile ground for innovation. The informatics regime drew on policy currents already present within the Brazilian state, but it bent them in novel ways that went well beyond the general thrust of Brazilian industrial policy. CAPRE/SEI went beyond redefining industrial policy; they restructured existing political and economic constituencies, acting as midwife in the creation of a new set of entrepreneurs and corporate organizations with vested interests in the development of local computer production.

To prevent CAPRE/SEI's midwifery from being overwhelmed by the contradictions of the custodial role, restrictive greenhouse regulations would have had to be carefully subordinated to an overall strategy of promotion, which, of course, was Korea's approach.

Korea

The Korean state's embedded autonomy was nicely reflected in its efforts to promote information technology. The custodial role was muted and behind the scenes. In comparison to the traumatic struggles with other parts of the state apparatus and with their own constituents that Brazil's técnicos faced, the lives of the Korean bureaucrats were a model of tranquility. In comparison to the continual flow of detailed prescriptions for individual firms and products required of their counterparts in India, their jobs were a model of simplicity.

Regulation of electronics production was thoroughly integrated in the general industrial policy apparatus. Within the Ministry of Trade and Industry, one of four industry-specific bureaus was devoted to electronics. Fiscal incentives and investments by foreigners had to be approved by the Ministry of Finance. The technology/energy division of the Economic Planning Board's Industrial Policy Coordination Bureau also played a role in setting electronics policy. When telecommunications production was involved, the Ministry of Communications joined the array of ministries. The Blue House was also involved, which, at least through the presidency of Chun Doo Hwan, meant substantial input from the security establishment.

In combination, the regulatory apparatus was formidable. The Ministry of Trade and Industry's Bureau for the Electronics Industry alone had a staff not much smaller than India's Department of Electronics. What was demanded of the apparatus, however, was qualitatively different. The regulatory apparatus did not have to process a license application every time an individual firm wanted to increase output of one of its products. If the state got involved in questions of output and product mix, it was in the style of "administrative guidance," negotiated with the major chaebol, or through the Korean Electronics Industry Association (EIAK). Firms were disciplined if they failed (Amsden 1989), but their production was not "micromanaged." The regulatory bureaucracy was a source of intelligence, a complement to other state strategies, but not the primary instrument of state influence. The state as regulator was strategically selective, conserving bureaucratic resources and minimizing contests with the private sector.

Since informatics policy was essentially consistent with Korea's overall industrial policy, conflicts within the state apparatus itself were minimal relative to the Brazilian case. There were, of course, tensions among the various agencies involved in regulating electronics. The MTI tended to be relatively more protective of domestic firms. The EPB was more insistent on market orientation. The two often disagreed. Still, it was not the kind of protracted struggle for political survival that consumed SEI's energies in Brazil.

Lower levels of internecine warfare made it easier to organize promotional policies. By fostering the growth of the chaebol conglomerates in the 1960s and 1970s, the state helped bring forth a versatile form of entrepreneurial organization that could move into new sectors as they became attractive. State policy in the 1970s was actively designed to make the electronics sector attractive. The Electronics Industry was selected by the Park Chung Hee regime as one of the six industries to be promoted under the Heavy and Chemical Industry Plan in 1973, despite the fact that it was neither heavy nor chemical (E. M. Kim 1987, 118; World Bank 1987a, 38–39). Targeted loans at below-market interest rates, use of government procurement, and careful though quiet control of foreign entry all helped shape the growth of the industry. Thus, the basic task of midwifery was accomplished in the 1970s, before information technology was a salient issue of industrial policy.

At the beginning of the 1980s, when local firms began producing PCs, the government provided them with an initial domestic market by ordering a large number of machines for educational use and also issued a decree protecting them from foreign competition (Chung 1986, 165). In 1983, when the domestic market was still only about U.S. $100 million (ITA 1981, 2; Chung 1986, 165), the government had already put forward a special developmental plan for the informatics sector (see NCCC 1988, 17–39). Despite having started much later than either India or Brazil, Korea was well on its way to having a formidable IT industry by the mid-1980s.

Structures, Roles, and Information Technology

Comparing Brazil, India, and Korea dramatizes the problems of trying to police for promotional purposes. Making custodial rules the primary instruments of industrial transformation demands more capacity than intermediate states like Brazil and India have to spare. Custodial rules do have a place in promotional efforts. Protected "greenhouses," a fundamental feature of custodial efforts, were essential to midwifery in all three countries. The problem is that maintaining a custodial approach becomes increasingly difficult as midwifery proceeds. Promotional success creates contradictions for custodial regulation. The more India and Brazil were successful in generating local computer industries, the more pressed their custodial agencies became.

At the same time, this comparison of IT sectors reinforces the general ideas about state structures and roles that have been raised in the last two chapters. What separates Korea from Brazil and India is not that Brazil and India constructed greenhouses while Korea did not. Nor is the difference that the Korean state intervened less than Brazil and India. The difference lies in the Korean state's blend of roles, which was in turn rooted in the structure of the state and the character of its ties to society. Internal coherence and close ties to entrepreneurial elites offered fruitful foundations from which to promote a new sector. Korea's embedded autonomy made it easier to adopt an effective combination of roles. The state devoted itself to the task of midwifery earlier and with more dedication.

Consequently, its informatics greenhouse took hold more quickly. Having fostered a group of powerful firms, Korea had to worry less about regulating their relations with transnational capital.

The logic of structures and roles played itself out in Brazil and India as well. The Indian state's generally ambivalent ties to industrial elites made it natural to adopt a custodial role and neglect midwifery even when a new, technologically dynamic sector called for the reverse emphasis. In Brazil, the fragmented character of the state found ample reflection in the IT sector. Likewise, conflicts in the IT sector reflected the divided character of the state's embeddedness. The state had no reluctance to engage in midwifery but could not easily combine the promotion of aspiring local capital with the realities of deep reliance on transnational capital. Efforts to sustain a greenhouse at the expense of TNC investors exacerbated the state's fragmentation, while at the same time the state lacked the autonomy to discipline local firms inside that same greenhouse.

Comparing state roles in information technology also brings home once again the ironic relation between roles and capacity that was raised at a general level in chapter 3. India and Brazil, whose intermediary state apparatuses were already strained to the breaking point, responded to the challenges of informatics with a combination of roles that required extraordinary if not impossible levels of capacity from their new regulatory bureaucracies, while Korea, whose bureaucratic capabilities were under less stress, chose a less demanding regulatory strategy. As the next chapter will show, this irony does not end with comparisons of custodial agencies. Both India and Brazil added the extremely difficult task of directly producing informatics goods to the already demanding role of custodian, while the Korean state focused on selectively husbanding the growth of local firms, a less demanding and more efficacious role.

Finally, comparing state roles in a specific sector helps bring state-society relations down to earth. Policing and promotion do not connect "the state" with "economic elites"; they connect specific state agencies and the people that run them with specific firms and their owners. Sectoral relations reflect larger structural patterns, but it is at the level of firm and agencies that roles really play themselves out, as will be even more evident once the discussion turns to state firms and husbandry in the next chapter.

6

State Firms and High-Tech Husbandry

It was the middle of an April night in 1989 when the phone rang in Ivan da Costa Marques's house in Rio de Janeiro, but he was happy to be dragged out of bed. The call was from Emeryville, California, and the news was good. A team of Brazilian software engineers from Costa Marques's company, Computadores e Sistemas Brasileiros SA (COBRA), was in Emeryville trying to make a point. They were trying to prove that they had designed, from scratch, a Brazilian clone of UNIX, an internationally standard operating system used around the world.

Emeryville was the site of Unisoft, an independent testing company commissioned by the X-OPEN, a consortium of European and American computer companies trying to establish international UNIX standards.[1] Passing Unisoft's "Verification Suite" would be internationally recognized proof of COBRA's claim that its operating system, SOX, was a legitimate, indigenously designed UNIX compatible. The team had gone to California once before without success, but this time they were phoning to tell Costa Marques that SOX had passed.

Later a letter from X-OPEN's London office would confirm COBRA's accomplishment, noting in addition that COBRA was the first company to pass the verification tests with a system developed completely independently of AT&T, which owned the international rights to UNIX. COBRA was now a potential player in the rapidly growing global market for UNIX operating systems and applications.

For Costa Marques, the letter was not just confirmation of compatibility, it vindicated a long and daunting technological struggle. Now that SOX was certified, COBRA was in an almost unique position. It could license its UNIX look-alike to Brazilian users without paying royalties to AT&T. It could also export the operating system to whatever country it wished without having to worry about AT&T's restrictions or U.S. export controls. Since COBRA had developed its own hardware platform to go along with SOX, it was even in a position to supply UNIX systems.

Ironically, COBRA's technological victory came at the most bitter and discouraging juncture in the company's history. The final years of SOX's development had been commercially disastrous for the company. COBRA was losing money. The chaos that reigned in the Brazilian economy overall made it an unauspicious time to try for a turnaround. Worst of all, the National Development Bank (BNDE), which had provided "deep pockets" and political support since COBRA's inception fifteen years earlier, had turned against it. For over a year, the BNDE had been pushing to sell the company to a private buyer and reinforcing its pressure for privatization by withholding the new infusion of capital that COBRA needed to get moving again commercially. COBRA still had strong political supporters scattered through the industry, the Congress, and the state apparatus, and it was later saved from dismemberment, at least temporarily, by another state bank, the Banco do Brasil. Nonetheless, the tide had clearly turned against it. The leading role that it had played in the initiation of local production of computers and software in Brazil had come to an end. Preserving the organizational and human resources it had amassed over the course of the 1970s and 1980s would be an uphill struggle in the 1990s.

What did the COBRA saga signify? For many, both in Brazil and in the rest of the world, it demonstrated the folly of state involvement in high-technology industries like computers. For those who had nurtured Brazil's infant computer industry, it showed how easily cowardly bankers and politicians fold under external pressure and sell out a developmental dream. Neither vision comes close to capturing the complex evolution of the Brazilian state's role in the information technology industry.

COBRA was never really intended to be a demiurge. It was supposed to be a demonstration project, a placeholder, and a vehicle for bringing local private partners into the industry. Yet it ended up selling commodity hardware in competition with Brazilian-owned firms, doing badly at it, and illustrating the pitfalls of the demiurge strategy. COBRA's story, together with those of India's state firms, shows clearly that the state's comparative institutional advantage does not lie in producing high-technology commodities.[2]

The lessons to be gained from looking at the state as producer are not negative only. While they reveal the contradictions of trying to replace private capital as a producer of commodity goods, Brazil's COBRA and India's various SOEs also illustrate innovative organizational forms and tactics that make better use of the distinctive nature of the state as a lever for fostering high-tech development. Korea extends these lessons by showing how efforts to support and prod local firms can involve just as much state entrepreneurship as producing goods directly.

The Demiurge Option[3]

Trying to replace private capital by taking the role of direct producer comes naturally to a state with more autonomy than embeddedness. Setting up state enterprises requires neither faith in the entrepreneurial initiatives of local private capital nor the continual negotiation of a joint transformative project. The state can play the role of "far-sighted helmsman"[4] without eliciting specific commitments and collaboration from local industrialists.

The "anti-Schumpeterian bargain" between the Indian state and local private capital[5] made sense only if the state was ready to take on entrepreneurial responsibility itself. Given the natural affinity between Indian patterns of state-society relations and the demiurge role, it is hardly surprising that this was India's initial option in information technology. Long-standing institutional proclivities were stronger than the sectoral logic that made high-tech industry look like a bad site for state firms.

As information technology made its way onto India's developmental agenda in the 1970s, state-owned enterprises dominated at the expense of local capital. Most of them were problematic entities. Nonetheless, as time went on, India's panoply of SOEs also offered some tantalizing examples of how state firms might define their role in ways quite different from the classic demiurge.

BEL began the saga of state-owned electronics production in India in 1954. Its principal mission was to supply the military's electronics' needs. Operating under the Defense Ministry's Department of Defense Production, it expanded rapidly, especially after the security scares of the early 1960s, becoming the largest producer of electronic goods in India (after Indian Telephone Industries, the state-owned phone company). Not a drain on the public coffers like the state-owned steel mills or railways, it always made a small profit (BEL 1989, 4).

BEL's contribution to the growth of India's capacity as an electronics producer went well beyond its products. It also developed substantial technical expertise. In the early 1970s it was the only company in India able to undertake the full cycle of semiconductor wafer fabrication. Like many high-tech public sector firms, it served as a training ground for engineers.[6] Its massive presence in Bangalore (almost twenty thousand employees by the end of the 1980s) helped lay the groundwork to make India's "silicon plateau" the country's most promising "technopolis" (see Pani 1987).

Despite its unquestioned contributions, BEL also illustrates the problems of having the state take on the role of direct producer. It never succeeded in getting its costs down to international standards of commercial competition. Insofar as it tried to compete commercially, its technological successes too often proved commercial failures.[7] Worse still, its presence seemed to be distort the way in which the state played the role of regulator.

In 1971 there were 150 electronics licensing requests that had been outstanding for one to three years. The Defense Ministry, which had responsibility for granting licenses,[8] seemed reluctant to allow newcomers into the industry, even other SOEs (Grieco 1984, 110–15). Since the Defense Ministry was also in charge of BEL, the state seemed to be using its regulatory prerogatives to protect its privileges as producer at the expense of the industry's overall growth. Once the DOE and the Electronics Commission, under the leadership of the BARC group, took over regulatory responsibility from the Ministry of Defense, BEL was no longer at the center of the regulator/producer equation, but the close links between the state as regulator and the state as producer continued.

ECIL was the DOE's favored instrument for developing local computer production. Unfortunately, it was also a good illustration of the difficulties of playing demiurge. The problem was not lack of entrepreneurship. ECIL was aggressive both technological and economically. It developed and produced an indigenously designed minicomputer, complete with operating system,[9] and it sold televisions in direct competition with the private firms.

The problem was that ECIL's entrepreneurial spirit did not translate easily into economic and technological success. Between 1971 and 1978, ECIL produced fewer than one hundred systems and only managed to sell four of them to the private sector (Grieco 1984, 127). Its hardware sold for several times the price of its competitors' hardware on the international market, and, to make matters worse, its indigenous operating system was woefully lacking in applications software.[10]

By the end of the 1970s there was understandable dissatisfaction with ECIL as the "national champion." Local private firms, attracted by the DOE's greenhouse, were quick to see that the "semiconductor revolution" brought the possibility of producing small machines, with performance comparable to ECIL's minis, within their grasp. To the degree that the greenhouse worked, the role of the state as demiurge became problematic. Once local private firms got into the act, ECIL found it difficult to compete with them in the market for personal computers.

Over the course of the next ten years, local firms completely outstripped ECIL in this market. By 1988–89 ECIL's PC sales were only about 1 percent those of commodity-oriented private newcomers like Sterling and Pertech (*Dataquest* 1989, 87, 88, 90). ECIL had also been forced to abandon completely its aspirations for technological autonomy in hardware. Producing competitive machines with novel architectures and indigenous operating systems had proved an impossible strategy.[11] ECIL's principal hardware in the 1980s was based on foreign licenses.[12]

What was surprising about ECIL was not its problems, which were exactly what a standard analysis of state-owned enterprises in high-technology industries would predict, but its resilience. By the end of the 1980s ECIL had found a new way of growing. "Special projects," which is to say large-scale systems integration efforts, became its new raison d'être.[13]

ECIL's special projects did more than keep the company alive, they provided solutions to important developmental problems. For example, ECIL played a lead role in the design and implantation of an automated monitoring system for India's far-flung offshore oil and natural gas wells, reputedly constructed for a fraction of the costs projected in bids received from international companies (Parthasarathi 1987, 17). ECIL also provided a computerized integrated control system to one of the state-owned steel plants (*Dataquest* 1989, 87) and was a principal supplier of computerized load dispatch systems to power companies (Parthasarathi 1987, 16).

ECIL's successes in the production of large-scale custom systems with large social returns and its failures at competing with small private firms in the PC market suggest a more general point. Having state firms produce commodity goods for individual consumers is a losing strategy, both for the firms themselves and for society, but this does not necessarily mean that there is no role for the state as a producer of high-technology goods. In a high-tech version of the state's traditional role as a provider of infrastructure, state firms may have advantages over both local private firms and TNCs.

CMC, formerly the Computer Maintenance Corporation, makes the same point more forcefully. Originally a by-product of India's fight with IBM, CMC was formed under the aegis of the DOE in 1975 and given a legal monopoly on servicing computer systems not manufactured in India (Grieco 1984, 80–81; Subramanian 1989, 226–27). At first IBM systems were its specialty, not surprisingly since 200 of the 230 engineers in IBM's customer engineering division joined CMC on IBM's departure (Subramanian 1989, 227). As companies like DEC and Hewlett-Packard increased their penetration of the Indian market, CMC found itself servicing an ever more diversified set of systems. By the end of the 1980s it was servicing hardware made by about forty different foreign firms as well as some manufactured by local companies.[14]

Well known for its corporate élan and disdain for orthodoxy, the company seemed to enjoy difficult contracts and challenging environments.[15] For example, in 1987 CMC won a "mission impossible" contract (beating ICL and Norskdata) to computerize the Tenth Mediterranean Games in Syria. In three months it had to produce a system, based on unfamiliar hardware, linking three different sites, operating in Arabic and French.[16] Later it set up an international headquarters in London, bagged a contract with the London subway, set up a long-term relationship to write software for ICL, and explored acquisition of a U.S. software company in order to "gain a foothold" in the U.S. market (*Dataquest* 1989, 85).

In 1989 CMC was the second largest informatics company in India, but not on the basis of its maintenance revenues. Maintenance accounted for less than a quarter of CMC's revenues (*Dataquest* 1989, 85). The company had become a systems integrator whose principal source of revenues was large turnkey projects, aimed mainly at improving the state's own capacity to deliver infrastructure services. Over half of its revenues came from such projects.[17]

The IMPRESS railway reservation system is the best example of the CMC's work. When CMC became interested in the problem of railway reservations, state-owned Indian Railways was running the second largest railway system in the world, carrying on the order of 100 million passengers a year. Issuing tickets was a bureaucratic nightmare involving "7 different categories of trains, 72 types of coaches, 7 classes of reservations, 32 types of quotas, and 85 kinds of concessional tickets" (CMC 1988a, 2). The railway company itself, one of the largest drains on the public coffers in the state enterprise system (World Bank 1987b, 34), was content to pass the nightmare on to its customers. Passengers in Delhi were reputed to resort to waiting in line overnight for reservations. CMC was attracted by the challenge and had put in two years of developmental efforts by the time the railway system decided to ask for bids to automate the system.

Writing the hundreds of thousands of lines of software code required to automate the first location (Delhi) took thirty-five engineer years. CMC's wide-ranging hardware experience complemented its software expertise. It used DEC hardware[18] and wrote the software system in DEC's proprietary operating system. By combining indigenous software and state-of-the-art hardware, CMC was able to produce a system that was both efficient and relatively inexpensive. The average waiting time for customers was brought down to less than twenty minutes, and the cost of the system was "far cheaper than what had been quoted by foreign companies" (Parthasarathi 1987, 20).

Like the railway reservation system, CMC's other projects were typically aimed at increasing the efficiency of India's infrastructure.[19] CMC has specialized in large projects that require a scale few local firms can muster and a feel for the idiosyncrasies of local systems and organizations that TNCs cannot easily provide. Such projects are in niches with high rates of social return for which state enterprises may have a "comparative institutional advantage."[20]

The general evolution of the role of SOEs in Indian electronics is consistent with the trajectories of ECIL and CMC. As the production of electronics commodities has grown, the role of the demiurge has shrunk.[21] To make a real contribution, state firms have had to redefine their role.

The **New Projects Division** initiated by Meltron, a relatively small firm owned by the state government of Maharastra, is another variation on the theme of adaptation.[22] Meltron's New Projects Division was set up to work with various private- and public-sector groups to promote the use and production of electronics in Maharastra. This could involve setting up working groups inside the state government to promote the utilization of electronics, setting up a training program for rural women who want to become electronics assemblers, or helping local manufacturers make contacts that would help them take advantage of the late 1980s' boom in hardware exports to the Soviet Union. In addition, New Projects produced Meltron's newsletter, which told local entrepreneurs about financing opportunities and incentive schemes, even providing sample application forms (Meltron 1988–89).

The head of New Projects, P. S. Sekhar, was a former industry consultant with an advanced degree in electronics who felt he had been able to get more projects off the ground in two years working inside Meltron than he could have in twenty years as a private consultant. His work style was more like that of the MITI men described by Okimoto (1989) or the IDB types described by Wade (1990) than of the distrustful custodians who are supposed to inhabit the Indian state apparatus. Sekhar considered the construction of public-sector/private-sector networks one of his most important accomplishments. Rather than keeping company heads waiting in his anteroom, he spent a substantial portion of his workweek out visiting companies. In short, Sekhar turned the idea of the demiurge on its head. The New Projects Division is an exercise in midwifery clothed in the organizational form of a state-owned enterprise.

C-DOT (Centre for the Development of Telematics) offers still another variation on the theme of state entrepreneurship. C-DOT managed to combine technological entrepreneurship with a focus on the development of infrastructure and support for local private firms.[23] It was formed in 1984 to produce a family of digital switches that would offer an alternative to the foreign technology on which Indian Telephone Industries was forced to rely.[24] The idea was to produce a switch potentially capable of handling advanced applications[25] yet still simple, rugged, and economical in the small-scale applications required by India's 650,000 villages.

Like CMC, C-DOT prided itself on having escaped the bureaucratic mold and created "an egalitarian organizational culture, as free as possible from bureaucratic strictures, emphasizing target-achievement through human resource management and strong leadership" (Singhal and Rogers 1989, 180).[26] Because it offered aspiring Indian engineers a unique organizational environment along with a state-of-the-art problem, it was soon able to attract between three and four hundred young, highly motivated engineers.[27]

The same kind of comparative advantage in large-scale software design that allowed CMC and ECIL to bid against TNCs for infrastructural systems enabled C-DOT to produce its switch design at a fraction of the investment typically required by international companies to design an electronic switching system (ESS).[28] The design relied on standardized chips[29] and the equally standard UNIX operating system and was modular to allow economical production of small-scale exchanges (Alam 1989, 66).[30]

One of the most interesting applications of C-DOT's technology was the rural automatic exchange (RAX). Based on a single switching module, the RAX was "ruggedized" so that it could operate without air conditioning under higher levels of heat and humidity. A "containerized" version came ready for immediate installation, complete with batteries, solar panels, and radio transmission equipment to connect it to a parent exchange, yet was still relatively inexpensive.[31] A pilot rural exchange installed in a village of twelve thousand in southern India in 1986 won high praise from the residents. Villagers credited their new phones with providing quicker medical attention and more law and order plus higher prices and increased sales for their agricultural product.[32]

By focusing on technological entrepreneurship rather than direct production, C-DOT was able to play technological midwife to potential private-sector producers of telecom equipment rather than confronting them as a competitor. Its electronic private branch automatic exchange (EPBAX) technology was licensed to about forty firms, which, given the modular design of C-DOT's switches, made them potential producers of rural exchanges as well.[33]

C-DOT's biggest problem was not its relations with the private sector, but its relations with the rest of the state apparatus, which had a hard time adapting to C-DOT's unorthodox definition of the state's role. For example, the Department of Telecommunications insisted on buying rural exchanges only from the state-owned telephone producer, Indian Telephone Industries (ITI). Consequently, only 25 of the 410 RAXes commissioned in the 1988–89 fiscal year were actually produced (*Computers Today*, January 1989, 10).[34]

From BEL to C-DOT, India's plethora of high-tech state enterprises run a full gamut of variations. Together they demonstrate that substituting for private capital in the production of routine commodities is not an effective strategy. At the same time, India's experience suggests that state enterprises, used in a creative and complementary way, may well have a role to play in the IT industry. Exploiting their "comparative institutional advantage"[35] in developing specialized large-scale systems based on intimate knowledge of the local environment offers better prospects of efficacy at the level of the firm and greater social return as well. Echoes of the same lessons can be found in Brazil, despite the Brazilian state's very different institutional style.

COBRA (Computadores e Sistemas Brasileiros SA) was originally intended to play a midwife role, drawing local capital into informatics production and anchoring an alliance between local and transnational capital. COBRA was also supposed to be a vehicle for technological entrepreneurship. Unfortunately, it had to combine both of these roles with the classic demiurge role, selling commodities[36] in competition with local private firms. Its efforts to combine these roles revealed the incompatibilities among them even more clearly than did the saga of India's SOEs.

Born in 1974 out of an alliance between the military and nationalist technocrats,[37] COBRA was intended to be a *tri-pé*, like those being initiated in the petrochemical industry at the same time.[38] The state would take the organizational initiative, but the ownership would be split equally among a state-owned enterprise, a local private firm, and a foreign company.

The search for private partners vindicated the importance of state initiative. When Ricardo Saur was done exploring the possibilities, the only local firm willing to come forward was a small military supplier by the name of E.E. Equipamentos Electrônicos, whose primary motivations seemed to be its desire to maintain good relations with the military and its hopes for an infusion of funds from the BNDE (Evans 1986a, 793). Maintaining good relations with its military customers also seemed to be the primary motivation of the foreign partner, Ferranti, the English defense firm that had provided the electronic gear for the Brazilian Navy's new frigates. Neither partner proved much of a contributor, though Ferranti did provide some important training for the first generation of COBRA managers. Within a year, Equipamentos Electrônico's share of the equity had sunk to 5 percent. Even worse, Ferranti's technology proved a commercial failure.

Surprisingly, COBRA's indigenously designed minicomputer, the COBRA 500,[39] proved a bigger commercial success than Ferranti's technology.[40] As the only Brazilian company to design an original computer architecture with its own indigenous operating system (as opposed to reverse engineering standard architectures), COBRA proved that locally generated innovation was a real possibility. Its 500 series ended up outselling all the foreign technology licensed in the 1977 mini competition.

In spite of its disappointing *tri-pé* partners, COBRA also achieved an early success in mediating between foreign and local capital. In 1976 the large Brazilian banks, looking for a way to solve their data entry problems, became interested in developing a local source of supply for the Sycor 400 (produced by a tiny American company and marketed in Brazil by Olivetti). Sycor proved willing to license its technology to COBRA, and eleven Brazilian banks were persuaded to take over almost 40 percent of COBRA's equity. The resulting COBRA 400, entering the market with an assured set of users from the beginning, was COBRA's second biggest commercial success.

Sustaining this combination of indigenous technological development and effective international intermediation grew successively harder as time went on. In 1982, when SEI initiated its second licensing competition, COBRA was in a difficult position. Competition within the protected market was increasingly intense, and COBRA's patrons in the BNDE were not interested in financing losses. The COBRA 500 could not compete with the new generation of foreign machines licensed in the supermini competition.[41] Trying to repeat its 1977 feat of developing a new indigenous machine would have been risky. In the end, COBRA decided to team up with Data General (DG).

From a distance the COBRA/DG tie-up looked like a strategic alliance that made sense.[42] DG needed to get back into the Brazilian market before it was too late.[43] COBRA needed larger, faster machines. Putting together COBRA's considerable installed base and the new DG technology should have allowed COBRA to exploit its existing market position by "migrating" customers up to the more powerful foreign technology.[44]

Relying on foreign technology might have been good business, but COBRA's tradition of indigenous development was still very much alive. In 1983, two years before the DG licensing agreement was finally put into operation, COBRA had begun developing a new workstation.[45] The new machine was designed to run both SOX, the new UNIX equivalent that COBRA was trying to develop, and SOD, the earlier, indigenously designed operating system that ran on COBRA's older machines.[46] Old customers could use their existing software on the new machine; new customers could enjoy a powerful system that ran internationally standard software. It was a promising project, and many members of the technical staff saw working on the DG machines as a distraction from their efforts at indigenous development. By 1988 COBRA still had only sold about fifty of the DG machines (Evans and Tigre 1989b).

COBRA's indigenous technology strategy was audacious. It required the company's software development team to construct, completely on their own, a legally legitimate clone of UNIX, arguably the operating system with the greatest worldwide diffusion at the time, together with a corresponding set of software utilities and applications,[47] thereby allowing Brazil "to secure its place in the standards market both as a buyer and as a seller"(Costa Marques 1988). It would have been considered a significant undertaking even by a major international firm.[48]

COBRA, which had at the time perhaps the largest concentration of software development engineers in Latin America (about two hundred), devoted fifty of them to developing its UNIX equivalent for six years. Twenty million dollars was invested in the project. As the cost for devel-

oping a UNIX equivalent, it was a sum that represented parsimony TNCs
might envy, but it was a huge investment for COBRA.[49] The magnitude
of the risk involved was what made success, and the call to Ivan da Costa
Marques with which this chapter began, so momentous.

Despite the project's technological success and SOX's certification as a
legitimate indigenous UNIX-compatible system, the undertaking proved
costly to COBRA's survival. The launching of the new workstation was
delayed while SOX was completed, which left COBRA without a presence in the advanced desktop market that was at the time the most rapidly
growing segment of the industry. Economically, the call from California
came too late. With no commercial return from the $20 million invested
and no innovative additions to the product line during the wait, COBRA
found itself in financial trouble.

Solving financial problems did not fit with a focus on indigenous technology. Facing declining sales volume and increasing losses in 1987,
COBRA fell back on producing a PC clone, which soon accounted for a
greater volume of sales than any of its large machines. By entering the PC
market, COBRA became a classic demiurge, competing with established
local firms in standard commodity markets. Its experience confirmed the
pitfalls of the role. The PC market was intensely price competitive, and
COBRA's PCs earned a very small margin of profit. The company continued to operate at a loss, but it garnered the enmity of local private competitors, which saw it using the financial resources of the state to bankroll
poaching on their turf. The movement to sell COBRA to the highest private bidder gained momentum.

COBRA's technological aspirations created political tensions as well.
Having invested so much in the creation of an indigenous operating system, COBRA became a fervent advocate of restricting the entry of foreign
software. Excluding licensed UNIX from the market would have put Brazil in an unusual position. Most industrializing countries, even
autarkically oriented India, saw UNIX as a means of breaking free from
proprietary, hardware-bound standards like IBM's. Many Brazilian firms
agreed. COBRA's stance divided it from part of the local industry. The
software issue also created higher-level tensions. Brazil's reluctance to
adopt a more open stance toward software became the focal point of its
ongoing feud with the United States, as well as a source of tension between SEI and the office of the president.[50]

COBRA's story reveals the contradictions of trying to be an agent of
indigenous technological development and a profit-making producer of
commodities at the same time. COBRA proved the caliber of Brazilian
software developers and created an invaluable pool of skilled, experienced human resources but was left without profits. It was evaluated,
even by its owners within the state, not as a research institution or the

bearer of the country's technological patrimony, but as a company with a responsibility to make a profit. If it was to be a demiurge, a stand-in for the local entrepreneurial class, it had to play by the rules of profit and loss.

Nor is it clear that COBRA maximized the social return on its investment by creating its own proprietary version of an internationally standard operating system. Developing locally relevant applications and utilities and trying to solve the myriad problems involved in maximizing local utilization of an international standard might have had a greater impact on Brazil's informatics users. The examples of ECIL and CMC certainly argue that a focus on local applications is a high-return option, for both countries and companies.[51]

Findings that cut across the quite different institutional environments of Brazil and India suggest a general conclusion. State firms may be the natural embodiment of the demiurge role, but the demiurge role rarely maximizes the contribution of state firms, at least not in the IT industry. Using state firms as substitutes for private production in the manufacture of commodity products is a mistake. It channels scarce state capacity into activities where the state has no comparative institutional advantage, generates relations of conflict rather than complementarity with local entrepreneurs, and complicates state firms' ability to serve as a font of indigenous technological capacity.

When a greenhouse will not suffice to bring forth local entrepreneurs, the demiurge may play an important transitional role in the process of midwifery.[52] Once an industry is under way, state firms are more likely to succeed if they focus on maximizing their comparative institutional advantage. They may well be able to build indigenous expertise and operate profitably if they focus on "niche markets," especially the provision of large systems designed to deal with local idiosyncrasies, like the projects of CMC and ECIL. State firms may also be able to provide organizational homes for activities completely outside the realm of demiurge role. They can supply technological entrepreneurship for the private sector, as C-DOT did, or they can follow in the footsteps of state agencies like Taiwan's IDB or Japan's MITI and work on building public-private networks, as Meltron's Special Projects Division did.

State enterprises are, almost by definition, more insulated from the pressure of the bottom line than are their private counterparts. In the production of routine commodities this is likely to put state enterprises at a disadvantage, but they still may be able to play a useful role in taking some of the burden of technological entrepreneurship off the shoulders of local entrepreneurs. India offers some examples of how separating the responsibility for technological entrepreneurship from the exigencies of day-to-day production might work. Korea offers many more.

High-Technology Husbandry

Husbandry fits the requirements of promoting high-tech industry as clearly as relying on the state as direct producer does not. Greenhouses do not dependably produce local firms able and disposed to sustain the levels of innovation and technological investment necessary to survive in a high-technology industry. Many of those induced to enter will not survive. Those that do will face strong pressure to migrate into more routine, less rewarding niches within the sector. Cultivating and supporting the capacities of new entrepreneurial groups and prodding them to make the most of available opportunities is an essential complement to midwifery, as the Japanese case illustrates so nicely.

Korea was more likely to focus on husbandry than Brazil or India for two reasons. First, the pattern of state-society relations that went with Korea's embedded autonomy made husbandry a natural choice. Second, Korea's early success at midwifery made the necessity of husbandry more obvious. Having accomplished the basic task of midwifery before information technology became a central issue, and therefore able to draw on manufacturers with world-scale production facilities, deep financial pockets, and substantial electronics experience, Korea could safely open up the greenhouse to competition from foreign imports by 1987, only about seven years after local production of PCs was initiated. Opening up the greenhouse did not mean the end of state involvement. It meant the state could focus on increasing the capacities of the local entrepreneurial groups that were committed to the industry, particularly their technological capacity.

The Korean Model of Husbandry

Korea's state planners continued to worry that their powerful manufacturers would become trapped in low-return commodity production, excluded from more design-intensive, higher-return markets. Entrepreneurship, particularly technological risk-taking, could not be taken for granted. In contrast to India's "anti-Schumpeterian bargain,"[53] the Korean state tried to strike a series of "Schumpeterian bargains" with local producers, aimed at inducing them to move to more technologically challenging products.

Stimulating entrepreneurship by local firms required entrepreneurship on the part of state organizations. Husbandry turned out to be just as "entrepreneurial" a form of state involvement as becoming a producer. Korea's "entrepreneurial bureaucrats" used a variety of instruments and strategies and created a variety of interesting institutions. All of them aimed at pushing the local information technology sector forward just a bit faster than it would have gone on its own.

The **4-Megabit DRAM Project**[54] is one good example. By the mid-1980s, Samsung's Lee Byung Chul had surprised the world by investing the vast sums necessary to make his company a world-class producer of commodity semiconductors. The other major chaebol, especially Goldstar, followed Samsung's lead. Despite their initial success, however, it was not clear that Korean companies would be able to keep up with the relentless march of the Japanese toward ever larger numbers of gates per chip. One-Megabit chips were already being produced, and the question was whether Korean firms would be able to follow the Japanese (and IBM) to 4 Megabits.

The 4-Megabit Project was organized through the Electronics and Telecommunications Research Institute (ETRI). With about 1,200 researchers and technicians and a budget of over $120 million, ETRI was the key research organization of the Ministry of Communications.[55] In this case, however, ETRI's job was not to do the research and development, its task was to stimulate and coordinate efforts by the major chaebol to develop the chips themselves.

The government would provide loans on generous terms (below-market interest rates, grace periods, etc.) to each of the companies to help finance the early development work. The loans were not large (estimates range from U.S. $30 to $200 million). If the companies had not been convinced that this was something they would have to do eventually, they might have resisted the offer of assistance. Since they knew that the 4-Megabit chip was on their agendas, it made no sense not to take advantage of the prod.

The research was "cooperative" in a way that heightened the pressure to keep up with competitors. Representatives from each company's team got together on a monthly basis and compared progress (without sharing any secret specifics). ETRI monitored progress and dispensed loans in accordance with each company's accomplishments. The pressure to keep abreast of the progress of the other participants was perhaps as important a prod as the monetary incentive itself. Even Samsung, clearly the most advanced, acknowledged the project's usefulness. Other companies admitted that, while they would have started work on a 4-Megabit chip sooner or later, the existence of the project made it sooner rather than later.

The 4-Megabit Project reinforced a call to technological entrepreneurship that already existed in the market. Other projects were bolder, pushing firms to get into technologically risky projects that they never would have embarked on without support. **Electronic switching systems** for telecommunications systems is an especially useful example because it highlights the role of one of Korea's most important complexes of entrepreneurial technocrats, the Ministry of Communications (MOC) and its associated state enterprises.

Entrepreneurship had been a central characteristic of MOC since the beginning of the 1980s. As the decade progressed, MOC added an average of a million telephone lines a year to move from less than three million lines in 1980 to more than ten million in 1987, financing most of the investment with revenues from its own operating company, the Korean Telecommunications Authority (KTA).[56] At the same time a nationwide direct distance dial system was established. All of this required, of course, massive investment in new switching equipment produced by a handful of transnational companies.[57]

Shifting to indigenously designed equipment would reduce the foreign exchange drain and open the possibility of future Korean participation in the huge worldwide market for telephone exchanges. The risk was beyond what the chaebol were willing to tackle on their own, but the formidable institutional structure that MOC had assembled made the attempt possible.

First, the ministry recognized that it was difficult to get funds for the initial stages of development out of the normal budgetary process. Therefore, 3 percent of the very healthy revenues (about U.S. $2 billion) that the KTA, its operating company, garnered from running the existing phone system were allocated to research and development. Second, MOC recognized that private companies would not become involved in developing ESS switches without some guarantee of future markets. The likelihood of getting a share of MOC's procurement of new exchanges was what made it worthwhile for the chaebol to participate. With MOC's extensive revenues subsidizing development costs and its massive procurement budget offering future markets, what would otherwise have been an impossibly daunting project became an attractive one.

Ministries, even aggressive ones, do not design electronic switching systems. Private companies are hard to draw into major basic research efforts even with a procurement carrot. Therefore, doing the research was ETRI's job.[58] Using its procurement leverage again, MOC persuaded international telecommunications manufacturers like Ericsson to transfer some of their switching technology and train ETRI personnel (Kim and Yoon 1991, 173–75). Ericsson's technology was a valuable springboard,[59] but the aim was to adapt it to local needs, not just copy it. Like C-DOT's engineers in India, ETRI defined its mission as producing a switch that was different from those favored by transnational firms—one that was smaller, suitable for expanding the network into rural areas, and built around commodity components rather than proprietary ones.

The big difference between India's efforts and Korea's was that in Korea powerful private actors were intimately involved from the beginning. The research was organized and managed by ETRI, but private companies were integrally involved even at the research stage. When it was time to produce the switch, private firms, not ETRI, would do the job.[60] Ernst and O'Connor (1992, 203–4) note the contrast between Korea's modus operandi and that of Brazil and India: "In the cases of Brazil and India, government research institutes appear to have operated with a minimum of collaboration with those firms which would ultimately manufacture the switches. Technology development and diffusion were treated as distinct activities, whereas in Korea they were closely inter-related."

By 1986 the chaebol were manufacturing the first version of the indigenous switch, the TDX-1A. It was a small switch by world standards[61] but more than adequate for the needs of rural villages. By 1987 it comprised the majority of the rural switching systems being installed in Korea. The local companies that were manufacturing the TDX-1A had already begun to bid for contracts to install their switch in other Third World countries. The next year TDX-1B, which could handle over twenty thousand lines, was developed, and Korea's first export success was achieved with a sale to the Philippines (L. Kim 1991, 39). To help local firms expand their market, the KTA set up an international marketing subsidiary and the Korean government initiated a fund to help foreigners finance their purchases.[62] At the same time, work began on the TDX-10, which was an international-scale system (100,000 lines) and would have the capacity to handle integrated service digital network (ISDN).

In retrospect, the TDX strategy looks simple. Private capital was assumed capable of producing even the most technologically sophisticated products, but its willingness to attack development tasks was not taken for granted. To push firms in the direction of classic Schumpeterian entrepreneurship, the state lowered the technological risk, taking on some of the development effort itself and subsidizing the firms' participation. At the same time, it lowered the commercial risk by assuring an initial market. The result was extension of telecommunications infrastructure to new areas at less foreign exchange cost, new indigenous technology with export potential, and a strengthened R&D infrastructure. In practice, putting together this "simple" strategy required an unusual combination of imagination, institutions, and state entrepreneurship.

An even more ambitious variation on the same theme, the **National Administrative Information System** (NAIS) project, took shape in the mid-1980s at about the same time as the electronic switching system project. The Blue House group[63] of technologically committed presidential advisers became convinced that manufacturing computers was not enough. Only with the construction of a full-fledged data network, eventually reaching millions of households, could Korea become an "information society."

The result was a plan for a national computer network built around indigenously developed hardware and software, designed to "enhance the administrative efficiency and the quality of public service."[64] Taking administrative systems and putting them on-line would reduce the time, expense, and opportunities for corruption involved in myriad administrative decisions. For example, according to one official, a computerized system for customs clearance would reduce clearance time from forty days to seven, which could save U.S. $7.5 billion over a ten-year period and represent a key gain for an export-dependent country.

NAIS was not just aimed at modernizing infrastructure. It was also intended to "boost up the local computer industry" (DACOM 1988, 18). In relation to local production at the time, the "boost" was considerable. Initial budgets called for buying about $100 million in hardware from local producers to set up a system of that would consist of around 100 supermini "host" machines connected to 10,000 workstations.[65] Since total Korean output of computers larger than PCs was only about U.S. $50 million in 1986 (*Business Korea* 1988, III-497), local manufacturers were being offered a chance to triple their market for larger machines with a single contract. As *Datamation* put it, "NAIS is the springboard that South Korean hardware and software suppliers have been looking for. It's their biggest opportunity yet to cut their teeth on designing and manufacturing more sophisticated systems" (Gadacz 1987, 68–2).

The NAIS project was more complicated than the TDX project, both organizationally and technically. MOC took the main responsibility and the chaebol were involved from the beginning,[66] but someone had to handle the network itself. MOC needed a small, agile company without responsibility for stringing phone lines to handle the new network. DACOM, formally a private company but owned 30 percent by the KTA, filled this role. With only a thousand employees, $70 million in sales (DACOM 1988, 28), and no responsibility for conventional phone lines, DACOM was in a position to focus on problems of computerization. In 1985 it was designated prime contractor for the NAIS system.

With an institutional base in place, technology became the issue. Like Brazil's SEI in 1982, DACOM was looking for a company that would give them complete access to a technology that used internationally standard hardware and software and would meet their networking needs.[67] In addition, the chaebol wanted an agreement that would allow them eventually to export the machine.

As Brazil had already discovered, the dominant transnational computer producers were not interested in this bill of particulars. DACOM ended up settling on "a lean and hungry San Jose–based startup with supermini technology for sale" (Gadacz 1987, 68–2) called Tolerant. DACOM bought about twenty-five systems from Tolerant in order to get the NAIS rolling and give the software companies something to work on. Tolerant transferred manufacturing technology to the four large chaebol (Samsung, Hyundai, Daewoo, Goldstar), and ETRI began the most ambitious part of the project, working on an indigenously designed successor to the Tolerant machine known as the TICOM or Jujonsanki II.[68]

The TICOM was clearly a challenge for ETRI, but ETRI researchers had already done considerable work on computer architectures.[69] A budget of about $40 million was set up for the project over a four-year period beginning in mid-1987.[70] ETRI's organizational structure was revised to allow the creation of a Computer Technology Division, whose human resources were devoted principally to working on the Tolerant machine and its successor (ETRI 1987, 33). One hundred researchers from the four chaebol would join 150 ETRI researchers under ETRI's management to develop the new machine (M. J. Lee 1988, 10).

The software side of the project was in some ways the most ambitious of all. There were no local firms with the kind of experience in writing software that the chaebol had in manufacturing, but DACOM contracted local firms to provide application software, assuming that they would somehow rise to the occasion.[71]

In the end, the hubris of their ambitions did cost NAIS's organizers some embarrassment. Automation of the National Pension System, the first NAIS project to be implemented, involved data processing of a magnitude beyond what the experts from Tolerant had dealt with before, and far beyond the experience of the local firms writing the applications software.[72] The result was a minor disaster. The operating system broke down, errors were rife, and there were reported to be "a million bugs in the system" (Baek 1988, 46–49). DACOM was forced to retreat and allow the Ministry of Health to use an IBM mainframe (see J. W. Kim 1988; Seo 1990; Park 1991). The path to development of an internationally competitive successor to the TICOM was equally rocky. ETRI did finally develop the Jujonsanki II, and its chaebol partners were set up for manufacturing it, but, by the time it was completed, even the head of the TICOM development project admitted that the machine was not internationally competitive.[73]

Despite its flaws and foibles, the NAIS adventure was surprisingly fruitful. As the 1990s began, the National Pension System was up and running (albeit not under DACOM's control). Four of the six other NAIS systems—Land Information, Employment Information, Customs Clearance, and Vehicle Information—were developed and ready for operation (DACOM 1991, 14–15). DACOM itself had become a sophisticated producer of networking services, including a packet-switched public data network (DACOM-NET) and various value-added services like e-mail, PC-serve, and a data bank service. It was constructing a new R&D center at Daeduk and also about to start offering its own international telephone service. With sales of over $120 million, DACOM was likely to be one of the local survivors once the telecommunications industry was opened to foreign competition.

At the same time, ETRI continued to play its role as a font of indigenous technology, working on a variety of projects. Its projects continued to be both ambitious (e.g., a neural network model parallel processor with 200 processors) and oriented toward local needs (e.g., a RISC processor for processing *Hangul* [Korean] characters).[74] There was even a new DRAM project in the works; this one aimed at a 16-Megabit chip.[75] More surprising still, work on the TICOM continued. The four chaebol had taken over leadership of the project from ETRI and brought in researchers from Seoul National University to help on the technical side.[76]

Comparisons with Brazil and India

From chips to telephone exchanges to data networks, the Korean state's efforts at high-technology husbandry share key characteristics with the efforts of state-owned enterprises in Brazil and India. An entrepreneurial approach to building infrastructure, the hallmark of Korea's Ministry of Communications, echoed the projects of CMC and ECIL. The determination to serve as a font for indigenous technology, which drove COBRA's corporate strategy, is equally evident in ETRI's endeavors.

The key difference between Korea's high-tech husbandry and the efforts of Brazil and India is worth underlining one more time. It lies in the nature of relations between the state and the private sector. Korea constructed a public-private division of labor based on complementarity. The embedded autonomy that characterized state-society relations in general created a matrix for public-private collaboration adapted to the special circumstances of building high-technology industry.

Specific efforts like the 4-Megabit Project, the TDX, and NAIS were nested in turn in a more general system of support for technological development. While MOC led the way in the support of specific information technology, the Ministry of Science and Technology (MOST) took the lead in general technological husbandry. MOST's efforts were in turn part of the general thrust of state policy. The state's efforts to enhance local technological capacities took many forms, ranging from strong support for technical education to the construction of Daeduk Science Town to the provision of fiscal incentives for research and development.

Technical education is the most basic infrastructure for informatics development, and Korea has excelled in its expansion. In the late 1980s Korea, with less than one-third Brazil's population, had one and a half times the number of postsecondary students studying mathematics, computer sciences, and engineering. In fact, there were twice as many students taking university degrees in engineering in Korea as in the United Kingdom (UNESCO 1991, sec. 3, 349, 356, 369).[77]

At the apex of this mushrooming system of technical education were two institutions set up by MOST: the Korean Institute of Science and Technology (KIST) at the graduate level and the Korea Institute of Technology (KIT) at the undergraduate level, both located in Daeduk Science Town, the state-sponsored technopolis.[78] These were later joined by the Pohang Institute of Technology (POSTEC), which was set up in Pohang by the state-owned steel corporation with the mission of becoming "Korea's MIT" and hooking up with the steel company's recent research emphasis on new materials.[79]

Investment in education is reinforced by burgeoning investment in R&D. Over the course of the 1970s and 1980s, Korea's investment in R&D moved from a level typical of developing countries to one that challenges advanced industrial countries. The contrast between Korea's evolution and that of Brazil and India is striking. All three countries started out at less than one half of one percent of GNP in 1970. Korea soon pushed up toward 2 percent while India remained at half Korea's level and Brazil got stuck even lower (see table 6.1).

Interaction between the state and private capital is crucial to achieving these levels of R&D spending. Starting at a general level and looking at the ratio of private and public R&D expenditures over the past twenty years in Korea shows the state providing initial leadership by supplying 97 percent of total R&D funds in the early 1960s (MOST 1987, 39). Over the 1970s and 1980s, the state increased its own expenditures over fiftyfold, but it also succeeded in inducing an even more rapid growth of private R&D until the private sector accounted for about 80 percent of total R&D expenditures in the late 1980s (Y. H. Kim n.d., 4). Organizational change paralleled increased expenditure. In 1970 there was only one firm with a corporate R&D laboratory; in 1987 there were 604 (L. Kim 1991, 26).

Pushing the local entrepreneurial class to increase its investment in research and development was the main motif in the state's strategy of husbandry during the 1980s.[80] Instead of using low-cost loans to entice firms into specific sectors as it had done in the 1970s, the state used them to

TABLE 6.1
Cross-Country Comparisons of R&D Effort

| | Research and Development as Percent of GNP | | | | |
Year	Korea	U.S.	Japan	India	Brazil
1970	0.4	2.6	1.6	0.4	0.2
1975	0.4	2.3	1.7	0.5	0.7
1980	0.6	2.4	2.0	0.6	0.6
1985	1.6	2.7	2.5	0.9	—
1987	1.9	2.6	2.8	1.0	0.6

Sources: Y. H. Kim (n.d., 4, table 3); DST (1989, 3); Dalhman and Frischtak (1990, 19, table 4.3); UNESCO (1990, 5–110, table 5.18).
Note: For Brazil, 1975 = 1977, 1980 = 1982.

stimulate increased attention to R&D. These loans were joined with special tax incentives and a series of "National R&D Projects" that offered grants, especially for cooperative research.

By combining various kinds of incentives, the government was able to leverage its own investment into substantial commitments on the part of the leaders of local industry. In 1987 the government's investment in National Research Projects was still only about U.S. $70 million, but this was used strategically, as in the 4-Megabit DRAM Project. Loans were much more substantial. Amounting to almost U.S. $900 million in 1987, they accounted for "64 percent of total R&D expenditure in manufacturing in 1987." Fiscal incentives, including deduction of current R&D expenses from taxable income and a set aside of up to 30 percent (in high-tech industries) of before-tax profits to be used for future R&D work, added to the effects of loans and grants (L. Kim 1991, table 4, 30, 31).

Daeduk Science Town illustrates the same kind of strategy. Starting in 1974, MOST began constructing facilities for public research institutes like ETRI in Daeduk, a greenfield site about 200 kilometers southeast of Seoul. Then it began to move its elite educational institutes (first KIT, then KIST) there as well. The public research institutes were joined by a few private R&D centers, most prominently the Lucky Central Research Institute, until there were nine public research institutes, three elite institutions of higher education, and four private research institutes. Projections for the 1990s indicate that at least twenty firms will locate their central R&D facilities in Daeduk, creating the agglomeration effect considered crucial to successful innovative environments.

There is no need to exaggerate the state's role in changing the private sector's attitude toward technological innovation. It was working with the tide of economic logic. As Korean firms grew more successful and sophisticated, technological borrowing became a less secure route to profits and the need for R&D more evident. At the same time, it cannot be taken for granted that the evolution of the market will automatically push firms in the direction of greater technological investment. R&D's share of the U.S. GNP stagnated over the same period that it was exploding in Korea, providing a useful reminder of what can happen in the absence of husbandry. Brazil and India illustrate the same point.

Why were Brazil and India left behind in the race to increase local technological effort? These states were certainly in favor of supporting technological innovation. Total state expenditures in Brazil were on the order of U.S. $1.5 billion in 1988 (Dahlman and Frischtak 1990, 18) and India's central government spent about the same in the mid-1980s (DST 1989, 3). Neither country could claim the fourfold rise in R&D funding that Korea had been able to muster, but the expenditures were still substantial. The difference was that neither Brazil nor India could generate the public-private symbiosis that was the key to Korea's success.

In **Brazil** the number of firms claiming R&D expenditures on their tax returns was virtually the same in 1985 as it had been in 1976 (Dahlman and Frischtak 1991, 14),[81] a stark contrast to the fiftyfold multiplication of private R&D facilities in Korea. Consequently the Brazilian state was still shouldering somewhere between 70 percent and 95 percent of the country's total R&D expenditures.[82]

The absence of institutional mechanisms for creating a public-private symbiosis was obvious in informatics. There were two organizations that might have played an ETRI-like role in the computer industry—COBRA and the Centro Technológico para Informática (CTI). Both were hamstrung.

COBRA could have been an important source of support for state agencies trying to modernize infrastructure or local hardware producers trying to offer new applications, but COBRA's management had little slack to devote to such husbandry. Its survival as an organization depended on competing in the hardware market, a task that left little room for other sorts of entrepreneurship. The CTI depended on SEI, to which it was attached, and SEI was preoccupied with its problems as a custodian and its conflicts with the rest of the state apparatus, hardly in a good position to promote a reasonable budget for the CTI that would have made it an effective complement to the technological efforts of local firms (Meyer-Stamer 1989, 23–24).

The only organization left to foster concrete development projects was the Center for Research and Development of the state telecommunications firm, Telebrás. Like ETRI, Telebrás's Center for Research and Development (CPqD) was given the mission of developing products that would then be transferred to locally owned firms for production. As in the Korean case, Telebrás designated a certain portion of its revenues (2.5

percent) to research and development, giving the CPqD a budget comparable to that of ETRI.[83] CPqD has in fact managed successfully to design a range of telecommunication products such as optical fibers and small digital switching systems (see Hobday 1984). Since it had no demiurge pretensions, it has also been able to pass them on to local firms. By 1987 the CPqD was responsible for the development of seventy-five products that were actually being manufactured by twenty-five different local firms (Frischtak 1989, 58), most important among them a small electronic switching system similar to Korea's TDX, called the Trópico. The Telebrás Research Center even supported work on software and semiconductors, but its ability to play an ETRI-like role in the computer industry was hampered by the intensity of interministerial rivalry between the Ministry of Communications and SEI.

The overall matrix of support for technological efforts in individual firms was as weak as the specific organizations that should have been taking the lead. The state's main gift to local entrepreneurs remained its provision of a protective greenhouse. The "market reserve" dominated the policy-making debate, and the perception that local informatics firms were being awarded a "rental haven" undercut political support for further subsidies to local entrepreneurs. Financial support for local innovation efforts, similar to that provided in Korea, had been written into the 1984 Informatics Law, but, except for some subsidies to encourage local capital to enter the semiconductor industry, it never materialized.[84] Later, the Collor regime offered a set of incentives for indigenous R&D called the Program for Technological Competence in Industry, but as the 1990s began there was no evidence that it would go beyond rhetoric (Meyer-Stamer 1992, 107).

Preoccupation with policing distracted attention from strategies of positive support for the technological efforts of local firms. The state's entrepreneurial energies ended up channeled into the production of routine commodities (e.g., COBRA's PCs), while its regulatory capacity was more than absorbed by quixotic efforts to avoid excessive reliance on foreign technology. High-tech husbandry remained a marginal activity. As a result, Brazil never built on the foundations of its success in bringing new firms into the industry. Midwifery without subsequent husbandry left Brazil's new informatics firms extremely vulnerable to the cold winds of global technological change as the 1980s drew to a close.

In India, lack of public-private symbiosis is even clearer. Within its own ambit, the state could certainly claim original initiatives, but evidence of state efforts to cultivate the growth of private technological capacity is hard to find. There is no equivalent to Korea's 4-Megabit DRAM Project or TICOM supermini project. Nor can India point to a growing private-sector involvement in research and development. Again, preoccupation with the roles of regulator and producer took the state's attention away from issues of husbandry. Funding a range of research and development projects was one of the roles of the Department of Electronics (DOE), but the projects were carried out primarily by organizations connected to the government. Reading the annual reports of Korea's ETRI and India's DOE shows the difference. ETRI never fails to cite the number of products transferred to the private sector; the DOE's reports do not mention the issue.

Private entrepreneurs hoping to carve out market niches based on indigenous product innovation were often frustrated by the contradiction between the state's support in principle for indigenous development and the weakness of institutionalized efforts on behalf of would-be local innovators. Vinay Deshpande, a former managing director of PSI Data Systems,[85] which seemed to be one of India's most promising local computer firms in the early 1980s, expressed it as follows: "Our own Government organizations, for example the DoT or ONGC,[86] only do lip service to indigenous technology. . . . Thinking our Government would support us was one strategic mistake we made at PSI Data Systems" *(Dataquest* April 1990, 99).

At a general level, the ironies of India's educational successes best illustrate the negative effects of neglecting public-private complementarity. India's investments in technological training are impressive by any standard of comparison. With a million degree-holding scientists and engineers at the end of the 1980s (DST 1989, 36), India was reputed to have produced the world's second largest pool of English-speaking scientific and technical labor. It had more than twice as many students studying engineering as the United States had (Singhal and Rogers 1989, 47–48). The graduates of its elite Indian Institutes of Technology (IIT) were so well trained that there was a brisk demand for their services in the United States. Indeed, a large proportion of IIT graduates emigrated, allowing the United States to reap the social return from India's extraordinary investment in their education.[87] Investment in human capital without equal attention to generating firms that will utilize it produces perverse results.

As in Brazil, there are some exceptions. Some, like C-DOT and Meltron's New Projects Division, have already been mentioned. The emergence of Bangalore as India's "silicon plateau" is another interesting example. State investment was certainly an important element in turning Bangalore into a center of high-technology industry. The concentration of state-owned high-technology firms, like BEL, generated depth in the local skilled labor force and supported the development of local technical education. When private informatics firms started looking for places to set up shop in the 1980s, Bangalore was a natural location. Even in this case, however, there does not seem to have been a conscious attempt to stimulate the emergence of private research by "seeding" the area with state research organizations, in the manner of Korea's Daeduk strategy.

In general, however, the state's efforts to foster technological efforts took place within the ambit of the state itself. N. Seshagiri's National Informatics Centre (NIC) is a good example. In the mid-1970s, a decade before Korea's NAIS project, NIC started working on a satellite-based communication system called NICnet. Among the projects implemented on the network was a system for the collection, compilation, and analysis of continually updated social and economic information from each of India's roughly 440 districts.[88] Obviously, this kind of information infrastructure is exactly what India needs. Nonetheless, in the 1980s NICnet remained "exclusively for government use" (Ernst and O'Connor 1992, 257) and involved none of the kind of public-private collaboration in hardware and software that was the hallmark of Korea's NAIS project.

Neither India nor Brazil could put together the institutional framework necessary to really engage in the task of husbandry. The combination of powerful firms and powerful state organizations tied together by webs of careful cooperation that allowed Korea to move smoothly from midwifery to husbandry was simply missing. In short, a close look at comparative husbandry amply confirms the advantages of embedded autonomy.

The Evolution of the State's Role

The story of state involvement in the IT industry during the 1970s and 1980s is a story of institutional proclivities operating in tension with sectoral exigencies. State structures and general patterns of state-society relations were reflected in state roles in information technology. In Korea the two fit well. Overall patterns of embedded autonomy made it easier to follow a midwifery-husbandry sequence in information technology. Close collaborative ties with local firms made it easier to balance of promotion and policing. The competence and coherence of state organizations enabled the state to pursue husbandry with entrepreneurial gusto.

In Brazil and India the fit was less felicitous. They were sidetracked, each for different reasons, by the contradictions of trying to play custodian and demiurge. Neither stayed completely stuck. There was institutional learning. In this sector at least, bureaucrats responded to the exigencies of the sector. By the end of the 1980s, old roles were being abandoned. In India, the attempt to substitute state-owned enterprises for a technologically engaged class of local entrepreneurs that had been the early hallmark of India's strategy was mainly a historic holdover. Brazil's fierce efforts to police flows of international technology were equally on the wane.

Unfortunately, both paid a lasting price for their earlier misadventures. Letting old roles fade is easier than constructing new ones, especially when the new roles imply substantial investments in institution building. In both India and Brazil, the overall fiscal environment made it hard to invest in state institutions. Brazil was reeling under an impossible burden of public debt, and India seemed determined to follow Latin America in the direction of a debt crisis. In both countries, the budgets of information technology agencies felt the bite of the state's larger fiscal problems. However interested India's Department of Electronics might be in pursuing a promotional role, it was constrained by further reduction in what had never been a large budget.[89] In Brazil, the possibilities for institution building were even weaker, not only because the state's fiscal crisis was much worse, but also because the political backlash was much more virulent.

Throughout the 1980s, SEI had reaped substantial political benefit from its efforts as a midwife. Political support from the firms that had grown up in its greenhouse allowed it to survive an incredible combination of domestic and international attack, but by the beginning of the 1990s it had reached the end of its rope. Its endurance seemed to intensify the degree to which it was demonized by its opponents. By the time the Collor regime formally announced that the informatics policy would not be extended past the 1992 deadline originally set in Brazil's 1984 informatics law, the informatics greenhouse was being pilloried as one of the main culprits in Brazil's lagging industrial growth.

Even without the negative political baggage that SEI and the Informatics policy had accumulated over the 1980s, it would have been very difficult to build new forms of state involvement at the beginning of the 1990s. Fernando Collor and his followers embraced the old neoliberal mantra with real fervor. "Openness to the international market will solve it" was their uniform response to all economic problems. Macroeconomic mismanagement and the consequent fiscal crisis in which the state found itself made planning for the future a dubious endeavor. The general decay of state institutions compounded the problem. Rhetorical commitment to the abolition of rental havens was accompanied by exceptional dedication to extracting the maximum possible rents from political office. The ironic contrast between the corruption of the new "economic reformers" and the abstinence of the old técnicos who constructed the "rental haven" of the market reserve was not lost on veterans of the informatics policy, but irony does not build new institutions.

Despite the fervor with which past policies were disparaged, especially in Brazil, their positive products were still undeniable. Greenhouse protection and state midwifery had fostered a local information technology sector where none existed before. The firms lured into informatics by CAPRE's 1977 "minicompetition" and SEI's 1984 "supermini competition," together with dozens of smaller firms that had found a place under the umbrella of the "market reserve," constituted an impressive legacy. Collectively, they had invested in corporate organizations and human resources that were extraordinary relative to those found in the rest of Latin America. In India as well, a host of local firms had emerged, grown, and invested in organizational infrastructure and human capital.

In all three countries, successful midwifery changed the political dynamics of the industry as well as its economic face. At the beginning of the 1970s, the initiative lay clearly in the hands of the state. By the end of the 1980s this was no longer true. Even in Brazil and India, where the effects of midwifery were partial and fragile, the political power and economic interests of private informatics firms, played out against the background of a changing global information technology sector, were crucial to defining the future. Just as the new entrepreneurial forces that came into being in informatics over the course of the 1970s and 1980s must be understood as having been shaped by state actors, so the subsequent role of these state agencies depended on the character of the sectors that they helped create.

The impact of state involvement cannot be appreciated without focusing on the firms it fostered. In this chapter, state organizations were the foreground while private industry was relegated to the background. It is time to reverse figure and ground, to put local firms and the international industry in the foreground, and to look at the dynamics of informatics from the perspective of the industry itself.

7

The Rise of Local Firms

If Simón R. Schvartzman had written his reminiscences at the end of the 1980s, they would have been about the pleasures of working as an engineer in the midst of an exciting period of technological change. They would also have been about the pleasures and frustrations of managing a Brazilian firm. They would also, by necessity, have been about the politics and economics of state involvement. By inclination, Schvartzman was no more interested in politics than the average citizen, but the course of his career could not help reflecting the evolution of Brazil's informatics policy.

Simón Schvartzman was exactly the kind of person the barbudinhos had in mind when they dreamed of implanting an informatics sector in Brazil. Without the impetus of the informatics policy, Schvartzman's job would not have been created. He might have become a salesman for IBM or he might have emigrated to an industrialized country where he could exercise his talents to the full, but he would not have ended up working on the design of super-minicomputers in Brazil. Without Secretary of Informatics Dytz's decision to embark on a supermini licensing competition, Schvartzman would not have spent a cold winter in New Jersey working with design engineers at the tiny Formation company and absorbing everything there was to absorb of the intricacies of IBM-compatible super-minicomputer architectures.

Indeed, without the informatics policy, the company he worked for, Itautec Informática, would not have been created. The Banco Itaú, Itautec's owner,[1] would have been involved in information technology, but the idea of creating a diversified computer manufacturing firm that engineered its own super-minicomputers as well as producing its own PCs and developing its own financial automation systems would have seemed fanciful. As it was, Itautec had grown into an impressive corporate organization. To be sure, it was small by the standards of the international computer industry, but as it closed the 1980s with sales approaching $200 million, it was the largest locally owned computer manufacturer in Brazil and one of the largest in the Third World. Many of the firms that grew up under the informatics policy would be dim memories by the time the "market reserve" officially expired in 1992, but Itautec would not be one of them. It seemed destined to be a permanent additional to Brazil's entrepreneurial landscape, a small but robust change in Brazil's position in the international division of labor.

The comparative history of informatics in Brazil, India, and Korea is really two tightly interwoven tales. One is the story that was related in the last chapter: how state policies and institution building shaped local possibilities for industrial transformation, calling forth new economic actors and generating new capabilities out of locally inherited resources. The other is the story of the evolution of the industry itself: how local entrepreneurs and industries responded, not only to the opportunities and incentives created by state policy but also to the threats and opportunities thrown up by global technology and transnational corporate strategies. The latter story is the focus of this chapter.

As state policies evolved, so did the orientations of individual entrepreneurs. Over the course of the 1980s, local firms in all three countries moved inexorably in the direction of more internationally oriented strategies. Describing the rise of the new internationalism is, however, the job of the next chapter. First, it is important to chronicle the results of the nationalist greenhouses that incubated the initial growth of local information technology sectors. Whatever the flaws and foibles of NIC informatics policies, they all accomplished the basic aim of midwifery. All three countries ended up with a new set of local participants in the information technology sector.

Looking at local firms takes the measure of state involvement better than do descriptions of the policies themselves. In each country, the collective entrepreneurial profile of local informatics firms reflected the distinctive character of state roles and policies as well as the general industrial heritage from which firms emerged.

Starting Points

Brazil, Korea, and India were not industrial neophytes at the beginning of the 1970s. They were poor, but they had manufacturing sectors producing billions of dollars of sophisticated industrial products. When they decided that locally controlled production of information technology was important, the question was whether and how existing entrepreneurial resources could be brought to bear on a new, technologically demanding sector. The answer depended on how prior state efforts at midwifery had positioned large local firms. It also depended on how transnational capital had been inserted into the local industrial structure and what strategies large local business groups had evolved over the course of post–World War II industrialization.

In India, initial problems were obvious. The state in its role of custodian had tried to wall off large business houses—the Birlas and the Tatas and their ilk—from consumer electronics production, hoping to turn the sector into a preserve of small firms that would use low-tech, labor-intensive methods (see Sridharan 1989). Consequently, the big houses lacked transferable manufacturing expertise when time came to mount an informatics industry. Even without this specific impediment, the traditions of the big houses were alien to the world of high technology. Having lived since independence under the terms of their "anti-Schumpeterian bargain" with the state,[2] they were used to sharing a protected domestic market for standardized goods, not to competing in markets with rapidly changing products and falling prices.

There were exceptions. The ever-prescient Tata group was one. In 1968, just as ECIL was getting started, the Tatas launched Tata Consultancy Systems Ltd., which would eventually become India's premier software exporter. Nonetheless, for the typical Indian industrial group, the difficult dynamics of the information technology sector created a very alien terrain.

The tribulations that faced the founders of what would eventually become India's largest local firm, Hindustan Computers Ltd. (HCL), were indicative of the attitudes of India's big business houses. Shiv Nadar, Arjun Malhotra, and the other founders of HCL were initially managers of a division inside the suffocating cocoon of the venerable Delhi Cloth Mills (DCM) group. Getting DCM's owners to understand the impossibility of applying generic directives designed for a sick textile industry to a fledgling computer operation finally grew so frustrating that Nadar and his friends decided to do without DCM's financial backing and go it alone.

Another oft-circulated story, perhaps apocryphal but still plausible, also captures the flavor of the problem. The board of one big house, which had entered the microcomputer business in the early 1980s, was asked by the marketing manager of computer sales to drop prices in order to meet the competition. The board was so taken aback by the possibility that the prices of any product might have to be lowered that it required the better part of a year to make a decision, by which time its chance to take a share of the market was gone.

Given the characteristic style of India's major manufacturing groups, it is not surprising that when the local private industry began to explode it was agile newcomers like HCL and WIPRO that explored the new possibilities of microprocessor-based hardware. Nor is it surprising that the manufacturing process itself never became a source of strength for Indian firms, despite what might have seemed an obvious comparative advantage in "cheap labor."

Brazil's large industrial groups were less insulated from the world of competition. They had considerable experience and success at producing manufactured products for export markets. Living with a much more liberal investment regime, they were used to being jostled by transnational competitors. Their experience made them less afraid of rapidly changing markets but also very conscious of the dangers of straying into areas where the comparative advantage of transnational capital was too great. A clear division of labor among state, local, and multinational capital was fundamental to Brazil's "dependent development." Within this division of labor, technology-intensive industries were the prerogative of the TNCs (see Evans 1979, 1982).

Natural wariness about poaching on the transnationals' turf was reinforced by specific state policies in the electronics sector. In contrast to sectors like machine tools or basic chemicals, where locals were encouraged to move in, electronics policies had worked strongly in favor of foreign firms. The late 1960s' decision to support the Manaus free zone as an "import platform" squeezed out local consumer electronics companies interested in using indigenous technology and made industrially oriented groups very cautious about entering the area.

The state's prior success at inducing local informatics production by transnational capital also made the industry less attractive to local groups. In comparison to India, Brazil was less inclined to exclude TNCs and more adept at eliciting their collaboration. Transnational capital had been supplying the needs of the domestic information technology market for decades. The state had successfully cajoled and prodded the dominant TNCs to increase the share of local value-added and balance their imports with exports. Both IBM and Burroughs had extensive, long-established, local manufacturing facilities, and IBM was a major contributor to Brazil's manufactured exports. Local entrepreneurs were unlikely to try to take a share of the domestic market away from these entrenched international giants.

Finally, any local industrial group that tried to become a producer of information technology would have faced the enduring prejudice of the Brazilian financial system against intangible assets. Real estate or perhaps machinery were acceptable collateral; skilled technicians, technological expertise, or ideas for new products were not. The private financial system was reluctant to provide venture capital to any kind of manufacturing investment. An industry where endowments were principally technological was beyond the pale.

No obvious natural path led Brazil's sophisticated industrial groups from the sectors they knew to informatics. Past state policies had helped destroy whatever path might have existed from consumer electronics and implanted formidable transnational guardians at the entrance to the local informatics market. It is hardly surprising that it took explicit promotional efforts on the part of the state to awaken local capital's interest in informatics.

Korea's industrial groups faced a situation that could hardly have been more different from Brazil's. The state-dominated financial system had put the major chaebol on the financial equivalent of a steroid diet beginning in the mid-1960s (cf. Woo 1991) but made its support contingent on increasingly competitive performance. Over the course of the 1970s, the state's "bodybuilding" program created a natural path in the direction of information technology by making support contingent on willingness to explore new sectors, with electronics one of the most highly recommended.

The possibility of exploiting a protected domestic market was crucial to this expansionary path into informatics. From the day in 1959 that Goldstar assembled the first Korean vacuum tube radio, the protected domestic market was crucial to the chaebol's acquisition of prowess (and profits) in consumer electronics. As Mody (1987b, 87) puts the case in general terms, "the domestic market in Korea . . . has been not merely a training ground for launching into exports but a substantial source of demand in itself."

Patterns of transnational investment in Korea, the result of both TNC strategies and state policy, made it easier for the chaebol to exploit their domestic base. Foreign capital was concentrated in the production of components for the export market. Semiconductor packaging was typical. Starting in the mid-1960s, companies like Motorola, Fairchild, and Signetics set up semiconductor packaging operations designed to take advantage of low-cost labor and supply their components needs in the United States and Europe. As Korea's industrial experience grew, transnational firms expanded the range of components they sourced from Korea, providing the country with useful windows on international cost/quality standards. But these firms had little interest in challenging the chaebol's preserve in the domestic market. The Korean division of labor, unlike Brazil's, left the domestic electronics market largely in the hands of local capital.

IBM did not install its first computer in Korea until 1967, when it finally decided to set up a subsidiary. Sperry and Burroughs did not consider Korea worth a subsidiary until the beginning of the 1970s. When state procurement policy began to create a local informatics market in the 1980s, the chaebol did not face the powerful, foreign-controlled local manufacturing capacity that would-be entrants had to confront in Brazil. In Korea restrictions on imports and government preferences for locally produced goods redounded to the benefit of local capital rather than providing a bonanza for foreign subsidiaries as they would have in Brazil.

From these three quite different starting points, three variegated and local informatics industries emerged. The firms that were established, like the process of state involvement that helped bring them forth, had their share of flaws and problems, but they represented a real transformation of the local industrial landscape.

By the beginning of the 1990s Korea was one of the world's largest semiconductor producers. The four big chaebol were also shipping over $2 billion worth of computer hardware.[3] While still not in the same league with the United States and Japan, Korea's information technology industry was out-producing many European countries. For example, at $3.45 billion in 1990, Korea's chip (IC) production, while less than 15 percent of Japan's output, almost equaled the combined total of Germany, France, and the United Kingdom.[4] The country had clearly changed its niche in the international division of labor.

More surprising was the growth of local computer production in Brazil and India. In Brazil, the output of locally owned computer producers had increased tenfold over the 1980s, from less than $200 million in 1979 to over $2 billion in 1989 (Evans 1986a, 796; DEPIN 1991, 52). In 1988 Brazil's overall production of "office automation equipment" was still greater than Korea's (Ernst and O'Connor 1992, 112). In India, a several hundred million dollar hardware industry was complemented by software exports that had quintupled over the last half of the 1980s, reported at over $100 million by 1990.[5]

In each country, entrepreneurs had seized on the space created by local greenhouses, building firms that reflected both the specific roles played by each state and the distinctive strengths and weaknesses of each country's industrial heritage. Each country's IT industry was as distinctive as each state's involvement. Subsectors that were outstanding examples of success in one country were disasters in another. No country had quite the industry that they would have liked, but they all had a local information technology sector.

Brazil—From Minicomputers to Financial Automation

From the local industry's official beginning in the 1977 minicomputer competition, the Brazilian industry focused first of all on hardware. The original winners of the 1977 contest were soon joined by literally dozens of small firms producing PCs. Creating a "market reserve" extended to local Brazilian firms the possibility of exploiting the same dramatic change in global technology that produced Apple, Compac, and dozens of other start-ups in the United States.[6] Within the market reserve, the fight was only among Brazilians. Microcomputers (PCs) quickly became the dominant form of local production. By 1983 they already represented over 60 percent of the sales of local firms. New firms like Microtec and Prológica seized this new opportunity and were added to the rolls of top local firms.

There were, of course, ambiguities as to the nature of the opportunity that was being offered. Some firms, like SCOPUS, took advantage of the freedom afforded by microprocessors to forge ahead, making local improvements on standard architectures and producing machines that were more than "reverse engineered" copies. These firms grew on the basis of innovation and enhanced performance. Others, allegedly including some of the largest makers of microcomputers like Prológica, took full advantage of the possibilities of free-riding, acquiring foreign technology without the sanction of SEI (and sometimes without the knowledge of the foreign firms themselves). They prospered even more.

The market reserve also created an ambiguous arena for forging new industrial skills. It was internally competitive, with dozens of firms turning out small computers. Consequently, internal prices followed international prices downward, and the pressure to cut costs was continual.[7] Nevertheless, competition among dozens of firms in a market only about 1 percent the size of the U.S. market made real economies of scale impossible. The problem was even worse in components production. While manufacturers in other countries shopped the world for price/performance in components, Brazilian manufacturers struggled to build local networks of suppliers that could reliably deliver technologically simple items like power supplies and fans.

Despite its problems, the market kept growing. By 1985 the sales of local informatics firms were almost a billion and a half dollars, on their way to sales of over $4 billion in 1989 (see table 7.1). Informatics sales had increased their share of Brazil's GDP from about one-half of 1 percent in 1979 to over 2 percent of GDP in 1989. There were now hundreds instead of dozens of firms producing information technology[8] and employing, just as the barbudinhos had hoped, thousands of technically trained Brazilian professionals (see table 7.2). Despite operating in an economy whose overall performance ranged during the early and mid-1980s from mediocre to disastrous, the informatics sector was impressive in its dynamism.

A look at the top Brazilian computer firms in 1986 is sobering in one respect (see table 7.3). At the very pinnacle of the industry, *plus ça change* . . . was the simplest summary. The wholly owned subsidiaries of IBM and Burroughs continued their dominance. Nonetheless, just below them a new set of actors had taken hold. SEI Secretary Dytz's aspirations to bring large capital into the industry had been realized. Traditional industrial capital still played a marginal role, but their absence was more than compensated by the direct involvement of the biggest banks.

From the beginning, the financial sector was where Brazil had come

TABLE 7.1

Growth of Informatics Revenues in Brazil, 1980–1989 (in millions of U.S. dollars)

	1979	1983	1985	1987	1989
Local firms					
Revenues	190	687	1,400	2,378	4,243
Percent of total	23%	46%	52%	59%	59%
TNCs					
Revenues	640	800	1,278	1,638	2,920
Percent of total	77%	54%	48%	41%	41%
Industry Total	830	1,487	2,678	4,016	7,163

Source: DEPIN (1991, 16) for 1983–89; Evans (1986, 796) for 1979.

TABLE 7.2

University-Trained Employment in the Brazilian Informatics Industry, 1979–1989

	1979	1983	1985	1987	1989
Locally owned firms	1,531	3,884	9,064	14,206	17,591
TNCs	2,521	2,810	3,467	5,147	6,522
Total	4,052	6,694	12,531	19,353	24,113

Source: DEPIN (1991, 26) for 1983–89; Evans (1986, 797) for 1979.

TABLE 7.3

Top Ten Brazilian Computer Firms, 1986 (in millions of U.S. dollars)

Firm	Sales	Firm	Sales
1. IBM Brazil[a]	731.4	6. SID Informática	87.0
2. Unisys[a]	211.4	7. Scopus	58.0
3. Itautec	111.7	8. Labo	48.6
4. Cobra	98.8	9. Microtec	38.3
5. Elebra Informática[b]	88.1	10. Racimec	37.8

Source: *Anuario Informática Hoje* 87/88, 14–21.

Note: Cruzados were converted into dollars at the midyear rate of Cz $15.425 per dollar.

[a]Foreign-owned.

[b]Includes peripherals and computers (Elebra Computadores) and excludes microelectronics and telecommunication equipment. If these were included, sales would be $126 million.

closest to achieving public-private relations approximating embedded autonomy. It began in the 1970s with the partnership in which COBRA provided the big banks with the data entry hardware that they needed[9] and the banks shored up COBRA's capital base in return. It continued in the early 1980s with Dytz's "supermini competition" in which the big banks provided the organizational and financial muscle to bring in a new generation of technology and got privileged positions in the local market in return.

Simón Schvartzman's employer, Itautec, was a prime example. As Brazil's second largest bank and one of IBM's biggest customers, Banco Itaú had first developed into a sophisticated user of financial information systems, designing its own internal networks and gradually automating its operations. With the advent of the informatics policy, it got directly into production of hardware, producing microcomputers. As a result of Dytz's supermini competition it began to produce larger machines as well. It also branched out into other information technology products, ranging from printed circuit boards to controllers and terminals. By the mid-1980s Itaú was thoroughly enmeshed in the computer industry, not only as a customer but as a manufacturer as well.

Bradesco, the country's biggest bank, was less systematically, but no less extensively, involved in information technology. Like Itaú it could not avoid being involved as a major user. Gradually it was drawn in as an investor as well: first through equity investment in one of the original mini competitors (SID), then through a wholly owned subsidiary called Digilab, later as a major investor in one of Dytz's supermini competitors (Elebra).

SID and Elebra embodied the involvement of major capital in their own right. SID was part of the empire of Mathias Machline, which used its ties to the Japanese Sharp brand to achieve commercial domination of local consumer electronics markets. Elebra was a new industrial adventure for one of Brazil's oldest financial families, the Guinle family, who had made its fortune by owning the docks at the port of Santos during the coffee boom at the turn of the century.

Brazil's leading firms were dwarfed by Korea's chaebol, as a quick comparison of overall sales of Korean electronics firms with the top Brazilian informatics firms shows (cf. tables 7.3 and 7.7). In the core of informatics production, however, the scales were much more balanced in the mid-1980s. On the one hand, computers continued to account for only a minor share of the Korean electronics firms' sales, most of which still came from consumer electronics.[10] On the other hand, by 1987 Itaú, SID, and Elebra had all created conglomerates in information technology, putting together computers and peripherals, semiconductors, telecommunications, and consumer electronics (see table 7.4). Brazilian firms were not

TABLE 7.4
Major Brazilian Electronics Groups, 1987 (approximate revenues in millions of U.S. dollars)

	Subsector			
Group	Computers and Peripherals	Semi-Conductors	Tele-communications	Consumer Electronics
Itau (ca.$420)	Itautec (ca.$110)	Itaucom (ca.$40)	SESA[a] (ca.$50)	Philco[b] (ca.$220)
Sharp (ca.$430)	SID Informatica (ca.$90)	SID Micro-electronica (ca.$40) Vertice[e]	SID Telecom[c]	Sharp Electronics[d] (ca.$300) RCA[f]
Elebra Electronica[g] (ca.$175)	Peripherals (ca.$80) Defense (ca.$10)	Semi-conductors (ca.$10)	Telecom. Equipment (ca.$70) Data Communications (ca.$5)	—

Source: Evans and Tigre (1989b, 28, table 12); see also Tigre (1988, 64); Annuario Informatica Hoje 87/88.

[a] 25 percent ownership.

[b] Purchased from Ford that year.

[c] Not yet operational.

[d] 83 percent ownership, 12 percent owned by Sharp Japan.

[e] Joint venture start-up in IC design.

[f] Recently purchased, manufactured CRTs.

[g] Unlike other Brazilian groups, Elebra had a divisional form of organization rather than being organized as separate companies.

international giants, but they had attained an impressive scale in the brief ten years since the market reserve had gone into effect.

No one could deny that a fundamental change had taken place in the fifteen years since the days when the only volunteer turned up in Ricardo Saur's search for local capital to enter the computer industry was E.E. Equipamentos Electrônicos. Informatics was on Brazil's entrepreneurial map. A prominent fraction of the local entrepreneurial class had invested significant capital in the industry. The role of midwife had been fulfilled.

The participation of major capital did not, unfortunately, wipe out the contradictions of combining promotion with regulatory policing focused on minimizing ties to the international industry. Even major firms lacked scale and specialization. Costs were high and quality lagged. Users, who first viewed the informatics policy as leverage against the local monopoly power of IBM, were disillusioned. In a study funded by IBM but reflecting the general view of outside analysts, William Cline (1987) accused the informatics policy of robbing Brazil's consumers, impeding the introduction of state-of-the-art information technology, and crippling the ability of other Brazilian industries to compete in international markets.

There was some truth to these accusations, but they also exaggerated the industry's shortcomings, laying the blame on the informatics greenhouse for problems that were not really its doing at all. Analyses that simply compared local PC prices to those in the United States and attributed the difference to the refusal to allow foreign subsidiaries to set up local manufacturing conveniently ignored the extent to which factors having nothing to do with the industry itself caused price differences.[11] Price comparisons with Europe rather than the United States showed the extent of the exaggeration.[12] Comparing prices charged by TNC subsidiaries in Brazil to U.S. prices showed the same thing. Differentials were as large or larger than those charged by local manufacturers (Schmitz and Hewitt 1992, 32).[13]

The ability of local firms to survive in competition with foreign subsidiaries at the upper end of the market reserve is also evidence that Brazil's new producers were not quite as inefficient as they were painted. For example, Elebra was able to compete directly with IBM machines whose price/performance was definitely superior[14] and still sell VAXs more rapidly than DEC itself was selling them in Korea,[15] which suggests that Elebra was offering some sort of service or "systems engineering" that local users found valuable.

Finally, it is worth pointing out that comparative data do not support the idea that Brazil's greenhouse has had a dramatically negative effect on overall levels of utilization of computers. Comparing Brazilian production for the domestic market with Korea's in the mid-1980s provides one test. The data suggest that the Brazilian domestic market was about double Korea's, that is, an equal share of GDP.[16] The discrepancy between Korean and Brazilian consumption of PCs is particularly interesting. Despite the world reputation of Korean PCs as low priced and high quality, domestic PC sales in Brazil were four times domestic consumption of Korean PCs.[17] In short, Brazilians were willing to spend about twice as much of their income on PCs as Koreans were, despite the fact that Brazilians were getting an inferior product in terms of international price/performance comparisons. The growth of the Brazilian market may have been stunted by high prices, but the emergence of local producers seems to have had compensating effects as well. The surprising levels of demand for information technology goods under the market reserve support the idea that the existence of local firms may enhance "user-producer linkages" and thereby stimulate demand (see Cassiolato 1992).

Banking, in which public-private collaboration had been most successful since the beginning of the state's involvement in information technology, provides the best evidence. Brazilian producers of financial automation equipment were not only genuinely innovative but also internationally competitive. According to Frischtak (1989, 32), the financial automation systems produced by the new Brazilian firms "were, by mid 1988, 30 percent less expensive than internationally available products of comparable quality and performance." This despite the fact that the individual hardware items going into their systems cost substantially more.

In addition to being competitive, Brazil's financial automation producers have changed the way that their users do business, exactly as information technology is supposed to. By the end of the 1980s, Brazil's leading banks were highly automated "even by developed country standards" (Frischtak 1991, 1). Increases in automation over the course of the 1980s were directly associated with increased productivity in retail functions like processing checks (Frischtak 1991, 32–45).

The importance of user-producer linkages was particularly obvious in this segment. Since the biggest banks were the biggest computer producers, user-producer linkages could not have been tighter, and the interest of producers in satisfying their customer/owners' needs could not have been greater. Local producers translated their intimate knowledge of the idiosyncrasies of Brazilian banking into information systems that were custom-designed to serve local needs. The result echoes the success of CMC and ECIL in providing large systems custom designed to solve local problems.

Financial automation also provides an interesting commentary on Brazil's comparative advantage in informatics. After looking at financial automation, Frischtak was convinced that Brazil's real comparative advantage lay in design and engineering intensive applications rather than in manufacturing per se. In his view (1989, 36), this advantage could be extended to the design of other, similar products, like point-of-sales systems. The evidence comes from a sector that the barbudinhos had no special interest in serving, but it supports their contention that midwifery could capture the productivity of skilled labor power that would otherwise go underutilized.

If financial automation demonstrated the potential power of midwifery, other subsectors revealed the policy's weaknesses. The software industry is one example (see Gaio 1992). From the beginning, the informatics policy privileged hardware, treating the software market as byproduct of hardware sales (which of course it had been for IBM in the 1960s and 1970s). This led to a preoccupation with indigenous operating systems, rather than a focus on developing local applications based on existing international standards. The operating system strategy proved quixotic, not just for COBRA but also SCOPUS, which invested first in its own operating system for microcomputers, SISNE, then in an indigenous version of MS-DOS, which was certified as genuine but never produced a commercial return.[18]

Symptomatic of the problems in the software strategy was the fact that, according to SEI's estimates, IBM and UNISYS still controlled over two-thirds of the Brazilian software market in 1990. Export performance even worse than the hardware sector's was another indicator of software's problems. The cumulative total of Brazil's software exports during the last four years of the 1980s was, according to SEI, only $100,000, a startling contrast to India's tens of millions each year, especially given the greater overall size of the informatics industry in Brazil (DEPIN 1991, 22, 97).[19]

Semiconductors (or microelectronics, as it is called in Brazil) were an even more vexing problem. Brazil was slow to consider the possibility of a local semiconductor industry. By the time it seriously broached the idea in the mid-1980s, entry demanded deep pockets well beyond the resources of any Brazilian firm. Only with the promise of massive government subsidies were the big informatics conglomerates enticed into the business. An informatics industry without semiconductor production was obviously incomplete, but it was clear that the new Brazilian entrants, who had bought out the relatively antiquated plants of Texas Instruments and Phillips, would never be in a position to compete in commodity markets. Entrepreneurs and policymakers debated the future of the industry, but before the debate could be resolved, the disastrous macroeconomic policies of presidents José Sarney and Fernando Collor descended on the informatics sector, as they did on the whole of Brazilian manufacturing. Inflation soared and investment in manufacturing dropped. Investing $100 million to jump start a semiconductor industry was unambiguously outside the possibilities of either the state or local capital.

The hard times of the late 1980s did more than derail semiconductors. As a capital goods industry, informatics was deeply affected by any drop in investment. Increasing uncertainty about new state policies and their effects compounded the industry's plight. Once Collor made it clear that the greenhouse itself was soon to be dismantled, local firms became more cautious about investing in technology and human capital.[20] The human and organizational resources that had been generated by the greenhouse were in jeopardy.

The hundreds of corporations and tens of thousands of skilled workers that had come to comprise the local informatics sector would not disappear overnight. Nonetheless, Brazil's informatics industry was going to have to find a new basis for survival. The question at the beginning of the

1990s was whether a new internationalization could be provide such a
new basis. It was the same question that was being asked in different ways
in India and Korea.

India—Hardware Design and Software Exports

Even though unleashing private capital had not been its principal aim,
India's greenhouse created an attractive opportunity for entrepreneurs
with an interest in new technologies. As in Brazil and Korea, the greenhouse gave local firms the market for smaller machines, protecting them
from international competition. Once policymakers were forced to retreat from reliance on ECIL as demiurge and ease restrictions at the end
of the 1970s, new firms began to emerge. They were small and technologically aggressive, relying on internationally standard INTEL or Motorola
microprocessors for their basic technology and on the pool of trained
manpower generated in the state sector for much of their technical cadres.
Because the state saw itself, not local entrepreneurs, as the vehicle of indigenous technological development, local firms were freer to exploit international standards than were their Brazilian counterparts. They could
not import foreign hardware, but they could build their strategies around
licensed UNIX. Gradually, they grew into a local industry that, while
much smaller than Brazil's or Korea's, had some impressive achievements
to its credit.

Once the state moved definitely from a custodial to a promotional posture in 1984, the growth of the industry was explosive. In the five years
after 1984, computer production increased dramatically (see table 7.5).
In contrast to Brazil, local computer producers were joined in India by
firms whose growth was based not on hardware but on software. Software exports grew almost as fast as the domestic hardware market, and
by 1990 three of the top ten informatics firms (CMC, Tata Consultancy
Systems, and Tata Unisys Ltd.) were software firms (see table 7.6).

The archetype of India's new information technology firms was Hindustan Computers Ltd. (HCL). Its founders got their start in informatics
working in marketing at DCM Data Products. Though they were engineers by training, their real genius lay in marketing.[21] In 1975, when it
became clear that DCM was an ungainly launching pad for a computer
company, they were in a tough position. They saw the opportunity the
computer industry offered, but they had no capital and no license to produce computers. Their solution was ingenious. They got out of DCM and
pooled about $20,000 to set up a company called Microcomp to make
electronic calculators, which then served as a means of generating the
capital to get into the computer business. Then they teamed up with a
small state-owned firm that had a license to make computers.[22]

TABLE 7.5

Indian Computer and Software Production/Exports, 1984–1988 (in millions of U.S. dollars[a])

	1984	1985	1986	1987	1988
Computer production	66	111	200	268	347
Hardware exports	0.6	0.5	3	3	34[b]
Software exports	17	20	30	41	61[c]

Source: DOE (1989, 58–59, Appendices II, III).

[a] Rupees were converted to U.S. dollars at Rs 14 per dollar, the approximate official exchange rate in 1988. This deflates the dollar value of sales in earlier years relative to the official value of the Rupee in those years.

[b] Figures for hardware exports are misleading due to massive sales to the Soviet Union, which could not be sustained. The following year hardware exports were only about 50 percent of the 1988 figure. See *Dataquest* (1992 10(7): 21).

[c] For a slightly more conservative estimate of software exports, see Schware (1992, 151).

TABLE 7.6

Top Ten Indian Informatics Firms, 1990

Firm	*Sales*
1. HCL (Hindustan Computers Ltd.)[a]	133
2. CMC[b]	89
3. WIPRO Information Technology Ltd.[c]	85
4. ECIL[d]	69
5. Pertech Computers Ltd.[e]	50
6. TCS (Tata Consultancy Services Ltd.)[f]	47
7. International Computers India Mfg. Ltd.[g]	46
8. Sterling Computers Ltd.[h]	43
9. DEIL (DEC India Ltd)[i]	26
10. TUL (Tata Unysis Ltd.)[j]	26

Source: Dataquest 1990(July):41.

Note: Sales are given in millions of U.S. dollars. Sales converted into Rupees at Rs 14 per dollar.

[a] The archetype of the local private entrepreneurial venture.

[b] State-owned software producer (see chap. 6).

[c] Associated with a small business house (A. Premji's WIPRO group), but still a typically enterpreneurial local private entry.

[d] The original demiurge (see chap. 6).

[e] Another entrepreneurial newcomer, specializing in PC clones.

[f] The Tata group's software company; India's premier software exporter.

[g] Created out of the old ICL subsidiary by selling 60 percent of equity to local investors, including the subsidiary's former Indian managers.

[h] Another PC clone specialist.

[i] DEC's new subsidiary in which DEC holds 40 percent, its old distributor 20 percent and individual Indians 40 percent.

[j] The Tatas' joint venture with Burroughs (Unisys), whose revenues are primarily from software and large projects.

HCL's first computer, launched in 1977 when microcomputers were just making their way onto the world market, was a huge success, so much so that they waited too long to move on to the next generation of PCs. So, they combined aggressive pricing of established machines with continual introduction of more advanced models that sold at a premium to get back into the PC market. Soon their Busybee was the leading seller in the PC market.[23] To gain a similar position in the minicomputer market they put together two standard international technologies in an innovative and, it turned out, commercially attractive way. HCL's Horizon 030 was reputed to be the first implementation of UNIX V.3 on a Motorola 68030 chip anywhere in the world. It was followed up with a variation on the theme, one of the first machines in the world to incorporate the Motorola 68030 chip in a multiprocessor design.

HCL's hardware design accomplishments were impressive, but probably less central to its survival than was its software expertise. Its specialty was in applying UNIX, used primarily for engineering work in most countries, to commercial applications. HCL's ability to claim 1,500 engineer years of UNIX experience at the end of the 1980s was not only the product of foresighted allocation of R&D efforts earlier in the decade. It was also a product of the greenhouse. IBM's departure in 1978[24] forced at least some banks and businesses to consider alternatives to IBM software environments. DEC, Hewlett Packard, and other proprietary systems were not prominently available. Thus, HCL could contemplate developing commercial UNIX applications in 1983–84, before commercial UNIX was considered a practical prospect in most developed countries.[25]

The contrasts between HCL's experience and that of COBRA are illuminating. The workstation COBRA planned in the late 1980s[26] was very similar in concept to the Horizon/Magnum series. Both used the same internationally standard chips and UNIX-type operating systems.[27] Both were being developed at the same time, but there was one critical difference. HCL was the first computer manufacturer in India to get a UNIX source code license directly from AT&T, and it immediately turned the energies of its UNIX development team (which was even bigger than COBRA's) to working on applications, including a UNIX commercial suite. HCL was selling Horizons and using the profits to expand into other areas, while COBRA was still waiting for its indigenous version of UNIX to be completed before launching its new hardware.

Obviously, HCL's success was not simply due to technological prowess. Shiv Nadar and his colleagues were astute in diversifying their empire. Early on, in 1981, they formed a separate company called the National Institute of Information Technology (NIIT), which later became India's largest private trainer of information management personnel and the fourteenth largest informatics firm overall (*Dataquest* July 1992, 35). In 1984 HCL formed Hindustan Reprographics and, using technology licensed from the Japanese, challenged Xerox in the plain-paper copier market. At the same time it formed a telecommunications division and began producing EPBAXs, telexes, and teleprinters. Then, in 1989, HCL bought up International Data Management (IDM), an early pioneer formed by former IBM managers after IBM pulled out.[28]

A genius for marketing and aggressive alliance building were at the core of HCL's success, but the company considered low-cost engineering talent to be its most important source of international comparative advantage. Echoing Frischtak's analysis of Brazil's comparative advantage, Shiv Nadar, HCL's president, once claimed that a given R&D project could be implemented by HCL for one-tenth of what it would cost a U.S. company to do the same thing in the United States (*Computers Today*, December 1988, 30).

HCL was the most successful of the newcomers that formed the basis for India's emerging informatics industry, but there were many others. The trajectory of WIPRO, India's number two hardware manufacturer in the 1980s, reinforces the lessons of the HCL case. Unlike HCL, WIPRO was the direct offspring of an established business house, not one of the largest but a successful, diversified firm that had moved from a secure position in cooking oils to explore the more technologically challenging area of precision hydraulic equipment. In 1981 Azim Premji, the group's owner and chair, decided the time was ripe to get into the computer business and authorized Ashok Narasimhan to set up WIPRO Information Technologies Ltd. WIPRO compensated for its lack of tradition in electronics by hiring away ECIL engineers. When HCL's initial entry into the minicomputer market stumbled, WIPRO was the company that best exploited the opening.

The minicomputer was WIPRO's focus from its founding. Its first mini was built improbably around the chip that powered the early IBM PCs,[29] but it stood up quite nicely in comparison to ECIL's massive and expensive minicomputers and offered access to a much wider range of software. By 1986, when INTEL launched a new world-standard microprocessor,[30] WIPRO was only two months behind Compac and well ahead of IBM in getting out a prototype machine. Three months later it had implemented the latest version of UNIX on a mini built around the new processor.[31] By the time INTEL launched its next new microprocessor[32] in 1989, WIPRO was designated as a "beta test site"[33] and could claim the first multiprocessor implementation of the chip worldwide (*Dataquest*, October 1989, 68).[34]

By the end of the 1980s, oils and other consumer products still constituted the WIPRO group's corporate "cash cow," but computers were already about a third of the group's total turnover. To maintain this volume, WIPRO, like HCL, relied on PCs as well as minis and even went into the manufacture of printers, using technology licensed from Epson.

For WIPRO, as for HCL, growth depended on combining engineering-intensive, high value-added products with the successful marketing of high-volume commodity manufactures. Other, smaller companies, like PSI Data Systems, tried to focus more exclusively on design intensive products. The brainchild of V. K. Ravindran (a Stanford Ph.D. in information systems) and Vinay Despande (also a Stanford engineering graduate), PSI excelled at the development of innovative systems. It got its start doing development contracts and gravitated to design-intensive products whenever it could. For example, it managed to underbid several international firms to get a contract for data acquisition systems to be used on offshore oil rigs.

HCL, WIPRO, and PSI all based their growth on India's low-cost, high-quality engineering resources. Most other local hardware manufacturers took a more conventional route. Major players like Pertech, Sterling, and Zenith, along with several dozen smaller firms, all focused almost exclusively on microcomputers. While commercially successful, none of these companies could claim real success as commodity manufacturers. Most of the smaller manufacturers and even some of the commercially oriented large-volume producers were engaged in what is pejoratively known as "screwdriver assembly," buying "semiknockdown kits" from Taiwan and Korea and reselling them at a profit accounted for only by tariff protection. Analysis by the Bureau of Industrial Costs and Prices (Kelkar and Varadarajan 1989, 16) concluded that when the import costs of the kits was compared to the price of importing the finished PCs themselves, "there is negative domestic value-added in these products."

The contrast between impressive accomplishments in design and innovation and negative value-added in simple assembly operations is counterintuitive in terms of traditional "product cycle" theories of the international division of labor. Activities that looked most appropriate for a low-wage country showed no evidence of comparative advantage, whereas the more competitive products incorporated indigenous design and engineering talent. This counterintuitive result stemmed from India's general weakness in commodity production. Like Brazil, India lacked a dense network of suppliers who could reliably deliver high-quality, low-cost parts and components. Even more than Brazil, India lacked the managerial and organizational traditions capable of executing commodity production at international costs.

State involvement fed into both India's problems as a manufacturer and its strengths in design-intensive activities. Manufacturing problems were compounded by lack of dependable high-quality infrastructure (transportation, communications, power, etc.), while the country owed its apparent advantage in design activities to the state's massive historical investment in educational infrastructure.

Nowhere was India's advantage in low-cost engineering and technical labor more obvious than in the software industry, without doubt the most dynamic segment of the local informatics industry. Software expertise was crucial to the survival of state-owned firms like CMC and ECIL and private hardware manufacturers like HCL, but it also helped generate new firms.

The classic example of India's software success is Tata Consultancy Services (TCS), an offshoot of the 120-year-old, four-billion-dollar Tata group and the best example of successful participation in the information technology sector by a big business house. By far the oldest major private firm in the informatics industry, TCS was, at the end of the 1980s, the biggest private player in the domestic software market, the country's largest software exporter, and the sixth largest firm in the informatics industry overall (see table 7.6).

If TCS demonstrates the possibility of participation by a big house in the industry, Datamatics, the creation of L. S. Kanodia, shows how the growth of software has been a vehicle for the rise of independent local entrepreneurs. Kanodia, an MIT Ph.D., came back to India to head up Tata Consultancy Services and then decided that he preferred individual entrepreneurship to working for a big house (*Computers Today*, October 1989, 29). Having started Datamatics with an initial capital of $12,000 in 1975, he was, by the end of the 1980s, the owner-manager of the country's fifth largest software company.[35]

One thing binds all participants in the new local software industry together. The industry was born internationalized. Software in India has burgeoned despite the fact that India's domestic market remains tiny.[36] Consequently, discussion of India's software industry really belongs in the next chapter with discussion of the new internationalization. First, this chronicle of local entrepreneurship needs to be completed with a review of the most successful set of local firms, those that emerged in Korea.

Korea—Leveraging Manufacturing Prowess

Korea's emerging informatics industry could not have contrasted more sharply with India's. In India, software was the only high-technology earner of hard currency and the best hope for continued export growth. Korea's software sector was about one-third the size of India's and an almost purely domestic endeavor.[37] Semiconductors, an unremitting failure in India,[38] are Korea's greatest export triumph. Commodity PCs, which generate negative value-added in India, are an important source of foreign exchange for Korea.

The subsectors of information technology in which the Koreans had the greatest success are, not surprisingly, ones in which the state's promotional efforts have already been discussed. PCs, the object of protection and special government procurement efforts in the early 1980s, became a mainstay of the industry in the late 1980s. The focus on semiconductors was presaged by the state's construction of a pilot wafer fabrication facility in the 1970s and reinforced by programs like the 4-Megabit DRAM Project in the 1980s.[39] Even more important in shaping the industry, however, was the generalized midwifery that produced the chaebol to begin with.[40]

The contrasts between Korea and India, like those between Korea and Brazil, flow from the fact that Korea began its foray into informatics with an entrepreneurial structure shaped by prior midwifery into an ideal instrument for attacking the commodity end of informatics production. In Korea, initiating production of computers and other informatics products did not require finding new entrepreneurs to start new companies. The country's chaebol had already made vast investments in facilities to manufacture consumer electronics products. It was only a question of convincing them to add informatics products to their repertoires. In contrast to both Brazil and India, the list of Korea's major informatics companies in the mid-1980s is also the list of its major electronics companies (see table 7.7).

Korea's vertiginous growth rates in computer and semiconductor production (see table 7.8) overshadow the rapid growth rates of the Brazilian and Indian industries. In a decade, Korean computer production went from nothing to over $2 billion. Semiconductor production was even more impressive, reaching $3.6 billion by 1988. By the late 1980s electronics had replaced textiles as Korea's most important export sector. Within electronics, exports of informatics goods had increasingly outdistanced traditional consumer goods like television sets as Korea's major export successes (see table 7.9). Informatics led a drive that turned high-technology production into a mainstay of Korea's industrial order.

The growth of semiconductor production and exports was, in fact, much more impressive than the raw numbers indicate. Korean semiconductor exports originally consisted of products that were imported, packaged in Korea, and then reexported. They were, in short, a low-tech, low value-added export. At first neither the foreign assemblers nor the chaebol attempted to get into the technologically difficult business of wafer fabrication (except for relatively simple watch chips). By the end of the 1980s the story was different. The chaebol, led by Samsung, had not just gotten into fabrication; they were a world power in the memory chip market.

It is hardly surprising that the chaebol should have gravitated to a sector in which competitive advantage depends first and foremost on cumulative manufacturing experience and by extension on the financial ability

TABLE 7.7

Sales by Korean Participants in the Computer Industry, 1986 (in millions of U.S. dollars)

Company	Total Sales
1. Samsung Electronics Co.	2,229
2. Goldstar Co.	1,755
3. Daewoo Electronics	606
4. SST (Samsung Semiconductor and Telecommunications)	447
5. Samsung Electron Devices	315
6. IBM Korea Inc.	222
7. Goldstar Semiconductor	196
8. Daewoo Telecom	152
9. Oriental Precision Co.	121
10. Hyundai Electronics	104

Source: Evans and Tigre 1989b:19 [Table 8]. Originally from *BK Electronics*, "Introducing the 1986 Top 300 Electronics Companies" 1, 1: (November 1987) 52–63. Original won figures converted to U.S. dollars at 878 won per dollar.

Note: Includes all companies from the listing in *BK Electronics* of the top 200 Korean Electronics companies that list "computers" among their products. Sales figures are for total sales and include sales of noninformatics products.

TABLE 7.8

Growth of Korean Computer and Semiconductor Production (in millions of U.S. dollars)

Year	Computers	Semiconductors
1981	31	342
1982	47	490
1983	207	850
1984	428	1,265
1985	519	1,005
1986	880	1,470
1987	1,655	2,300
1988	2,665	3,678

Sources: Computers, 1981–86, KIIA (1987, 86); 1987–88, Ernst and O'Connor (1992, 112), originally from *Yearbook of World Electronics*. Data for these two years is for "office automation equipment," which is a somewhat broader category and therefore exaggerates 1986–87 growth.

Semiconductors, 1981–82, EIAK (1987, 14) (data are for ICs only); 1983–88, FKI (1991, 592).

TABLE 7.9
Korean Exports of Televisions, Computers, and Semiconductors, 1980–1989 (in millions of U.S. dollars)

Year	Televisions	Computers[a]	Semiconductors
1980	415	6	445
1983	624	112	812
1986	955	707	1,359
1989	1,355	2,042	4,023

Sources: 1980–86, EIAK (1987, 16–18); 1989, EIAK (1991, 21, 25, 37).
[a] Computers includes peripherals and software, but the latter is negligible, accounting for only $16 in 1989.

to invest continually in the new capacity. The magnitude of the risk involved is still impressive. The Japanese firms that dominated the industry during the 1980s drove the product cycle at ever faster rates, forcing all producers to make new investments in more sophisticated equipment and then struggle to regain yields. The intensity of competition drove most independent U.S. producers out of the memory business, but the chaebol remained undaunted.

Investment in wafer fabrication facilities ranged from about $250 million to roughly $600 million a year from 1984 to 1988, hitting a peak of over $1.5 billion in 1989.[41] Samsung, under the leadership of Lee Byung Chul, gambled earliest and most heavily on semiconductors, moving quickly from 64K to 256K DRAMs.[42] By mid-1988 Samsung was the among the top half-dozen producers of 256K DRAMs in the world, had begun producing 1-Megabit DRAMs, and was ranked among the world's top twenty semiconductor producers overall (*Electronics Korea* 3(2), 15). In November 1989, with some help from the state-sponsored 4-Megabit DRAM Project,[43] it was able to announce that it was producing 4-Megabit DRAMs, only six months after the Japanese had begun to ship, and had completed construction of a new research institute, dedicated to the development of "ultra large-scale integration," chips with 16 to 256 Megabits of memory capacity. Finally, at the beginning of the 1990s, it was third in the world in the production of memory chips, topped only by IBM and Toshiba.

Semiconductors show the potential power of the entrepreneurial structure that was constructed in the 1970s.[44] Massive local semiconductor production helps satisfy an even larger domestic demand[45] and provides an important boost to local computer firms.[46] Without local firms capable of producing of semiconductors, Korea's negative balance of trade in electronics parts would be almost as large as its positive balance of trade in consumer electronics.[47]

Finally, it is worth underlining once again that Korea's challenge to the advanced industrial powers in semiconductors is based almost completely on the entrepreneurial élan of local capital, encouraged and supported by the backing of the state. None of the foreign firms that were involved in assembling semiconductors in Korea in the 1960s and 1970s made any attempt to invest in local wafer fabrication facilities.

The PC clone industry replays the semiconductor story in a minor key. By the early 1980s PC clones were a commodity product rather than a design-intensive one. Price competition increased correspondingly, making the PC an ideal product for firms like the chaebol, whose forte was in mass production of electronics goods, as long as they could find a way to market what they produced. Daewoo Telecommunications was the first to venture into the U.S. market. By getting Leading Edge, a small, aggressive U.S. distributor, to market its dependable, well-configured clone, Daewoo was able generate a market of 200,000 units a year. Hyundai was even bolder, going in under its own brand name. By 1988 Korea was exporting PCs at an annual rate of over two million units. Hyundai and Daewoo ranked sixth and eighth, respectively in the U.S. clone market, while machines produced by Trigem, a smaller Korean firm for Epson and sold under Epson's own brand name, ranked fifth (B.K. Electronics 2(1), 27–28).

The formidable entrepreneurial structure built up in the 1970s had, by the 1980s, been thoroughly engaged in the project of turning Korea into a major information technology producer. Despite its success, however, there were surprising lacunae in the development of Korea's informatics industry. In 1986 production of computers larger than PCs in Korea was less than half that of local Brazilian firms (see Evans and Tigre 1989b, 12, 15). The chaebol had failed to make much headway in selling larger computers in the domestic market, say nothing of abroad. Even in production of PCs using more advanced processors,[48] the next step up in the mid-1980s, the chaebol could not boast an outpouring of innovative designs like those of Indian or Brazilian companies.[49]

Staying out of the development of larger machines may have shown sharp commercial acumen, but it diminished the chaebol's capacity to move from "making boxes"[50] to "selling solutions."[51] PC production, however commercially successful, could not produce the kind of innovative systems integration achieved by makers of financial automation systems in Brazil. Systems integration, a market with rates of return potentially much higher than those in clone production, required software expertise and technical command over more powerful architectures. Making PC clones provided neither.

The chaebol's amazing success in penetrating advanced countries' markets with high-technology commodities did not change the fact that selling commodities on the basis of price competition is a low-return niche, especially if they are sold OEM[52] rather than under the firm's own name. The competitiveness of Korean manufacturers was too often bought at the price of reducing local value-added. Value-added in the production of PC clones at the end of the 1980s was estimated as low as 10 percent (*Electronics Korea* 3(9), 12), in part because Korean PC products were paying 10–15 percent of their receipts as licensing fees (EIAK 1991b, 10). Korean OEM producers were especially vulnerable because of their dependence on Japanese parts and technology.[53]

In short, the Korean industry, despite its well-deserved world renown, was not immune from the self-doubts and second thoughts that were the rule in Brazil and India. On the one hand, Korea was not sure that it had really constructed the kind of industry that it needed for long-run development. As Jeon Byeong-Seo of the Daewoo Research Institute put it, "In simple 'screwdriver' operations, original manufacturing equipment (OEM) suppliers tend to squeeze most of their profits out of low labor costs, not technological breakthroughs" (*Electronics Korea* 3(9), 11). On the other hand, not even commercial success could be taken for granted. In 1990 computer exports suddenly dropped by 36 percent,[54] sharply reminding Korea that its informatics industry, like those of the other NICs, was still vulnerable to changes in the global character of the industry.

Greenhouse Firms in a Global Industry

In Korea, as in India and Brazil, the local industrial panorama in the mid-to late 1980s represented an impressive change in scenery. The dreamers who had formulated informatics policies in the three countries could not claim that all their hopes were fully realized, but the array of local firms and locally designed products went well beyond what would have been predicted by a skeptical outside observer at the beginning of the 1970s.

State involvement had produced substantial fruits. A plethora of greenhouse firms vindicated midwifery. The results were all the more impressive because they revealed local resources that conventional analysis would not have predicted in advance, especially in India and Brazil. In retrospect, it makes sense that these countries might have had a comparative advantage in tasks that required skilled professionals, like engineers and software designers, but it took on-the-ground experimentation to create a convincing demonstration.

State involvement did not have to be flawless to produce results. Even in India and Brazil, where the efficacy was undercut by experiments with roles that did not work, the promotional aspects of involvement still had substantial effects. Brazil and India could not boast of industries as powerful and internationally competitive as the one that grew out of Korea's more felicitous blend of roles, but they did show that it was possible to make mistakes and still get results.

Some skeptics will still want to argue that the rise of local firms and the state's efforts at promoting information technology production are only coincidentally connected, that the apparent relation is spurious, and that local firms would have come into being and grown just as rapidly if the state had ignored information technology. Unfortunately, disproving this counterfactual argument would take evidence from a range of countries vastly broader than the range that has been considered here. Nonetheless, believers in spuriousness have a lot to explain away. There are too many instances where the connection between the initiation of a policy and the initiation of an investment is undeniable.[55] Some local firms would have started anyway, but to argue that the information technology industries that existed in these three countries at the end of the 1980s were only coincidentally related to patterns of state involvement over the prior twenty years strains credulity.

Certainly, equating state involvement with the creation of stagnant rental havens does not help explain this evidence. Rental havens were created, but they were anything but stagnant. A neo-Schumpeterian analysis comes closer to the mark than does a neo-utilitarian one. In all three countries local firms used the greenhouses the state provided as an opportunity to engage in entrepreneurship and innovation. Not all local firms responded in such a Schumpeterian fashion, but an impressive number did.

All three industries could claim significant successes. Brazil had put together a new set of diversified informatics producers who were significant actors on the local industrial scene. Local entrepreneurs commanded experienced organizations that sold billions of dollars of informatics goods and employed thousands of technically trained professionals. Local técnicos had demonstrated their technological bravura and even managed to turn their talents into internationally competitive products in the financial automation sector. In India the design successes of local hardware firms were even more impressive, and the prospect of a real international comparative advantage in certain kinds of software engineering did not seem at all fanciful. In Korea production of information technology products had become a cornerstone of the country's overall industrial strategy. The chaebol were going head to head with the world's leading firms in memory chips and had also succeeded in becoming a force in the world PC market. For three countries that many economic theorists would have categorically excluded from having a chance at real participation in the globe's leading sector, the results were impressive.

This is not to say that declarations of victory were in order. As the new informatics entrepreneurs looked out from local greenhouses at the industry they faced, they saw a sector that was changing even more rapidly than the one they had entered, an industry whose technological transformations made clinging to proven strategies perilous, especially strategies that had worked inside the greenhouses.

If technological change at the beginning of the 1980s opened new space for national industries to develop, trends in the latter part of the decade wrote the obituary for any policy with autarkic aims. It was a confusing world in which openness and standards forced alliances across national boundaries and across corporate divides.[56] For firms in the NICs the logic was inescapable. Survival meant a "new internationalization" based on the fusion of local and transnational capital.

By the late 1980s internationalization became the prevailing tide in all three countries. Aspirations to autarky were quaint memories, and transnational influences and alliances were the dominant theme. Internationalization seemed to be the only way to confront the challenges of a changing global informatics industry. Yet in all three countries—even Korea, which seemed most successful at shaping its insertion into the global economy—internationalization was rife with problems. Did the new internationalization offer a way of extending and deepening the growth of local information technology industries? Or was it a trap, one that would the consign NIC industries to low-return niches within information technology, reimposing the old international hierarchy in a slightly more subtle guise? Understanding the outcome of state policies had come to mean understanding the new internationalization.

8

The New Internationalization

A STARTLING newcomer hit the Indian computer scene in the winter of 1992. Called Tata Information Systems Ltd. (TISL), the company was not just another extension of the Tatas' flowering information technology empire. It was IBM. Fifteen years after refusing to stay in India unless it could have 100 percent ownership of its local operations, Big Blue was back.

The reappearance of IBM had been predicted by industry experts for some time,[1] but its form was still surprising, especially to those who still remembered IBM's earlier incarnation. TISL was not just a joint venture; it was a 50/50 joint venture, something unthinkable for IBM in the 1970s. In the 1990s, India's regulations would allow IBM to take a majority in the company, and the Tatas were ready to go ahead on that basis. Legally, IBM could even have split up the Indian side of the equity among a set of passive individual investors. But the 1990s' IBM was not interested in either option. The 50/50 split was a deliberate gesture. IBM's general manager for the ASEAN region was emphatic: "We will start this partnership on the basis of partnership. . . . 50–50 is an emotional signal of that" (*Dataquest* March 1992, 105).

Why was IBM back? Why was it back as a joint venture? For IBM, coming back made eminently good sense. Its rivals, DEC and HP, had already set up new subsidiaries. Bull and UNISYS were there too. Letting its transnational competitors carve up the Indian market in IBM's absence did not make any sense. From the Indian perspective, IBM's return was less momentous than it might have appeared. Local firms (and later other TNCs) had occupied space that otherwise would have gone to IBM, especially at the lower end of the market. UNIX had taken off more rapidly. Nonetheless, IBM was a persistent presence in the Indian market throughout the 1980s even without a local subsidiary. Large Indian users, including state enterprises, had continued to buy imported IBM mainframes, and most of the country's software exports continued to be written for IBM users.

IBM's return made sense in retrospect, but what did it say about the 1970s and 1980s? Did it demonstrate that the greenhouse policies of the 1970s had failed? Was India's relation to the international industry back to where it had been at the beginning of the 1970s? Or did the fact that IBM had come back as a joint venture represent a victory for the Indian policymakers who had refused to allow it to stay as a wholly owned subsidiary? After all, wasn't IBM coming back essentially on India's terms?

A satisfactory interpretation should go beyond the Indian case. Even though IBM never left Brazil or Korea, the evolution of its role in those countries brought it to positions that echoed its new role in India. In Korea it was involved in a joint venture with Samsung, the largest of the local computer manufacturers. In Brazil it had formed a business partnership with Itautec and a joint venture with SID, both firms that grown up since IBM lost its right to sell into the lower end of the Brazilian market. The similarities arose from the common elements in the policies of the three countries, but they also reflected trends in the global environment that shaped the structure of the IT industry in all countries.

From the beginning, national efforts to instigate informatics production were powerfully influenced by the changing global industry. At each step of the way, global technological standards inexorably imposed themselves. Transnational firms were the bearers of global technological influence. Their changing corporate strategies introduced an additional layer of coercive external context. As local resources, capacities, and interests evolved over the course of the 1970s and 1980s, national dramas were played out against a continually changing background of global technology and transnational corporate strategies.

The centrality of international influences was a constant, but the character of internationalization changed sharply over the course of the 1980s, as exemplified by IBM's shifting strategy. The changes created new opportunities for local firms, but their implications for state involvement were more ambiguous. Did the roles that had helped produce the rise of local firms still make sense? Or did the new internationalization finally signal the obsolescence of the state?

Internationalization—Old and New

Before the Bhabha Committee, the barbudinhos, and the Blue House group, information technology in the NICs was thoroughly internationalized. Brazil, India, and Korea consumed imported finished products. The minor amount of local informatics manufacturing that existed was in the hands of the wholly owned subsidiaries of transnational firms. Exports were either conjunctural results of pressure on subsidiaries to counterbalance imports, as in Brazil and India, or restricted to simpler components and packaging operations, as in Korea. That was the old internationalization.

Looking at the thrust of policy pronouncements, at least in Brazil and India, one might have predicted that greenhouses would move these countries closer to autarky. The prediction could not have been more wrong. Even the most traditional kinds of international ties—imports—grew as greenhouses were implanted. Stimulating the growth of information technology increased imports along with local production. The proportion of imports to total informatics sales may have fallen, but imports still rose absolutely.

Brazil is a good case in point. Between 1979 and 1985 when the market reserve was being implanted, computer-related exports from the United States to Brazil grew two and a half times, faster than U.S. computer exports to the world as a whole, and in sharp contrast to the overall stagnation of U.S. exports to Brazil (see Evans 1989c, 215). Because the upper end of the market was still supplied by imports, the majority of newly installed capacity in the early 1980s was imported (Erber 1985, 296). Overall trade figures show that the same is true for India and Korea. The growth of local industries was import substituting, but it also created new demands, especially for imported components but also for final products beyond the reach of local firms. In all three countries, growing imports were one aspect of the persistence of the old internationalization.

Old investment persisted as well. With the one famous exception of IBM's 1978 departure from India, subsidiaries were not dislodged. To the contrary, they grew. In Brazil, IBM and UNISYS were the two largest computer producers when the market reserve started in 1977, and they were the two largest producers as it drew to a close at the beginning of the 1990s.[2] Some even argued that Brazil's market reserve turned out to be first and foremost a market reserve for IBM.

If the trade and investment ties that characterized the old internationalization persisted, what changed? How did the emergence of local informatics industries change the way in which these countries related to global markets and the international industry? Three principal changes took place.

First, even though imports continued to be central to supplying local informatics needs, local firms became important mediators between users and the global market. They turned imported components into final products, integrated imported hardware into systems, and figured out ways to translate an international menu of products into local solutions. Locally controlled firms turned importing information technology into an active process.

The second and more dramatic change was the emergence of exports. Local firms became exporters as well as importers; exporters not just of minor components or imported inputs that were packaged and reexported, but of final products, sometimes highly complex and sophisticated ones. In Brazil the process was limited to a few niches, but in India and Korea it was more substantial. In certain segments, like Korean semiconductors and PC clones or Indian software, a large part, if not the majority, of local production was sold on international markets. This was a an unmistakable departure from the old internationalization.

Third, the relation between local and transnational capital was transformed. While wholly owned subsidiaries remained, the old model of transnational capital operating with splendid independence from local firms became anachronistic. Instead, local informatics industries were populated more and more by alliances of transnational and local capital, sometimes in the form of technology or licensing agreements, sometimes in the form of joint ventures or "business partnerships." The fusion of local and transnational capital, as exemplified by the Tata/IBM tie-up, is the real hallmark of the new internationalization.

In short, the old internationalization was a world of wholly owned TNC subsidiaries supplying local markets, importing most of what they sold, and engaging in a limited gamut of exports. The new internationalization was a world of alliances between local and transnational capital, with substantial amounts of vertically integrated local manufacturing and an increasing emphasis on exports by both alliances and local firms.

The new internationalization was not simply the negation of nationalist development strategies. In many ways it built on the foundations laid by those strategies. Local firms had to exist before they could make alliances. They had to develop their own organizations, marketing skills, and installed base in order to have something to offer potential transnational allies. Without midwifery there would not have been local groups with which to ally.

Greenhouse policies also gave TNCs an incentive to look for allies. Greenhouse rules in all three countries, explicitly in Brazil and India, implicitly in Korea, made certain kinds of foreign entry contingent on finding local partners. These policies were local capital's the biggest single bargaining asset. Ironically in retrospect, the most important "rent" generated by nationalist greenhouses may have taken the form of leverage to negotiate the internationalization of the industry.

The global evolution of the industry complemented local dynamics, giving transnational firms additional incentives to negotiate alliances with local firms. In the 1960s, the heyday of the IBM System 360, when proprietary architectures were the most important asset, there was little incentive to make alliances that would dilute proprietary rents. The old internationalization of imports and the 100 percent foreign-owned subsidiary was the natural form of global expansion.

As the global panorama of information technology had moved from a world of proprietary hardware rents to a world where components and software were the key inputs, alliances became essential.[3] In this new world even alliances with NIC firms that were tiny by international standards, like HCL or Itautec, made sense. Some NIC allies, like COBRA in Brazil with its nationwide installed base and service network, offered access to a new set of customers. Others, like PSI in India, offered low-cost engineers that could work on problems for which Silicon Valley engineering talent was no longer cost-effective. Still others, like the Korean chaebol, offered low-cost, high-quality manufacturing crucial to staying in price competitive markets.

The new internationalization of local information technology sectors shared generic characteristics across the three countries, but its specifics in each country were as different as the local industries themselves. The adaptations of local firms, their participation in exports, and the forms of fusion that joined them with international capital all depended on how the local industry had been shaped by prior state policies and the responses of local firms.

Brazil: Alliances or Subsidiaries?

Brazil started with the most internationalized of the three informatics industries when it began its efforts to generate local firms. Consequently, it also had the most defensive of the three greenhouses. By the mid-1980s Brazil's industry was arguably the least internationalized. No appreciable exports had developed beyond IBM's original contribution. Joint ventures were not allowed.[4] The technology licensing agreements of the 1984 supermini competition were the closest approximation to alliances allowed.

By the end of the decade things had changed. Entrepreneurial strategies had moved in an internationalist direction. Then, at the beginning of the 1990s, the Collor administration's revision of the National Informatics Law provided a legal framework that opened the floodgates. The evolution of Elebra, Itautec, and SID—the three big conglomerates of the mid-1980s—illustrates the change. Each of them formally left the 1980s behind by forming new associations with transnational capital at the beginning of the 1990s.

Elebra's transition was abrupt and thorough. In 1989 the company gave up any pretense of developing an indigenous successor to its licensed VAX 750 and received permission to license DEC's new MICROVAX. Then in 1991, under the new rules promoted by Collor, Elebra became a joint venture, with DEC taking an equity position for the first time. There was every indication that DEC would take an increasing management role, eventually merging the Elebra organization with DEC's wholly owned subsidiary to form a new firm, clearly part of the DEC organization but with some Brazilian equity participation. By 1993 DEC controlled 83 percent of Elebra's equity, the maximum amount that it could control if Elebra was to continue to be a "Brazilian" firm under the new law.[5]

The case of Itautec was more complex. Ironically, Itautec's earlier efforts to achieve "technological autonomy" had vastly deepened its expertise relative to IBM compatible systems.[6] These efforts also prompted it to accelerate work on indigenously designed equipment, like controllers and communications devices, which could be used with IBM systems. By the end of the 1980s, Itautec was using the expertise acquired and its stature as Brazil's largest locally owned producer to negotiate an associative arrangement with IBM that gave it the rights to manufacture and sell IBM's most successful mid-sized computer line, the AS-400, one of the few clear winners that IBM had developed during a difficult decade (Meyer-Stamer 1989, 46, 53–55).[7]

Itautec's new internationalized strategy had other elements as well. On the one hand, as a leading manufacturer of microcomputers, it looked forward to being able to use internationally competitive components. On the other hand, it could continue its role in financial automation and consider expanding into point-of-sale and commercial automation with aspirations to penetrate European markets. In addition to its AS-400 deal, it was also working on a deal to become one of two worldwide manufacturing centers for IBM communications controllers.[8]

Itautec remained a sophisticated producer of a full gamut of hardware and financial automation software. With the AS-400, it had a state-of-the-art hardware platform to drive what had already become a formidable informatics empire. If it was not the independent national entity that the barbudinhos might have dreamed of, it was still an indigenously owned and managed enterprise with over $200 million in annual sales and a decade of experience in engineering its own products.

For other firms, the new internationalization required no adjustment of philosophy. SID, the country's second largest local hardware producer in 1988 (after Itautec), found the intensification of international ties natural. Born from the Machline group, which had built its fortune in consumer electronics by allying with Sharp of Japan, and led by Antonio Carlos Rego Gil, a veteran of twenty-two years in IBM, SID had always found nationalist impediments to building international alliances frustrating.[9] When things opened up at the beginning of the 1990s, SID negotiated a joint venture with IBM, called MC&A. The new joint venture's mission, like that of IBM's joint venture with the Tatas in India, was the local manufacture of PS/2s. At first the joint venture was 51 percent owned by SID and 49 percent by IBM, but IBM's share was later increased to 70 percent.

The other veterans of the 1984 supermini competition represent different variations on the same theme.[10] Even firms that had epitomized the quest for technological autonomy in the 1970s ended up exemplifying internationalization in the 1990s. For SCOPUS, founded by archetypal "frustrated nationalist técnicos," the intrinsic benefits of technological autonomy were an article of faith. Nonetheless its owners, hit hard by the 1987 downturn, were forced to relinquish control to Bradesco. At the beginning of the 1990s SCOPUS found itself along with Digilab as part of a new joint venture with NEC.[11]

Insofar as the barbudinhos had dreamed of "technological autonomy," the new internationalization clearly was a negation. At the end of the 1980s, trying to participate in global technology, not trying to achieve autonomy from it, was the definition of local technological efforts. Perhaps more galling was the old internationalization's persistence in the form of control of the local market by wholly owned TNC subsidiaries.

Even though local firms accounted for the majority of informatics sales at the beginning of the 1990s, 100 percent owned subsidiaries continued to dominate the local pecking order. In 1990, a dozen years after the initiation of the market reserve, UNISYS had made a strong comeback and had its largest market share since the beginning of the 1980s.[12] It was second only to IBM, which was doing even better. IBM's 100 percent owned operation had five times the revenues of the largest Brazilian computer firm in 1990 (DEPIN 1991, 52). In fact, looking at the structure of the Brazilian market, it was clear that the market reserve had operated strongly in IBM's favor in many respects. Large machines, still IBM's forte, held a much larger share in Brazil than in other markets. Furthermore, in Brazil, IBM had been able to rent a larger share of its machines rather than selling them outright, a practice that competition had forced it to abandon in other markets.

Should the new internationalization be seen then as a defeat? Not necessarily. The core of the barbudinhos' vision was to create a local industry that not only would be responsive to local needs for information technology but also would give Brazilians opportunities to take on technologically challenging roles in developing that responsiveness. Whether this part of the vision was viable depended on the survival and the future character of the firms that had come into being as a result of the state's midwifery.

For local firms, successfully negotiating the new internationalization meant combining a multiplicity of international linkages with indigenous innovation, increasing local value-added, offering superior solutions for local users, and exploiting niches in international markets. The other possibility was devolution to the role of distributors for transnational firms, depending on the technological capacity of foreign parent's research organizations and relying on commercial margins for their own returns.

At the beginning of the 1990s the verdict was still out. The downside was obvious. The diversification of the three large conglomerates of the mid-1980s (Itautec, SID, Elebra) was put on hold by their problems with semiconductors. All three groups regretted their attempts to enter the semiconductor business, felt betrayed by the state's retreat from its mid-1980s' ambitions, and were primarily concerned with cutting losses. Elebra's owners were retreating from informatics more generally. In addition to allowing DEC to gain effective control over its computer operations, Elebra had sold off its telecommunications operations to a group with European ties. SID and Itautec seemed to be in the computer business for the duration, but whether they would be able to resist the pressure to become commercial rather than industrial participants was unclear.

Itautec exemplified the ambivalent possibilities best. It was a company whose three-hundred-person research and development team could claim a considerable record of accomplishment.[13] Financially, it was hard to justify the maintenance of its 1980s' levels of investment in research and development in the environment of the 1990s. The obvious alternative was to become in effect a "value-added retailer" for IBM, concentrating on maximizing the huge potential sales volume of its AS-400 line, moving back toward the days when the barbudinhos were confronted with the choice of working in the university or being salespeople for IBM.

Brazil's overall macroeconomic problems made it harder to choose investment. In some subsectors, like semiconductors, local firms began the 1990s expecting sales to drop dramatically (Tigre 1993, 15). Only in the financial automation sector did sales of local firms seem to be holding up. Given these trends, most firms in the industry were beginning to think twice about the value of indigenous technological efforts. Expenditures on research and development by locally owned hardware firms dropped by a third between 1989 and 1990, while expenditures in industrial automation and software were cut by more than half). Expenditures on the training of personnel by local informatics firms showed a similar trend, dropping to less than half their 1989 level in 1990 (DEPIN 1991, 39, 32).[14] The government's new program for the "formation of human resources in strategic areas" found the industrial sector's interest in the program's students plummeting.[15]

Despite these inauspicious trends, Brazilian informatics firms were hardly comatose. There was substantial evidence of adaptive responses to the new internationalization. Claudio Frischtak (1992) catalogs a number of examples. Two will suffice here, both based on a combination of ingenuity and alliances.

The first comes, as might be expected, from the financial automation sector. Among the top ten computer producers in 1990, there was one newcomer, PROCOMP, which was founded in 1985 and only began substantial production in 1988. Three years later PROCOMP was not only the fourth largest firm local firm in Brazil in terms of sales, it was also the only firm among the top four that reported profits instead of losses.[16] It was universally acknowledged to be one of the most successful entrants in the successful financial automation subsector. PROCOMP was a classic systems integrator, relying on Digilab to produce its hardware. Having developed conventional financial systems into a $100 million a year business, it was pushing forward in the direction of point-of-sale terminals, which it estimated could cut the cost of processing a transaction to half of what it cost to process a check in the United States. It was convinced that its equipment would be price competitive on international markets if it could set up adequate marketing channels.

Sistema, a producer of industrial automation systems, and Rima, its associated peripherals manufacturer, were another example of successful adaptation to the new internationalization. Rima, which operated in association with the big informatics banks (Itaú and Bradesco), shared domination of the local printer market for years with Elebra. Eventually it decided that the production scales and technology of its indigenously designed printers were competitive with those of European producers. It broke into the Italian market by setting up an alliance with a local Italian producer of microcomputers (Frischtak 1992, 179). At the same time, the Sistema group decided to build on its strong position in the Brazilian market for process controls[17] by getting into the European market. To overcome the hurdles involved in exporting into the European Community, it set up a German joint venture that soon had process control sales amounting to two-thirds Sistema's Brazilian sales. Like PROCOMP, Sistema was basically a systems integrator. It licensed technology from Reliance, a U.S. company. In Brazil it used equipment built by one of its biggest rivals (Villares) as a hardware platform. In Germany it used a foreign hardware platform. As Frischtak (1992, 184) puts it, Sistema's secret is "the identification of a niche in which the Brazilian firm can use its competence and specific comparative advantage in software and systems engineering."

If cases like PROCOMP and Sistema could be multiplied over the course of the coming decades, Brazilian informatics would have transformed itself into an internationalized version of the barbudinhos' dream. If, on the other hand, local enterprises gravitate toward becoming TNC distributors, the arduous process of greenhouse construction will look like a very costly way of enhancing the commercial possibilities of local entrepreneurial groups. Which occurs will depend, at least in part, on whether the Brazilian state can muster the institutional and political resources necessary to engage in husbandry.

India: The Ambiguities of Software

India's local private sector found the transition to the new internationalization less traumatic than did their Brazilian counterparts. Since responsibility for defending technological autonomy was allocated primarily to state firms, local hardware manufacturers had always been more open to internationalized strategies. At the same time, the growth of the export-oriented software industry was a strong stimulant to an internationalist perspective.[18] While Brazil's custodial efforts aimed initially at making information technology *less* internationalized than other advanced manufacturing sectors in Brazil by adding restrictions on TNC investments, India's shift from policing to promotion resulted in a burgeoning of intricate international alliances and an influx of TNC subsidiaries that made Indian informatics in the 1980s, a major departure from India's autarkic industrial traditions.

Hindustan Computers Ltd. (HCL) illustrates the complexities of international ties on the hardware side.[19] Already in 1981, HCL had created a subsidiary in Singapore (Far East Computers Ltd.) to test out its microcomputer technology.[20] Later, a tie-up with Apollo allowed HCL to manufacture Apollo's low-end workstations and get into the computer-aided design and manufacture (CAD/CAM) market. A distribution agreement with Mentor Graphics gave it a powerful set of CAD/CAM software to go with its Apollo workstations, especially in the area of electronic design automation.[21] By acquiring another local firm (IDM), they got a tie-up with Prime computers as well, providing them with a high-end transaction-processing machine.[22] An agreement with National Advanced Systems (NAS) allowed them to compete occasionally in the mainframe market with Hitachi mainframe technology. And these were only the ties of the computer division. HCL's other divisions—communications, instruments, and reprographics—all had their own foreign tie-ups.

In 1989 HCL added a new kind of internationalization to its repertoire by setting up HCL America, a wholly owned, Silicon Valley subsidiary. HCL America was, first of all, an attempt to get more return from its investments in product development for the Indian market.[23] U.S. operations were essentially systems integration, not manufacturing.[24]

The beginning of the 1990s saw yet another metamorphosis of HCL's international ties. The entire computer division (minus HCL America) was merged with Hewlett-Packard's newly initiated Indian operations to become HCL-HP. The combination of HP's product line and manufacturing experience with HCL's legendary skill at playing the Indian market will undoubtedly make this fusion a potent player in the Indian market. One of its first initiatives was a state-of-the-art[25] manufacturing plant in the new Noida industrial zone.

The decision to form a joint venture represented movement toward the new internationalization, not just for HCL, but also for HP. Attracted by the post-1984 growth of India's market, Hewlett-Packard decided in the mid-1980s to set up its own manufacturing operations in India. Formally, they stuck to the FERA rules that had driven IBM out ten years earlier, limiting their equity to the required 40 percent. In practice, the other 60 percent was sufficiently dispersed among local stockholders to give HP with effective control.[26] The creation of HCL-HP turned the operation from a relatively traditional subsidiary into a real alliance.[27]

The HCL-HP alliance raised the same questions that IBM's hook-up with Itautec raised in Brazil. Was this the first step in the gradual transformation of HCL into India's HP distributor? Or will the alliance's new market power allow HCL to focus on its strengths as a systems integrator and its comparative advantage in low-cost, high-quality engineering talent, resulting in new solutions for Indian users and expanding sales in the United States for HCL America? Positive answers would vindicate the new internationalization as a vehicle for extending the achievements of the nationalist greenhouse. Negative ones would leave India's greenhouse without its prize product.

The late 1980s' trajectories of WIPRO and PSI raised the same themes in a slightly different way. The early histories of both firms showed how international ties can support the development of indigenous technological capacity. Yet neither found an easy way to translate internationally connected indigenous innovation into long-term commercial success. The point is clearest in the case of PSI.[28]

PSI's original operating capital was provided by a development contract with a small Silicon Valley start-up looking for someone to build a microprocessor-based telex monitor. Later, in 1985, an order to develop prototype systems for a Japanese company using Motorola 68020 processors gave PSI a head start on a minicomputer, which became its most important hardware platform.[29] Unfortunately PSI's technological acumen was not coupled with the kind of marketing ability that propelled HCL. The company gained a reputation for being technologically innovative but commercially inept and announced losses of $5 million in 1989.[30]

Nonetheless, PSI's demonstrated capacity for technological innovation continued to serve as a key asset. Groupe Bull, which had been attracted to PSI by its technological reputation, responded to PSI's financial problems by cementing the joint-venture agreement originally initiated in 1988 with an equity investment. Explaining why, Ove Lange, vice president of Bull International, said, "The software development of PSI when compared to its turnover is the highest in the world including France, which is a strategic factor in this alliance with PSI" (*Dataquest*, April 1990, 98). PSI was expected to develop software for Bull's operations abroad, thereby covering the hard currency costs of importing components for the Bull mainframes that the joint venture intended to assemble and sell in India. Expectations were quickly fulfilled. By the beginning of the 1990s, two-thirds of PSI's revenues came from software exports (*Dataquest*, July 1992, 111).

WIPRO demonstrated the same synergy between international alliances and local development that appears in the history of PSI. A processing "board" that it developed for a small California company became the basis of its own Landmark 386 minicomputer.[31] The international contract underwrote the cost of developing an indigenous machine. In addition, since WIPRO engineers worked on the board in California, close to the source of supply of the new components, they were able to speed up the design process, which helped insure the timely launching of WIPRO's machine.

Other international ties strengthened WIPRO's commercial position. A licensing agreement with Epson allowed it to provide printers along with its computers and added another 8 percent to its sales. Tie-ups with Tandem and Convex gave it the possibility of moving into the market for large machines. Still other ties improved its access to microprocessors and software.[32]

WIPRO's most important international alliance by far was with Sun Microsystems. It negotiated an agreement to manufacture Sun workstations under license, do some software development work for Sun to help cover the foreign exchange costs, and market Sun's new risk-based SPARC-stations in India. The Sun line soon comprised a large share of its midrange hardware sales (*Dataquest*, July 1992, 67).

At the beginning of the 1990s, WIPRO was still independent in terms of both management and equity, but the basic questions were the same. Would WIPRO devolve in the direction of becoming a value-added retailer for Sun workstations? Or could the relationship with Sun be leveraged to allow WIPRO to become an internationally competitive systems integrator, capable of purveying innovative solutions to the India market and sometimes selling them abroad as well?

For the technologically entrepreneurial pioneers that formed the initial wave of informatics entrants, the new internationalization was an equivocal benefit, but for the big business houses that had been slow to move into information technology it was an unambiguous boon. The alliance of the Modi group with Olivetti, the largest producer of PCs in Europe, is a good example. The Modi contribution was not a history of innovation in information technology; it was wide-ranging experience in doing business in India. Since Modi-Olivetti targeted volume sales, the kind of engineering experience that PSI or WIPRO might have offered was less relevant than Modi's general business clout and commercial skills.

The Tata-IBM alliance, with which this chapter began, was the most interesting of all. On the manufacturing side, the Tata-IBM deal mirrored the Modi-Olivetti venture and the IBM-SID venture in Brazil. Tata Information Systems Ltd. was slated to get IBM back into the Indian PC market by producing PS/2s (*Dataquest* March 1992, 98–102). For the Tatas, however, the payoff was more likely to be in software than in manufacturing profits.

TISL was slated to handle software development for internal IBM projects and for major worldwide users, subcontracting with local developers where necessary. It would join the Tata's two other major software producers: Tata Consultancy Services and Tata Unisys Ltd., the Tatas' joint venture with UNISYS, whose software exports were surpassed only by TCS.[33] As the local software industry's largest player and the most prominent exception to the big houses' ineptitude in information technology, TCS had very early on developed a diversified and highly internationalized strategy.

At the end of the 1980s, three-fourths of TCS's business was for foreign customers (*Dataquest* 1990, 58, 75). In India it did custom design work, marketed "packages"[34] by prominent American manufacturers (SPSS, Oracle, Lotus, etc.), and developed some packages of its own, though, like most other Indian firms,[35] it had found that packages, no matter how impressive technologically, would not provide the volume to sustain a major firm.

A large portion of TCS's business consisted of traditional service contracts in which its engineers wrote code to solve specific problems designated by customers. Given twenty years of experience and a reputation for quality, TCS was gradually able to shift about half of its work from labor contracts to project management. For example, it designed a comprehensive banking system for a British bank, a screen definition system for one of Citibank's on-line banking applications, and a turnkey information and management system for the Kuwaiti port authority.

The highly internationalized strategy that characterized the Tatas' software empire was a privilege of not only the big houses. New entrepreneurial entrants like L. S. Kanodia's Datamatics were even more internationally oriented.[36] Eighty percent of Datamatics' revenues were from exports, and most of these were generated by strategic linkages with U.S. firms. Kanodia's first partner was Wang. His company became the largest developer of Wang software outside of the United States. From its Wang base, the company moved into UNIX. Its UNIX expertise allowed it to develop a relationship with AT&T. At the end of the 1980s it opened a dedicated satellite linkup with Bell Laboratories, which allowed Datamatics developers to work directly on AT&T's hardware in New Jersey. In addition, Datamatics was an authorized AT&T training center. To round out his strategy, Kanodia decided to add a new focus on IBM software, setting aside part of his facility in the Santa Cruz special export processing zone for IBM work and buying some midsized IBM hardware on which to work.

Like the growth of TCS and Datamatics, much of the expansion of software exports is based on alliances. Some of it, however, represents a modernized resuscitation of the ownership strategies of the old internationalization. Even in the 1980s, foreign firms could retain 100 percent ownership of software companies as long as their business was purely exports. Subsidiaries like Texas Instruments' wholly owned operation in Bangalore, which pioneered the use of dedicated satellite connections to export software, were among the most successful entries in the internationalized software industry.[37]

Citicorp Overseas Software Ltd. (COSL) is one of the most interesting of the wholly owned software subsidiaries. Started in the state-subsidized Santa Cruz special export processing zone in 1987, it came close to doubling its business every year in the first three years of its operations, until it was the fourth largest software company in the country. COSL has been exemplary in moving its exports in the direction of high value-added markets. By putting the credibility of its international pedigree together with the productivity of its Indian engineers, it has been able to expand the consulting/systems-design end of its business aggressively.[38]

Taken as a whole, India's new software exports go to the heart of the ambiguities of the new internationalization. Software is really a variety of disparate activities lumped together under the same rubric. Leaving aside packaged software, a business that is almost impossible to break into unless a company starts with major marketing clout in the United States, the custom side of the business ranges from routine code writing, which is a low-return use of skilled intellectual labor, to the design and implementation of complex information systems, which is essentially very high-level consulting work and reaps commensurately high returns. The difference between the low end and the high end in returns per programmer day is even greater than the difference in the returns to proprietary as opposed to commodity hardware. Some estimate it as high as fifteenfold.[39]

India had tremendous comparative advantage at the low end of the software business. Beginning programmers' wages were on the order of

10–15 percent of U.S. wages, and for most low-end jobs labor still consti-tuted more than three-fourths of the total cost of production in developed countries. The high-return end of the software business was a different story. Inexpensive technical programming skills provided limited advan-tage in bagging custom projects where the secret of success lay in under-standing the activities of potential users and identifying the information needs that flowed from them.

A few large firms like TCS and Datamatics were able to secure higher-return project management contracts, but a substantial proportion (per-haps the majority) of India's software "exports" were in reality contracts for migrant intellectual labor, pejoratively known as "bodyshopping." Indian companies contract with foreign firms, providing them with skilled "bodies" who work at the foreign site to solve the foreign firm's software problems, returning to India when the work is done. Indian en-trepreneurs earned their return by putting skilled Indian programmers together with foreign customers who were unable otherwise to cope with the worldwide gap between demand for new software and the supply of software engineers.

Bodyshopping produced neither proprietary return nor a contribution to organizational or entrepreneurial infrastructure of India's domestic in-dustry. It also exacerbated India's "brain drain." Working alongside of foreign programmers who were making multiples of their wages, a sub-stantial proportion (perhaps 20 percent) of the Indian programmers de-cided to jump ship and become direct, permanent participants in the more lucrative labor markets to which they had been exposed. The main ad-vantage of bodyshopping was that the barriers to entry were low, which was why most of the multitude of tiny firms that coexisted alongside gi-ants like TCS and Datamatics survived on the basis of bodyshopping.

Small local producers may well have no option other than bodyshop-ping, but transnational hardware subsidiaries, like DEC and HP, are also charged with concentrating on the less rewarding (and less challenging) end of world markets. Local critics accuse these firms of generating "soft-ware exports" by directing their local software engineers to routine tasks that U.S. software people would like to avoid, like debugging existing software, extending the life of old operating systems, or porting existing applications to different platforms. They are accused, in effect, of con-structing an intangible high-tech version of the low-wage export strate-gies of the old internationalization.

One international expert, Robert Schware (1992a, 153–54), has lev-eled an additional criticism against low-return software exports. He ar-gues that they absorb skilled labor power that would produce a much greater social return if its energies were applied to domestic problems. There are large potential increases in domestic productivity from software systems of the kind on which CMC and ECIL have focused—systems that would improve freight transport, distribute electric power more efficiently, or improve predictions of monsoon waterflows. Insofar as the labor involved in exports would otherwise be underutilized there is no problem, but, even in India, the demand for well-trained software engineers probably exceeds the supply. Taking programming talent that could be used to increase the utilization of India's scarce rolling stock and devoting it instead to enabling an American insurance company to shift its data base from Burroughs to IBM hardware may suit the interests of transnational firms and avoid the need for the construction of more sophisticated Indian software firms, but it has a substantial social cost.

Overall, it is not hard to look on India's software exports with a jaundiced eye. One Indian executive characterized the international flows of software generated by the new internationalization as a reversion to earlier colonial trading patterns. For him, the export of inexpensive lines of code and the import of expensive foreign software packages had a familiar feel. "It's the old story," he said. "We are exporting cotton and buying back the finished cloth."

Perhaps the most fascinating thing about the debate on the Indian software industry is that it bears a strong resemblance to the debates generated by a totally different kind of export boom—Korean penetration of world markets for memory chips and PC clones. By some criteria, Indian software is at the opposite end of the economic spectrum from Korea's exports: intangible rather than the result of manufacturing expertise; produced by highly educated white-collar labor, not a blue-collar proletariat; generated by both small firms and large ones. Nonetheless, Korea and India share the same worries over getting trapped at the low-return end of the international division of labor.

Korea: The Dilemmas of Manufactured Exports

Korea looked at the internationalization in the late 1980s from a different perspective than did Brazil and India. The closure of Fairchild Semiconductor Korea Ltd. in 1989 was as emblematic for Korea as the arrival of IBM in 1992 was for India. Fairchild had been the first of the foreign assemblers to set up in the late 1960s (*Electronics Korea* 2(9), 17–18). Its operations had been built on the assumption that Korea's comparative advantage lay in low-wage labor. It had assumed that strategic alliances with the chaebol were superfluous, envisioning Korea as a source of simple subassemblies, not complex finished products. By 1989 its assumptions were anachronistic, out of touch with Korea's new relation to the international economy.

Fairchild was typical of the old internationalization in Korea, where the role of wholly owned subsidiaries was quite different from what it had been in Brazil and India. Korea's TNC subsidiaries were interested in export markets, not the domestic market as in Brazil and India. Consequently, they focused on a narrower range of simpler products in which they felt Korea's cheaper labor gave them an advantage.

In Brazil and India, the end of the 1980s saw a new emphasis on exports, both rhetorical and real. In Korea, where exports had been central to earlier development strategies, there was a renewed appreciation of the importance of the domestic market as a source of growth. In computers, the domestic market was already over $600 million by 1986, almost as large as Korea's computer exports. Given that exports were almost exclusively low value-added products, often sold under other companies' brand names, returns in the domestic market were increasingly attractive. Three-quarters of this substantial, comparatively higher-return market was still supplied by foreign imports.[40]

More important, the future growth in export markets could not be taken for granted. Between 1976 and 1986, Korea's domestic market for electronics had grown at about one and half times the rate of its export markets (see Mody 1987b, 131). Between 1988 and 1989, overall domestic electronics sales grew 29 percent while exports grew only 5.4 percent (*Electronics Korea* 3(6), 6). In semiconductors, Korea's most successful export subsector, the domestic market grew more than twice as fast as overall production between 1984 and 1988 (*B. K. Electronics* 1(12), 22). In computers, growth of the domestic market completely overshadowed the growth of exports at the end of the decade. Between 1989 and 1990, when computer exports were shrinking, the domestic market continued to grow at a rapid rate (see EIAK 1991a, 21).

Overall, Korea's experience in information technology export markets at the end of the 1980s provided concrete evidence for analysts increasingly skeptical of the wisdom of trying to base IT industry growth on commodity exports. Ernst and O'Connor (1992, 280), for example, conclude their analysis of the NICs competitive position by saying that "an export-led growth strategy targeted on major OECD markets appears increasingly problematic."

The issue of local value-added was as worrisome as the question of how much exports could grow. Over the course of two decades, the Korean electronics industry had been unable to reduce substantially its dependence on imported parts. In 1970 70 percent of the parts used by local manufacturing operations were imported; in 1987 the figure was 60 percent (*Electronics Korea* 3(9), 17). The worrisome implications of this dependence became particularly evident in 1987 when Japanese parts exporters, disturbed by Korean competition in the VCR market, engaged in concerted restriction of supplies to Korean competitors (*Electronics Korea* 3(9), 16).

Just as the virtues of foreign sourcing were becoming canonical wisdom in India and Brazil, Korean analysts were pointing out the virtues of more nationalist strategies, saying that "self-sufficiency in technology and key parts production are the only way for Korea's electronics industry to survive in the heightening competition in the world market."[41] Korea would never approach the degree of self-sufficiency that Brazil and India were trying to shake off, just as Brazil and India would never rely on exports as much as Korea did, but it was still ironic that India and Brazil were emulating what they thought was the Korean model, while Korea was rethinking what the model should be.

Just as the earlier importance of exports to the Korean informatics industry led Korea to rethink export strategies, the less dominant role of wholly owned TNC subsidiaries under the old internationalization made it easier for Korea to sustain a more nationalist version of the new internationalization when it came to investments. Brazil required over a decade of intense struggle to increase the share of the informatics industry controlled by domestic companies from 23 percent to 59 percent (see table 7.1). Domestic producers in Korea started by controlling of the 49 percent of the electronics industry at the beginning of the 1980s and ended up with 71 percent, while wholly owned subsidiaries controlled just 9 percent of overall electronics production (see table 8.1).

As the 1980s ended, IBM Korea was a power in the local market, but it was still "doing a feasibility study on the establishment of a factory in Korea" and using components sourced from the chaebol as a major part of its contribution to Korea's exports (*Electronics Korea* 3(3), 12). Rather than towering over local firms as it did in Brazil, IBM's rapidly growing informatics sales entered the 1990s still smaller than those of Goldstar (*Wolgan Computer*, May 1991, 100, 102). No other foreign subsidiary could claim to be a power in the local market in the way that UNISYS was in Brazil and DEC was becoming in India.

The absence of dominant foreign subsidiaries was historical, but it also reflected a quiet continuation of the policy of midwifery toward locally owned firms. Even after formal restrictions on foreign ownership had largely disappeared, informal ones continued to be important. The American Chamber of Commerce in Korea complained particularly about "localization requirements," which they described as "a collection of usually unwritten policies and practices—enforced by formal and informal government pressure—requiring firms to transfer technology and expertise to Korean producers" (*Electronics Korea* 2(9), 14). When, for example, DEC, which had long worked through a distributor in Korea, decided to

TABLE 8.1

Foreign Firms in the Korean Electronics Industry: Share of Production by Type of Ownership and Subsector, 1980–1988

	Year	
	1980	1988
Electronics Overall		
Locally owned	49%	71%
Joint Ventures	27%	20%
Foreign-owned	4%	9%
Components (Including Semiconductors)		
Locally owned	28%	50%
Joint Ventures	38%	36%
Foreign-owned	34%	14%
Industrial Electronics: (Principally Computers and Telecommunications)		
Locally owned	38%	72%
Joint Ventures	54%	12%
Foreign-owned	8%	16%

Source: KIET, as reported in Electronics Korea 3, 9 (July 1990):12.

set up a 100 percent owned subsidiary, it found itself engaged in arduous negotiations with state officials as well as its private counterparts over what contributions DEC would have to make to the development of local informatics capacities in order to justify the switch.

Nationalist preferences persisted, but investment patterns still shifted from those of the old internationalization to those of the new internationalization. Traditional export-oriented foreign assemblers, like Fairchild, found that successful industrialization made Korea a less supportive environment for their kind of operations. Foreign dominance declined in the more traditional areas of the electronics industry at the same time that TNCs were showing new interests in information technology. Table 8.1, which shows declining foreign ownership in electronics overall but a growing foreign presence in "industrial electronics," illustrates the trend.[42]

As the role of foreign investors shifted, alliances between local capital and TNCs, the hallmark of the new internationalization, became increasingly important. Each of the chaebol maintained myriad international alliances. Their number and diversity accelerated over the course of the 1980s. They ranged from joint ventures with foreign firms to technology agreements that gave the chaebol access to foreign product technology, to OEM agreements through which the chaebol played a key role as low-cost suppliers. Looking across the pattern of international ties from Samsung to Goldstar to Hyundai to Daewoo shows the advantages of having gotten an early start on alliance building.

In 1984 Samsung, after having been a distributor for Hewlett-Packard for eight years, formed a joint venture to market HP's products in Korea. It also had "arrangements" with NEC (Samsung Electronics 1985, 19). In telecommunications, in addition to being involved in the indigenous TDX-1 project, Samsung produced the Acatel S-1240 digital switching system. Like WIPRO in India, it had a joint venture with General Electric to produce medical imaging equipment. Its original entry into semiconductors involved a technological alliance with Micron Devices.[43]

Most interesting were Samsung's links with IBM. When IBM introduced its "Asian PC,"[44] Samsung Electron Devices got the contract to make the monitors (*Business Korea*, August 1985, 42). In 1987 Samsung and IBM formed a joint venture called Samsung Data Systems to develop value-added data networks in Korea (*Business Korea*, August 1987, 69). In addition, in 1989 Samsung and IBM announced a long-term cross-licensing agreement that "gives each company free access to the other's current portfolio of patents relating to the design and manufacture of semiconductor devices" (*Electronic Engineering Times*, April 3, 1989, 1).[45]

Goldstar's most important alliance was with AT&T, its partner in Goldstar Semiconductors and a source of technology in both semiconductors and digital switching. Goldstar was the local supplier of AT&T's 1AESS and 5ESS switching systems to the Korean Telecommunications Authority. Goldstar's close technological relation with AT&T was important to its ability to develop 1 megabit DRAM capacity. Goldstar also had agreements with Hitachi in memory chips and mainframes.[46] A joint venture called Goldstar-Hitachi Systems developed software for use on Hitachi mainframes in the Korean market. Goldstar and Hitachi were also reputedly working together on application-specific integrated circuit (ASIC) technology, though a deal with LSI Logic was also important in getting Goldstar into the production of ASICs.

A joint venture with Electronic Data Systems was designed to get Goldstar into the software and systems integration business (*Business Korea*, August 1987, 69). To boost its entry into the PC business, Goldstar developed an arrangement with Olivetti (Ryavec 1987, 10). In addition, Goldstar had a joint venture with Honeywell to produce controls and instruments and was listed as selling Honeywell-Bull's DPS-6 minicomputer (*Computer Mind* 1988, 210–11).

Hyundai Electronics is a newcomer relative to Goldstar and Samsung, but just as aggressive in constructing international ties. It got its start in semiconductors by producing 256K DRAMs under license from Vitelic.[47]

The mainstay of its production later became huge OEM semiconductor orders from Texas Instruments. It also used ties with Inmos, Western Design Center, and Motorola to increase its semiconductor expertise (Ryavec 1987, 19). A contract to make the CPU of IBM's "Asian PC" was important to its entry into computer production. Another step on its way to breaking into the U.S. PC market under its own name was a large OEM contract with a small U.S. company called Blue Chip Computers. In addition, Hyundai set up an arrangement to act as a distributor for Sun.

Daewoo's most important tie in computers was its marketing link with Leading Edge (through which it became a major supplier of U.S. PC clones). It also had an arrangement with Fujitsu. In semiconductors, it purchased an entire production line from Zymos (a small, troubled U.S. semiconductor manufacturer) and agreed to OEM for Zymos the products that Zymos found it could no longer produce for itself.[48] In addition, Daewoo was a major OEM manufacturer for IBM, producing, for example, $100 million worth of automatic banking terminals and later a million PS/2 monitors.[49]

The chaebols' technological tie-ups and joint ventures bore a family resemblance to the ties that Indian and Brazilian firms were trying to develop, with the crucial difference that none of the chaebol was in danger of being swallowed by their TNC partners. They had resources that local entrepreneurs in India and Brazil could not claim. With their manufacturing prowess they could win large-scale supplier contracts with major TNCs, using them to build volume and manufacturing expertise. Their long-standing international experience allowed them to operate directly in developed country markets rather than relying completely on TNC allies to create access.

The chaebols' international experience did not stop at technological tie-ups, joint ventures in their home countries, and exports. By the end of the 1980s they had also set up a variety of subsidiaries in developed countries. In the context of India and Brazil, operations like HCL's Santa Clara subsidiary or Sistema's German partnership were examples of unusual imagination and entrepreneurship. For the chaebol, foreign subsidiaries were a standard strategy.

Some of the chaebols' foreign subsidiaries simply produced routine consumer products. In 1982 Goldstar led the way by constructing its first major American production facility in Huntsville, Alabama. Producing a million color televisions and half a million microwave ovens, it was a wholly owned Goldstar subsidiary (see Goldstar 1987, 55). Since then, other chaebol have also set up a series of production facilities in advanced industrial countries. Samsung has plants in Portugal and New Jersey, and Goldstar followed up its Alabama plant with a similar facility in West Germany. Such plants were economically important in sustaining consumer electronics markets, but in informatics there was also a distinctly different set of foreign operations that was equally important for different reasons. Informatics subsidiaries were, as Linsu Kim (1991, 33–34) has put it, "outposts in the Silicon Valley," which served as "antennas for information on research activities in advanced countries and as training posts for scientists and engineers from R&D centers and manufacturing plants in Korea." Daewoo Electronics maintained a laboratory in Tokyo and a "product design and engineering institute in Santa Clara, California, called International Design Focus" (*Korea Herald*, June 7, 1987). In addition to its U.S. production facilities and its various U.S. marketing offices, Samsung also had a research-oriented Santa Clara subsidiary—Samsung Semiconductor Inc. (Samsung 1987, 45). Goldstar maintained a Silicon Valley base called Goldstar Technology (*Electronics Korea*, 3(2), 16).

Even when developed country subsidiaries failed, they could still be valuable experiments. Hyundai's $300 million investment in an advanced semiconductor plant in the United States, known as Hyundai Electronics America, was a flop, the "kind of mistake that would send most companies to bankruptcy court."[50] Nonetheless, the plant itself was eventually reincarnated in Inchon as Fab.3, a combination research and production operation using engineers who had worked in the U.S. facility. For a latecomer trying to break into the semiconductor business, the learning experience was probably worth the price (*B.K. Electronics* 1(6), 38–41).[51]

None of the chaebols' ventures was as adventurous as HCL America. They made no pretense of penetrating advanced industrial markets with technologically original products like HCL's UNIX suite. Nonetheless, like India's HCL and Brazil's Sistema, the chaebol saw international technological ties as complementing and reinforcing indigenous technological capacity rather than as replacing indigenous efforts. Likewise, they saw indigenous technological capacity is an important asset in negotiating transnational alliances. The Samsung-IBM cross-licensing is a good example. When it was announced American observers commented, "Access to Samsung technology could help IBM trim valuable design and manufacturing time off of the long lead time that products like the 3090 series demand. . . . Samsung's portfolio of semiconductor patents are believed to contain valuable surface-mount packaging techniques, techniques that play a critical role in streamlining complex manufacturing processes, such as those called for in IBM's mainframe-production operations" (*Electronic Engineering Times*, April 3, 1989, 2).[52]

Looking at the chaebols' multifaceted assault on technological prowess, it is tempting to conclude that they had developed the optimal strategy for adapting to the environment of the new internationalization. Most Korean observers, including the management of the chaebol them-

selves, considered such optimism premature if not false. Like Korean academic analysts who emphasized the country's difficulty in improving
value-added and pointed to the 1989 downturn in the computer market
as a portent of the fragility of export sales, managers were acutely aware
of the difficulties of breaking out of commodity markets into higher-return kinds of activities. They knew that Korean informatics could not
afford to rely on memory chips and clones indefinitely.

Korea confronted the new internationalization with tremendous assets, but it could still envy India's software exports and Brazil's success at
design-intensive systems integration. If Korea's experience in the 1980s
showed anything, it showed that more international alliances and more
attention to exports were means, not ends in themselves. The new internationalization, even in its robust Korean version, only provided a new
context for the fight to secure more rewarding niches in the hierarchy of
the international division of labor.

Internationalization and State Involvement

The new internationalization was not an end point. Neither new ties between transnational and local capital nor new export efforts were laurels
on which to rest. Like the nationalist greenhouses that preceded them,
they were ambiguous achievements whose long-run implications were
not easy to project.

The transnational links that were the hallmark of the new internationalization epitomized the ambiguities, especially in Brazil and India. Seen
as alliances, they were victories, allowing local entrepreneurial groups to
make use of international technology in devising indigenous solutions to
local IT needs. Less optimistic interpretations were equally plausible. The
agreements and mergers of the new internationalization could also be
seen as replacing real entrepreneurial entities with de facto subsidiaries,
dedicated to sales and service and without any commitment to the development of local manufacturing or independent technological capacity.

Some alliances will unquestionably devolve into de facto subsidiaries,
but in all three countries some local firms will survive as real entrepreneurial entities. The survivors raise another set of questions. If local firms
survive, but adopt subsidiary-like strategies, there is no difference between "real alliances" and "de facto subsidiaries." Ownership and managerial control are of interest only insofar as they have implications for
what kind of niche a firm will try to carve for itself in the global division
of labor. The real question is how local firms (or, for that matter, subsidiaries) behave. Will they take an interest in increasing local value-added?
Will they make investments in local technological capacity that can lead

them in the direction of higher return niches? Will they create the kind of productive organizations that stimulate the development of local technical cadres?

A local informatics industry built around international alliances can mean very different things. Sistema, with its European joint ventures, has a different relation to world markets from SID's PC assembly joint venture with IBM. Itautec's survival as a value-added retailer of AS-400s would have quite different implications for Brazil's place in the international division of labor from its survival as a producer of innovative, proprietary point-of-sale systems that can compete in international markets. The difference between being an internationally connected systems integrator and being an internationally dependent assembler is the difference between the positive potential of the new internationalization and a return to the industry the barbudinhos were trying to escape.

The exports associated with the new internationalization are only slightly less ambiguous than the alliances. Indian software exports epitomize the ambiguities. Do software exports represent India's leapfrogging into the global markets of the twenty-first century? Or does the combination of bodyshopping and consumption of imported packages mean a return to trading cheap cotton for expensive textiles? If bodyshopping is the twenty-first-century equivalent of cotton-picking, then software exports are the old international division of labor in a more modern guise. Korea's PCs raise similar issues. In the beginning of the 1990s, as technology payments and components imports shrank the value-added on PC exports, Koreans had to wonder whether PCs were wigs and wallets dressed as "high-tech."

Low-return exports are not bad in themselves. Bodyshopping beats being a redundant bank clerk or joining the swollen ranks of the educated unemployed. Assembling low-end PCs for Leading Edge at Daewoo beats being a peasant, trapped on a plot of land too small to provide a living. Nonetheless, low-return exports do raise two questions. The first is the old question of constructing comparative advantage: Do these exports generate skills and experience that will enable the country to keep pace with a changing international division of labor? The second is Robert Schware's question: Is the total social return from these exports greater than the return that could be had if the same labor were engaged in producing domestic systems and solutions? In other words, do such exports maximize information technology producers' contribution to "development" in the broader sense of overall levels of national welfare and positive social structural changes?

This brings us back to the role of the state. The changes encompassed by new internationalization do not derive their impetus from state action in the same obvious way that the old greenhouses did, but the importance of state involvement should not be underestimated. Old greenhouse rules remained a crucially important bargaining chip when local firms started trying to form alliances with TNCs. Likewise, there are continued examples of husbandry. The Indian state's international promotional efforts on behalf of its software producers are one. Korea's provision of financing and marketing support to help it land foreign contracts for indigenously designed telecommunications products is another.

Some would argue that both the legacies of earlier midwifery and continued efforts at husbandry are simply the remnants of earlier involvement, lagging indicators of a withering away of state involvement. They would also argue that such withering makes sense. Even if the emergence of the information technology sector did not signal the obsolescence of state involvement, its intensified internationalization does. Having helped midwife the emergence of local firms and seen them grow to the point where they could become plausible allies for TNCs, the state should step back.

If the new internationalization were an unambiguous avenue for mobility vis-à-vis the global division of labor, the argument for obsolescence would be compelling, but the analysis of the new internationalization that has been offered in this chapter suggests otherwise. Given the ambivalent and contradictory prospects offered by the new internationalization, considering state involvement obsolete makes no more sense at the end of the 1980s than it did at the beginning of the 1970s.

Looking at the new internationalization does strengthen previous arguments about the relative efficacy of different roles in the IT sector. The new internationalization certainly removes any possibility of a return to the demiurge as a dominant strategy.[53] The new internationalization also seals the coffin of the kind of custodial regulation that was possible in earlier phases of the sector's development. At the same time, husbandry and midwifery redefined in part as the mediation of alliance building seem likely to be permanent features of successful responses to the new global context. Indeed, it can be argued that husbandry in the context of the new internationalization demands a higher level of sophistication and resources than it did before, that instead of diminishing the need for state capacity, the new internationalization has increased it.

One thing is clear. The new internationalization clearly complicates the politics of state involvement. Once enmeshed in alliances with transnational firms, local entrepreneurs no longer comprise a political constituency as they did under the old greenhouses. Their interests are much less clearly bound up with the growth of local demand and the enhancement of local productive capacity. Getting some share of the proprietary rents generated by their partner's global technological and marketing assets is increasingly important. Consequently, embeddedness is more problematic. At the same time, the political vacuum that allowed early "guerrilla" initiatives from inside the state has been filled. Once local firms have established themselves, the sector is no longer an empty space politically. The kind of autonomous action that propelled the initial development of the sector is no longer possible.

What this analysis suggests, then, is that the new internationalization places new demands on the state yet leaves it less politically able to pursue transformative ends. Far from bringing consideration of state involvement to a close, the new internationalization forces us to think anew about the political roots and economic consequences of the state's role.

9

Lessons from Informatics

As THE 1990s began, Mario Dias Ripper was looking for work again. He was no longer president of Elebra Computadores, the company he had helped put together in the early 1980s which joined the formidable Brazilian financial resources of the Bradesco and the Docas de Santos groups with the equally formidable technological clout of the DEC VAX. The rules had changed. DEC was allowed to become a part owner of Elebra and wanted to take a more direct managerial role. Ripper had decided he was too closely associated with the old informatics policy to fit in with the new venture. Nor did it make sense for Ripper to try to return to his earlier vocation as an entrepreneurial technocrat, working inside the state apparatus. All that was left from CAPRE and SEI was the Departamento de Política de Informáticae Automaçâo (DEPIN), a modest department whose power and prospects were so reduced that it was having a hard time even getting access to the data it needed to publish statistical bulletins.

Ripper needed a new niche. His search for a new job revolved around trying to find a way to make entrepreneurial use of newly available "open" technologies. It mirrored Brazil's own search for a new niche in the global information technology sector, which was hardly surprising. Ripper's two decades in the Brazilian informatics industry had often reflected the changing currents of policy and technology. From his early engineering training at the air force's elite Institute of Technology (ITA), to the years he spent getting a doctorate in computer sciences at Berkeley, to the exciting days in CAPRE when the informatics policy was being constructed, to the years at Elebra helping to put together what seemed for a time likely to be one of Brazil's leading information technology conglomerates, Ripper's trajectory had mirrored the transformation of Brazil's participation in the global IT industry.

Should Mario Ripper's job search be taken as simply another bit of evidence confirming the quixotic character of Third World aspirations to participate in the informatics industry? Such an interpretation would be more plausible except that other, loftier figures in the world computer industry were in equally difficult straits. At the end of 1992 John Akers was forced out of IBM after losing a record $4.9 billion. Brazil's share of world markets may not have grown as it should have during the 1980s, but at least it was not cut in half like IBM's was.[1] Nor was IBM unique. Kenneth Olsen, the engineering genius and entrepreneurial spirit behind DEC's rise to second place in the world computer industry, was also in the process of being forced out. DEC's 1992 losses were only about half of IBM's, but its future was less secure.

Reconciling Third World citizenship and continued participation in the information technology industry required agility, fortitude, and the periodic search for a new niche, but so did survival as a leading TNC. The stories of Ripper and his Brazilian colleagues, like those of their counterparts in India and Korea, are full of twists and turns, but so is any narrative set against the background of the tumultuous information technology sector. Despite the twists and turns there is a logic that runs through these histories, a logic with implications for both the theoretical debates with which this book started and the societal-level propositions that oriented my investigation of the IT sector. It is time to synthesize the myriad specific lessons that are inlaid into the history of these three information technology sectors and set overall conclusions in relief.

The question is, how has looking at the IT sector helped us better understand the relation between state involvement and industrial transformation? The simplest answer is that the expectations of earlier chapters were generally confirmed. Coherent, connected state structures were an advantage. Custodial policies and reliance on the state as demiurge eventually gave way to a more promotional emphasis. Focusing on the midwifery-husbandry sequence worked best. That, however, is only the simplest answer.

The IT industry also generated unanticipated state-society interactions. As local firms took hold, they provided political support for the agencies that helped midwife their emergence, especially in Brazil, but state strategies in both Brazil and India had to change to accommodate the industry they had helped bring into being. Later, nationalist policies ended up producing internationalized industries in all three countries. Internationalization made state promotional efforts less relevant to the strategies of local entrepreneurs. The separation of clients from the policies that created them not only contradicts neo-utilitarian images of a simple symbiosis built around a mutual benefit from rent creation but also raises questions about the idea of "joint projects" that was central to my initial formulations of "embedded autonomy."

This chapter begins by reviewing patterns of state involvement in information technology. Then it recapitulates the rise of local industries and their subsequent internationalization. With sectoral dynamics recapped, the discussion turns to implications. First, the various ways in which information technology narratives contradict a neo-utilitarian vision of state-society relations are underlined. Then the chapter asks what these sectoral results imply for the societal-level ideas that got the whole investigation started.

Roles and Structures in Information Technology

A close look at the information technology sector did not support the idea that state involvement becomes anachronistic as rapid technological changes become more central to industrial transformation. To the contrary, Flamm's dictum that government involvement is inevitable and ubiquitous in high-technology industry holds, even in NICs where technology is borrowed rather than invented. All three states intervened, but each intervened in its own way, setting up a "natural experiment" on the consequences of different forms of involvement.

Divergent information technology trajectories flowed first of all from general differences in state structures and state-society relations. The extraordinary growth of the information technology sector in Korea confirmed the advantages of embedded autonomy. A robust, coherent bureaucratic apparatus and dense ties to private industrial capital proved itself a potent combination in high technology, just as it had in other industrial sectors. Networks of concrete ties connecting the state and the relevant firms were crucial to developing local information technology capacities. Korea had the advantage of these kind of relations from the beginning. The complex ties among MOC, ETRI, and the chaebol that were used to nurture technological entrepreneurship epitomized embedded autonomy.

The pitfalls of insufficient embeddedness were also well illustrated, nowhere better than in India. The aloof, semiadversarial relation that characterized state-industry relations in the early days of informatics policy was consistent with India's bureaucratic tradition, but not with promoting the growth of local informatics production. Aloofness eventually gave way until, by the end of the 1980s, promoting software exports was a project shared by the state and private entrepreneurs.

The Brazilian state connected better with local entrepreneurs, but fragmentation made it hard to pursue a coherent program of transformation. Individual agencies acted like cohesive corporate entities, but the state apparatus as a whole was badly divided. Lack of coherence made it hard to use ties with local firms effectively. SEI's inability to keep "free riders" from exploiting the market reserve, which turned its genuine supporters into "suckers," exemplified the flawed nature of the Brazilian state's autonomy.

Differences in overall structures were reflected in the roles adopted in the sector. Embedded autonomy made pursuit of the midwifery-husbandry sequence easier; its relative absence made it hard to get from midwifery to husbandry. Lack of embeddedness increased the attractiveness of the demiurge role and exaggerated custodial efforts.

Once adopted, roles were differentially effective. Direct entrepreneurial interventions aimed at replacing local private capital in the production of normal commodities—playing the role of demiurge—proved untenable (though state enterprises were sometimes effective in other ways). The key to facilitating the growth of a new sector was midwifery, creating the conditions that led entrepreneurial groups to identify their interests with the growth of the sector and commit resources to it. Restrictive regulation played a part in midwifery, but when detailed custodial regulation became the dominant form of state involvement, the capacity of state agencies was overwhelmed. To be effective, state involvement had to move from midwifery to husbandry—prodding firms to move forward within the sector and supporting their efforts to do so. Together the three countries offered a rich set of illustrations for all of these patterns.

Brazil and India demonstrated the contradictions involved in trying to use restrictive regulation as the principal strategy for managing the implantation of a new sector. Relying primarily on custodial strategies was problematic first of all because it ignored the importance of conserving scarce bureaucratic capacity. Effective implementation of restrictive regulation would have required much more state capacity than either country could mobilize. In both India's DOE and Brazil's SEI, small numbers of professional staff were asked to evaluate an almost impossible number and variety of proposals for new products and production plans. There were also contradictions in the content of the rules themselves. In both cases, the attempt to police ended up contradicting efforts to promote. Making and enforcing rules is unavoidable, but primary reliance on the custodial role is counterproductive, at least in this industry.

India's system of licensing products and output levels was completely unrealistic in the context of a dynamic industry like informatics. The state's custodial efforts made sense only as long as it could be assumed that the state-owned enterprises would be able to provide the entrepreneurial thrust the industry needed. Once it was clear that the state as demiurge could not keep up with the rate of global progress in the industry, custodial rules had to take a back seat.

In Brazil, the principle source of the overload was the attempt to regulate technological ties with TNCs. Trying to play the conscientious custodian by insulating local industry from dependence on international technological ties while at the same time avoiding a gap between the technology available domestically and internationally proved impossible. SEI's regulatory efforts created an incentive structure that alienated even those committed to the policy. "Free riders" using illicitly acquired international technology benefited from a protected market, leaving genuine adherents resentful of being asked to pay their dues in the form of investment in indigenous research. Users still complained of lack of access to internationally state-of-the-art information processing capacity.

The contradictions of a directly productive role were as evident as those of the restrictive regulation. Lack of agility and efficiency were part of the problem, but contradictory mandates were more fundamental. Both ECIL in India and COBRA in Brazil were given incompatible missions. They were supposed to be fonts of indigenous technology, taking on technological challenges that no private entrepreneur could sensibly take on, pushing the envelope of local technological possibilities outward at every opportunity. Yet both companies were also supposed to compete as "normal" firms. The two roles undermined each other. The focus on technological autonomy made it hard to exploit the growth of the market in a competitive way. Producing commodity hardware distracted from their potential technological contribution and created an antagonistic relationship with local firms.

The state was more effective when it complemented local firms than when it tried to replace them. The division of labor in which organizations like India's C-DOT or Korea's ETRI took central responsibility for technological entrepreneurship but disavowed productive-commercial ambitions worked better. This combination freed technological efforts from the distractions of making a profit in routine commodity markets, yet at the same time helped connect technological entrepreneurship to the needs of local firms and markets, inhibiting pursuit of the "state of the art" for its own sake.

Focusing on technological entrepreneurship and leaving production and commercialization to local entrepreneurs is not the only kind of complementarity. CMC and ECIL proved quite successful in the development of large customized systems designed to speak to the complex idiosyncrasies of local problems. Given the potential social returns from such systems, the possible gains from this kind of complementarity are great. Unfortunately, disillusionment with the demiurge makes exploration of more creative uses of state enterprises unlikely.

In all three countries, the core of creating a new sector was convincing local entrepreneurs to enter. Hirschman's basic insight that inducing decision making is the key to industrial transformation in the Third World is well supported in the IT industry. Positive impact on the sector came largely through playing midwife, convincing local entrepreneurs that it was a sector in which they could and should become involved. All three states played the role, but they had different entrepreneurial endowments to work with, in part because of their own past efforts.

In Korea, playing the midwife in informatics was easy because the role had been played so well in a more generic way before information technology became an issue. With large, powerful firms well positioned to move into the industry, a temporary greenhouse, combined with sectorally specific financial incentives and use of government procurement, quickly provided the sector with a strong set of local participants. The relative ease with which local firms became entrenched made it easier for the state to avoid getting bogged down in policing.

The failure of prior midwifery to build a foundation in consumer electronics put Brazil at a disadvantage. A preexisting set of powerful firms with transferable industrial experience was missing. To make matters worse, the domestic market was more or less monopolized by IBM's wholly owned subsidiary (with some help from Burroughs). Still, the success of midwifery in Brazil was striking, relative to its starting point. A dramatically initiated set of greenhouse rules in the form of the 1977 "market reserve" got the ball rolling. The 1984 "supermini licensing" complemented earlier efforts and drew some of Brazil's largest capital groups firmly into the sector.

In India, the role of midwife was accepted grudgingly at first, but the greenhouse still provided space, and local firms emerged to fill it. The state's adamant commitment to restricting the TNCs' domestic operations, best symbolized by the standoff that led to IBM's withdrawal in 1978, provided local firms with sheltered space in which to start growing. There was also positive spillover from the state's own productive efforts in the form of engineers with experience in production and design.

Midwifery was at the core of fostering transformation in all three countries, but it was not enough. Even after large capital had been drawn into the sector, there were still strong pressures for local firms to settle into routine low-return activities or retreat in the direction of a purely commercial role. Continued development of local IT capacity required husbandry. Korea was able to move most easily into this role, prodding firms to explore niches that were more challenging but potentially more rewarding, lowering the risks of indigenous technological development, and generally promoting the exploration of higher-return avenues of growth.

High-tech husbandry involves a variety of techniques. Specific nudges to try more advanced and difficult products, as exemplified by the Korean state's support of new chip designs, indigenous digital switching systems, and advanced minicomputers, complement general support for research and development and investment in human capital. More important than the specific products that result from these efforts is inculcating a general sense that investing in technological capacity and taking technological risks hold the promise of rewards, both in the form of state favor and in terms of market advantage. Soaring investments by Korean firms in research and development facilities showed the extent to which this aim was accomplished.

Investment in high-technology infrastructure complemented both general support for knowledge creation and specific support for new products. High-technology infrastructure like telecommunications networks offered powerful possibilities for using state procurement to stimulate local production of high-technology goods. Since IT producers and the state itself were among the most important users of such infrastructure, there was also strong potential for synergy through user-producer linkages.

By the end of the 1980s there was considerable consensus that midwifery and husbandry were the best ways to foster local IT capacity. India had retreated from its reliance on the demiurge and given up its highly restrictive custodial role. Brazil had eschewed its custodial preoccupation with controlling technological links to TNCs. Policing was on the wane. Promotion was the primary focus in all three countries. Nevertheless, the residue of past roles was a heavy heritage in both Brazil and India.

The costs of past choices did not disappear when the state adopted new roles. In India state-owned firms remained the most visible symbols of state involvement in the sector. In Brazil, intense struggles over regulating the inflows of foreign technology bequeathed a political culture in which state involvement was equated with policing. Existing state organizations from SEI (now reduced to a department) to COBRA were demoralized and on the defensive. Husbandry might be the obvious next phase in a promotional strategy, but the political and institutional resources that had been absorbed by old strategies could not be recuperated quickly or easily.

Overcoming the negative legacy of past policies required more than learning on the part of the agencies involved in informatics. Regardless of what they might have learned, informatics agencies were still operating in the context of larger state structures that not only retained their old flaws but were besieged in new ways. At the beginning of the 1990s, the Brazilian state, staggering under the accumulated consequences of macroeconomic mismanagement, was incapable of major positive initiatives. The Indian state was less obviously crippled, but still facing growing fiscal pressure and a growing threat of political instability. None of this, however, erased the record of what had been accomplished over the previous two decades. In Brazil and India, as in Korea, new local industries had been created and were still there.

The Rise and Internationalization of Local Industries

Viewed one step at a time, the twenty-year entrepreneurial history of informatics in Brazil, India, and Korea flows easily and plausibly. Reflecting on the beginnings and ends of these trajectories makes them more surprising, especially in Brazil and India. Was the locally owned, multibillion-dollar hardware industry that existed in Brazil in the mid- to late 1980s an outcome that would have been predicted in 1977? Hardly. India's growing participation in international software markets would have seemed equally implausible. To get a similar sense of disjuncture in Korea would mean going back a decade earlier, when the chaebol were still fledglings, good at wigs, wallets, and construction but hardly high-tech threats. Even so, a prediction that Samsung would be third in the world in memory chips by 1992 would certainly have been scoffed at fifteen years earlier. The aspirations of the Bhabha Committee, Brazil's barbudinhos, and the Blue House group in Korea turned out to be more than nationalist delusions.

The case of England, which opened chapter 5, is a reminder of how surprising these industrial trajectories are. The English computer industry at the end of the 1980s would have to envy Korea's. As an advanced industrial country with a per capita income of $15,000 a year, England was, of course, still a much more sophisticated and intensive user of information technology. Yet with Fujitsu's purchase of ICL leaving no major independent hardware manufacturers afloat, England's entrepreneurial participation in the production of informatics hardware was in some ways more comparable to that of Brazil and India. When three countries that had virtually no locally controlled information technology producers at the beginning of the 1970s can boast a brand new set of local producers while a world leader in computer sciences at the close of World War II was dependent on firms headquartered in other countries, it is hard to deny that a country can change its position in the international division of labor.

Efforts to change local industrial profiles had effects, even when the forms of state involvement were only partial approximations of optimal strategies. Information technology sectors emerged not only in Korea, where roles and structures "fit," but also in India and Brazil, where initial entrepreneurial endowments were less promising, state structures less well articulated, and the choice of roles less apt. To be sure, the Korean state's greater structural capacity and more appropriate strategies were reflected in a more extensive, competitive, and promising industry. Nonetheless, the core elements of midwifery that were present in India and Brazil sufficed to get local industries off the ground.

The emergence of these industries is also an affront to traditional renditions of comparative advantage. What was most surprising was that low-end production did not really turn out to be the principal strength of any of the three countries. Korea was good at clones, good enough to be internationally competitive, but it was better at semiconductor fabrication where production engineering, not low-cost assembly workers, was the key to survival. Brazil and India, where wages were lower, found themselves at an unmistakable comparative *dis*advantage in low-end, labor-intensive activities like clone assembly.

India illustrates the point most starkly. With a national income of less than $300 per capita, India's comparative advantage should have been in the most labor-intensive production of the simplest products. It was not. Not only were routine assembly operations internationally uncompetitive; they typically generated "negative value-added." Whatever comparative advantage might have been conferred by low wages was more than wiped out by the lack of appropriate organizational forms, managerial expertise, supplier networks, and infrastructure.

India's comparative advantage turned out to be in highly skilled intellectual labor, as exemplified by the software engineer, not in routine manual labor as exemplified by the assembly line operator. Some firms managed to create internationally competitive software. Others came up with a variety of innovative hardware designs, which, if they had been coupled with commensurate low-cost manufacturing capacity and commercial networks, might have been internationally competitive as well.

Brazil confirms the Indian results. Where Brazil came closest to being internationally competitive was not in the assembly of commodity goods but in design-intensive products like financial automation systems. Tight linkages between the big banks who were the principal users of financial automation and the new companies that produced information processing equipment combined with relatively abundant high-quality, low-cost engineering talent to enable Brazil to produce systems that were competitive despite being built from excessively expensive hardware components. In this subsector at least, the barbudinhos' dream that Brazil could generate jobs for design engineers was not as fanciful as traditional economic analysis would have predicted.

Korea reinforces the point. Memory chips and PC clones are mass produced commodities, not design-intensive, customized products. Yet what Amsden (1989) says of Korea's strategy more generally is also true in informatics: production engineering, not cheap labor, is the real root of success. This is especially obvious in the case of semiconductors. Wafer fabrication is one of the most quality-sensitive, capital-intensive production processes in the information technology industry. The engineers may be production engineers rather than design engineers, but the quality of human capital, not low wages, is still the key ingredient.

The three countries together suggest a vision of comparative advantage that leads away from conventional wisdom. Entry into new sectors, not just in advanced industrial countries but in the NICs as well, seems to depend on investing in human capital and enhancing local technological capacities, rather than on containment of routine manufacturing wages. Despite the fact that NIC technological efforts consist almost entirely of imitation, reverse engineering, adaptation, and incremental advances on existing designs, the prescription for success in high-technology industry remains remarkably similar to the one usually associated with advanced industrial countries.

The importance of human capital and general support for research and development does not contradict the Brazilian barbudinhos' original insight that skills without jobs produce frustration rather than development. The secret of Korea's success lay in the fact that investment in human capital went hand in hand with the growth of entrepreneurial organizations that could put technological skills to productive use. Support for technical education and research is necessary but not sufficient. Unless entrepreneurial behavior is affected at the same time, such efforts are ineffectual. Without a connection between educational effort and industrial growth, NICs can end up using scarce state resources to provide "foreign aid" to the United States in the form of highly educated emigrants, as India has been doing for years.

In sum, the emergence of NIC information technology production over the course of the 1970s and 1980s, the form that production took, and the capacities that lay behind it all vindicated the idea that explicit efforts to change a country's position in the international division of labor can bear fruit. These narratives suggest that the hopes of nationalist technocrats may sometimes be more useful than the expectations generated by traditional theories of comparative advantage. This is not to say, however, that the information technology industries of Brazil, India, and Korea fulfilled nationalist dreams.

Nationalist canons were contradicted along with conventional theories. Nationalists, at least in Brazil and India, had assumed that establishing local firms and local productive capacity was the hard part. They bet that local entrepreneurs, once established, would be able to wean themselves from reliance on foreign technology, gradually diminishing the extent of TNC domination over local markets. What actually happened was almost the reverse. With the growth of local companies came more, not less, involvement with international markets, global technology, and transnational capital.

As the 1990s began, alliances between transnational capital and local firms were burgeoning in all three countries. From India, which had dreamed of autarky, through Brazil, where "technological autonomy" was the early rallying cry, to Korea, which had assumed the necessity of strategic alliances from the beginning, NIC informatics industries converged around a new internationalization.

The new internationalization was not based on wholly owned TNCs subsidiaries, as the old internationalization of the early 1960s had been. It was built instead around alliances between local capital and TNCs. Where local entrepreneurs had been fixed on domestic customers, it shifted their focus more to global markets.

The new internationalization was a result of both global changes and local political dynamics. Globally, all firms large and small began to depend more on strategic alliances and "network transactions" rather than relying on their customers' exclusive dependence on particular proprietary computer architectures. As the search for allies intensified, it spread from the advanced industrial countries to the NICs. Even TNCs like IBM and DEC, which had always relied on wholly owned affiliates selling proprietary technology, decided that they could not survive without participating in a variety of strategic alliances. An alliance-based strategy opened up possibilities for NIC entrepreneurs that had not existed in an earlier world where maximizing control over proprietary assets was the central strategic principle.

Ironically, the nationalist politics that enabled the creation of local greenhouses also contributed to the new internationalization. When TNCs went looking for allies at the end of the 1980s, they found local counterparts with something to offer. Local informatics enterprises were seasoned organizations with intimate knowledge of local markets and hands-on experience in producing new technological solutions. Local managers and technicians had decades of experience. Midwifery had helped build the foundations for the new internationalization.

Nationalist policies not only helped create local partners; they also endowed those local partners with their most important source of bargaining leverage. Even in their waning years, greenhouse politics provided local industrialists with their single most crucial bargaining advantage. Whether it was Itautec negotiating with IBM for rights to the AS-400, HCL defining its joint venture with Hewlett-Packard, or Goldstar looking for DRAM technology from AT&T, alliance formation took place against a historical backdrop in which connections with local capital were an important asset for a TNC interested in securing full citizenship in NIC markets. In the end, greenhouses turned out to be an indirect strategy for internationalization, not a means of escaping it.

Internationalization was not necessarily the negation of nationalist aspirations that it appeared to be. Local firms in all three countries showed that the relation between international ties and developing indigenous technological capacity could be synergistic. Exploiting international ties for nationalist ends had been at the core of Korea's strategy from the beginning. It was also crucial to the strategies of the most successful firms in India, like HCL and WIPRO, and of the rising stars in Brazil, like PROCOMP and Sistema. Nevertheless, the new internationalization also carried seeds of the negative features of the old internationalization. The devolution of alliances to subsidiaries, the relegation of local operations to commercial outlets rather than industrial operations, and the concentration of exports on low-return, routinized commodities were all real possibilities.

Openness did not in itself ensure the positive evolution of local IT capacities. Analysis of NIC attempts to develop IT exports, which epitomize the struggle to seize a more advantageous position in the international division of labor, argued for the importance of continuing state support for efforts to challenge the apparent logic of international markets.

The specter of getting trapped in the high-tech equivalent of trading "cheap cotton for expensive cloth" remained real, not only for the Indian software industry but for Korean manufacturers as well. Even the most powerful chaebol face difficult choices between struggling in price-competitive markets for standardized commodities and attempting more technologically challenging products where returns are potentially higher but risks greater. While analysts of Korean informatics may inveigh against low value-added strategies, the chaebol themselves show little affinity for moving beyond "me too" products. Whether the new internationalization brings with it a better position within the international division of labor is likely to depend on the quality of future state involvement.

Aggressive state involvement helped reveal possibilities in "design-intensive" production, especially in India and Brazil. Exploiting this kind of comparative advantage in the future is likely to require further sophisticated intervention, primarily in the form of "high-tech husbandry." Being able to move into attractive niches in an industry that moves as fast as the IT sector requires continuing technological efforts that strain the capacities of any individual firm, especially one located at a distance from the leading edge of the market. Supportive state institutions are no guarantee of success, but they are one way of shifting the balance. Indeed, given the ubiquity of state involvement in information technology in advanced industrial countries, it would be perplexing if such involvement had already become anachronistic in NICs.

Future forms of industrial organization are also likely to depend on state involvement. Absent the leverage provided by nationalist policies, the deals cut by individual local firms will be different. HCL, Itautec, and other greenhouse products are likely to be pushed by allies and economics in the direction of becoming commercial rather than industrial actors.

Despite arguments in favor of continued state involvement, nothing about the politics of state-industry relations predicted that what was "necessary" was likely to happen "naturally." To the contrary, promoting industrial transformation and maintaining a political constituency seemed increasingly contradictory projects. Nationalist policies created foundations for the new internationalization, but once alliances had been negotiated, interests changed. Firms had, in effect, traded the rents associated with state protection of the local market for those associated with their TNC allies' proprietary technology and global market power. State support became less central to corporate strategies while freedom to take advantage of global ties became more crucial. Local entrepreneurial groups no longer constituted a dependable political constituency for state efforts to enhance technological capacity at the local level. Instead they became potential recruits to the campaign to make the establishment of "openness" the overriding aim of state involvement.

What all of this suggested was that state involvement would be difficult to sustain, despite its potential importance to the future development of local industries. Policies favoring devolution in the direction of the old internationalization might not be developmentally advantageous, but they made sense politically.

In Brazil, this result seemed already confirmed as the 1980s closed. The negative political heritage generated by custodial conflicts played neatly into the general romance with neoliberal policies, lending apparently irresistible political momentum to the proposition that unmodified "openness" was the best policy for informatics. With the industry's leading entrepreneurial groups looking to international allies as their key to the future, there was no politically effective group in civil society committed to supporting a strategy of husbandry. The institutional exhaustion of the state made the possibility that future barbudinhos might somehow reconstruct a new political constituency from inside the state remote at best.

In India there was more ambiguity, but the dynamics looked similar. State involvement was equated historically with the custodian-demiurge combination. The shift to a more promotional policy was followed in rapid succession by an emphasis on openness. There was still support for husbandry insofar as it could be connected to the drive to increase software exports, but no effective political constituency for a more general policy of husbandry.

Korea was obviously in the best shape. To be sure, the symbiosis between state institutions and the firms they had helped create was threatened by the same forces that had undercut possibilities for future state action in Brazil and India. The major chaebol were increasingly convinced that they could handle the problems that might be addressed by state institutions by themselves while the problems that were likely to overwhelm them required international rather than local allies. Nonetheless, focusing the capacity of a coherent state apparatus on a mid-wifery-husbandry sequence had created a robust inheritance, both in state institutions and in the industry itself. Even if the Korean information technology sector proved unable to sustain its past momentum in the direction of more technologically complex products, the foundations that have been laid would not disappear quickly. The positive legacies of the past continued to compensate for current political contradictions, negating at the same time the neo-utilitarian model's dire predictions that state involvement would bring uniformly negative consequences.

Informatics and the Neo-Utilitarian Vision of the State

Discontent with neo-utilitarian visions of state-society relations provided the initial impetus for looking more closely at states and industrial transformation. Having completed a closer look, it makes sense to ask how neo-utilitarian expectations fit what actually happened in the informatics sectors of Brazil, India, and Korea. In general, they do not. Neo-utilitarian assumptions make it harder, not easier, to see what is going on. Despite its looser, more eclectic conceptual frame, a comparative institutional perspective provides a better basis for interpreting IT trajectories.

Conventional neo-utilitarian analyses tend to assume that they have unlocked the secret of the relation between state policy and industrial development by uncovering the state's ability to generate rents and the private sector's predilection to seek them. They equate state involvement with the construction of opportunities for self-aggrandizing, antidevelopmental "deals" between state officials and private clients. The more state involvement, the more lucrative the "rental havens" and the less likely that anyone will expend energy on entrepreneurial efforts to create new productive capacity.

If neo-utilitarian visions of the nature of the state apparatus were correct, then the officials in the agencies dealing with informatics, especially in Brazil and India, should have been exceptionally corrupt. They were dispensing access to a rapidly growing, highly protected industry, a desirable rental haven. They had extensive power over private "clients" who in turn had the ability to offer substantial rewards in return for regulatory favors.

In fact, the organizations that had prime responsibility for the regulation and promotion of information technology conformed to a surprising degree to Weberian norms. Despite the fact that their rules and decisions conferred crucial rents on local entrepreneurs, none had reputations as bastions of clientelism or hives of individual profiteering. To the contrary, they were acknowledged as remarkably free from corruption, relative to other parts of the state apparatus. The relative lack of corruption in agencies like Brazil's SEI or India's DOE does not make sense in neo-utilitarian terms. It supports instead the notion that predatory behavior depends less on the degree of intervention and more on the absence of bureaucratic cohesion. Looking at these organizations even suggests that a positive project of explicit involvement can create a sense of élan or mission that increases bureaucratic cohesion and reduces corruption.

Not only were state technocrats less corrupt than neo-utilitarians would predict, they were also more flexible, willing to abandon policies they themselves had formulated when these policies became outmoded. The standard neo-utilitarian assumption that bureaucrats develop a vested interest in particular forms of intervention, which turns them into resolute opponents of policy change, did not fit the evidence. State agencies sometimes defended policies that had outlived their usefulness, but they also initiated changes that reduced their own power. The best example is India's DOE, which broke out of the traditional custodial mold, embracing a promotional role that diminished its own ostensible power and made it more accountable to the firms it had formerly controlled.

The neo-utilitarian perspective's obsession with the dangers of state power distracts attention from the possible benefits of having a cohesive, coherent state apparatus. The costs of fragmentation and problems of insufficient capacity are pushed out of consideration by the assumption that the less states are able to act the better. The advantages of increased state capacity and the possibility of state entrepreneurship remain unexplored.

"Entrepreneurial bureaucrat" did not turn out to be an oxymoron. The entrepreneurial vision of state agencies implicit in the Gerschenkron/Hirschman version of the comparative institutional perspective fit information technology agencies. Following a set of general policy rules was not enough to induce growth in a new sector. Initiative and imagination were required as well. In all three countries, initiation of informatics policies depended on small groups of individuals using the state apparatus as a locus of leverage. India's BARC group, Brazil's barbudinhos, and Korea's Blue House group had much in common. These strategically located groups formulated ideas about the possible futures of the sector and convinced the rest of the state apparatus to try them out.

Entrepreneurship did not necessarily, or even primarily, mean engaging directly in production. Entrepreneurial initiatives could be found everywhere, from regulatory agencies like Brazil's CAPRE to infrastructure providers like Korea's Ministry of Communications. If anything, engaging directly in production, or at least trying to produce commodities in competition with the private sector, worked against the state's ability to deliver technological entrepreneurship. Neither COBRA nor ECIL succeeded in combining efforts at technological innovation with profitable commodity production. Korea's Ministry of Communications, on the other hand, was one of the most entrepreneurial of any of the organizations, private or public, involved in the informatics industry in any of the three countries, successfully engineering both a multiplication of the country's telecommunications infrastructure and the development of indigenously designed equipment.

Entrepreneurial behavior within the state apparatus was important but not enough. Small numbers of individuals were surprisingly effective at pushing new initiatives, but realizing the full potential of these policies depended on relations with the rest of the state apparatus. When the state apparatus as a whole was more fragmented than coherent, as in Brazil, it was hard to put entrepreneurial initiative together with the bureaucratic momentum necessary to sustain new policies.

The "guerrilla" character of Brazil's original CAPRE group was fundamental both to the visionary character of its early initiatives and to its subsequent problems. CAPRE's early success at creating an industrial policy for informatics is the best example of how, given the right conjuncture of circumstances, a relatively small and formally powerless group of individuals can make a large difference in the direction of state policy. The subsequent history of CAPRE and its successor SEI is the best example of how hard it is to sustain policies that are not backed by a clear consensus of the relevant parts of the bureaucratic apparatus. Internecine struggle within the state apparatus undermined Brazil's capacity to adapt its informatics policy as the global face of the IT industry changed. Persistent warfare between SEI and the Ministry of Communications crippled the possibility of a unified policy toward information technology. The eventual isolation of SEI from the rest of the economic policy-making apparatus made things worse.

Again, Korea provides a useful contrast, illustrating the advantage of coherence and cohesion. Korea's information technology bureaucrats were well integrated into a larger bureaucratic structure. While this structure was hardly conflict-free, the policies that promoted the IT sector were consistent with an overall framework, not anomalies.

Just as it distracts attention from problems of fragmentation, the neo-utilitarian perspective put the analysis of capacity on the wrong track. It focuses on the problem of excess capacity, whereas the problem in informatics was the reverse. The bureaucratic capacity of information technology agencies was never sufficient to carry out the tasks demanded of them. The problem was particularly obvious in Brazil. As the custodial role with its excessive demands was jettisoned, resources were withdraw from the organizations in charge of informatics, making it impossible for them to take up the role of husbandry. Enjoying greater capacity to begin with, Korean technocrats in charge of informatics compounded their advantage by pursuing a less burdensome blend of roles. Relative to their counterparts in Brazil and India, they enjoyed a balance of demand and capacity heavily weighted in their favor. The result was more effective promotion, not the greater rent seeking and inferior performance that a neo-utilitarian vision would predict.

On almost all counts, the neo-utilitarian vision fails to facilitate an understanding of what happened in the information technology sector. The state's role in information technology cannot be recounted without discussing state entrepreneurship, problems of fragmentation, and the disadvantages of insufficient capacity. Yet these are all issues that a neo-utilitarian perspective obscures. The weakness of the neo-utilitarian account when it comes to accounting for relations between bureaucrats and their private "clients" is even more surprising.

Actual relations between private capital and the state in the IT sector, like the internal character of state agencies, stand in sharp contrast to neo-utilitarian expectations. The neo-utilitarian fixation on rents misses the point because it assumes that rent seeking inherently entails stagnation, that all rental havens have the same developmental impact, that rents and transformation cannot coexist. A Schumpeterian perspective is a more appropriate starting point. All rental havens are not equal. They arise for different reasons and have different effects.

Did state policies generate rents in the information technology sector? Of course. Did private entrepreneurs take advantage of the rents that the state created? Of course. Does this suffice to convey what went on in information technology in the NICs during the 1970s and 1980s? Not at all. Some rental havens were associated with stagnation, others with transformation. Some were generated by nationalist efforts to implant local industries, others were generated by the absence of such efforts.

Before the barbudinhos, the traditional law of similars ensured IBM a very comfortable set of monopoly rents. Brazil's protection of the rents of the original set of local minicomputer producers slowed the introduction of new technology, but it also created long-term investment in human capital. The preservation of ECIL's monopoly position in the late 1970s hampered the introduction of microprocessor-based machines, but the protection of India's fledgling local entrepreneurs against imported computers helped generate an industry that was technologically dynamic. Korea assured the chaebol of an initial set of rents if they went into PCs, and a dynamic center of clone production was born. Analyzing the creation of rental havens makes sense if it is connected to the dynamics of industrial transformation. Otherwise it is sterile.

Political dynamics escape a simple rent-seeking model as surely as economic ones. Seen through the neo-utilitarian lens, relations between rent-generators inside the state and rent-seekers outside it take the form of a static symbiosis. The state creates rental havens that speak to the interests of politically powerful private clients; clients benefit economically from state action and respond with political support. Static symbiosis is the natural political result of state involvement.

The histories of these three informatics sectors reveal a political dynamic that is anything but a static symbiosis. Local entrepreneurial groups were at first indifferent bystanders, then tempted entrants, then supportive but difficult clients, and eventually ex-clients with other, more attractive options. As the process of industrial transformation unfolded, the power and interests of private entrepreneurial groups changed. Their relations with the state shifted accordingly. The state's success in fostering industrial change undermined the political constituency that its earlier efforts had fostered.

Informatics policies did not start out as an attempt to reward political clients by speaking to preexisting interests. They started out trying to create interests, trying to bring forth a group of entrepreneurs who would identify their interests with the growth of the sector. Entrepreneurial engagement with informational technology did not spring automatically to life. Interests, like decision making in Hirschman's schema, had to be induced. The whole idea of midwifery is that creating a new sector means creating a social group who come to identify their future with the future of the sector. The neo-utilitarian perspective is correct in suggesting that this means creating a political constituency as well as an economic group. Where it misleads is in suggesting that the constituency's identification with state policies and agencies is stable and self-reinforcing.

Once informatics policies had succeeded in creating a set of local industrialists whose assets and interests were committed to producing information technology goods, political support was indeed the result, as neo-utilitarian models would predict. This was most obvious in Brazil, where informatics was a salient public issue. Also obvious, however, was the ambivalent character of this support. The interests of individual economic beneficiaries coincided only partially with the goals of the policy. At the same time, policies designed to promote local informatics producers stimulated the growth of a variety of other interests, most obviously users and international producers excluded from what had been turned into an interesting market. Generating rents created contestation, not stable symbiosis.

With internationalization, political dynamics departed even further from neo-utilitarian projections of stable symbiosis. Former clients formed alliances with the very TNCs that had been the initial targets of state-initiated restrictions. In doing so, they opened up the possibility of new kinds of rents, derived from TNC proprietary rights rather than state regulation. Neo-utilitarian logic was turned on its head. Instead of clientelistic relations between the state and private capitalists impeding economic progress by generating state involvement, the erosion of political symbiosis between the state and the local industry seemed likely to derail further industrial transformation by impeding state involvement.

Unfortunately, while a comparative institutional approach may have facilitated uncovering these contradictory political dynamics, they were certainly not predicted in my initial discussion of state-society relations. My version of the comparative institutional approach offered some ideas about how states might affect industrial transformation but had relatively little to say about how this transformation would change the basis of subsequent state involvement.

In sum, while the evolution of political dynamics from nationalist greenhouses through internationalization thoroughly contradicts neo-utilitarian expectations of a self-reinforcing cycle of rent seeking and rent creation, it also reveals a serious lacuna in my own version of the comparative institutional framework. The initial account served nicely as a lens to focus attention on variations in state involvement and their consequences, but it did not do justice to the political dynamics of state-industry relations. Given this failure, reconsideration of the same dynamics at the societal level is certainly in order.

Sectoral Results and Societal Implications

The purpose of delving into the information technology sector was to see whether my general ideas about how states were connected to transformation would be echoed in concrete relations between specific state agencies and individual firms. The general proposition was that a coherent, cohesive state apparatus with close, institutionalized links to an economic elite would be more effective at producing industrial transformation than were other kinds of state-society relations.

The results were reassuring. Informatics showed that patterns at the societal level translated into specific roles and ties at the sectoral level. These in turn associated with corresponding variations in the dynamism, competitiveness and robustness of local information technology industries. Sectoral specifics vindicated the general framework.

At the same time, sectoral specifics brought to light an issue that was not highlighted in the initial general vision of states and industrial transformation. Looking back over the evolution of these three informatics sectors, it is clear that the growth of the sector shaped state roles and strategies just as surely as state roles and strategies shaped the sector. Sometimes the two mutually reinforced each other, but the reverse also occurred. Groups brought to life in part by state policies developed interests that undercut the very policies and agencies that helped create the conditions for their emergence.

If successful state involvement in the information technology sector helps generate new entrepreneurial structures that makes future state involvement more difficult, what are the implications for state-society relations more generally? Is there a more general contradictory dynamic that undermines political support for states that successfully promote transformation?

Looking back, the interplay in information technology does seem to parallel patterns of state-society relations in other contexts. It echoes, for example, the changing relations between Nasser and the middle peasants during the process of land reform that were taken as paradigmatic in my initial discussion of state-society relations.[2]

The sectoral results demand further exploration of the idea that transformative states help create actors who then recreate the conditions under which future state involvement takes place. If successful state action at the sectoral level produces new agents and conditions that make it hard to sustain involvement, then why shouldn't the same be true for industrial transformation overall? The idea is particularly relevant to developmental states. Maybe the internal structures and state-society relations that characterize developmental states are less robust than they seem. In short, looking closely at the information technology sector forces a rethinking of embedded autonomy.

10

Rethinking Embedded Autonomy

As THE 1980s drew to a close, Seoul's ultramodern subway system was one of Korea's most prized pieces of new infrastructure, symbolic of the developmental state's efficacy. In March 1989 the Seoul subway briefly became a different kind of symbol, a dramatic reminder that, along with infrastructure and new industrial prowess, the state had helped bring to life social forces that it could not always control.[1]

On March 16, six thousand subway workers went on strike, paralyzing Seoul's new transportation system and turning the city's morning rush hour into chaos. Three thousand workers occupied the round house from which subway locomotives were dispatched. The workers were demanding that the Seoul Subway-system Public Corporation live up to an agreement the company had made with them earlier to restructure the organization, modify methods of payment and get rid of the company president. It was a strike over control and power, not economic survival.[2]

The government of former General Roh Tae Woo responded with the full repressive power of the state. Over 6,000 police swarmed over the locomotive roundhouse and took more than 2,300 of the occupying workers off to the police station. Within a few days the strike was crushed and the subway system resumed the impressive efficiency of its normal operations, but crushing the strike could not erase the social and political changes that lay behind it.

Defeating individual strikes was well within the state's capacity, but neither the repressive power of the state nor the cooptive abilities of the government-sponsored Federation of Korean Trade Unions (FKTU) seemed capable of stopping the growth of insurgency among Korea's workers in the late 1980s. Insurgency mushroomed as impressively as the country's industrial output. According to the International Labor Organization, workdays lost to strikes in the last three years of the decade totaled more than eighteen million, almost a two-hundred-fold increase relative to the first three years of the decade (E. M. Kim 1992, 14, table 4).

By the end of the 1980s, Korea's workers looked more militant than their supposedly more politically powerful Latin American counterparts (cf. Deyo 1989). Their militancy helped reshape the process of industrial transformation. Strikes like the bitter dispute that shut down Motorola

Korea Ltd.[3] helped push export strategies away from the old focus on low-wage, low value-added components. The new militancy was also a challenge to the developmental state. It challenged political legitimacy along with economic strategy.

At first glance, rising labor militancy and the shifting strategies of Korean IT firms discussed in the last two chapters may seem unconnected. In fact, they are arguably part of the same general phenomenon. In both cases, state policies helped effect industrial transformation that brought new actors onto the social stage. Once there, these actors developed their own agendas, reshaping the process of industrial transformation and challenging the state itself. Having delved at length into the dynamics of a single sector, it is time to look at the logic of change on the societal level.

This chapter will begin by speculating on the future prospects of the developmental state, arguing that its transformative success threatens the stability of the state-society coalition that made success possible to begin with. Re-examining the developmental state means rethinking embedded autonomy. In developmental states, connectedness has meant ties with industrial elites. Can embedded autonomy also be built around ties to other groups? Are alternative constructions more or less politically stable than the original version? What sort of joint projects fit with different kinds of state-society links? The next section explores these questions, using the improbable combination of Kerala and Austria to illustrate alternative forms of embedded autonomy. The basic argument in this section is that expanding the scope of state-society links to include a broader range of groups and classes, however difficult that might be to accomplish, should result in a more politically robust and adaptive version of embedded autonomy.

Having made this argument, I will consider the implications of the analysis for intermediate states like Brazil and India which, after all, constitute the bulk of Third World states. Finally, I will close the chapter with a brief reprise highlighting the overall contributions of this study to the analysis of states and industrial transformation.

The Future of the Developmental State

State and society are not just linked together: each helps constitute the other. Sometimes they reinforce each other. Mutual reinforcement, it was argued in chapter 3, lies at the core of the developmental state's success. A robust and coherent state apparatus facilitates the organization of industrial capital; an organized class of industrialists facilitates a joint project of industrialization, which in turn legitimates both the state and industrialists.

Mutual reinforcement is not the only possibility. State strategies can also create social groups whose agendas conflict with the state's original project. The relation between labor militancy and the developmental state in Korea is one good example of such a process, but it is not the only one. Seidman (1994), for example, argues for a very similar process in both South Africa and Brazil. State-led efforts to "deepen" industrial development helped produce factories that "manufactured militance" along with their other products.[4]

Viewed this way, the Korean state's role in producing militant workers brings to mind Marx's vision of the bourgeoisie as "calling forth its own gravedigger" in the form of the proletariat. In Marx's view, the bourgeoisie needed an industrial working class to accomplish its project of accumulation. It therefore had no choice but to produce a group whose interests and agenda conflicted with its own. The same could be argued in the case of the developmental state and the social constituencies that it helps bring into being.

Successful transformation, not failure, is what produces gravediggers. Korea, as a successful developmental state, is more susceptible to the gravedigger problem than Zaire as a stagnant predator. The subway workers are products of the state's successful efforts to create new infrastructure, but industrial growth has produced other gravediggers as well. Marx assumed that gravediggers and their creators came only in dyadic pairs, but the challenges to the developmental state are multiple. They include not only workers, who might be considered an inadvertent product of the state's transformative project, but also industrial capital, whose strengthening was one of the state's central aims.

Korea's 1992 presidential campaign offered a perfect symbolic representation of this other challenge. Among the most outspoken of the opposition candidates for president was Chung Ju Yung, the founder of Hyundai, one of Korea's largest chaebol. The growth of Hyundai was no less clearly an example of the transformative success of the developmental state than was the Seoul subway system. Yet Chung Ju Yung did not consider himself a "creature of the state" any more than the leader of the Seoul subway workers' union did. To the contrary, he styled himself explicitly as a gravedigger, running on the slogan "Get government out of business."

A third sort of challenge came from within the state apparatus itself. At the end of the 1980s some of the strongest pressure for diminishing the state's interventive role came from precisely those elite agencies, like the Economic Planning Board, that had been most central to the state's past contribution to industrial transformation. Incumbents in these agencies, often American-trained economists, far from being "statists," tended to embrace neoliberal policy prescriptions, even if they did not necessarily subscribe to neo-utilitarian theories of the state. Kim Jae-Ik, acknowledged prior to his untimely death to be one of Korea's most brilliant economic bureaucrats, was simultaneously a state manager and a tireless crusader for reducing the state's role. He provides a symbolic representative of the internal challenge in the same way that Chung Ju Yung represents the industrialist as challenger.

The existence of challenges does not necessarily mean that the state's institutional character will change. Inertia alone makes rapid change implausible. Change could be limited to adopting new roles without restructuring either the internal organization of the state or the fundamental nature of its relations with society. Nevertheless, if state and society are mutually constitutive, having changed society the developmental state itself must change. The question is what form the state's own transformation will take.

The most fundamental challenges would be those aimed at reducing the state's capacity to behave as a coherent corporate actor. If successful, such challenges would dismantle the developmental state. It might seem that dismantling should be a fate reserved for apparatuses that have failed in their own terms, like the government of the former Soviet Union, but the gravedigger argument suggests that success as well as failure creates pressure for dismantling. It is a prospect that needs to be taken seriously.

Taking dismantling seriously means analyzing the forces and motivations that might drive the process. The connections between social transformation and pressure to dismantle are most obvious at the bottom of society. As long as the bottom consisted primarily of the peasant beneficiaries of land reform, serious political opposition from below was improbable. As the ranks of industrial workers swelled, their level of organization increased as well, despite (or perhaps because of) the repressive political climate in which industrialization took place (cf. Yun and Folk 1990). The eventual result was the politically militant unionism described at the beginning of the chapter—eighteen million workers on strike during the last three years of the 1980s.

From the point of view of industrial labor, which now outnumbers what is left of the peasantry,[5] the drive to dismantle the developmental state makes sense. Workers may benefit from the state's ability to provide predictable rules and collective goods, but for them the most salient form of state action is repression. Its organizational capacity is manifested in the ability to mass six thousand police at a moment's notice. For those who must face six thousand policemen, separating state capacity in general from repressive capacity is an unlikely intellectual exercise. Since exceptional repressive capacity is a cost, not a benefit, challenges from below are likely to take the form of calls to dismantle state capacity.

Not only the state's internal coherence but also its external networks are a disadvantage from the point of view of those at the bottom. These networks are remarkable not only for their density but also for their narrow focus. Capital is connected, labor is excluded. The apparent connections provided by government-sponsored trade union confederations are more means of repressive cooptation than channels for pursuing collective goals.[6] Viewed from the perspective of conflict between labor and capital, embedded autonomy increases the coherence of capital at labor's expense.

In Korea, a combination of repression and rising real wages served to forestall pressure for dismantling.[7] Developmental success diminishes the potency of both. The increasing difficulty of relying on repression has already been discussed. Sustaining the real wage increases that were possible during the transition from peasant agriculture to manufacturing jobs or during the initial movement to more capital- and technology-intensive forms of production is equally difficult. A period of adjustment during which real wages grow more slowly is eventually unavoidable.

There are manifold reasons for predicting that the developmental state will be under increasing pressure from below, but states are rarely dismantled from the bottom. The vulnerability of the developmental state comes not so much from the militancy of the subway workers as from their implicit coalition with Chung Ju Yung and the ghost of Kim Jae-Ik.

The idea that industrialists might end up on the side of dismantling seems at first to contradict the very description of the developmental state. Entrepreneurial groups are thoroughly included in the networks of embedded autonomy. The operation of the developmental state has unquestionably worked to their advantage. Why should they be anything other than dedicated supporters? The evolution of the information technology sector provides the obvious answer. Successful industrial transformation makes industrial capital less dependent on the state and opens up options for alternative alliances.

Accounts of the general trajectory of state-capital relations suggest that the informatics sector is not a special case.[8] Even the World Bank notes (1993, 183) that in the Korea of the late 1980s and early 1990s "relations between government and business have become more distant and the meetings [between them] less frequent." Firms that were dependent on the state to channel foreign loans in their direction in the early 1970s could go after them directly at the end of the 1980s (cf. Woo 1991). The growth of international marketing channels and overseas production facilities made the chaebol less dependent on the domestic market to which the state could control access. At the same time, the domestic market power of large firms expanded tremendously. In the mid-1970s the combined sales of the top ten chaebol amounted to 15 percent of

Korea's GNP; in the mid-1980s they amounted to 67 percent (Amsden 1989, 116).

The degree of autonomy that characterizes developmental states is the product of historical circumstance rather than a social pact between capital and the state. It has already been well argued that the extraordinary weakness of local capital following thirty-five years of colonialism and a devastating civil war was a precondition for the degree of autonomy enjoyed by the developmental state.[9] Barring this kind of weakness, individual industrialists always prefer a state less able to infringe on managerial prerogatives. At the same time, the propensity of entrepreneurs to see economic success as derived from their own virtues makes them less likely to see diminished state capacity as threatening to the process of accumulation.

None of this is to say that capital is unambivalently opposed to the existence of a powerful state apparatus. Even if corporate leaders dismiss the importance of the state in promoting accumulation, they are likely to find value in its ability to promote their interests vis-à-vis other social groups, like labor. The same repressive face that makes the developmental state an anathema to labor makes it useful to capital. Useful, that is, as long as traditional repressive methods work. Once labor gains enough power to make peace depend on more sophisticated forms of industrial relations, the absence of legitimate ties to labor becomes a disadvantage. The developmental state may begin to look more like an albatross than a valued protector of entrepreneurial interests.[10]

What about Kim Jae-Ik? Challenges to the state from within its own ranks make no sense at all from the point of view of neo-utilitarian theory. Self-interested bureaucrats should cling to the preservation of state privilege at any cost. Kim Jae-Ik's behavior is, however, quite consistent with the character of the state technocrats as it was revealed in the IT sector. For state technocrats in the IT sector, pursuing a long-term project was as important as enhancing their power or perquisites. Technocrats who are also economists, especially those trained in the United States, are likely to share their mentors' conviction that minimizing the state's role is the best way to promote development. Reducing the scope of state involvement is a long-term project for them just as initiating local informatics production was for the barbudinhos, the BARC group, or the Blue House group.

None of these challengers to the developmental state is necessarily arguing for dismantling. Internal challengers may well see themselves as promoting strategic reduction of the state's role as the best route to increasing the state's efficacy. Industrialists like Chung Ju Yung may also see their criticisms as aimed at reducing the state's intrusiveness but not necessarily its capacity. Even the subway workers may see themselves as only trying to reduce the state's capacity to repress the interests of the majority of the population. It is the combination of challenges and changing context that produces the possibility of dismantling.

Spreading elite perception that the state is superfluous and increasingly fierce popular rejection of *kwanjon minbi* (the government's primacy over the people) as an odious vestige of colonial ideology combine to undercut one of the most important incentives to choosing a career in the civil service. If the bureaucratic apparatus of the state is not an instrument for the realization of national goals but an impediment to their achievement, then "bureaucrat" becomes synonymous with opprobrium rather than prestige.

Social structural changes reinforce ideological ones. The dynamic growth of private capital has undercut the material incentives for the best and the brightest to choose a career within the state. In September 1989 the *Kookmin Ilbo* noted that "the gap [in salaries] between civil service and private sector has been conspicuously widened." Figures from Korea's Ministry of Government Administration (MGA 1986, 54) confirmed the observation, showing that the salaries of top civil servants were already less than half those of the upper management of big private companies in 1986.

Without prestige and remuneration, job security becomes the principle incentive to undertake a civil service career, not the best incentive for recruiting individuals capable of formulating and implementing a collective project of transformation. In this scenario, the bureaucratic apparatus of the developmental state is transformed into an "American-style" civil service. Instead of a coherent, attractive career that attracts the "best and the brightest," the bureaucracy becomes either a second best option for the risk-averse or a temporary exercise in diversification for what are really private-sector careers.

Diminished material rewards also increase the possibility of corruption. This at least was the *Kookmin Ilbo*'s conclusion. The paper speculated (September 25, 1989) that as a result of the changing incentive structure, "superior manpower's refusal to join the state bureaucracy would be accelerated" and "worries about corruption and other deviant behavior by civil servants become more realistic."

If the quality of the civil service erodes, the ability of state institutions to perform their current roles must erode with it. Deteriorating performance reinforces perceptions that the state is superfluous and therefore parasitic, further lowering the prestige of the civil service, making it harder to justify investing in bureaucratic salaries, and propelling a vicious circle of dismantling.

From some theoretical perspectives, of course, the circle is not vicious at all. Instead, dismantling is "functional" to future transformation. Just as Marx assumed that the bourgeoisie, having played its role in creating the forces of production, had to be done away with in order for further progress to take place, so critics of the developmental state may assume that, having created the conditions for the emergence of new forces of production, the state must now be dismantled in order for industrial transformation to proceed further.

Looking at the information technology sector was a nice way of exploring this hypothesis. If there were compelling evidence for the obsolescence of state involvement at the sectoral level, information technology was certainly the sector in which it should show up. My conclusion was different. Despite diminished political support, state involvement remained crucial to the continued progress of local industries. This conclusion is consistent with the impressions of those who have focused at a more general level. There is nothing in the analysis by Amsden and Wade and their ilk to suggest that industrial transformation has made state involvement anachronistic—more difficult and politically sensitive perhaps, but still central to the process of seeking a more desirable niche in the global division of labor.

If dismantling is a bad idea, then reconstruction moves to the fore of the theoretical agenda. If society has changed too much for the state to remain the same, are there paths for reconstructing state-society relations that avoid the prospect of dismantling? Reconstruction must involve rethinking embedded autonomy, particularly the nature of the networks that connect state and society.

Variations on Embedded Autonomy

For developmental states, connections with society are connections to industrial capital. Since the growth of industrial production is the overriding goal, this makes sense. Indeed, it was argued in chapter 3 that other kinds of state-society ties, like those to traditional agrarian powerholders in Brazil, undermine the state's capacity for transformation. Connections that privilege industrialists allow the developmental state to focus on a project of industrial transformation, to keep its involvement selective, and to avoid having its bureaucratic capacities overwhelmed in the way that those of intermediate states have been overwhelmed. Be this as it may, the social consequences of industrial transformation have increased the political liabilities associated with this kind of embeddedness. Exclusionary links limit what the developmental state can do and contribute to pressure for dismantling.

The most obvious alternative, and the one that Korea is currently attempting to emulate, is Japan's "Liberal Democratic party (LDP) model."

The aim is to complement the embedded autonomy that connects industry and bureaucracy with a political network, based on a single, broad, conservative party. This strategy reflects the increased power of private industrialists in relation to the state. The political network provides additional channels of elite influence, changing the relative weight of autonomy and embeddedness. It increases connectedness at the expense of insulation. Yet at the same time it provides some possibility of connection for nonelites, especially farmers, and dampens pressures from below for dismantling.

The LDP model gives the political side of the developmental state a softer face, but it is remodeling rather than reconstruction. Since it increases the ability of elite groups to push their bargain with the state in an anti-Schumpeterian direction, it does little to enhance economic dynamism. Since connectedness remains very skewed in favor of elite actors, it offers little in the way of increased external scrutiny to compensate for diminished insulation. Degeneration in the direction of clientelism is a potentially serious problem.

Japan's problems, both political and economic, in the early 1990s have discredited the LDP model (along with the LDP itself) but some would argue that it remains the only real alternative to explicitly exclusionary politics. In a market society, the argument goes, the state can only be linked to capital. Such arguments are plausible. They may well offer a descriptively accurate gloss for most of the comparative evidence. Nonetheless, there are at least a few cases that suggest the generalization is not a law, that embeddedness does not necessary take the form of exclusionary ties to entrepreneurial elites. The best illustration comes from an unlikely quarter—the Indian state of Kerala.[11]

Kerala

Levels of social welfare that belie its economic impoverishment and intense social mobilization are Kerala's two claims to fame. The connection between the two runs directly through a form of embeddedness that is almost the mirror image of the developmental state. Kerala's accomplishments reflect the difference.

Kerala is not a developmental state if development is defined narrowly as economic growth. Its levels of per capita income, which are about a third lower than India's overall average, locate it in the developmental vicinity of Chad or Burundi. Only if the definition of development is weighted very heavily on the side of welfare can Kerala claim success. Infant mortality runs less than half the level of Brazil and a third the levels of the rest of India, almost at the same level as Korea. Life expectancy is likewise closer to Korea than to Brazil or the rest of India. Birthrates are low, literacy is high, especially among women. In short, Kerala's success in welfare terms is no less striking than that of the East Asian NICs in terms of industrial transformation.[12]

In most accounts, Kerala's welfare results are seen simply as a consequence of its historically high levels of mobilization. Franke and Chasin (1989, 63), for example, emphasize that advances in land reform were not produced "simply as a result of enlightened government" but required "the organized and activist strength of large numbers of people with dedicated leaders and a willingness to struggle."

From the Moplah Rebellions of the nineteenth and early twentieth centuries through the bloody Alleppey general strike of 1938, the peasants and workers of Malabar gained a reputation for combativeness (see Herring 1991, chaps. 1–2). Peasants' associations, like the Kerala Karshaka Sangham (KKS), led by Congress party militants turned Communist, channeled the energy of peasant "jacqueries" into an institutionalized movement for structural change. The eventual consequence of institutionalized political mobilization was to transform Kerala's class structure. The land reform of 1969 and other reforms, such as the Kerala Agricultural Workers Act of 1974, decimated the old landlord class, created a new class of peasant proprietors, and gave new rights to landless laborers.

While the centrality of mobilization to Kerala's gains is undeniable, Kerala also demonstrates why mobilization is not sufficient in itself. Without adequate state capacity, neither the changes in Keralan social structure nor the construction of new welfare institutions would have been possible, regardless of the level of protest. Mobilized constituents cannot, by themselves, deliver the reforms and services they have fought for, no matter how militant they might be. They require an administrative apparatus.

Kerala's welfare performance cannot be understood without looking at the institutional and administrative infrastructure that underlies it. Lower infant mortality and longer life expectancy depend on high levels of state expenditure on health care, which is in turn reflected in a much more effective network of local health care facilities than most Third World countries enjoy. Kerala has more health centers per capita than the rest of India and about eight times the hospital beds per capita in its rural areas (Franke and Chasin 1989, 42). Even more important, it has a health delivery system that actually functions, with doctors at their posts serving clients rather than enjoying their professional perquisites elsewhere.[13]

Nutrition, another pillar of improved health, is supported by a network of government-organized ration or fair-price shops.[14] These shops redistribute the rice levy collected from larger farmers and ensure that the poorer segments of the population have access to food grains.[15] In addition, the state provides free hot lunches for primary school children and for mothers and infants at local village nurseries (Franke and Chasin 1989, 29). Obviously, the state is also responsible for providing educational facilities and other infrastructure like roads and post offices, which Kerala has in abundance relative to the rest of India.

Delivery of these services, like the original execution of the land reform, depends on the existence of a competent bureaucratic apparatus. Most Third World countries would find it impossible to administer the range of services provided in Kerala given the strict resource constraints under which the state must operate. One can easily imagine what would happen to a rice levy in Zaire. Even in Mexico, keeping Conasupo, whose functions are similar to those of the fair-price shops, from being itself consumed by the clientelistic tendencies of the Partido Revolucionario Institucional (PRI) regime has been a constant struggle (see Grindle 1977).

Fortunately for Kerala, it was in a position to put the relatively well developed bureaucratic autonomy that characterized the Indian system as a whole together with its own brand of embeddedness to produce a quite different combination. The result was an idiosyncratic version of "embedded autonomy," extremely well suited to accomplishing a transformative project aimed at increased levels of welfare.

Kerala's Communist-led regimes made full use of the competence built into the Indian civil service. When they first gained office in Malabar in the early 1950s, they received several distinctions from Nehru for good administration of local government (Herring 1991, I-15). At the same time, the government's mobilized constituencies, whose relation to the state was institutionalized through the various Communist parties (and eventually their competitors on the left and right who were forced to recognize the advantage of having an organized base), enforced new standards of performance on the state apparatus.

Just as researchers at ETRI are rapidly made aware when their efforts are considered ineffectual by local industry, likewise those who run Kerala's social services are rapidly made aware when their systems are not delivering. According to one researcher (Mencher 1980), "if a PHC [Primary Health Center] was unmanned for a few days, there would be a massive demonstration at the nearest collectorate [regional government office] led by local leftists, who would demand to be given what they knew they were entitled to." Likewise, officials in the agency in charge of dealing with land reform openly affirmed to Herring (1991, V-4) that, "without mass pressure and exposures of fraud and bureaucratic misbehavior, implementation might well have moved in the sluggish and corrupt manner typical of subcontinental [Indian] reforms."

"Embeddedness Kerala-style" is clearly crucial to insuring the state's performance. It should not, however, be taken to imply that the state in Kerala is simply a "passive register," responding directly to the interests of peasants and workers in a mirror image of "the capitalist state" as conceived by "instrumentalists."[16] In fact, the structure of relations between state and society in Kerala provides a solid basis for autonomy, from subordinate groups as well as elites.

Autonomy in relation to subordinate groups is provided in part by the fact that the bureaucracy itself is subject to the rules and authority of the national bureaucratic apparatus. Central government funds form an important part of the state budget. In those agencies that are subunits of national ministries, administrators who simply did what constituents told them to do (as opposed to being pressured by constituents into doing what they were supposed to be doing in the first place) could find themselves subject to transfer or even, in theory, demotion. Neither local bureaucrats nor leftist politicians can afford to ignore political opponents for whom leverage at the national level is a principal weapon. Providing grounds for charges of "corruption" risks bringing intervention from the center.

As in the East Asian cases, autonomy also grows out of the social origins of the bureaucrats themselves. Local recruits into the bureaucracy are likely to be ideologically committed to the state's redistributive project, given the long-standing ideological hegemony of left-wing ideas among the local university population, but they are less likely to be of peasant origin themselves. Historically, at least, there was also a certain amount of social distance between those who were recruited into the state apparatus and those who dominated the local agrarian structure, the former often being the less privileged Nairs and the latter being the high-caste Brahmin Namboodiripads (Herring 1991, III-13).

Overall, state-society relations in Kerala embody the same sort of contradictory combination of close relations with a particular social constituency and insulation from it that characterizes the ideal-typical developmental state. Given that Kerala's "redistributive state" is almost the mirror image of the East Asian "growth states," the analogy is surprising. Looking at the way state-society relations evolve over time reveals additional parallels.

Even more obviously than in the East Asian NICs, state and society in Kerala are mutually constitutive. The existence of a mobilized class of tenant farmers and landless laborers was a precondition for changing the character of state action. In turn, state action in the form of land reform transformed the class structure. It not only destroyed the old rentier agrarian class, it also created a new class of small property holders—the "former tenants." The class structure that emerged as a result of state action changed, in its turn, the political conditions of future state action.

As in East Asia, the results of successful midwifery make future pursuit of the transformative project problematic. Herring (1991) demonstrates how the state-assisted emergence of new classes threatens to undermine the political foundations of the state that made class transformation possible in the first place. What had been, for political purposes, a single unified class composed of agrarian tenants and landless laborers became two separate groups with conflicting interests. After land reform, landless laborers, instead of being the tenants' allies against landlords, became their adversaries in agrarian struggles and the principle advocates of further state intervention. Further redistribution in favor of landless laborers now comes at the expense of the new class of small proprietors. Correspondingly, former tenants, having received their land as a result of state action, became convinced that an active state was irrelevant to their interests even more quickly than did East Asian capitalists who achieved industrial preeminence.

As in East Asia, state-sponsored transformation diminished the loyalties of the groups that had benefited from the transformation and created new groups whose social and economic agendas were more difficult to respond to. In the East Asian NICs, a state with an agenda of capital accumulation served as midwife to the emergence of two groups: a class of industrial entrepreneurs, which then came to prefer its own quest for profitability over a state-directed project of accumulation, and a working class increasingly determined to give redistributive goals priority over state-sponsored accumulation of capital. In Kerala, a state with redistributive aims was midwife to a class of small proprietors. Assured of their own position, small proprietors then opposed redistribution from themselves to the agricultural laborers.

The limits of further redistribution were clear. In the 1980s the average agricultural laborer was already working less than 150 days per year. Alleviating underemployment by expanding the acreage of cultivated land would have meant intensifying a process of ecological degradation that had been under way for some time.[17] Increasing agricultural productivity has proved difficult. The former tenants have not been motivated to make new, productivity enhancing investments. In fact, the productivity of paddy land stagnated completely during the 1980s (see Herring 1991, table 6.1). To make matters worse, the new class of former tenants proved a more politically formidable opposition than the old landlords since "they are both more numerous and better connected in the villages than were the rentiers"(Herring 1991, II-26).

Future improvements in welfare must be grounded in accelerated accumulation, including industrialization. Yet the existing pattern of embeddedness makes it difficult for the state to take on such a project. The problem of adding a project of accumulation to a redistributive agenda is even more daunting than the problem of adding a redistributive agenda to a project of accumulation. At least in the case of the developmental state, a potential political constituency for a new redistributive project, the industrial working class, was generated by the old accumulation-oriented strategy. In the case of Kerala, the decimation of the old agrarian elite was accomplished without opening space for the emergence of a class of industrial entrepreneurs. Calling forth such a group at this point would require a radical reconstruction of state-society relations.[18] In short, Kerala in its own very different way demonstrates the contradictions of ties that connect the state with only one constituency.

This is not to say that Kerala's version of embedded autonomy is collapsing. Just as East Asia's embedded autonomy continues to make prospects for future industrial growth much brighter than they are in India or Brazil (to say nothing of Zaire), so Kerala's version of embedded autonomy remains a vast improvement on the deterioration of state institutions that characterizes most Indian states (cf. Rudolph and Rudolph 1987). Compared to the rising tide of communal violence and political disarray that characterized some other Indian states at the beginning of the 1990s,[19] Kerala has been relatively calm, despite its religious and ethnic diversity. Furthermore, Kerala's political leadership has already had some success in using its deeply institutionalized connections with industrial and agricultural workers to increase levels of labor peace (Heller 1994). As in East Asia, embedded autonomy, however skewed, is better than its absence, but, as in East Asia, moving forward will require reconstruction.

Kerala contributes two important general propositions to the debate over the possible futures of the developmental state. First, it demonstrates that the embeddedness is not necessarily restricted to connections with industrial capital. Second, it shows that being linked to a single group is problematic, whatever the group. In short, the Kerala case reinforces the idea that reconstruction must involve a more encompassing definition of embeddedness.[20] What Kerala does not offer is guidance on how embedded autonomy might be built on ties to constituencies with diverse interests. For clues as to how a more encompassing embeddedness might work, small European social democracies are an obvious site. Peter Katzenstein's (1984, 1985) description of Austria during the 1970s provides one of the best illustrations.

Austria

Like the East Asian NICs, Austria has a highly organized private industrial sector closely linked to the state apparatus. Large industrialists are united in the Federation of Austrian Industrialists (VÖI), while business more generally is brought together under the umbrella of the Federal Economic Chamber (Katzenstein 1984, 60). As in the model of the developmental state, this highly organized class confronts a sophisticated state apparatus that enjoys an exceptional degree of economic leverage.

Like the East Asian NICs, Austria inherited a formidable bureaucratic tradition. During the post–World War II period, the state bureaucracy expanded steadily and became more technocratic in character (Katzenstein 1984, 63, 69). As in the case of Taiwan, nationalization of the property of former occupying powers (in this case Germany and the Soviet Union) left the Austrian state in control of the commanding heights of industry. In fact, Austria had a higher level of public ownership than its Communist neighbor, Yugoslavia. State-owned banks and federal and regional authorities accounted together for about two-thirds of all joint stock companies in the country, whereas local private capital accounted for only 13 percent.[21] The state's role as a producer explained, however, only part of its importance vis-à-vis private capital.

As in Kerala, embedded autonomy did not entail the marginalization of subordinate groups. To the contrary, the links between labor and the Austrian state were as intricate as those that connected the state and capital. The Austrian Trade Union Federation (ÖGB) matched the industrialists' federation in comprehensively uniting those who worked in major firms, and represented about 60 percent of the overall work force (Katzenstein 1984, 36). The ÖGB was in turn inextricably linked to the Socialist party (SPÖ), which not only shared electoral hegemony with the more conservative People's party (ÖVP), but had influence via the thorough penetration of the bureaucracy by its members (Katzenstein 1984, 76). When the organization of labor is combined with the strength of the state-owned sector, capital looks less than overwhelming despite its high level of organization. Katzenstein's own conclusion (52) is that "Private business plays a subordinate role compared to both Austria's vast nationalized sector and its trade union."

Even more clearly than Kerala or the East Asian developmental states, Austria exemplifies the way in which the state and classes mutually constitute each other. The existence of a coherent state apparatus helps call forth an internally organized entrepreneurial class in Austria just as it does in the developmental states. The existence of a comparably organized working class reinforces the process. If labor cannot be marginalized or ignored, a dependable arena for centralized bargaining between capital and labor is essential. A competent, corporately coherent state apparatus provides that arena. Far from making the state irrelevant, the comprehensive organization of class interests makes it essential. As actors in civil society become more organized, a solid and sophisticated state apparatus becomes more rather than less necessary.

Being connected to multiple groups does makes the state's autonomy ambiguous. In the Austrian case this ambiguity is epitomized by the Joint Commission, which serves as a state-sponsored forum for translating the interests of capital and labor into policies. According to Katzenstein (1984, 67), everyone agrees that the Joint Commission is the linchpin of policy formation, but diametrically opposed views of its character coexist. Some see it as "an executive organ of the government's economic policy," others as the crystallization of interest group politics.[22]

Once the state is connected to all major social actors, the image of independent bureaucrats forging their own project and imposing it on society becomes implausible. At the same time, the notion that transformative projects are forged independently of the state apparatus becomes even more implausible. Since any strategy for change must reconcile conflicting interests, the necessity of a strong mediating institution is obvious. The state's independent influence depends on a balance of forces in civil society, but the balance is actively constructed rather than the result of exogenous stalemate.

But what is this intriguing structure good for? Katzenstein is quite clear about what encompassing embeddedness achieved during the period on which he focuses. During the 1970s Austria, like most of Europe, was threatened by adjustment problems far more serious than those currently facing the East Asian NICs. Austria's encompassing embeddedness gave it the capacity to respond adaptively. The costs of a more competitive international environment were borne in a way that improved the country's prospects for competitiveness in the future and did not threaten its political stability.

To be sure, Austria's adaptation was not neutral. According to Katzenstein, it involved "substantial losses in the relative share of gross domestic product accruing to labor" (1984, 39). Nonetheless, this loss must be balanced against the fact that capital's share of income at the beginning of the decade was "by far the lowest among the OECD States" (49). It must also be balanced against the fact that the strategy adopted produced an unemployment rate of only 2 percent combined with high rates of growth in "the technological competitiveness of its export products, total exports, real annual investment, productivity, real economic growth, and the growth of per capita income" (34–35).

It may, of course, be argued that the model Katzenstein describes is already outmoded in its countries of origin. Streeck and Schmitter (1991, 144) talk about the "demise of national corporatism in the early 1980s." Most analysts would agree that the rise of the European community puts national political institutions like Austria's in jeopardy. Pontusson (1992) makes the additional argument that the "post-Fordist" evolution of industrial production undercuts the labor solidarity that is the backbone of Social Democracy.

All of this may well be true, but it is somewhat beside the point. The point is that the skewed version that currently prevails in East Asian developmental states is not the only possible version of embedded autonomy. Neither dismantling the current developmental bureaucracy and replacing it with a weak American-style civil service nor the quiet LDP-style descent into clientelism is the only alternative to the status quo. More radical reconstruction is possible, at least in theory.

If reconstruction of the developmental state occurs, it will undoubtedly take the form of an indigenous innovation. Implausible institutional innovation is, after all, central to the process that produced the developmental state to begin with. A sober, knowledgeable analyst of East Asia at the end of World War II would have seen the future in terms of a debilitating blend of the formally imposed norms of Anglo-American liberal democracy and the informal persistence of traditional Asian authoritarianism. The creatively eclectic combination of market capitalism and state bureaucracy that emerged instead only makes sense in hindsight.

Awareness that more encompassing forms of embedded autonomy exist may provide useful clues for the reconstruction of the developmental state, just as rumors of Chinese bureaucracy inspired the original European bureaucrats and glimpses of Prussian administration served as a source of new ideas for the renovators of the Tokugawa state. As in the past, exogenous inspirations will no doubt build on indigenous institutional foundations. Future forms will build on current institutions in unexpected ways, just as current developmental states made old antimarket bureaucratic traditions into unexpectedly effective weapons in dealing with the challenges of global markets.

Equally important, looking at variations on the theme of embedded autonomy should remind intermediate states that they cannot allow their visions of reconstruction to become transfixed by East Asian models. Reconstruction is a desperate need, but the starting point is different. The flawed combinations of embeddedness and autonomy found in intermediate states do not provide the same institutional foundation on which to build, and there is no decades-long history of unparalleled economic success to cushion the problems of a transition. What then do arguments about different kinds of embedded autonomy have to offer states like India and Brazil?

Implications for Intermediate States

For intermediate states like Brazil and India, the dismantling scenario is not a worrisome compilation of potential problems; it is a description of decay well under way. The vicious circle has been in operation for some time. Local combinations of internal organization and societal ties produced only partial transformation. Performance could not keep up with demands, and the shortfall discredited the state. The neo-utilitarian vision, with its conviction that the health and capacity of state organizations were irrelevant, made the problem worse.

The evidence from Korea argues that an imbalance of demands and capacity is not inevitable. Greater initial capacity, conserved by strategies that reduced demands, allowed the Korean state to escape the discrediting gulf between demands and capacity that plagued its counterparts in Brazil and India. This was true both in the informatics sector and more generally.

For intermediate states, replicating the embedded autonomy of the developmental state would represent a giant step forward. Someday they might eventually have to confront the challenges that developmental states currently confront, but these would be problems of success, problems that it would be a pleasure for Brazil and India to have to confront. The assertion of World Bank Vice President Karaosmanoglu[23] that the developmental state's successes at industrial transformation are worth trying to emulate is vindicated. What remains to be answered is how.

Would-be emulators must begin by recognizing that full replication is unlikely. The East Asian amalgam depends on special historical circumstances. The concept of embedded autonomy is a useful analytical guidepost, not an engineering formula that can be applied, with a few easy adjustments, to states in other regions and historical periods in the same way that the formula for a suspension bridge can be applied regardless of where a river or chasm is located. Nevertheless, ignoring potential comparative lessons would be foolish.

Some things are obvious. Selectivity makes sense. Decisions about what roles to adopt must always assume that state capacity is in short supply. In this respect, neoliberal ideologists can be allies. At the same time, increasing capacity must be an explicit goal. Even with rigorous selectivity, demands on intermediate states will exceed current capacities. Efforts to increase state capacity must go along with selectivity. Meritocratic recruitment and reward systems with incentives for the long-term pursuit of collective projects are essential. It is hard to make bureaucracies effective even when bureaucrats are the best and the brightest; it is impossible when they are incompetent cousins and nephews. Building (or in some cases rebuilding) robust, coherent bureaucracies is a daunting task but an essential one for intermediate states.

Connecting state and society is the more difficult problem. Embeddedness is essential. Capacity without connection will not do the job. Yet the model of the developmental state becomes hardest to follow when it comes to the special kind of state-society connectedness that is rooted in East Asia's unique historical experience.

East Asian developmental states began the post–World War II period with legacies of long bureaucratic traditions and considerable prewar experience in direct economic intervention. World War II and its aftermath in the Pacific region produced a very special kind of "massive societal dislocation."[24] Traditional agrarian elites were decimated, industrial groups were disorganized and undercapitalized, and external resources were channeled through the state apparatus. The outcome of the war, including, ironically, American occupation,[25] qualitatively enhanced the autonomy of these states vis-à-vis private domestic elites. The combination of historically accumulated bureaucratic capacity and conjuncturally generated autonomy placed these states in an exceptional position.

At the same time, the state's autonomy was constrained by the international context, both geopolitical and economic. Their political leaders were certainly not free to make history as they chose. The end of World War II left Japan, Korea, and Taiwan caught between a powerful Communist giant, China, as their immediate neighbor and the world's military hegemon, the United States, as their occupier and patron. The international context precluded military expansion, leaving economic expansion the only basis for shoring up legitimacy.

The imposition of American hegemony, reinforced by the threatening alternative of expansionary Asian communism, also left these states no choice but to rely on private capital as a primary instrument of industrialization. The environment conspired to create the conviction that regime survival depended on rapid, market-based industrialization. Their small size and lack of resources made the necessity of export competitiveness obvious.[26] Commitment to industrialization made a joint project with local industrialists plausible. Initially, exceptional autonomy allowed the state to dominate the alliance with private capital. Later, increasing involvement with international markets helped discipline local industrialists and provided a brake on the descent into clientelism. Embedded autonomy was by no means an inevitable outcome, but the circumstances were certainly propitious for its emergence.

Once the difficulty of replicating the historical patterns that gave rise to the developmental state is accepted, the two conventional responses are decidedly unhelpful. One is to dismiss calls for any kind of emulation as utopian. This fits nicely with traditional neoliberal policy prescriptions. Since effective states cannot be replicated, policies that presume ineffectual states are a good second best. The other is to focus on political exclusion as a substitute for historical circumstance. In this case, authoritarian repression is presented as a way of insuring that embeddedness does not degenerate into clientelism.

Thinking about variations on embedded autonomy helps get beyond these unhelpful conventional responses. Kerala and Austria show how embedded autonomy can emerge from historical circumstances quite different from those of the original developmental states. They also offer some specific insights that apply to the problems of intermediate states.

First, Kerala and Austria show that mobilization of subordinate groups can serve as a substitute for the exogenously created weakness of elites that was so important for the balance of autonomy and embeddedness in the East Asian cases. If only capital is organized, then only exceptional external events on the order of World War II are likely to allow the state to remain autonomous while at the same time connected. Multiple organized constituencies make it easier to balance embeddedness and autonomy.

This proposition reverses the standard neo-utilitarian response to the political organizations that bring together labor or other subordinate groups. In the standard neo-utilitarian vision, these are dismissed as "distributional coalitions" interested in rents and detrimental to development (cf. Olson 1982). A more institutional perspective suggests that the organization of subordinate groups may be an important bulwark against a degeneration of narrowly focused state-society connections into an elite clientelism that is ultimately more threatening to development.

Broadening the focus of embeddedness means that bureaucratic agencies and the personal networks that grow out of them are no longer sufficient to connect state and society. In both Kerala and Austria, state-society connections run primarily through parties. If intermediate states are to follow this route they will need party organizations capable of providing coherent support for long-term collective aims.

The idea that the mobilization of subordinate groups by strong parties may provide an alternative basis for embedded autonomy will be met by skepticism in intermediate states, where electoral politics is usually associated with clientelism and the capture of the state. Parties with long-term agendas are even harder to build than state bureaucracies. Any possibility of building political organizations that are encompassing and efficacious depends first of all on finding a "joint project" that unites the state apparatus and its societal constituencies in the same way that the project of industrial transformation brought together industrial capital and the developmental state.

When specific subordinate groups, such as agricultural laborers in Kerala, are mobilized, defining a joint project is not difficult: redistribution makes sense. When mobilization includes multiple groups, as is likely in intermediate states, formulating a joint project is harder. The Austrian case offers one suggestion. Maintaining an open economy's competitiveness vis-à-vis other open economies is a joint project with an encompassing ring to it. Clearly, seeing industrial transformation in these terms was central to East Asian joint projects. Conversely, it has often been argued that continental-sized intermediate states like India and Brazil are at a political disadvantage because of their inability to define local economic welfare as depending on competition with an uncontrollable external world. Here again, neoliberal ideology might be useful, providing, paradoxically, part of the ideological foundation for a joint project that could facilitate the construction of a more encompassing embedded autonomy.

Finally, both Kerala and Austria also reinforce the point that has been made repeatedly in relation to developmental states. Intermediate states that are successful in promoting societal transformation will inevitably face the necessity of changing the very structures that enabled them to succeed. Having provided the basis for one of the world's most successful attacks on distributional issues, Kerala must broaden its version of embedded autonomy to include industrial capital if it is to succeed in confronting problems of accumulation. Having successfully adapted to the challenge of preserving competitive openness, Austria must now confront the challenges of a more powerful form of supranational integration. In each case transformation means finding new ways to use hard-won institutional assets. If intermediate states are to succeed, they will have to do the same thing.

Predators and Midwives

This book began with a fantasy of bureaucrats as lion fodder. The rest of the analysis contested the story's premise. Contesting the premise meant contesting simplistic neo-utilitarian visions of the state and using a comparative institutionalist approach to demonstrate the value of seeing states in a different way. Analyzing societies and analyzing sectors produced the same message: industrial transformation is possible, and states make a difference. The character of state institutions helps determine whether and how countries change their position in the international division of labor. State apparatuses are potential sites for agency. Sturdy structures make agency easier. Agency changes the structures that made it possible.

There are, of course, good reasons for sympathy with lion fantasies and neo-utilitarian theories. Predatory states justify cannibalistic dreams. Without coherent bureaucratic institutions, states do indeed reduce themselves to the horrifying caricature predicted by simplistic versions of the neo-utilitarian vision. Rules and decisions are commodities, to be sold like any other commodity to the highest bidder. Without a predictable environment of political rules and decisions, long-term investment is foolish. State power, used for capricious extraction and wasteful consumption, diminishes private productive capacities rather than enhancing them. Welfare and growth both suffer.

Extracting a larger share from a shrinking pie is not the optimal way to maximize revenues, but it may be the only way consistent with the survival of predatory states. The disorganization of civil society is the sine qua non of political survival for predatory rulers. Generating an entrepreneurial class with an interest in industrial transformation would be almost as dangerous as promoting the political organization of civil society. For predatory states, "low-level equilibrium traps" are not something to be escaped; they are something to be cherished.

The predatory state is an ideal type, but empirical approximations like Zaire under Mobutu exist. Neo-utilitarians are not wrong in pointing out the existence of predation; they are wrong in their diagnosis of its roots. For neo-utilitarians, state power is the cause of predation. Diminishing state power is therefore its cure. Predatory states are not a perverse variation; they are the ideal-typical state. Actual states will approximate the predatory ideal unless their power is curtailed. The only good state is an eviscerated one.

The ideal type of the developmental state turns this logic on its head. Developmental states show that state capacity can be an antidote to predation. To deliver collective goods, states must act as coherent entities. Institutionalized bureaucratic power keeps individual incumbents from peddling rules and decisions to the highest bidder. Being a coherent actor involves more than just reining in the greed of individual officeholders. It involves entrepreneurship as well. Developmental states help formulate projects that go beyond responding to the immediate demands of politically powerful constituents.

Autonomy is fundamental to the definition of the developmental state but not sufficient. The ability to effect transformation depends on state-society relations as well. Autonomous states completely insulated from society could be very effective predators. Developmental states must be immersed in a dense network of ties that bind them to societal allies with transformational goals. Embedded autonomy, not just autonomy, gives the developmental state its efficacy.

The power of embedded autonomy arises from the fusion of what seem at first to be contradictory characteristics. Embeddedness provides sources of intelligence and channels of implementation that enhance the competence of the state. Autonomy complements embeddedness, protecting the state from piecemeal capture, which would destroy the cohesiveness of the state itself and eventually undermine the coherence of its social interlocutors. The state's corporate coherence enhances the cohesiveness of external networks and helps groups that share its vision overcome their own collective action problems. Just as predatory states deliberately disorganize society, developmental states help organize it.

Comparative analysis leads to a vision that stands in contrast to the old neo-utilitarian assumptions. A few of the general propositions that go with this perspective are worth reiterating.

First and most crucially, the fate of civil society is inextricably bound to the robustness of the state apparatus. Deterioration of state institutions is likely to go hand in hand with the disorganization of civil society. Sustaining or regaining the institutional integrity of state bureaucracies increases the possibility of mounting projects of social transformation.

The second proposition follows from the first. Predation is not a function of state capacity. The idea that eviscerating state bureaucracies will wipe out predators is misguided. To the contrary, constructing state apparatuses that are bureaucracies in Weber's positive sense should help prevent predation.

Finally, bureaucracy is not enough. Even the most bureaucratically coherent state cannot effect transformation without a network of ties to social groups and classes with which it shares a project. Connectedness is as important as coherence and cohesion.

The concept of embedded autonomy is useful because it concretizes the structural relations that lie behind the efficacy of the ideal typical developmental state, but it does not fully capture variations in state involvement across sectors and circumstances. States play an array of roles that work or do not work depending on their fit with specific goals and contexts. Transformation depends on turning structural strengths into the effective execution of a well-selected blend of roles.

Exploring roles and strategies in the information technology sector helped put flesh on abstract ideas about how states affect industrial change. Looking at informatics reinforced general propositions about the consequences of bureaucratic capacity, but it also led to a sharper focus on state-society relations.

The idea of the state as midwife came to the fore. States foster industry by assisting in the emergence of new social groups and interests. The consequences of midwifery were remarkably robust across countries. From the impressive institutional constructions that went with embedded autonomy in Korea to the often inconsistent strategies of Brazil and India, state efforts to generate local entrepreneurial groups committed to a local information technology industry produced results.

The findings were encouraging for those who would like to see the state as an agent of transformation, but they were also sobering. Industries emerged, but they were not the industries that had been expected. In caricature, the outcome can be summarized in a paraphrase of an old aphorism: States can make industries, but not as they choose. Nationalist initiatives ended up contributing to the emergence of internationalized industries that were, for at least some of the initiators, mirror images of what they had hoped for.

Results were sobering for a second reason. Social structural changes, even if partially put in motion by the state itself, supersede the organizations and policies that created them, forcing changes in the state itself. The reciprocal shaping of state and society is not always mutually reinforcing. Informatics agencies were transformed and sometimes marginalized by the industries they helped create. At a more general level, the social structural bases of the developmental state have been at least partially undercut by the new industrial society it helped create.

None of this negates the prospect that the state will continue to be an instrument for social transformation. New generations of barbudinhos undoubtedly lie in wait. State apparatuses will provide launch sites for their projects. They will find niches within the bureaucracy, and sometimes these niches will provide the leverage to make them midwives. The results of their work may well surprise them. Any successes will end up redefining the possibilities for future state action, and the cycle will begin again.

In the end, then, the lessons to be drawn from this complicated analysis are simple ones. Uniformly treating bureaucrats as lion fodder is a mistake. Disdain is often deserved, but state bureaucracies can also be homes to creative entrepreneurial initiatives. Used imaginatively, they can spark new sources of social energy. Fewer predators and more midwives should be the goal.

Notes _____

Chapter 1
States and Industrial Transformation

1. See, for example, Boli-Bennett (1980).

2. Skocpol (1985, 7). For Weber's original discussion of the state, see Weber (1968 [1904–1911], chaps. 10–13).

3. For a brief summary of the most influential version of the "neorealist approach," see Waltz (1979, chap. 2).

4. See Tilly (1985); Mann (1984, 1986, 1993); Giddens (1987).

5. Thereby achieving something analogous to what Gramsci (1971) called "hegemony."

6. Compare with Rueschemeyer and Evans (1985).

7. Cf. Rueschemeyer and Evans (1985) on the state as "an arena of social conflict."

8. For Wallerstein, of course, the existence of a single division of labor that encompasses multiple cultural and political units is what sets "world-economies" like the contemporary capitalist world-system apart from "mini-systems" and "world-empires." See Wallerstein (1974b, 391).

9. See Chase-Dunn (1989) for a recent overview of the world-system approach.

10. For a brief, accessible summary of the theory of comparative advantage, see Todaro (1977, 277–91).

11. Hamilton's (1817) "Report on Manufactures" remains a classic defense of state support for "import-substituting industrialization."

12. List (1885) set out German suspicions that Ricardian formulations of comparative advantages represented England's interests rather than "objective" economics.

13. Prebisch (1950) and his Economic Commission on Latin America (ECLA) school of economists led the earliest attacks on comparative advantage from the perspective of the contemporary Third World.

14. This is, of course, the position of the dependency approach (see Cardoso and Faletto 1979) and world-system theory. Wallerstein paints the picture with the broadest strokes. In his vision, occupying different productive roles in the world-system entails a comprehensive set of sociopolitical differences ranging from the kind of labor control to the extent of division among dominant elites to the efficacy of the state. See Wallerstein (1974a, 1974b); Chase-Dunn (1989).

15. See Vernon (1966) and Wells (1972). The idea of the "product cycle" has been expanded from the more "economistic" versions of Vernon and Wells to a full blown sociopolitical schema by Kurth (1979) and Cumings (1987).

16. "Niches" do not necessarily have to be equated with sectors or products. A "commodity chain" perspective suggests that the process of production and

commercialization in any sector includes a set of interlinked niches, some of which are more desirable than others. See Gereffi (1991); Gereffi and Korzeniewicz (1990, 1993); Hopkins and Wallerstein (1986). In this perspective, it is not what you produce that counts so much as what role you play in producing it. The difference is one of emphasis, since the distribution of available "links" depends on the sector. Some sectors involve chains with very few high return links; others offer a variety of possibilities. Nonetheless, the commodity chain perspective is a good reminder that what is important in the final analysis is not the sector per se but the set of productive roles that go with it.

17. Cited in Wade (1990, 355).

18. Both authors emphasize the contrast between their arguments and a world-system approach that assumes that class relations and the character of the state are consequences rather than determinants of position in the international division of labor. See especially Zeitlin (1984, 217–37) and Brenner (1977).

19. Obviously the reverse argument is also possible. In the same article that looks at sectors as "multidimensional conspiracies in favor of development," Hirschman (1977) also uses the term "micro-Marxism" to describe the idea that sectoral specialization shapes sociopolitical institutions. The implications of "micro-Marxism" are certainly worth exploring (cf. Evans 1986b; Shafer 1990, 1994; Karl forthcoming). Nonetheless, in a world dominated by manufacturing and services rather than by primary production, single products rarely determine the shape of a country's economy. The degree of specialization required for a "sectoral determinist" argument to be plausible is increasingly hard to find.

20. See, for example, Arrighi and Drangel (1986), who found that only a handful of nations actually changed their general position in the international division of labor as defined in world-system terms (i.e., shifted between periphery and semiperiphery or semiperiphery and core) during the post–World War II period.

21. Korea, Taiwan, Singapore, and Hong Kong.

22. While the bulk of the analysis focuses on the 1970s and 1980s, the period actually begins in the late 1960s in India and runs into the beginning of the 1990s.

23. Since the "demiurge" in its original usage was the creator of material things, the term is an appropriate label for a state that takes on directly productive activities itself rather than leaving them to private capital. Credit for first applying the term to the state should go, I believe, to Luciano Martins (1977), who used it to describe Brazil's national development bank. For a different usage of the demiurge rubric, see L. Frischtak (1992).

24. *Técnico* translates roughly as a professional whose expertise is technical.

25. The *chaebol* are the large conglomerate firms that dominate Korea's industrial economy.

26. IBM actually came back in 1992, but the move was clearly in the works at the end of the 1980s.

27. Emanuel Adler (1986, 1987) uses this term in talking about Brazil.

28. Some years ago John Stephens and I (Evans and Stephens 1988a, 1988b) proposed using an approach we called "the new comparative historical political economy." The approach used here is essentially the same, but the label "compar-

ative institutional" avoids confusion with contemporary definitions that equate "the new political economy" with neoliberal extensions of economic analysis to political issues, as in the Buchanan/Tullock tradition.

29. This is essentially the perspective on the state that is set out in Evans, Rueschemeyer and Skocpol (1985).

30. March and Olsen's 1984 article is one marker of the resurgence of "institutionalism." Powell and DiMaggio's 1991 collection offers a good summary of the contemporary sociological perspectives subsumed under "institutionalism."

31. By training, the political economists include political scientists (Johnson and Bates), economists (Bardhan, Amsden), and one social anthropologist (Wade).

32. The list of sociologists includes two joint authors not officially sociologists: Faletto, who is officially a historian, and Evelyne Huber Stephens, whose training was in political science.

Chapter 2
A Comparative Institutional Approach

1. As reported in the *Financial Times*, October 7, 1991.

2. See, for example, Dutkiewicz and Williams (1987).

3. Hernando de Soto's *The Other Path* (1989) is probably the best-known indigenous manifesto of disillusionment.

4. At the heart of the neo-utilitarian vision was "public choice theory" as developed by Nobel Laureate James Buchanan and his collaborators Tollison and Tullock (see Buchanan, Tollison, and Tullock 1980). Niskanen (1971) is also a pioneer in the attack on the state, and Auster and Silver (1979) offer a particularly clear-cut example of the genre. The recent reemergence of "neoclassical political economy" (see Collander 1984) represents a similar, though usually less extreme, perspective.

5. For a similar perspective, see Nelson and Winter (1982).

6. If we look at the most general level and compare performance in the "statist 1960s" with performance in the "market-oriented 1980s," it is hard to argue that the "neoliberal revolution" had dramatic consequences for development. In retrospect, the performance of developing countries in the 1950s and 1960s looked quite impressive. Killick (1986, 105, table 1) notes that during the 1950s and 1960s the growth performance of developing countries was superior both to the contemporary performance of the original industrializers and to their historical performance. Conversely, whatever positive effects widespread market-oriented reforms might have had in the 1970s and 1980s were more than overwhelmed by other factors in Latin America and Africa.

7. Callaghy (1989, 133) cites the World Bank's 1988 report on adjustment lending as an example of the new emphasis on institution building.

8. See Evans and Stephens (1988a) for a more general version of this critique.

9. For an excellent compilation of recent work on institutions, see Powell and DiMaggio (1991).

10. Particularly in the case of late-nineteenth-century Russia.

11. There is an obvious affinity between the Gerschenkron/Hirschman perspective and "neo-Schumpeterian" approaches to growth (eg., Nelson and Winter 1982).

12. Cf. Granovetter (1985) for a discussion of "embeddedness."

13. See Powell and DiMaggio (1991, 5–6) for a discussion of the rise of institutionalism among followers of the "rational choice" tradition in political science.

14. For example, the operation of the residential housing market in the United States is used to illustrate an "efficient" institutional framework (North 1990, 61–63).

15. Pyrethrum, where politicians anxious to "achieve the status of spokesmen" for the small growers "fight for higher and more prompt payments for crop deliveries," is an archetypal case (Bates 1989, 87). This case is particularly interesting because, as Bates himself notes (86), it contradicts the generic "Olsonian" logic (cf. Olson 1965) that dominates much of Bates's argument in his 1981 book.

16. Toye makes the point (1991b, 329) that "very few development economists forty years ago believed that the state in developing countries was concerned unreservedly to maximize social welfare." The "benevolent state assumption" was "a convenient myth" adopted for reasons of "pure diplomacy or of 'reformist hope.'"

17. For a review of changing conceptions of the state in Marxist theories, see Carnoy (1984).

18. See the introductory chapter by Skocpol in Evans, Rueschemeyer, and Skocpol (1985).

19. See, for example, the literature cited in Rueschemeyer and Evans (1985) as well as the discussion of "developmental states" that follows here. By focusing on studies that have the Third World as their empirical focus, I have, of course, neglected the resurgent literature on the role of the state in advanced industrial countries that took a comparative institutionalist approach, starting with Katzenstein's classic 1978 volume and continuing to the present. See Zysman (1993) for a recent review of some of this literature.

20. In his recent work, Migdal (1994) moves in the direction of a more explicit recognition of the possibility of shared projects, seeing "zero-sum" relations as contingent rather than generic.

21. To be sure, Bates and Migdal focus on different cases. Migdal uses Sierra Leone as his principal case, and Bates says explicitly that state-society relations in Kenya are different from those in West Africa. Nonetheless, even when one compares Bates's earlier analysis of West Africa with Migdal's description of Sierra Leone, the difference is striking.

22. Amsden and Wade are, of course, only two exemplars of a burgeoning set of analyses of East Asia using a comparative institutional approach. These range from Haggard (1990), who uses an analysis that privileges the role of political institutions to revise traditional neoclassical interpretations of East Asian growth, to Cumings (1987), who focuses on the political history of the region, to Hamilton and Biggart (1988), who emphasize cultural and institutional differences among the countries in the region. (See also the works cited in chapter 3 below.)

23. It should be noted that what Amsden labels "late industrialization" is the mid-twentieth-century industrialization that Hirschman called "late late industri-

alization," as distinct from Gerschenkron's nineteenth- and early-twentieth-century "late industrialization."

24. For an extended discussion of her differences with Gerschenkron, see Amsden (1992).

25. The World Bank did continue to deny the value of interventions designed to foster the growth of specific industries, Nevertheless, this position represented a definite retreat from asking "how much" to asking "what kind" of state involvement works. In addition, subsequent critiques raised doubts about whether even this more restricted claim could be successfully defended in the long run. See Rodrik (1994, 12–21).

26. For recent elaborations on the "insulation hypothesis," see, for example, Haggard (1990) or Haggard and Kaufman (1992).

Chapter 3
States

1. The term "developmental state" is sometimes used with a meaning quite different from the one intended here. Dutkiewicz and Williams (1987), for example, used professed intentions rather than achieved results to identify developmental states. A state is "developmental" if it professes an interest in development, regardless of whether there is a plausible argument that state actions have had any positive "developmental" consequences, or, for that matter, whether a plausible case can be made that the professed interest is more than rhetorical.

2. For some interesting efforts to understand origins, see Cumings (1987) and Kohli (forthcoming).

3. It is important to note that this "vernacular" way of conceptualizing the "predatory state" is quite different from the way the term is used by Levi (1981, 1988) whose "predatory" state is simply a revenue maximizer. In Levi's use, states may maximize revenue in ways that promote development or in ways that impede it. Thus, the term "predatory" in her usage does not necessarily entail negative developmental implications. Levi's predatory states might also be "developmental" as long as their horizon for revenue maximization was sufficiently long run so that they saw increasing societal wealth as the best way of maximizing their own returns.

4. Zaire is not the only example of this combination. Argentina experienced a similar combination in the late 1970s and early 1980s under a military regime that combined brutal control over political dissension with fierce imposition of market logic on the surrounding society.

5. As Gould (1979, 93) puts it bluntly, "the bureaucratic bourgeoisie owes its existence to past and continued foreign support." Aid from the World Bank as well as from individual Western nations has played an important role, but French and Belgian troops at critical moments (e.g. in Shaba in 1978) have been the sine qua non of Mobutu's remaining in power (Hull 1979). By the beginning of the 1990s, the symbiotic relation between Mobutu and his foreign allies seemed to be breaking down. "Freelancing" on the part of the repressive apparatus had begun to affect even foreigners (e.g., five Europeans including the French ambassador killed by disgruntled army troops in Kinshasa in January 1993—*San Francisco*

Chronicle, January 30, 1993, A9), thereby threatening to deprive Mobutu of his foreign support.

6. Tshitenji-Nzembele, quoted in Lemarchand (1979, 249).

7. See White and Wade (1984), which later appeared in revised form as White (1988). Duvall and Freeman's (1983) discussion of "entrepreneurial states" represents a parallel strand of theorizing.

8. For example, Jones and Sakong (1980) on Korea.

9. See, for example, Johnson's description (1982, 236) of MITI's nurturing of the petrochemical industry in the 1950s and 1960s.

10. Johnson (1982, 57) reports that in 1977 only 1,300 out of 53,000 passed the Higher-Level Public Officials Examination. He cites an overall failure rate of 90 percent for the years 1928–1943. See also World Bank (1993, 175).

11. In 1965 an astounding 73 percent of higher bureaucrats were graduates of Tokyo Law School.

12. Calder (1993) offers a similar characterization of Japan's "strategic capitalism," but with an even greater emphasis on the importance of private-sector organization.

13. See, for example, Kang's (1989) description of the Hanahoe club, founded by members of the eleventh military academy class.

14. Except for the very highest ranks, like minister and vice-minister, which continued to be treated as political appointments.

15. For example, according to Choi (1987, 50), "four out of five Ministers of the Ministry of Trade and Industry between December 1973 and May 1982 were former Vice-Ministers of the EPB."

16. Cheng (1987, 231–32) claims that MTI rather than EPB dominated industrial policy making in the early 1970s, but clearly by the late 1970s the EPB was again dominant.

17. The importance first of foreign aid and then of foreign loans, both of which were channeled through the state and allocated by it, was a cornerstone of the state's control over capital. See E. M. Kim (1987); Woo (1991); Stallings (1992).

18. K. Y. Yin was forced to resign in July 1955 and returned after being cleared in court in 1956. See Pang (1987, 193) for an account. While struggles between factions were obviously involved in the case and not simply questions of corruption, the fact that the taint of corruption could serve as grounds for removal of such a powerful figure is in striking contrast to mores in most developing countries.

19. The discussion that follows draws primarily on Wade (1990).

20. According to Wade (1990, 272–73), the pool of NRC technocrats provided, among other leading economic bureaucrats, eight out of fourteen ministers of economic affairs.

21. Even in the 1980s, the state accounted for almost half of Taiwan's gross domestic capital formation, and state enterprises accounted for two-thirds of the state's share (Cheng 1987, 166).

22. According to Wade (1990, 275), "most ministers of economic affairs have had management positions in public enterprises."

23. Taiwan was, of course, quite willing to use a demiurge strategy in other sectors like steel and petrochemicals.

24. See also Gold (1986, 70); Pang (1987, 167–69).

25. The same strategy continues to be used. Wade (1990, 207–8) recounts the IDB's efforts to induce local VCR production at the beginning of the 1980s. Two local companies were at first given a monopoly, but when, after a year and a half, they were still not producing internationally competitive products, Japanese firms were allowed to enter the market (with local joint-venture partners) despite the protests of the original entrants.

26. Including city states like Singapore and Hong Kong would extend the range of variation. Singapore, which combines a high degree of autonomy with a pattern of embeddedness that centers on transnational rather than local capital, is a particularly interesting case (see, for example, Lim 1993).

27. For a very similar formulation of the structural characteristics of the developmental state, see Önis (1991, 123).

28. Cf. Heller (1990, 10–13).

29. For some, such as Castells (1992, 56), the decision to base legitimacy on promoting and sustaining development is what defines states as "developmental." The problem with this definition is that it conflates a desire to build legitimacy on this basis and the ability to do so. Many states might wish to use development as a basis of legitimacy but are unable to produce necessary results.

30. Among historical studies, those by Murilo de Carvalho (1974) and Uricoechea (1980) are particularly relevant to this discussion. Important recent contemporary studies include Abranches (1978), Barzelay (1986), Hagopian (1986), Geddes (1986), Raw (1985), Schneider (1987a), Shapiro (1988, 1994), and Willis (1986). The discussion that follows draws especially on Schneider.

31. The BNDE later became the National Bank for Economic and Social Development (BNDES). Its history is discussed by both Geddes and Schneider, but the fullest discussions are Martins (1985) and Willis (1986).

32. Among the agencies highlighted by Geddes (1986, 117) are the BNDES, the trade authority (CACEX), the monetary authority (SUMOC), the Departmento Administrativo de Servico Publico (DASP), Itamaraty, Kubitschek's Executive Groups and Work Groups, and the Foreign Exchange Department of the Bank of Brazil.

33. According to Willis (1986:4) the bank has "virtually monopolized the provision of long-term credit in Brazil, often accounting for as much as 10 percent of gross domestic capital formation."

34. DASP was established by Vargas in 1938 as part of the "Estado Novo."

35. This was the goal of Roberto Campos (Schneider 1987a, 575).

36. This figure is based on Schneider's (1987a) survey of 281 Brazilian bureaucrats.

37. Schneider (1987a, 106). As Schneider points out, there are positive as well as negative features to this pattern. It discourages organizationally parochial perspectives and generates a web of interorganizational ties among individuals. The main problem with these career patterns is that they provide insufficient counterweight either to the idiosyncratic decision making from the top political leadership or to the tendencies toward individualized "rent seeking."

38. It is worth noting that there is a striking resemblance between this symbiosis and the pattern described in one of the best detailed analyses of a Latin American elite, Zeitlin and Ratcliff's (1988) study of Chile. There as well, the tradi-

tional oligarchy escaped displacement and forged a symbiotic relationship with the state apparatus (see also n. 49 below).

39. See Evans (1979, 1982) for a discussion of the consequences of foreign capital in Brazil. For a more general contrast between Latin America and East Asia with regard to the role of foreign capital, see Evans (1987) and Stallings (1992).

40. As a cohesive corporate group whose lack of combat opportunities brought technocratic (i.e., educational) criteria for internal mobility to the fore, the Brazilian military seemed at first to have potential for reinforcing the coherence of the state apparatus (see Stepan 1971 and especially Geddes 1986, chap. 7).

41. See, for example, Brooke (1992) and *Business Latin America*, April 6, 1992, 105–6.

42. On the early role of the state, see, for example, Furtado (1965); Topik (1980); Wirth (1970).

43. Given Brazil's current economic agonies it is easy to forget that its overall record during the post–World War II period until the late 1980s was close to a 6 percent annual rate of GDP growth and that this was accompanied by a shift of GDP from agriculture to industry followed by a rapid increase in manufactured exports during the 1970s and 1980s. For the best overall summary of the evolution of the Brazilian economy, see Baer (1989).

44. Brazil's state power-generating enterprises still seem to be relatively efficient even by international standards. For example, Schneider (1987a, 87–88) notes that one of them, Furnas, is reputed to employ fewer employees per gigawatt/hour of electricity than either the TVA or major European power companies.

45. Figures are from Gargan (1993). The 12,000 final exam takers have already been winnowed from 200,000 who take the initial phase. Taub (1969, 29) reports that in 1960, 11,000 college graduates competed for 100 places.

46. An example of the solidary created is the statement by one of Taub's (1969, 33) informants that he could "go anywhere in India and put up with a batch mate [member of his IAS class]," a possibility that the informant considered "unheard of" in terms of normal relations with non-kin.

47. Take, for example, the question cited by Taub (1969, 30): "Identify the following: Venus de Milo, Mona Lisa, the Thinker, William Faulkner, Corbusier, Karen Hantze Susman, Major Gherman Titov, Ravi Shankar, Disneyland." Gargan (1993) notes that 1992 exam takers needed to know, among other things, who won the Olympic gold medal in tennis as well as "something about chukkars, coxswains, and jiggers."

48. See also, for example, Wade (1985).

49. It is interesting to contrast this vision with a quite different social structural dilemma, equally difficult for a would-be developmental state. In Zeitlin and Ratcliff's (1988) analysis of Chile, united agrarian and industrial interests were found to control the state. The prominent political role of landowning families within this amalgamated elited ensured that the elite as a whole would resist both transformation of the agrarian sector and the kind of single-minded focus on industrialization that characterized East Asian cases.

50. One indication of the lack of competitive pressure on large firms is the relative stability of market shares (see World Bank 1987b, 63).

51. This traditional stereotype has shifted substantially in recent years. Brahman families are more likely to encourage their offspring to go into business, and applicants are increasingly "middle class" (see Gargan 1993).

52. This lack of selectivity is not always evident in aggregate comparisons. For example, the distribution of public enterprises in Korea and India looked quite similar when Jones and Mason (1982, 22) considered "manufacturing" a single sector rather than disaggregating it.

53. For a good discussion of problems in the inefficiency of state investments in terms of extraordinarily high capital/output ratios and so forth, see Ahluwalia (1985).

54. According to Rudolph and Rudolph (1987, 80–81), "The real salaries of senior officials both in the public services (IAS, Indian Foreign Service, Indian Police Service) and in public-sector enterprises declined significantly in the 1970s." Schneider (1987a, 152) notes that in Brazil real salaries at the top of the bureaucracy were cut 40 to 60 percent under Figueiredo, driving a number of the more competent state managers to look for work in the private sector. After a respite under Sarney, the erosion of salaries has been even more severe during the Collor administration.

Chapter 4
Roles and Sectors

1. D'Costa (1989, 42, n. 10) cites this as the opinion of Western European engineers visiting the Kwangyang plant.

2. This discussion of POSCO is based on D'Costa (1989) and Amsden (1989); see also E. M. Kim (1987).

3. See discussion of Hirschman (1958) in chapter 2.

4. Giving "husbandry" this traditional agrarian connotation obviously makes it quite different from "husbanding" in the sense of simply conserving resources.

5. See, for example, Encarnation (1989).

6. Johnson's (1982, 19–23) contrast between the "regulatory" American state and the "developmental" Japanese state focuses on the custodial character of American rule making. The label unfortunately distracts attention from the use of regulatory powers for developmental ends.

7. According to Hirschman (1958, 83), social overhead capital is "usually defined as comprising those basic services without which primary, secondary and tertiary productive activities cannot function."

8. Cf. discussion in chapter 1, n. 23.

9. Cf. discussion of Yin's textile entrustment scheme in chapter 3.

10. The difference between "husbandry" and the contemporary connotations of "husbanding" in the sense of simply conserving existing resources is worth underlining one more time (cf. n. 4 above).

11. Complexes of activities that produce related products can be bounded narrowly, as in "athletic shoes" versus "dressshoes" or very broadly as in "secondary sector" versus "primary sector." The scope used here is in between, as in "steel" or "informatics."

12. See Schmitter (1990) for an excellent overview of variation in modes of governance across sectors.

13. Michael Shafer (1994) and others (e.g., Schmitter 1990) have argued compellingly that there is a powerful "sectoral logic" that transcends national boundaries. Shafer takes Hirschman's "micro-Marxism" a step further. He argues that producing certain products creates social forces and institutions, including particular types of states, which in turn prevent emergence of new kinds of production. Such an argument is persuasive primarily for countries in which a single, clearly defined product dominates the economy (as in mineral extraction), but even in these cases it is easy to overstate the degree to which products determine institutional arrangements. As Hirschman (1977) points out, even the production of primary commodities like coffee and sugar is organized quite differently in different social and political contexts (cf. Paige 1987 on coffee in Central America). Furthermore, in a world where most exports are manufactured and most economies are dominated by the service sector, it is much harder to imagine particular products shaping political and social institutions, except perhaps among mineral exporters (cf. Karl forthcoming). See also chapter 1, n. 19.

14. My thanks to Isu Fang via Mario Dias Ripper for this insight.

15. See chapter 1, section on "global context."

16. See, for example, Tugwell (1975) and Karl (forthcoming) on oil in Venezuela; Moran (1974) and Becker (1983) on copper in Chile and Peru; and Stephens and Stephens (1986) on bauxite in Jamaica.

17. The extent to which "revealed institutional advantage" favored the role of demiurge during the 1960s and 1970s can be seen in the proportion of Third World capacity with significant government ownership at the beginning of the 1980s: 71 percent in aluminum, 73 percent in copper, and almost 95 percent in iron ore (Brown and McKern 1986, 137).

18. See also E. H. Stephens (1987), which provides a comparative analysis across a range of countries and mineral markets, and Shafer (1994).

19. In Zaire, the mines' financial circumstances forced the government to grant "tax relief," which came to account for a substantial part of the government's own deficit. In Zambia, the combined costs of mining inputs and debt service (largely incurred by the mines themselves) was soaking up 80 percent of all foreign exchange earnings (Shafer 1983, 112).

20. See Shafer (1983, 104). Underlining the general problem of vulnerability is sufficient for our purposes here, but it should be noted that the extent to which this increased vulnerability undercuts the state's ability to take on the role of producer depends in part on the specific commodity involved. E. H. Stephens argues (1987, 67) that despite the fact that bauxite and primarily aluminum production are more highly monopolized and vertically integrated than is the case for copper, Jamaica still did better with state participation and the imposed bauxite levy than it would have if it had left the TNCs alone. In the case of iron ore, Vernon and Levy (1982, 177) note that "any given seller of iron ore, unless strongly linked to some specific buyers, was exposed to a high degree of market risk" in international markets. Nonetheless, only 20 percent of iron ore trade consists of intracompany transfers (Brown and McKern 1986, 56), which makes

it a much more open market than for minerals like bauxite, where intracorporate transfers account for about 70–80 percent (Stephens 1987, 74).

21. Even at the beginning of the 1980s, after most of the LDC state-owned capacity had come on stream, developing countries imported about 65 million tons of steel while exporting 305 million tons of iron ore (Brown and McKern 1986, 56).

22. For example, the projected costs of producing steel in new facilities in Latin America were less than in projected U.S. facilities, according to Crandall (1981, 91).

23. This began with the Industrial Policy Resolution of 1948 and was reiterated in the Industrial Policy Resolution of 1956.

24. Local production was only 43 percent of local consumption by 1957. Tata Iron and Steel (TISCO), founded at the turn of the century (1907), was by 1939 one of the largest, lowest-cost steel producers in the British empire (Johnson 1966, 11–12), but not all private-sector firms had TISCO's record of relative efficiency. IISCO (Indian Iron and Steel Co.), another early private entry (see Moorthy 1984), had such poor performance that Lall (1987, 80) characterizes it as having been "rescued by nationalization" in 1973–74.

25. According to D'Costa (1989, 136), Japan "lost 12 out of 14 major shipbuilding contracts to Korea" in 1986 in part because plate steel in South Korea cost $190 per ton less than in Japan.

26. The World Bank and the U.S. Import-Export Bank both turned down the initial Pohang venture as overly ambitious and uneconomic (D'Costa 1989, 127).

27. Taiwan is, of course, another successful case of developing steel by means of the demiurge. The experience of Taiwan's state-owned steel company (China Steel) has been very similar to (though less spectacular than) that of Pohang. China Steel, which was also built in spite of advice to the contrary from Western experts, "runs at a handsome profit" and "has been efficient enough to make Taiwan the second biggest steel exporter to Japan" (after Korea) (Wade 1990, 99).

28. Werner Baer's (1969) economic analysis of the CSN's performance in the 1960s suggested that the CSN remained a positive example of institutional advantage twenty years later. Baer (1969, 125) reported that CSN was making a better return on investment than U.S. Steel while producing plates and hot-rolled sheets at lower than U.S. prices. Trebat's later evaluation (1983, 197) essentially supported Baer's assessment. A 1978 study by Carl Dahlman (D'Costa 1989, 97) found output per person-year at Usiminas (another of Brazil's newer plants) to exceed U.S. levels. Overall, Brazil's labor and materials costs for hot-rolled products were, in fact, lower than Korea's (D'Costa 1989, 135). Evidence of the efficiency of Indian steel plants, even in the early days, is harder to come by, but Sanjaya Lall (1987, 80), usually a stern critic of Indian state policies, evaluated Indian steel in the 1950s and 1960s as "fully competitive" and noted that domestic steel was "considerably cheaper than imported steel."

29. Brazil's production had increased almost tenfold until it was producing twenty million tons a year and had surpassed France to become the world's seventh largest producer. Korea, starting from almost nothing, had also become a

major power. When the next phase of Kwangyang came on stream at the beginning of the 1990s, it would surpass Brazil in terms of total capacity. The combined production of the developing world was greater than production in the United States. Ten new major plants were scheduled to go on stream in the late 1980s and early 1990s with a combined capacity of over twenty million tons. Every one of them was in the developing world.

30. Even with the massive increases in state-owned capacity, domestic users had to import growing amounts of finished steel to supply their needs: $240 million in the late 1980s in the case of Brazil, over $1 billion in the case of India, and almost $2 billion in the case of Korea. Figures for Brazil and Korea are for 1987; for India, 1985 (*International Trade Statistics Handbook* 1990, 1:107, 424, 499).

31. By 1985 India exported only $46 million worth of steel (one-third less than it had exported at the beginning of the 1970s) while importing $1.15 billion. In most cases, 1986 output per person year was only about 50 percent of 1966 output (D'Costa 1989, 118, 120).

32. Another analyst (Sengupta 1984, 208) characterized state steel as "a peculiar social mode of production where both labor and management are alienated from State capital and neither has been able to act as the agent of technical progress."

33. In addition, India's state steel companies suffered from an inabiilty to create the kind of international alliances that were central to Pohang's success. The British, German, and Soviet technology for India's older plants was never fully adapted to local conditions (e.g., poor-quality coking coal), and even in the construction of its most recent plant (Vizag), the Steel Authority of India was forced to use Soviet and Eastern European technology in order to avoid hard currency loans (D'Costa 1989, 115).

34. Schneider notes (1987a, 278) that in the 1960s jurisdiction over state steel was divided among four ministries, two state banks, and at least one regional development agency.

35. In the case of Acominas, "political indecision and inordinate delays in plan implementation" resulted in capital costs of over $2,000 per ton capacity, as opposed to around $1,000 for Kwangyang (D'Costa 1989, 48). Higher financial charges resulting from inflated capital costs accounted for a substantial portion of the difference between Brazil's operating costs and those of Korea.

36. An internal report by the holding company in charge of Brazil's state-owned steel companies (SIDERBRAS) argued that price controls on flat steel products had been responsible for losses of U.S. $5.5 billion between 1978 and 1986. Lack of revenues forced state steel to borrow, generating an additional $2.7 billion in financial costs over the period (D'Costa 1989, 108). From 1979 to 1985, SIDERBRAS always had a loss, sometimes as high as 75 percent of sales. By 1986 it was $17 billion in debt (D'Costa 1989, 108).

37. Usiminas, generally regarded as one of Brazil's most efficient plants, was a joint venture with Nippon Steel (Schneider 1987a, 308). Tubarão, the newest plant, was a joint venture with Kawasaki Steel and Finsider (a subsidiary of Italsider, the Italian state-owned steel giant). Tubarão's international ties run the gamut from technology to marketing. California Steel Industries (a joint venture

of Kawasaki and Brazil's state-owned iron ore exporter, the CVRD) was its most important foreign customer (D'Costa 1989, 98).

38. Obviously, international ideological trends and not just poor performance contributed to the attractiveness of privatization. Even Korea chose to finesse the appearance of supporting a demiurge strategy by placing the majority of Pohang's shares in the hands of the public while leaving a controlling block with the Ministry of Industry.

39. Basic chemicals respresent an interesting variation on the steel case. See, for example, Brian Levy (1988) on the demiurge in fertilizers or my own work on petrochemicals (Evans 1979, 1981, 1982, 1986b).

40. See chapter 3, section on "variations on the developmental state."

41. Import quotas for raw cotton were based on past export performance, and without cotton there was no way to compete in the domestic market.

42. New synthetic fiber capacity depended in turn, of course, on state promotion of intermediate chemical production.

43. From almost 80 percent in the 1950s to about 30 percent at the beginning of the 1980s (Lall 1987, 114).

44. What is surprising is that there are still pockets of dynamism in the industry. The growth of the Reliance group is one example.

45. In 1973–74 cotton textile prices were about 50 percent of U.S. prices, but by the beginning of the 1980s they had risen substantially relative to U.S. prices.

46. According to Lall (1987, 114), per capita availability of woven cloth has shrunk from 16.8 meters in 1964 to 13.5 in 1982.

47. Exports were $259 million in 1950–51 and $278 million in 1982. Quantity of exports peaked at 631 million meters in 1973 and fell back to 199 million in 1982 (Lall 1987, 117).

48. There are, of course, exceptions. At the very beginnings of the industry in Brazil and even in Korea (see Wade 1990, 309), there were some attempts at direct state involvement in production. Taiwan also explored the possibility of a *tri-pé* including important SOE participation, but this plan was aborted before getting off the ground (Wade 1990, 102).

49. Shapiro (1988, 1994) is the single best source on the foundation of the industry.

50. Bennett and Sharpe (1985) make the same point in their analysis of the growth of Mexican auto production. Getting the TNCs to expand their local production in the 1960s and 1970s took considerable political will and skill. Getting them to make the initial commitment to export from Mexico at the end of the 1970s required the same sort of energy and determination. TNCs not only had to be persuaded to undertake what seemed to them a very risky venture, but also had to act in opposition to the policies of their own state (see Bennett and Sharpe 1985, 220–24). Only at the end of the 1980s did U.S. firms come to share the Mexican state's conviction that Mexico was a reasonable place to produce autos. After twenty years of successful production, U.S. firms finally decided that even the most technologically complex auto components could be internationally competitive if produced in Mexico and began investing on their own (see Shaiken 1989).

51. The following discussion of the Korean industry relies heavily on E. M. Kim (1987, 197–206) and Doner (1992).

52. By the end of the 1980s, Korea was not only the largest auto producer in the world outside of the United States, Japan, and Western Europe, but was also exporting about half a million cars a year, making automobiles a major source of export earnings (Bello and Rosenfeld 1990, 129–30). Doner (1992, 402) estimates Korea's percentage of localization at above 90 percent.

53. It is worth noting the contrast with the initial phases of the auto industry in most Latin American countries where local industries were hopelessly fragmented, with large numbers of local firms assembling cars from imported components for tiny domestic markets.

54. In 1974 the Ministry of Trade and Industry announced the ambitious if not fanciful goal of exporting 75,000 cars by 1981. At the same time, the inclusion of autos among the priority industries of the 1973 Heavy and Chemical Industry Plan made it clear that support (financial and otherwise) would be forthcoming for those that took the state's ambitious goals seriously. The commitment to support was renewed in 1979 when autos were included in the ten target industries for the 1980s.

55. Private resistance was particularly strong when it came to efforts at consolidation. First industrialists resisted the Park regime's early efforts to consolidate assembly in a single company—Sinjin (Doner 1992, 407). Later Hyundai refused to be cajoled into merging its operations with the Daewoo/GM partnership (Doner 1992, 408). Then Ssangyong elbowed its way into passenger car production, and Samsung threatened to do likewise. See Lew (1992) for an analysis of the industry's evolution that stresses the importance of the varying responses of the different chaebol.

56. Hyundai sold 10 percent of the equity in its auto operations to Mitsubishi and relied on its joint-venture partner Mitsubishi for key imported components (e.g., transmissions) as well as for design and production technology.

57. The rate of technological progress in cotton textiles in the late eighteen and early nineteenth century was a "mere" 3.1 percent per annum (Flamm 1988b, 1).

58. The "fifth generation project" was funded by MITI for ten years, starting in 1981, to develop new computer architectures (see Flamm 1987, 142–43). ESPRIT stands for European Strategic Program for Research and Development in Information Technologies and involved investment of about $1.5 billion by the EEC and European firms over the latter half of the 1980s (see Flamm 1987, 163). Sematech, funded in part by the Department of Defense, describes itself as "a unique public/private partnership formed to provide the U.S. semiconductor industry the domestic capability for world leadership in semiconductor manufacturing" (*Sematech Update*, October 1991).

Chapter 5
Promotion and Policing

1. Apricot Computers, which once seemed like Britain's best hope for having a niche in the PC market, was "gobbled up" by Mitsubishi (*Wall Street Journal*, August 13, 1990, B1). At the same time that the Fujitsu buyout was announced,

Ferranti, the mainstay of British defense electronics capabilities, admitted that despite having sold off a steady stream of nondefense assets, it was making losses and unlikely to pay any dividends for another two years (*Financial Times*, July 20, 1990, 18). A month later, Atlantic, the leasing company that had enjoyed the second largest revenues in the British computer industry, collapsed, leaving its customers in the lurch (*Datamation*, August 15, 1990, 94–95; June 15, 1989, 9). This left Amstrad, a company which "has always insisted it is a marketing company rather than a technology company or even a computer company," as Britain's principal locally owned representative in the computer industry (*Datamation*, June 15, 1990, 136).

2. The comparison is Sabashi Shigeru's, head of MITI's Heavy Industries Bureau in the early 1960s (see Anchordoguy 1988, 515).

3. The discussion that follows relies primarily on Flamm (1987, 1988a).

4. By 1974, foreign computer manufacturers held 70–75 percent of the British market. Later efforts at direct support for the industry, principally the Alvey Program, had some effect in semiconductors (DOI 1982; *Financial Times*, June 26, 1985) but could not reverse the industry's general decline.

5. The following discussion of Japanese policy relies heavily on Anchordoguy (1988).

6. British tariffs were a "stiff" 14 percent prior to entry into the common market, then went down to 7 percent (Flamm 1987, 167), but Japanese tariffs were 25 percent beginning in 1960 (Anchordoguy 1988, 513).

7. Joint ventures or technological licensing agreements were also set up with other American firms, but (with the exception of NEC's agreement with Honeywell) these proved less useful. GE (linked to Toshiba) and RCA (linked to Hitachi) both dropped out of the industry, forcing their partners to reorient their strategies.

8. This can be contrasted with Britain at the same time, where 44 percent of government computers were foreign (Flamm 1987, 167).

9. Fujitsu, Hitachi, NEC, Mitsubishi, Toshiba, and Oki.

10. Before JECC, rentals accounted for only 4 percent of computer revenues; by the time JECC had been in operation for four years this jumped to almost 80 percent (Anchordoguy 1988, 520; see also Flamm 1987, 252–53).

11. Anchordoguy (1988, 521) estimates the firms' total investments at 103.9 billion yen, and the difference between the cash flow received under the JECC system and that which would have been available if the firms had run their own rental system at 97 billion yen.

12. The Very Large Scale Integration (VLSI) project was aimed at enhancing the ability of local firms to design and produce semiconductors.

13. Oki, for example, was dropped because it did not commercialize the products it developed in the "3.5 Generation" project (Anchordoguy 1988, 530).

14. Despite Japan's success it is important not to assume that the Japanese state was somehow superhumanly prescient. Kent Calder (1993, 116), for example, argues that "Until well into the late 1950s, the electronics industry had to struggle against a range of government measures intended to supress it and redirect its financial resources elsewhere."

15. Kenneth Flamm's two books (1987, 1988a), on which this section is

based, are the best sources for anyone wishing a more detailed account of the global industry. I am also indebted to Mario Dias Ripper (1988) for his "three waves" vision of how the industry changed.

16. Ernst and O'Connor (1992) provide a compelling description of competitive strategies that characterize the new world of information technology. See for example, their discussion of "network transactions," pp. 34–37.

17. Ernst and O'Connor (1992, 38) estimate that gross margins in PCs are only about 30 percent as opposed to the estimated 70 percent enjoyed by mainframe producers.

18. Officially known as the "Electronics Committee of India," it was unofficially known by the name of its chair, Dr. Homi J. Bhabha, who was also head of the Atomic Energy Commission (Grieco 1984, 21).

19. Sridharan (1989, 328, 355–58); Grieco (1984, 20–23, 110).

20. According to Subramanian (1989, 176–77), 600 percent.

21. See Evans (1986a). Adler (1986, 1987) gives this group the more dramatic label of "ideological guerrillas." See also Dantas (1988); Langer (1989).

22. For example, Prof. M. G. K. Menon headed both the DOE and its supervising Electronics Commission from its founding in 1970 until 1978, and Dr. A. S. Rao, the managing director of ECIL and a strong advocate of the national champion position, was also a member of the Electronics Commission.

23. The requirements were set down in the Foreign Exchange Regulation Act (FERA) passed under Indira Gandhi. The struggle over whether IBM would allow Indians to own a share of the equity in its 100 percent owned subsidiary was not, of course, only the responsibility of the DOE. It was conducted at the highest levels of government, e.g., Prime Minister Morarji Desai in 1977. See Grieco (1984, 89–97).

24. For example, S. R. Vijayaker (secretary, Department of Electronics, 1984–86) was a former managing director of ECIL. P. P Gupta (1981–82) and K. P. P. Nambiar (1987–88) were both former executives from state-sector firms.

25. Vijayaker was secretary of the DOE from May 1984 to December 1986. See Sridharan (1989, 406).

26. There are two informatics companies in the WIPRO group, WIPRO Information Technology, Ltd., the country's second largest producer of microcomputers and minicomputers, and WIPRO Systems Ltd, a new software company. Tata Unisys Ltd. and Tata Consultancy Systems are the country's two largest private software firms.

27. Texas Instruments' subsidiary in Bangalore was the first company to engage in software exports via satellite link.

28. Adler (1987) develops this theme well in his portrayal of the frustrated nationalist técnicos as "ideological guerrillas."

29. In addition to the three firms using licensed technology (EDISA, LABO, and SID), COBRA (the state-owned firm) was allowed to enter the market using indigenous technology developed at the University of São Paulo, and SISCO presented as indigenous what was probably a "reverse engineered" older Data General machine (see Evans 1986a, 806, n. 11).

30. The law of similars, put in place before World War I, was a cornerstone of Brazil's strategy of "import-substituting industrialization" (see Bergsman 1970).

31. Operationally, "small" meant machines of the size of the System 32 or smaller. As technology evolved, "small" computers became more and more powerful and harder to distinguish from "large" computers, complicating the definition of the market reserve.

32. *Tri-pé* is the term used for companies owned one-third by local capital, one-third by foreign capital, and one-third by the state. The idea had been pioneered in the petrochemical industry, in part by the same individual (José Pelúcio) who was responsible for setting up the special working group on the computer industry (see Evans 1979, 1981, 1986a, 793).

33. Artur Pereira Nunes, a CAPRE cadre who remained in SEI through the passage of the National Informatics Law in 1984, was one important exception.

34. While Octávio Gennari, the first head of SEI, was a civilian, his successors, colonels Joubert Brízida and Edison Dytz and Commander José Ezil, were all drawn from the military.

35. The computer industry employed about seven thousand university-trained employees by 1983. See table 7.3.

36. A small version of the 4331.

37. Basically, Brazil was left with 16-bit minicomputers while the rest of the world moved on to 32-bit "supermini" machines.

38. Known as the "supermini" competition, its aim was to move Brazil from 16-bit technology to the 32-bit technologies now dominant in the rest of the world.

39. DEC was at that time the second largest U.S. manufacturer and the largest manufacturer of minicomputers. A spin-off from DEC, Data General was an important challenger to DEC's preeminence in the market for minicomputers. DEC licensed its classic VAX750. Data General licensed its "Eclipse" machines. Honeywell-Bull and Hewlett-Packard technology was also licensed. This new technology was several cuts above what the TNCs had been willing to part with in the 1977 competition.

40. Critics of the policy would, of course, point out that the indigenous designs were in fact "clones," that is, locally engineered variations on standard international architectures, but this is only to say that the engineering accomplishments of local firms were analogous to those of COMPAC or NEC rather than those of Apple or IBM.

41. SCOPUS, which had been engaged in designing and selling indigenous hardware since before CAPRE's original mini competition, was working on 32-bit microprocessor-based machines, which it felt would be able to compete with the licensed "superminis." Subsequent history vindicated SCOPUS's sense of where hardware technology was headed but not its conviction that indigenous systems could compete with the combined software and hardware advantages of licensed technology.

42. SEI *Comunicado* 007/82, published December 12, 1982, signed by Colonel Dytz as *secretário executivo*.

43. Formation had designed a machine equivalent to an IBM 370-138, at the time roughly competitive with the 4331. Formation's machine was "software equivalent," which means that applications would run the same way on Formation's machine as they would on the IBM machine, but it was not architecturally

the same. Formation needed a successor machine and was anxious to find some-one with the financial resources that might enable them to develop one. Itaú looked like a good candidate (Evans and Tigre 1989a, 1755).

44. Roughly 70–80 out of an overall staff in the neighborhood of 120.

Chapter 6
State Firms and High-Tech Husbandry

1. X-OPEN was formed in 1986 to "establish a standard version of the UNIX operating system for use in European markets" (Flamm 1987, 166).

2. By "commodities" I mean goods that are mass-produced on an undifferenti-ated basis, such that one manufacturer's products are essentially undistinguish-able from another, and must therefore compete largely on the basis of price, as opposed to customized or proprietary products that compete on the basis of spe-cial properties or features hard to obtain from other producers.

3. This section is draw from Evans (1992a).

4. See Waterbury (1993, 260), cited in section on "roles" in chapter 4 in this volume.

5. The implicit bargain in which private industry accepted the restrictions im-posed on it by the state and in return the state used its regulatory capacity to protect the comfortable oligopolistic redoubts of the big houses from the threat of either upstart internal competition or, more seriously, foreign competition. See chapter 3, discussion of India in the section on "intermediate states."

6. Singhal and Rogers (1989, 164) call BEL the "mother hen" of India's elec-tronics industry since 10–15 percent of its engineers left each year to join the technical teams of private firms.

7. For example, its TTL logic chips in the 1970s and its liquid crystal display (see Sridharan 1989, 312).

8. It was given responsibility for overseeing import substitution in electronics after the 1965 war.

9. In 1971 ECIL had started producing the TDC-12 minicomputer and was on its way to designing the more advanced TDC-316.

10. The TD-316 was selling for around $200,000, while international hard-ware of equivalent performance (e.g., DEC's PDP-11/04) went for $15,000 (Grieco 1984, 126).

11. In fact, ECIL had been forced to abandon its strict adherence to the princi-ple of self-reliance as early as 1973 and resort to reverse engineering of a Hon-eywell-Bull machine in order to come up with more advanced (32-bit) hardware (Subramanian 1989, 206–7).

12. Licenses for large machines were from Control Data Corporation, whose CDC 930 series was produced and sold by ECIL as the Medha. Licenses for mini-computers (sold as the Super 32) were from Norsk Data (Subramanian 1989, 218–22).

13. ECIL's shift in emphasis is nicely illustrated by *Dataquest*'s (1988, 32; 1989, 87) comparison of ECIL's 1988–89 computer group revenues with the prior year. According to *Dataquest*, ECIL's overall growth of 78 percent between the two years was achieved by putting together very disparate trends in different

segments of the company's business. While sales of small computers shrank, income growth from special projects increased ninefold to comprise more than half of the computer group's total revenues. Precise interpretation of the *Dataquest* data (1988, 32; 1989, 87) is difficult since their categories for the two years are not exactly equivalent. In 1987–88, turnover of 464.9 million Rupees is divided into four categories: projects, 47.9; large systems, 98.7; small and medium, 248.7; maintenance, 70.9. In 1988–89, turnover of 828.3 million Rupees is divided into five categories: special projects, 457.5; large systems, 231.9; minis, 10.9; maintenance, 105.2; and other, 22.8. It seems likely that some of the Norsk Data machines were counted as "small and medium" in 1988 but counted as part of "large systems" in 1989. In addition, since "projects" involve the provision of integrated systems that include both hardware and software, reporting of sales in the two categories may have shifted between the two years, exaggerating the changes. However, even making generous allowance for possible reporting shifts, the trend remains dramatic. Subramanian (1989, 211–12) presents a different set of data which shows a similar trend over the long term. He shows service income growing from about 5 percent of the value of hardware deliveries in 1975–76 to over 40 percent of hardware deliveries in 1986–87. Since a substantial proportion of hardware deliveries are part of large scale-projects, this underestimates the shift away from commodity production.

14. In 1988 CMC maintained 657 systems of which 218 were DEC systems and 161 were HP. Other systems included IBM, Honeywell-Bull, Unisys, Control Data, Data General, NAS, Prime, Perkin Elmer, Wang, and Harris (see CMC 1988b, 10–11).

15. See *The Times of India*, October 14, 1989, I-1.

16. It was forced to implement the system on unfamiliar hardware (NCR Towers), since the companies whose hardware it knew better could offer no customer support in Syria.

17. CMC's new revenue profile was the result of a long-term strategy of complementing the company's initial hardware engineering capabilities by hiring a growing number of software engineers.

18. First VAX 750s and later 6250s.

19. The on-line container management system for the Nhava Sheva port in Bombay, a contract won under the competitive bidding procedures of a World Bank tender, is one example (DOE 1989, 44). Others include a computerized load dispatch system designed for the Tamil Nadu State Power Board, a traffic management system for the Bhilai Steel Plant (*Dataquest* 1989, 85), and SAILNET, a communications network provided for the state-owned steel authority.

20. Some would say that the company's entrepreneurial verve and inside track with the state in its role as regulator still make it a threat to the growth of local capital. CMC's success in winning a contract for the Bombay stock exchange over the country's largest private software company (TCS) prompted accusations of this kind, especially since TCS's bid was undercut by the failure of the DOE to approve import of the Tandem hardware that TCS had proposed using (*Business India*, October 16, 1989, 64). This may be true, but as long as the demand for large public-sector information systems exceeds the supply of companies with the

capacity to produce them, the benefits of an aggressive entrepreneurial approach to these projects are likely to far outweigh the costs.

21. From the beginning of the 1970s to the end of the 1980s the public sector's share of gross electronics output was cut almost in half (Sridharan 1989, 295). ECIL's smaller counterparts, enterprises owned by individual states rather than the central government, had a more difficult time shifting out of commodity production and suffered accordingly.

22. Meltron's overall profile is that of a typical demiurge, producing everything from semiconductors to microcomputers to private branch telephone exchanges to sophisticated communications equipment for military and police.

23. C-DOT was the brainchild of S. R. "Sam" Pitroda, a native of the impoverished state of Orissa who had culminated a successful entrepreneurial career in the United States by selling his telecom switch manufacturing company to Rockwell International. He became intrigued with the problems of Indian telecommunications and returned to India at the beginning of the 1980s, becoming closely involved with the Rajiv Gandhi administration (Singhal and Rogers 1989, 179–80).

24. ITI's electronic switching system (ESS) capacity depended on the E-10B, licensed from CIT-Acatel. The E-10B was relatively old technology, and the version licensed to ITI required upgrading in order to allow use of ISDN. In addition, reliance on the E-10B meant reliance on components imported through Acatel against which there were allegations of over-invoicing (*Dataquest* April 1989, 37).

25. For example, ISDN.

26. While it was supported by DOE and other government funds (DOE 1988, 70, 1989, 57; C-DOT 1987, 9), C-DOT was set up as a "Scientific Society . . . vested with total authority and flexibility outside Government norms" (C-DOT 1987).

27. Singhal and Rogers (1989, 180) report that C-DOT had 400 young engineers in 1984 with an average age of twenty-three. C-DOT's annual report shows a slower growth of personnel and a slightly older age distribution, but even according to the annual report the modal age of C-DOT's 328 professionals in 1986 was between twenty and twenty-five, and almost no one at the operational level was over forty (C-DOT 1987, 4).

28. According to Ernst and O'Connor (1992, 202), it cost $40 million for C-DOT to design its switch.

29. The Motorola 68000.

30. In contrast, the French ESS produced by ITI was considered uneconomical for exchanges less than four thousand lines (Alam 1989, 69).

31. According to C-DOT, a containerized RAX cost only about U.S. $25,000 (C-DOT 1988). According *Computers Today* (January 1989, 10), this is "about half of what the Western counterparts would cost."

32. See Singhal and Rogers (1989, 182). According to Singhal and Rogers, deposits in the local bank increased 80 percent and local business incomes rose 20 to 30 percent.

33. See Alam (1989, 71); Parthasarathi (1989). Some of the licensees were other state firms, but most were in the private sector.

34. By the beginning of the 1990s, half a million installed lines of its electronic switches (*Pioneer*, January 5, 1992) gave C-DOT a certain credibility, but it was weakened politically by bad relations with the Department of Telecommunications. At the end of Rajiv Gandhi's administration, Sam Pitroda became a politically beleaguered figure and his brainchild, C-DOT, suffered accordingly (see *Dataquest*, June 1990, 22; August 1990, 25). C-DOT was attacked for not meeting its deadlines and was put under the control of the Department of Telecommunications, creating rebellion in the C-DOT ranks (*Dataquest*, March 1990, 62; August 1990, 25; September 1990, 33). In addition, C-DOT's critics argued that delays in the availability of its technology were holding up the desperately needed expansion of telecommunications. C-DOT charged in return that the Department of Telecommunications was a "pro-import lobby" on behalf of Acatel and other foreign suppliers (*Dataquest*, August 1990, 25).

35. Cf. discussion of Jones and Mason (1982) in chapter 4, section on "sectoral variations."

36. By "commodities" I mean undifferentiated products sold primarily on the basis of price competition. Cf. n. 2 above.

37. See chapter 5. The special working group that put together the plan for COBRA, known as the Grupo de Trabalho Especial-111 (GTE-111), was the brainchild of José Pelúcio, who was working at the BNDE. The navy's representative was Commander José Guaranys. The BNDE's representative, Ricardo Saur, later went on to become executive secretary of CAPRE. The best accounts of this history are Helena (1980, 1984); Adler (1986, 1987); and Langer (1989).

38. See chapter 4 and Evans (1979, 1981, 1982, 1986b) for a discussion of the *tri-pé* as it evolved in the petrochemical industry. José Pelúcio (see n. 38 above) was also a key figure in the construction of the petrochemical *tri-pés*.

39. The 500 was a direct descendent of the G-10, a bit-slice machine that had been developed at the University of São Paulo under the auspices of the BNDE Special Work Group.

40. The hardware Ferranti brought to the partnership (the Argus 700) was an industrial process control machine, poorly suited to the commercial and government uses that constituted the bulk of the potential market in Brazil at the time (Evans 1986a, 794; Helena 1984, 27).

41. Most obviously the DEC VAX.

42. This despite the fact that the alliance was filled with historic irony since it had been Edson de Castro, president of Data General, who had publicly called on the U.S. government to retaliate against Brazil for creating the market reserve in 1977 (see Evans 1989b, 218).

43. DG had pulled out of the Brazilian market. Its installed base consisted primarily of about a hundred old Novas and was stagnant (see SEI 1985, 26; 1985, 42).

44. The Eclipse MV series.

45. In local parlance, the machine was considered a "supermicro." It was a multiprocessor design, based on the 32-bit Motorola 68000 series of microprocessors.

46. The UNIX system V equivalent (SOX) is described at the beginning of the chapter. Cf. Ivan da Costa Marques (1988).

47. See Costa Marques (1988, fig. 3, parts 2–6).

48. One indication of the magnitude of what COBRA was attempting is the fact that when IBM, Digital, and other major U.S. firms decided to develop a challenger to AT&T's UNIX, they felt it necessary to join together, forming the Open Software Foundation.

49. Costa Marques (1988, fig. 2, part 3).

50. See Bastos (1992). It should, of course, be noted that Brazil's nationalist position was to some extent thrust upon it by AT&T's refusal to negotiate a general agreement for licensing UNIX in Brazil, a decision that was reinforced, if not prompted, by the Reagan administration's ongoing attempt to get Brazil to retreat on the informatics policy more generally. See Evans (1989c, 228–32).

51. Cf. Ernst and O'Connor (1992, 277), who argue that there is a "huge application potential for NITs [new information technologies] in the management of agriculture and other primary sector activities in developing countries."

52. Taiwan's use of state firms to spark the emergence of local wafer fabrication capacity in the semiconductor industry is an excellent example of how direct production can be an important component of a strategy aimed at complementarity with the private sector. See Ernst and O'Connor (1992, 214–16) and Hong (1992).

53. See note 5 in this chapter.

54. Dynamic Random Access Memory (DRAM) chips are the principal form of memory chips used in computers and other electronic processing devices. A 4-Megabit chip contains roughly four million "gates" or binary switches.

55. See Kim and Yoon (1991, 163–64); *Gin Donga* (May 1991, 485). ETRI is also the largest and best funded of the specialized government research institutes that had been set up in the late 1970s. See Ministry of Science and Technology (1987, 35–36) for a listing of all the institutes.

56. See MOC (1987, 66); E. H. Lee (1987, 7). Beginning in 1982 the Korean Telecommunications Authority became the ministry's operating company in charge of providing telephone services (see MOC 1987, 3). MOC's performance stands in contrast to the deterioration of Brazil's telecommunications system during the 1980s (see Ernst and O'Connor 1992, 201). India was in still worse shape. In the late 1980s, India had one-third the number of phone lines to serve its 800 million people that Korea did to serve one-twentieth as many (Parthasarathi 1987, 32; Evans and Tigre 1989a, 1989b). The technological level of the switching system was even more embarrassing. Until 1987 the bulk of the switch equipment produced was ancient Strowger and Cross-bar exchanges, incapable of handling the functions usually assumed to be part of a modern telecommunications system (Alam 1989, 63; Sridharan 1989, 284). Existing lines were concentrated among the urban rich. Only 12 percent of India's phones are in the rural areas (where three-fourths of the population lives), and only one Indian village in twenty had any phone service whatsoever (Kelkar and Kaul 1989, 2; Parthasarathi 1987, 32). The privileges of urban dwellers should not, however, be overestimated since, according to Singhal and Rogers (1989, 177), "At any given point of time, four out of every ten phones in Delhi and seven out of ten in Calcutta do not work."

57. AT&T, Acatel (formerly IT&T), and LM Ericsson are the major competitors in the large-scale electronic switching systems (ESS) market.

58. At the beginning of the digital switch project the institute involved was called KETRI (Korean Electrotechnology and Telecommunications Research Institute), which was a descendant of KTRI (Korean Telecommunications Research Institute). At the end of 1984 it was decided to merge KETRI with KIET (Korean Institute of Electronics Technology) to form ETRI.

59. According to Ernst and O'Connor (1992, 199), Ericsson's AXE-10 switch provided the basic design on which the ETRI team constructed their own "TDX" switches.

60. Private participation in this case included three of the four principal chaebol (Daewoo Telecommunications, Goldstar Semiconductors, Samsung Semiconductor and Telecommunications), but instead of Hyundai the fourth company was Oriental Telecommunications (Dongyang) (*B. K. Electronics* 1(2), 32).

61. With a capacity to handle ten thousand lines.

62. See Ernst and O'Connor (1992, 220). The financing provided by Korea's Economic Development Cooperation Fund was not limited to telecommunications equipment, but it was nonetheless an important resource in securing telecommunications contracts from hard-strapped Third World governments.

63. See chapter 5, discussion of Korea in the section on "the roots of state involvement."

64. The seven systems were the Economic Statistics Information System (ESS), Resident Information System (RIS), House and Land Information System (HALIS), Customs Clearance Information System (CCS), Employment Information System (EIS), Vehicle Management Information System (VMS), and National Pension Information System (NPIS). See DACOM (1988, 18).

65. Estimates of the number of supermini host machines run from 66 (EIAK 1988, 406) to 105 (DACOM 1987, 4), with the expected number growing over time. Total projected cost for hardware through 1988 was 83.4 billion won, with an additional 35.5 billion won spent for software (EIAK 1988, 402).

66. In this case (as opposed to the TDX), the four regulars (Samsung, Goldstar, Daewoo, and Hyundai) (cf. note 60, this chapter).

67. Concretely, they were looking for a 32-bit, "supermini" machine that would use standard microprocessors, not proprietary ones. They also wanted a machine oriented toward "on-line transaction processing" (OLTP) using a UNIX-based operating system.

68. A number of the researchers involved spent several months in San Jose assimilating Tolerant's expertise, but the indigenous machine would not be simply a copy of Tolerant's Eternity system. The projected differences even included the possibility of using different microprocessors. The Eternity used NSC 32032 series processors, generally considered to be outmoded. ETRI personnel were considering moving to Motorola 68000 series processors. While the Tolerant machine was considered by the Koreans as roughly equivalent to the DEC VAX 8600, the TICOM was intended to be equivalent to the successor to the DEC VAX 8600 (see M. J. Lee 1988, 7), a state-of-the-art machine. In addition, it was supposed to support five times the external memory and cost 40 percent less.

69. See KETRI (1984); ETRI (1985, 1986, 1987). Successful development of a 32-bit UNIX "supermicro" machine (see ETRI 1985, 17; 1986, 16; 1987, 12) was followed by an even more ambitious project to develop a 64-bit supermini machine in conjunction with a small California company called AIT (see ETRI

1986, 28). While this later project was not successful, it gave a dozen or more ETRI scientists a chance to spend an extended period of time in the Silicon Valley working on problems of computer architecture.

70. The funds came from a combination of the KTA, MOST, one of the venture capital funds associated with MOST (the Industrial Technology Development Fund), and the private companies themselves. See M. J. Lee (1988, 9).

71. In the same vein, Korea decided to use the 1988 Seoul Olympic games to showcase indigenously designed software rather than simply purchasing the existing system (as the United States had for the 1984 games).

72. The problems of the pension application were further complicated by the fact that it was essentially a batch operation for which the Tolerant machine's OLTP orientation was a disadvantage.

73. Interview in *Kyongongkwa Computer* (August 1991, 161); see also I. S. Cho (1991). It should also be noted that Tolerant itself was unable to keep up with the accelerating pace of improvements in hardware performance and dropped out of the hardware business.

74. See *Hanguk Kyongje Sinmun*, December 24, 1991; EIAK (1991b).

75. The project was slated to involve "the establishment of a new government laboratory in collaboration with the three major DRAM manufacturers— Samsung, Goldstar, and Hyundai" with about half the financing to be provided by the government in the form of low-interest loans (Ernst and O'Connor 1992, 254).

76. The "Main Computer Development Team" hoped to have an internationally competitive Jujonsanki III ready for production by the end of 1993 (see I. S. Cho 1991). Whether the Jujonsanki III will be a commercial success remains to be seen, but it is still one of the chaebols' most important efforts to develop indigenous computer technology.

77. In 1961 there were less than 15,000 students studying engineering in Korea. By 1989 there were more than 225,000 (Y. H. Kim n.d.).

78. See MOST (1987, 34–35, 43, and passim). KIST (whose primary mission is advanced research training) has at various points been merged with KAIS (the research/contract-oriented institute) and called the Korean Advanced Institute of Science and Technology (KAIST).

79. It should be noted that however successful Korea may appear in comparison with other countries, local analysts remain far from satisfied. Linsu Kim, for example, considers "under-investment in higher educational institutions" to be "one of the major mistakes made by the Korean government in developing a national system of innovation" (Ernst and O'Connor 1992, 273).

80. The discussion that follows draws heavily on L. Kim (1991, 29–31).

81. If the data were limited to private firms, it would look even worse. A few state-owned enterprises like Petrobrás and Telebrás account for the majority of R&D expenditures (see Dahlman and Frischtak 1991, 14–15).

82. Dahlman and Frischtak (1991, 30) estimate 70 percent; Brazil's Ministry of Science and Technology (SCT 1990, 48) estimates 95 percent.

83. U.S. $65 million a year in 1988. See Tigre (1993, 11).

84. Only U.S. $3 million went to non-semiconductor projects during the first three years after the law was passed (Meyer-Stamer 1989, 24).

85. See the discussion of PSI Data Systems in chapter 7.

86. Department of Telecommunications and Oil and Natural Gas Corporation (both of whom had been beneficiaries of PSI's innovative products).

87. Each IIT graduate represents a public investment of $25,000 (for the IIT training alone) (Singhal and Rogers 1989, 47). Calculated in terms of the local GNP per capita, this would be equivalent to an expenditure on the order of $1.5 million in the United States (i.e., 100 times the GNP per capita).

88. Known as DISNET, the system, which was designed and written at NIC, allowed users at the district level to input and access information easily, while at the same time ensuring consistency of coding across districts (see NIC n.d.).

89. For example, between 1991–92 and 1992–93, the DOE budget was cut between 25 and 35 percent. The percentage of cut depends on whether only funds received from the government itself are counted or whether foreign aid channeled through the DOE is included (*Dataquest* March 1992, 92).

Chapter 7
The Rise of Local Firms

1. The Banco Itaú does not own Itautec directly. Itautec is a publicly traded company. ITAUSA, the Itaú group's holding company, is its largest shareholder. The Banco Itaú is in turn the cornerstone of the Itaú group.

2. See chapter 6, note 5.

3. *Wall Street Journal*, July 14, 1992, B-1; FKI (1991, 592); *Wolgan Computer* (May 1991, 102).

4. See Ernst and O'Connor (1992, 123). Of course, countries like Malaysia also had high levels of output, but it consisted almost exclusively of assembling and packaging wafers produced elsewhere, whereas Korea's production, like that of the advanced countries, involved wafer fabrication, not just assembly and packaging.

5. DOE (1989, 58–59); *Economic Times*, June 5, 1992.

6. See chapter 5, discussion of Brazil in section on "greenhouse construction and custodial institutions."

7. On falling prices, see Schmitz and Cassiolato (1992, 27–29).

8. In 1990 DEPIN (1991, 13) estimated the population of firms, including hardware and software, telecommunications, industrial automation, semiconductors, and instruments (but not including purely service firms), at 682 firms, over 90 percent of which were locally owned.

9. The Sycor 400. See discussion of COBRA in chapter 6, section on "the demiurge option."

10. *Wolgan Computer* (May 1991, 102) estimates computer shipments as accounting for only about 5 percent of Samsung Electronics' total sales, 23 percent of Goldstar's sales, and 16 percent of Daewoo Electronics' sales. Only in the cases of Hyundai Electronics and Daewoo Telecommunications, whose sales were substantially smaller, did computers account for a substantial portion of sales (42 percent and 43 percent, respectively). EIAK's estimates for computer sales of the major electronics chaebol in 1986 show even smaller shares. According to EIAK, Daewoo Telecommunications was the only firm with substantial computer sales

in 1986 (about U.S. $93 million), while Samsung and Goldstar each had only about $20 million in computer sales. See Evans and Tigre (1989b, 27, table 11).

11. For example, tariffs on imported components, excise and sales taxes, and so forth.

12. For example, price comparisons between Brazil and Germany in the late 1980s found Brazilian informatics prices only 15–25 percent higher (see Meyer-Stamer 1992, 103). Schmitz and Hewitt (1992, 27, 33) suggest a differential of 25–40 percent between Brazil and Great Britain.

13. It is, of course, difficult to prove that TNC prices reflected "what the market would bear" rather than costs, but the lack of difference does undercut arguments that changing the policy's novel aspect—its refusal to allow TNC subsidiaries to produce locally—would have resulted in substantially lower local prices.

14. IBM was selling used 4341s, which were more powerful than the VAX750s (and normally more expensive), at bargain basement prices. (IBM's 4341 was a small mainframe and therefore outside the market reserve.) See Evans and Tigre (1989a, 1755).

15. In 1987, after the VAX had been on the market almost ten years, the total accumulated stock of VAX 750s (and 780s) in Korea (where DEC machines were imported instead of being made by a local licensee) was only 150, whereas Elebra sold 88 750s in Brazil in only three years. See Evans and Tigre (1989b, 22; 1989a, 1754).

16. If we add local Korean production for the domestic market of $156 million to imports of $473 million (see Evans and Tigre 1989b, 14, table 6, 15, table 7), the result is a total domestic hardware market of about $630 million. If we add imports of roughly $150 million to total Brazilian hardware production for 1986 revenues of $2,126 million and subtract $267 million of exports (DEPIN 1991, 16, 22) and deflate by about 30 percent to account for nonhardware revenues of hardware firms, this gives an estimate of about $1.4 billion, or double the Korean domestic market. The Brazilian figures do not, of course, take into account contraband, which by the mid-1980s was already considerable.

17. Korean production of PCs for the domestic market was $46.5 million in 1986. Brazilian production of PCs was $192.3 million in 1985 (Evans and Tigre 1989b, 12, table 5, 15, table 7). Again, this comparison considers only consumption of locally produced Brazilian PCs, not the more "internationally competitive" and untaxed contraband PCs.

18. Obviously, if SEI had been able to hold the line on licensing international systems, COBRA and SCOPUS would have gotten a better return on their investment, but between losses to contraband software, pressure from local users, and international pressure from the United States, such a policy was untenable (see Evans 1989b; Bastos 1992).

19. For a more positive assessment of the development of Brazil's software sector, see Schware (1992a, 1992b).

20. See the discussion of trends in R&D and training expenditures in chapter 8, section on "Brazil: alliances or subsidiaries."

21. For a detailed history of HCL see Computers Today (December 1988, 30–47).

22. Their partner, UPTRON, was one of the electronics companies set up by a state government (Uttar Pradesh) rather than the central government.

23. For example, their Busybee PC was launched at a price of RS $50,000 in 1985 and its price was cut by 60 percent the next year. By the following year it led the industry in PC sales.

24. See discussion of India in chapter 5, section on "greenhouse construction and custodial institutions."

25. According to some Indian market researchers, about 85 percent of India's minis were UNIX systems by 1988.

26. See discussion of COBRA in chapter 6, section on "the demiurge option."

27. Both used the Motorola 68000 series microprocessors and projected an eventual 68030 multiprocessor implementation.

28. IDM steadily lost momentum since its formation but was still ranked eighteenth in overall sales when HCL stepped in.

29. The INTEL 8086.

30. The 80386 chip.

31. The new mini was called the Landmark.

32. The 80486.

33. That is, selected by INTEL as a site for early testing of a new product.

34. An ironic footnote to the 486 story is that the company that beat even WIPRO off the mark in designing a single-processor 486 machine was a revitalized DCM Data Products, the company that Shiv Nadar and his colleagues had left behind fifteen years earlier.

35. With CMC considered a systems integrator rather than a software company, Datamatics ranked fourth in 1989–90 (*Dataquest* 1990, 57). See *Dataquest* (1990, 104) for a brief description Datamatics.

36. Looking at the packaged software market, Schware (1992a, 146, table 1) estimates Brazil's domestic market at $360 million, Korea's at $107 million, and India's at $90 million in 1989. *Dataquest* (July 1992, 26) estimates 1989–90 total domestic software sales at only about $72 million (Rs 1,010 million, using an exchange rate of Rs14 to the dollar) compared to DEPIN's (1991, 17) estimate of $389 for Brazilian software revenues in 1989.

37. Ernst and O'Connor (1992, 134–35) estimate India's software production at $160 million in 1986–87, with exports accounting for $60 million, whereas Korea's total production was only $50 million, with exports of only $6.3 million, one-tenth India's.

38. No private Indian firms dared venture into the semiconductor industry. The Semiconductor Complex Ltd. (SCL), India's attempt at the demiurge in semiconductors, was a disaster. When it came on stream in 1984, the SCL was completely underscaled in an industry where cumulative economies of scale are crucial. Looking at Indian semiconductor production in 1987, Sridharan (1989, 290) estimated that "minimum economic scale for any one device in ICs [integrated circuit chips] would be about ten times the total number of all ICs produced." The disadvantages of uneconomic scale were exacerbated by the tendency toward "chasing micron barriers instead of the market" (Subramanian 1989, 327). While SCL did manage to develop a 3-micron process, the only product produced in large scale was watch chips (Subramanian 1989, 328). In February 1989 a major

fire destroyed SCL's wafer fabrication facility and R&D area. The DOE could close its 1988–89 report on the SCL by saying only, "Steps are being taken to ensure that the highly trained personnel at SCL, who have been affected by the fire in terms of employment, are not dispersed, and their services continue to be available" (1989, 46–47).

39. See discussion of Korea in section on "greenhouse contruction and custodial institutions" in chapter 5.

40. See Ernst and O'Connor (1992, 253) and chapter 6 in this volume..

41. *Electronics Korea* (3(2), 16). Figures are from the Ministry of Trade and Industry. Goldstar is reputed to be investing in a $2.2 billion wafer fabrication facility that will come on line in 1996 (Ernst and O'Connor 1992, 216).

42. Dynamic Random Access Memories (the most standard form of memory chips) with 64,000 and 256,000 bits of memory capacity.

43. See chapter 6.

44. As is usually the case in the success of risky ventures, some luck was involved as well. The U.S.-Japanese semiconductor agreement, restricting Japanese exports to the United States (see Prestowicz 1988; Krauss 1993), drove up prices and increased Korea's share of the U.S. market, boosting the fortunes of Korean producers; some would argue saving them from disaster.

45. While Korea was exporting $4 billion worth of semiconductors at the end of 1980s it was importing $3.6 billion worth (EIAK 1991, 25). Figures are for 1989.

46. As Taiwanese firms discovered to their chagrin, the absence of local semiconductor production can be a serious disadvantage to the local computer producers. According to Ernst and O'Connor (1992, 206), industry experts estimate that Taiwan's ACER could have come closer to shipping 500,000 instead of 400,000 PCs in 1988 if it had had sufficient access to DRAM.

47. Korea's positive balance in consumer electronics equipment was about $4 billion in 1989 (EIAK 1991, 37).

48. E.g., INTEL's 80386 or Motorola's 68030 at that time.

49. E.g., WIPRO's Landmark, HCL's Magnum, or COBRA's Linha X.

50. "Making boxes" is the pejorative term used to describe the manufacture of commodity informatics hardware that must be sold on a strictly price-competitive basis.

51. "Selling solutions" is another way of describing systems integration activities. It means selling whole systems, including hardware and software, integrated and customized in such a way as to meet a customer's information-processing needs, and is a more sophisticated, higher-return kind of participation in the informatics sector.

52. "Original equipment manufacture" is the term used when a product is manufactured for another firm, which then sells it under its own brand name, as for example when Daewoo sold PCs to Leading Edge, which then sold them as its own, or when Trigem produced printers to be sold by Epson under Epson's brand name.

53. For example, in 1987, while they managed a $3.5 billion export surplus in electronics trade with the United States, they also had a $2.5 billion deficit in their trade with Japan.

54. See EIAK (1991a, 21). Fortunately for the companies involved, peripherals exports continued to grow so that total exports for computers and peripherals remained constant from 1989 to 1990.

55. Dytz's supermini competition and the Brazilian banks' commitment to becoming supermini producers, for example.

56. On the one hand, Machines Bull, a product of French nationalist aspirations, decided it could not survive without closer ties to NEC. On the other hand, Apple and IBM announced an improbable strategic alliance in the PC market.

Chapter 8
The New Internationalization

1. For example, Prem Shivdasani, in a seminar in Bangalore in the fall of 1990, predicted that by the end of 1991 IBM would be back in India. In fact he was right, since the deal with the Tatas was substantively in place by December 1991.

2. Evans (1986a, 802); DEPIN (1991, 52). See also table 7.3.

3. See the discussion in the section on "the changing IT industry" in chapter 5.

4. The rules on joint ventures were actually complicated. In theory a foreign firm could have up to 30 percent of the voting capital as well as substantial nonvoting capital, but "technological control" was also supposed to rest with the local firm, which effectively precluded a TNC setting up a joint venture to use its proprietary technology.

5. Under the new Informatics Law (8.248 of October 23, 1991, which went into effect in April 1993), a firm had to have 51 percent of the voting shares owned by persons living in Brazil, but since two-thirds of the total equity could be nonvoting, total foreign ownership of 83 percent (all the nonvoting plus just under half of the one-third voting) still qualified. See Tigre (1993).

6. See discussion of Itautec's strategy in chapters 5 and 7.

7. The AS-400 not only provided the link between IBM mainframe architectures and PCs but was a hugely successful line in its own right. At the beginning of the 1990s, Itautec and IBM created a joint venture, ITEC, owned 51 percent by Itautec and 49 percent by IBM, to do the manufacturing, marketing, and second-level support of the AS-400 line, with Itautec and IBM both doing the sales and service.

8. The communications controllers deal was brought to successful fruition and the operation won a quality award from IBM in 1993.

9. In the mid-1980s it tried to negotiate a broad technological alliance with AT&T, only to have its efforts founder on the bitter fight between the United States and Brazil. See Evans (1989c); Bastos (1992); and chapter 6 in this volume. Despite this setback, SID eventually became one of the early licensees of AT&T's UNIX, and its sister telecommunications company also developed technological ties with AT&T. At the same time, SID negotiated an agreement to manufacture Fujitsu's large-scale disk drives.

10. LABO continued its relationship with Nixdorf (now folded into Seimens), which had lasted since the 1977 mini competition. ABC Telematica continued its reliance on Honeywell-Bull, which included both licensing of superminis and a joint venture in mainframes. The Iochpe group, owners of Edisa, consolidated

their relationship with Hewlett-Packard in much the same way that Elebra's owning groups had done with DEC. HP/Tesis, whose ties to HP appeared in practice to be almost like those of a subsidiary (see Meyer-Stamer 1989, 56), was folded into Edisa. Edisa became a joint venture with the Iochpe owning 51 percent and HP owning 49 percent, and the company was integrated more firmly into HP's global organizational structure (Tigre 1993, 17).

11. At the beginning of the 1990s, NEC controlled 33 percent of SCOPUS, which was trying to make a place for itself in the local notebook market (see Tigre 1993, 17).

12. See DEPIN (1991, 52) for the 1990 share. For earlier shares, see Evans (1986a, 802) and table 7.3, above.

13. For example, as it entered the AS-400 agreement with IBM, Itautec had just developed its own communications board designed to link the AS-400 to PCs. Those involved in the development claimed that their board was half the size and significantly cheaper than the existing international standard. It was also an archetypal example of the strategic use of international ties. At its core was a chip designed by a tiny U.S. firm. Seeing the chip described in an early trade journal report and recognizing its potential, Itautec had helped finance its development because Itautec knew it would need such a board and the rules at that time would have prevented its importation.

14. It should be noted that there was no immediate evidence of compensating trends in the foreign-owned sector of the industry. Training expenditures by foreign firms dropped by more than two-thirds between 1989 and 1990 (DEPIN 1991, 31).

15. By 1990 the number of fellowships requested by industry dropped to a little over one-third its 1988 level, from 283 to 103 (DEPIN 1991, 33).

16. Tigre (1993, 14), reporting sales and profit data from *Computerworld* (Brazil), November 30, 1992, 21.

17. It had about 30 percent of the local market for programmable logic controllers (see DEPIN 1991, 76–81).

18. One other intriguing, though ephemeral, stimulant to an international orientation in India was the brief burgeoning of hardware exports to the Eastern bloc at the end of the 1980s, between the opening of markets in the Soviet Union and its collapse. To be sure, Eastern bloc exports involved selling, for very soft currency, PCs whose components were purchased for hard currency, and therefore made sense only so long as India's demand for rubles to import Soviet defense equipment and other goods justified the exchange. More sophisticated hardware like HCL's Horizon or Magnum or WIPRO's Landmark were excluded by U.S. export controls (which applied because they used microprocessors produced in the United States), but smaller producers of PCs, ATs, and peripherals, especially new firms looking for a way to break into the business like Pertech in microcomputers and Essen in peripherals, found an unprecedented new source of growth in the opening of the Soviet market.

19. See also the discussion of HCL in chapter 7.

20. The Singapore subsidiary allowed them to take an Indian-designed machine, try it out in a more demanding market, and then modify it for reintroduction in India.

21. Mentor Graphics was the world's largest supplier of tools for VLSI design and printed circuit board (PCB) layout (*Computers Today*, December 1988, 15).

22. HCL also put together a technology agreement with Tolerant Systems, suppliers of technology to the Korean NAIS system.

23. Most specifically its UNIX commercial suite and the Magnum hardware platform that went with it.

24. Any manufacturing of boards for HCL's hardware platform would be done by an American company (SCI) (reversing the stereotypical industrialized country/less-developed country division of labor). Typical of its early contracts was one with Sybase, a U.S. software producer.

25. E.g., surface mount board stuffing.

26. The biggest block was held by HP's former distributors (Blue Star), who were transformed into a financial partner without managerial input.

27. The launching of HCL-HP also set up an interesting comparison with DEC's strategy. Prior to HCL-HP, DEC and HP had seemed embarked on a similar trajectory. Like HP, DEC had replaced it old distributor relationship with a 40/60 manufacturing venture in which the old distributor was a financial partner. As in the HP subsidiary, the majority of the 60 percent equity that was locally held was distributed to the public, so that DEC retained managerial control. This in itself was a precedent-breaking move for DEC at the time, since (with the exception of Brazil) it made it a rule to retain complete control over the manufacturing of its products. At the end of the 1980s the local DEC operation was already the ninth largest informatics company in the country, and, having achieved 421 percent growth in its first year of operation, it was expected to be in the top five within a few years (*Dataquest* 1990, 79). Hewlett-Packard was slower to get off the ground. Its software company was in operation, exporting three-quarters of a million dollars back to the parent, but its hardware operation was still getting under way. If HP's more radical new internationalization outperforms DEC's more conservative strategy, it will be a vindication of new internationalization from the TNCs' point of view.

28. See the discussion of PSI in chapter 7.

29. Known as the Sirius.

30. NB: the accusation of Vinay Despande, one of the founders of PSI, that the absence of husbandry lay at the root of the failure of PSI's technological strategy, cited in chapter 6.

31. Since it also got royalties on sales of the board itself, the deal was doubly profitable.

32. WIPRO also became a Beta test site for INTEL (which gave it better access to new INTEL technology) and was a distributor of Autodesk CAD systems (*Dataquest*, April 1989).

33. See the discussion of TCS in chapter 7.

34. Prepackaged software sold on a commodity basis as opposed to customized software systems designed to fit the needs of specific customers or types of customers.

35. A prominent example here is WIPRO Systems Ltd., the software counterpart to WIPRO's hardware venture. WSL had aspirations to develop packages in India and market them in the United States using links to U.S. firms. It found,

however, that the packaged software market was extremely difficult to crack and was forced to retreat to a more conventional strategy.

36. See the discussion of Datamatics in chapter 7.

37. By the end of the decade TI's subsidiary was supplying its parent with several million dollars a year in software.

38. For example, having been called in (along with a number of competing firms) with a Third World central bank to consult on a financial information system, COSL was able to say, "We can put 20 people on the job of implementing our proposals." None of the other consultants could make the same offer, so COSL got the contract, which led in turn to additional high-level work.

39. Obviously, the returns from creating a successful packaged software product, like Lotus 1-2-3 or MS-DOS, which generates an extended flow of proprietary returns, are orders of magnitude larger still.

40. Domestic production was $880 million and exports were $723 million, leaving $157 million available for the domestic market. Imports were $473 million, creating a total domestic market of $630 million (see Evans and Tigre 1989b, 10, 14, tables 4 and 6.

41. Views attributed to Bae Jong-Ki and Joo Dae-young (*Electronics Korea* 3 (9), 17).

42. In consumer electronics only 8 percent of total production was controlled by firms with even partial foreign ownership, and most of that was controlled by joint ventures (*Electronics Korea* 3(9), 12). Between the end of the 1970s and the end of the 1980s, the number of companies operating in the Masan free export zone (the archetypal haven for simple electronics assemblers) declined by about 20 percent (*Electronics Korea* 2(9), 16).

43. A small U.S. firm that subsequently found itself unable to keep up with the pace of change in the memory business and had to drop out.

44. Known as the 5550.

45. Samsung also has cross-licensing agreements with Texas Instruments, Motorola, Phillips, Hitachi, and Unisys, but its agreement with IBM is the broadest and probably the most significant.

46. The chip agreement with Hitachi was to OEM 1-Megabit DRAMs (and eventually 4- and 16-Megabit DRAMs) for Hitachi (*Electronics Korea* 3(2), 16), but according to Ernst and O'Connor (1992, 163) it involves no significant exchange of technology. The mainframe agreement allows Goldstar to assemble and sell M-series mainframes.

47. A small Silicon Valley producer.

48. According to Ernst and O'Connor (1992, 165), Daewoo ended up with a controlling interest in Zymos.

49. *Korea Herald*, May 19, 1987; *Electronics Korea* 3(3), 11.

50. *IEEE Spectrum*, quoted in *B. K. Electronics* (1(6), 38).

51. Hyundai benefited in an analogous way from its OEM with Blue Chip (see above). In the short run, the Blue Chip experience was a disaster. The Arizona distributor contracted for many times the volume it was capable of selling, and Hyundai got stuck with inventory.

52. Ernst and O'Connor (1992, 163) have a less flattering view of the tie-up, arguing that Samsung was chosen not for "technological excellence" but because

its "mundane capabilities" made it a good second source for IBM. Even if this interpretation were true, it remains the case that Samsung has developed capabilities unique in the Third World and that its capabilities have given it leverage in forging an exceptionally strong set of international alliances.

53. State-owned firms may still play some role. In addition to the examples set out in chapter 7, the Taiwanese government's strategic use of state ownership in the construction of transnational alliances in semiconductor production is a good case in point. See Ernst and O'Connor (1992, 214–16); Hong (1992); and chapter 6, note 52.

Chapter 9
Lessons from Informatics

1. According to *The Economist* (1993, 5,15), IBM's share of world computer and software revenues was 38 percent in 1980 and less than 19 percent in 1992.

2. See Migdal (1988, 204–5), as discussed in chapter 2, section on "comparative institutional variations."

Chapter 10
Rethinking Embedded Autonomy

1. The description that follows is based on reports in the *Chungang Ilbo*, March 17–19, 1989, and research by Young Min Yun.

2. The subway workers' union was the biggest local in the Seoul area. More important, it had decided two years earlier to secede from the government-sponsored Federation of Korean Trade Unions (FKTU) and form an extralegal Seoul Area Council of Trade Unions (Senohyop). Senohyop in turn provided a key building block for an extralegal national council of trade unions, the Junnohyop, which attained a membership of 200,000, challenging the hitherto uncontested dominance of the FKTU.

3. See *New York Times*, February 19, 1989, 3-1, 10

4. For another version of the argument in relation to Brazil, see Stepan (1985).

5. For a careful quantitative analysis of Korea's changing class structure, see Yun (1994).

6. An incident involving some women textile workers during the regime of Park Chung Hee provides an excellent illustration. In 1978 the official Labor Day celebrations of Korea's National Union of Textile Workers (NTWU) turned into an embarrassment. Union leaders, government officials, and a national television audience were shocked when eighty women workers from the Dongil Textile Company rallied to protest the company's efforts to reimpose an ŏyong (literally, company-tool) leadership on their union and the collusion of the government and the NTWU in the company's efforts. The workers' protests garnered support of both Catholic and Protestant church hierarchies. A special Labor Day Mass at the Dapdong Catholic Church in Inchon provided the occasion for the beginning of a hunger strike by fifty workers, while the Protestant Urban Industrial Mission housed a second hunger strike. The Catholic cardinal even met with President Park Chung Hee on their behalf. In the end, the efforts of the workers and their

supporters were unrequited. Despite a promise from President Park to reinstate the union's elected leadership, the workers were fired by the company and black-listed throughout the textile industry by the National Union of Textile Workers. (This account is taken from M. S. Kim (1987, 198–202), who in turn relies on research by J. N. Lim.)

7. See, for example, Deyo (1989); M. S. Kim (1987); Koo (1987); Yun and Folk (1990).

8. See, for example, Amsden (1989); E. M. Kim (1987); M. S. Kim (1987); Woo (1991).

9. See the discussion of the literature in chapters 2 and 3, especially Migdal (1988).

10. Again, this speculation follows closely Seidman's (1994) account of the way industrialists' attitudes toward the usefulness of the state changed in Brazil and South Africa over the course of the 1970s and 1980s.

11. This discussion of Kerala relies heavily on Herring (1991) as well as the recent research of Patrick Heller (1994).

12. For an early discussion of Kerala's welfare successes, see Bardhan (1974). For later statistics see Heller (1994).

13. Mencher (1980) notes the contrast between Kerala, where the expected number of doctors were in fact on duty in the primary health centers she visited, and Tamil Nadu, where half the centers she visited were without doctors because those assigned were on leave, off at conferences or training sessions, or attending to personal matters (see Franke and Chasin 1989, 45).

14. It is interesting to note that the shops are actually run by private owners, in contradiction to the usual Indian practice of emphasizing the state as demiurge and relying on SOEs.

15. According to a United Nations study (1975), fair-price shops accounted for two-thirds of the rice and wheat consumed by the poorest 30 percent of Kerala's population (Franke and Chasin 1989, 31).

16. In "instrumentalist" versions of Marxist theories of the state, there is a "principal-agent" relation between the state and capitalists, in which the latter are the principals and the former is the agent. See Carnoy (1984) for a discussion.

17. According to Franke and Chasin (1989, 39–40), the proportion of forest land in Kerala has dropped from 27 percent to 7–10 percent over the course of the last twenty-five years, threatening Kerala's water supply.

18. None of this is to say that such a reconstruction is impossible. In some ways Kerala is in a better position than Brazil or the rest of India. Unless current tendencies toward the fragmentation of politics go further, it still has the advantage of a state capable of behaving as a coherent corporate actor. Its proven ability to deliver infrastructure is also an advantage. Perhaps most important, it has shown the ability to generate a reservoir of extraordinarily inexpensive skilled labor. The basic issue is whether it can create the kind of pact between capital and labor that allowed industrialization to coexist with mobilization in advanced industrial countries (see Heller 1994). Speculation on this issue goes well beyond what can legitimately be attempted here.

19. See the discussion in chapter 3. See also Kohli (1990) on the "ungovernability of India."

20. For a complementary perspective on the virtues of "encompassing" forms of social organization, see Olson (1982).

21. Data are from Lacina, as cited in Katzenstein (1984, 50).

22. Katzenstein's evaluation of the importance of the state reflects this ambivalence. Anxious to demonstrate that the state does not dominate the system in a unilateral way, he portrays it as only one actor in "a broadly based policy network" (1984, 64).

23. See the opening discussion in chapter 2.

24. See the discussion of Migdal in chapter 2.

25. American occupation is, of course, one of the common denominators in the historical development of these developmental states. On its effects in Japan, see Johnson (1982); on Taiwan, see Pang (1987); on Korea, see Jun (1991).

26. It is important to underline the full configuration of circumstances that pushed these states in the direction of a focus on industrialization in order to avoid the simplistic assumption that somehow small size and minimal resource base are sufficient to produce industrialization. The path of stagnation or decay is always open to small countries, as so many small Third World countries painfully demonstrate.

References

ORGANIZATIONS are often cited in the text by acronym (e.g. MOC, DOE), but are alphabetized here by their full name (e.g. Ministry of Communications, Department of Electronics). In case of difficulty, the reader should check the list of acronyms at the beginning of the book.

Books and Articles

Associação Brasileira da Indústria de Computadores e Periféricos (ABICOMP). 1987. "O Mercado De Bens De Informática: Evolução Das Importações Autorizadas Em 1985 E 1986." Rio de Janeiro: ABICOMP.

———. 1988. *Informe* 24 (June).

Abranches, Sergio. 1978. "The Divided Leviathan: The State and Economic Policy Making in Authoritarian Brazil." Ph.D. diss., Department of Political Science, Cornell University.

Adler, Emanuel. 1986. "Ideological Guerrillas and the Quest for Technological Autonomy: Development of a Domestic Computer Industry in Brazil." *International Organization* 40, 3 (Summer): 673–705.

———. 1987. *The Power of Ideology: The Quest for Technological Autonomy in Argentina and Brazil*. Berkeley and Los Angeles: University of California Press.

Agarwal, S. M. 1985. "Electronics in India: Past Strategies and Future Possibilities." *World Development* 13, 3 (March): 273–92.

Ahluwalia, Isher Judge. 1985. *Industrial Growth in India: Stagnation since the Mid-Sixties*. Delhi: Oxford University Press.

———. 1987. "The Role of Policy in Industrial Development." In *The Development Process of the Indian Economy*, ed. P. R. Drahmananda and V. R. Panchamukhi. Delhi: Himalaya.

Alam, Ghayur. 1989. "A Study of India's Electronics Industry." Report Prepared for OECD Development Centre Research Project on Technological Change and the Electronics Sector—Perspectives and Policy Options for Newly Industrializing Economies. Paris: OECD.

Ames, Barry. 1987. *Political Survival: Politicians and Public Policy in Latin America*. Berkeley and Los Angeles: University of California Press.

Amsden, Alice. 1979. "Taiwan's Economic History: A Case of Etatisme and a Challenge to Dependency Theory." *Modern China* 5, 3 (July): 341–80.

———. 1985. "The State and Taiwan's Economic Development." In *Bringing the State Back In*, ed. Peter Evans, Dietrich Rueschemeyer, and Theda Skocpol. New York: Cambridge University Press.

———. 1989. *Asia's Next Giant: South Korea and Late Industrialization*. New York: Oxford University Press.

———. 1992. "A Theory of Government Intervention in Late Industrialization." In *State and Market in Development: Synergy or Rivalry*, ed. Louis Putterman and Dietrich Rueschemeyer. Boulder: Lynne Rienner.

———. 1994. "Why Isn't the Whole World Experimenting with the East Asian

Model to Develop?: A Review of *The East Asian Miracle,*" *World Development* 22, 4 (April) 627–33.

Anchordoguy, Marie. 1988. "Mastering the Market: Japanese Government Targeting of the Computer Industry." *International Organization* 42, 3 (Summer): 509–43.

Anuário Informática Hoje 87/88. 1988. "Listing of Brazilian Informatics Firms." Rio de Janeiro: Informatica Hoje.

Appelbaum, Richard, and Jeffrey Henderson, eds. 1992. *States and Development in the Asia Pacific Region.* Newbury Park, Calif.: Sage.

Arrighi, Giovanni, and Jessica Drangel. 1986. "The Stratification of the World-Economy." *Review* 10:9–74.

Auster, Richard D., and Morris Silver. 1979. *The State as a Firm: Economic Forces in Political Development.* The Hague: Martinus Nijhoff.

Baek, Jun Ho. 1988. "Computerization of the National Administrative Network." *Kumpyuta Jungbosa* (Computer world) (May): 46–49.

Baer, Werner. 1969. *The Development of the Brazilian Steel Industry.* Nashville: Vanderbilt University Press.

———. 1989. *The Brazilian Economy: Growth and Development.* New York: Praeger.

Baptista, Margarida A. C. 1987. "A Indústria Eletrônica De Consuma a Nível Internacional E No Brazil: Padrões De Concorrência, Inovação Tecnológica E Caráter Da Intervenção Do Estado." Tese de Mestrado, Universidade Estadual de Campinas, São Paulo.

Bardhan, Pranab. 1974. "On Life and Death Questions." *Economic and Political Weekly* 9, 32–34 (August): 1293–1304.

———. 1984. *The Political Economy of Development in India.* Oxford: Basil Blackwell.

Barzelay, Michael. 1986. *The Politicized Market Economy: Alcohol in Brazil's Energy Strategy.* Berkeley and Los Angeles: University of California Press.

Bastos, Maria Ines. 1992. "The Interplay of Domestic and International Constraints on the Informatics Policy of Brazil." UNU/INTECH Working Paper no. 6.

Bates, Robert H. 1981. *Markets and States in Tropical Africa: The Political Basis of Agricultural Policies.* Berkeley and Los Angeles: University of California Press.

———. 1989. *Beyond the Miracle of the Market: The Political Economy of Agrarian Development in Kenya.* Cambridge: Cambridge University Press.

Becker, David G. 1983. *The New Bourgeoisie and the Limits of Dependency: Mining, Class, and Power in "Revolutionary" Peru.* Princeton: Princeton University Press.

Bello, Walden, and Stephanie Rosenfeld. 1990. *Dragons in Distress: Asia's Miracle Economies in Crisis.* San Francisco: Food First, Institute for Food and Development Policy.

Bennett, Douglas C., and Kenneth Sharpe. 1985. *Transnational Corporations Versus the State.* Princeton: Princeton University Press.

Bergsman, Joel. 1970. *Brazil: Industrialization and Trade Policies.* New York: Oxford University Press.

Bhambiri, C. P. 1986. "Bureaucracy in India." In *A Survey of Research in Public Administration, 1970–79*, ed. Kuldeep Mathur (sponsored by Indian Council of Social Science Research). New Delhi: Concept Publishing Company.

Bharat Electronics Ltd. (BEL). 1988. *34th Annual Report 1987–88*. Bangalore: BEL.

———. 1989. Company Brochure. Bangalore: BEL.

Biggart, Nicole Woolsey. 1991. "Explaining Asian Economic Organization: Toward a Weberian Institutional Perspective." *Theory and Society* (Fall): 199–232.

Bloom, Martin. 1989. "Technological Change and the Electronics Sector—Perspectives and Policy Options for the Republic of Korea." Paper presented at the Workshop on Technological Change and the Electronics Sector: Perspectives and Policy Options for Newly Industrializing Economies, June. Paris: OECD Development Centre.

Boli-Bennett, John. 1980. "Global Integration and the Universal Increase of State Dominance: 1910–1970." In *Studies of the Modern World-System*, ed. Albert Bergesen. New York: Academic Press.

Brenner, Robert. 1976. "Agrarian Class Structure and Economic Development in Pre-Industrial Europe." *Past and Present* 70 (February): 30–75.

———.1977. "The Origins of Capitalist Development: A Critique of Neo-Smithian Marxism." *New Left Review* 104:24–92.

Brett, E. A. 1987. "States, Markets, and Private Power in the Developing World: Problems and Possibilities." *IDS Bulletin* 18, 3 (July): 31–37.

Brooke, James. 1992. "Looting Brazil." *The New York Times Magazine*, November 8, 30–33.

Brown, Martin, and Bruce McKern. 1986. *Aluminum, Copper, and Steel in Developing Countries*. An OECD Development Centre study. Paris: OECD.

Buchanan, James M., Robert D. Tollison, and Gordon Tullock, eds. 1980. *Toward a Theory of Rent-Seeking Society*. College Station: Texas A&M University Press.

Bureau of Industrial Costs and Prices, Government of India (BICP). 1987. *Report on Electronics*. New Delhi: Government of India.

Business Korea. 1987. *Business Korea Yearbook*. Seoul: Business Korea (published in collaboration with James Capel & Co. and Tongyang Securities Co. Ltd.).

Calder, Kent. 1993. *Strategic Capitalism: Private Business and Public Purpose in Japanese Industrial Finance*. Princeton: Princeton University Press.

Callaghy, Thomas. 1984. *The State-Society Struggle: Zaire in Comparative Perspective*. New York: Columbia University Press.

———. 1989. "Toward State Capability and Embedded Liberalism in the Third World: Lessons for Adjustment." In *Fragile Coalitions: The Politics of Economic Adjustment*, ed. Joan Nelson. Washington, D.C.: Overseas Development Council.

———. 1990. "Lost Between State and Market: The Politics of Economic Adjustment in Gambia, Zambia, and Nigeria" In *Economic Crisis and Policy Choice: The Politics of Economic Adjustment in the Third World*, ed. Joan M. Nelson. Princeton: Princeton University Press.

Cardoso, Fernando Henrique. 1975. *Autoritarismo E Democratização*. Rio de Janeiro: Paz e Terra.

Cardoso, Fernando Henrique, and Enzo Faletto. 1979. *Dependency and Development in Latin America*. Berkeley and Los Angeles: University of California Press.

Carnoy, Martin. 1984. *The State and Political Theory*. Princeton: Princeton University Press.

Cassiolato, José. 1992. "The User-Producer Connection in Hi-Tech: A Case Study of Banking Automation in Brazil." In *Hi-Tech for Industrial Development*, ed. Hubert Schmitz and José Cassiolato. London: Routledge.

Castells, Manuel. 1992. "Four Asian Tigers with a Dragon Head: A Comparative Analysis of the State, Economy, and Society in the Asian Pacific Rim." In *States and Development in the Asian Pacific Rim*, ed. Richard Appelbaum and Jeffrey Henderson. Newbury Park, Calif.: Sage Publications.

Centre for the Development of Telematics (C-DOT). 1987. *Annual Report, 1985–86*. New Delhi: C-DOT.

———. 1988. *C-DOT DSS: Family of Digital Switches, Gateway to ISDN*. New Delhi: C-DOT.

Chase-Dunn, Christopher. 1989. *Global Formation: Structures of the World Economy*. Cambridge, Mass.: Basil Blackwell.

Chatterjee, Bhaskar. 1990. *Japanese Management: Maruti and the Indian Experience*. New Delhi: Sterling Publishers.

Cheng, Tun-jen. 1987. "The Politics of Industrial Transformation: The Case of the East Asia NICs." Ph.D. diss., Department of Political Science, University of California, Berkeley.

Cho, In-Su. 1991. "Haengmang Jujonsaki, Aproei Haenglonun" (Whither NAIS main computer?). *Kyongyongkwa Computer* (August): 158–65.

Choi, Byung Sun. 1987. "Institutionalizing a Liberal Economic Order in Korea: The Strategic Management of Economic Change." Ph.D. diss., Kennedy School, Harvard University.

Chung, Joseph S. 1986. "Korea." In *National Policies for Developing High Technology Industries*, ed. Francis W. Rushing and Carole Ganz Brown. Boulder: Westview Press.

Cline, William. 1987. *Informatics and Development: Trade and Industrial Policy in Argentina, Brazil, and Mexico* (study funded by IBM). Washington, D.C.: Economics International, Inc.

Colclough, Christopher. 1991. "Structuralism versus Neo-liberalism: An Introduction." In *States or Markets?: Neo-liberalism and the Development Policy Debate*, ed. Christopher Colclough and James Manor. Oxford: Clarendon Press.

Collander, David, ed. 1984. *Neoclassical Political Economy: The Analysis of Rent-Seeking and DUP Activities*. Cambridge, Mass.: Ballinger.

Computer Maintenance Corporation (CMC). 1988a. *IMPRESS: Railway Passenger Reservation System*. New Delhi: CMC.

———. 1988b. *The Possibilities Are Infinite (Twelfth Annual Report, 1987–88)*. New Delhi: CMC.

Computer Mind. (Computer Annual). 1988. Seoul: Jusighoesa Minkom.

Costa Marques, Ivan da. 1988. "Developing Indigenous Systems Software in Latin America: The Sox Operating System Case." Paper presented at the International Symposium on Technology Policy in the Americas, December. Stanford University.

Crandall, Robert W. 1981. *The U.S. Steel Industry in Recurrent Crisis: Policy Options in a Competitive World.* Washington, D.C.: The Brookings Institution.

Cumings, Bruce. 1987. "The Origins and Development of the Northeast Asian Political Economy: Industrial Sectors, Product Cycles, and Political Consequences." In *The Political Economy of the New Asian Industrialism*, ed. Frederic Deyo. Ithaca, N.Y.: Cornell University Press.

Dahlman, Carl J. 1990. "Electronics Development Strategy: The Role of Government." Industry and Energy Dept. Working Paper, Industry series paper no. 37. Washington, D.C.: World Bank.

———. 1992. "Information Technology Strategies: Brazil and the East Asian Newly Industrializing Economies." In *High Technology and Third World Industrialization: Brazilian Computer Policy in Comparative Perspective*, ed. Peter B. Evans, Claudio R. Frischtak, and Paulo Basos Tigre. Berkeley: Institute of International Studies.

Dahlman, Carl J., and Claudio Frischtak. 1990. "National Systems Supporting Technical Advance in Industry: The Brazilian Experience." Industry and Energy Dept. Working Paper, Industry series paper no. 32. Washington, D.C.: World Bank.

———. 1991. "National Systems Supporting Technical Advance in Industry: The Brazilian Experience." Ms. (revised version of the paper above)

Dantas, Vera. 1988. *Guerrilha Tecnológica: A Verdadeira História da Política Nacional de Informática.* Rio de Janeiro: LTC Editora

Data Communications Corporation of Korea (DACOM). 1987. "NAIS Project" (mimeo). Seoul: DACOM.

———. 1988. *1987 Annual Report.* Seoul: DACOM.

———. 1991. *1990 Annual Report.* Seoul: DACOM.

Dataquest. 1988. "The Dataquest Top Ten—1987–88." Special issue (n.d.).

Dataquest. 1989. "The Dataquest Top Twenty—1988–89." Special issue (July).

Dataquest. 1990. "The Dataquest Top Twenty—1989–90." Special issue (July).

Data Sources. 1986. *Hardware and Data Communications, 3rd Qrt.* New York: Ziff-Davis.

D'Costa, Anthony P. 1989. "Capital Accumulation, Technology, and the State: The Political Economy of Steel Industry Restructuring." Ph. D. diss., University of Pittsburgh, Graduate School of Public and International Affairs.

Dearlove, John. 1987. "Economists on the State." *IDS Bulletin* 18, 3 (July): 5–11.

Dearlove, John, and Gordon White. 1987. "Editorial Introduction." *IDS Bulletin* 18, 3 (July): 1–3.

Departamento de Política de Informática e Automação, Government of Brazil (DEPIN). 1991. *Panorama do Setor de Informática.* Brasilia: DEPIN.

Department of Electronics, Government of India (DOE). 1984. "New Computer Policy." *Electronics Information and Planning* 12, 2 (November): 89–94.

————. 1988. *Annual Report, 1987–88*. New Delhi: Government of India.

Department of Electronics, Government of India (DOE). 1989. *Annual Report, 1988–89*. New Delhi: Government of India.

Department of Industry, United Kingdom (DOI). 1982. "A Programme for Advanced Information Technology: The Report of the Alvey Committee." London: Her Majesty's Stationary Office.

Department of Science and Technology, Government of India (DST). 1989. *Pocket Data Book 1989*. New Delhi: Government of India.

Desai, Anita. 1991. "India: The Seed of Destruction." *New York Review of Books* 38, 12 (June 27): 3–4.

Deyo, Frederic, ed. 1987. *The Political Economy of the New Asian Industrialism*. Ithaca, N.Y.: Cornell University Press.

————. 1989. *Beneath the Miracle: Labor Subordination in the New Asian Industrialism*. Berkeley and Los Angeles: University of California Press.

Doner, Richard F. 1992. "Limits of State Strength: Toward an Institutionalist View of Economic Development." *World Politics* 44 (April): 398–431.

Dutkiewicz, Piotr, and Gavin Williams. 1987. "All the King's Horses and All the King's Men Couldn't Put Humpty-Dumpty Together Again." *IDS Bulletin* 18, 3 (July): 39–44.

Duvall, Raymond, and John R. Freeman. 1983. "The Techno-Bureaucratic Elite and the Entrepreneurial State in Dependent Industrialization." *American Political Science Review* 77, 3 (September): 569–87.

Dytz, Edison. 1986. *A Informática No Brasil*. São Paulo: Editora Nobel.

The Economist. 1993. "Within the Whirlwind." Special survey of the computer industry, 326 (February 27–March 5): 58.

Edquist, Charles, and Staffan Jacobsson. 1987. "The Integrated Circuit Industries of India and the Republic of Korea in an International Techno-Economic Context." *Industry and Development* 21 (November): 1–62.

Electronics and Telecommunications Research Institute (ETRI). 1985–87. *Annual Reports, 1985, 1986, 1987*. Daedog: ETRI.

Electronics Industry Association of Korea (EIAK). 1987. *Information Industry Annual—1987*. Compiled under supervision of Information Industry Division, Ministry of Trade and Industry. Seoul: EIAK.

————. 1988. *1987–1988 Electronic Industry of Korea*. Seoul: EIAK.

————. 1991a. *Statistics of Electronic and Electrical Industries—1990: Production, Export, Import*. Seoul: EIAK.

————. 1991b. *Jeongbo Saenop Yongam* (Annual of the informatics industry in Korea). Seoul: Korea Herald/Naeway Economic Daily.

Encarnation, Dennis. 1989. *Dislodging the Multinationals: India's Strategy in Comparative Perspective*. Ithaca, N.Y.: Cornell University Press.

Enos, J. 1984. "Government Intervention in the Transfer of Technology: The Case of South Korea." *IDS Bulletin* 15, 2 (April): 26–31.

Erber, Fabio. 1983. "O Complexo Eletrônico: Estrutura, Evolução Histórica E Padrão De Competição." Texto para Discussão no. 19. Rio de Janeiro: IEI/UFRJ.

————. 1985. "The Development of the 'Electronics Complex' and Government Policies in Brazil." *World Development* 13, 3 (March): 293–309.

Ernst, Dieter, and David O'Connor. 1992. *Competing in the Electronics Industry: The Experience of Newly Industrialising Countries.* An OECD Development Centre study. Paris: OECD.

Evans, Peter. 1979. *Dependent Development: The Alliance of Multinational, State, and Local Capital in Brazil.* Princeton: Princeton University Press.

———. 1981. "Collectivized Capitalism: Integrating Petrochemical Complexes and Capital Accumulation in Brazil." In *Authoritarian Capitalism: Brazil's Contemporary Economic and Political Development,* ed. Thomas C. Bruneau and Philippe Faucher. Boulder: Westview Press.

———. 1982. "Reinventing the Bourgeoisie: State Entrepreneurship and Class Formation in Dependent Capitalist Development." *American Journal of Sociology* 88 (supplement): S210-S247.

———. 1986a. "State, Capital and the Transformation of Dependence: The Brazilian Computer Case." *World Development* 14, 7 (July): 791–808.

———.1986b. "A Generalized Linkage Approach to Recent Industrial Development in Brazil: The Case of the Petrochemical Industry 1967–1979." In *Development, Democracy and the Art of Trespassing: Essays in Honor of Albert Hirschman,* ed. Alexandro Foxley, Guillermo O'Donnell, and Michael McPherson. South Bend: University of Notre Dame Press.

———. 1987. "Class, State and Dependence in East Asia: Lessons for Latin Americanists." In *The Political Economy of the New Asian Industrialism,* ed. Frederic Deyo. Ithaca, N.Y.: Cornell University Press.

———. 1989a. "High Technology Industry in the Americas: Corporate Strategies and Government Policies." La Jolla, Calif.: Institute of the Americas.

———. 1989b. "Predatory, Developmental and Other Apparatuses: A Comparative Political Economy Perspective on the Third World State." *Sociological Forum* 4, 4 (December): 561–87.

———. 1989c. "Declining Hegemony and Assertive Industrialization: U.S. Brazilian Conflict in the Computer Industry." *International Organization* 43, 2 (Spring): 207–38.

———. 1989d "The Future of the Developmental State." *The Korean Journal of Policy Studies* 4:129–46.

———. 1992a. "Indian Informatics in the 1980s: The Changing Character of State Involvement." *World Development* 20, 1 (January): 1–18.

———. 1992b. "The State as Problem and Solution: Predation, Embedded Autonomy and Adjustment." In *The Politics of Economic Adjustment: International Constraints, Distributive Politics, and the State,* ed. Stephan Haggard and Robert Kaufman. Princeton: Princeton University Press.

Evans, Peter, and Chien-kuo Pang. 1987. "State Structure and State Policy: Implications of the Taiwanese Case for Newly Industrializing Countries." Paper presented at the International Conference on Taiwan: A Newly Industrialized Country, September 3–5. National Taiwan University.

Evans, Peter, Dietrich Reuschemeyer, and Theda Skocpol, eds. 1985. *Bringing the State Back In.* New York: Cambridge University Press.

Evans, Peter, and John Stephens. 1988a. "Studying Development since the Sixties: The Emergence of a New Comparative Political Economy." *Theory and Society* 17:713–45.

———. 1988b. "Development and the World Economy." In *The Handbook of Sociology*, ed. Neil Smelser. Beverly Hills: Sage Publications.

Evans, Peter, and Paulo Tigre. 1989a. "Going Beyond Clones in Brazil and Korea: A Comparative Analysis of NIC Strategies in the Computer Industry." *World Development* 17, 11 (November): 1751–68.

———. 1989b. "Paths to Participation in 'Hi-Tech' Industry: A Comparative Analysis of Computers in Brazil and Korea." *Asian Perspective* 13, 1 (Spring-Summer): 5–35.

Fayad, Marwan, and Homa Motamen. 1986. *The Economics of the Petrochemical Industry*. London: Frances Pinter.

Federation of Korean Industries (FKI). 1991. *Hankukei Juyosanop: Hyonsangkwa Kwaje* (Major industries in Korea: Current situation and task). Seoul: FKI.

Fishlow, Albert. 1987. "Some Reflections on Comparative Latin American Economic Performance and Policy." Working Paper no. 8754. Department of Economics, University of California, Berkeley.

Flamm, Kenneth. 1987. *Targeting the Computer*. Washington, D.C.: The Brookings Institution.

———. 1988a. *Creating the Computer*. Washington, D.C.: The Brookings Institution.

———.1988b. "Trends in the Computer Industry and Their Implications for Developing Countries." Paper presented at the International Symposium on Technology Policy in the Americas, December. Stanford University.

Fortune. 1988. "The International 500: The Fortune Directory of the Biggest Industrial Corporations Outside of the US." (August 1): D7-D37.

Franke, Richard W., and Barbara H. Chasin. 1989. *Kerala: Radical Reform as Development in an Indian State*. Food First Development Report no. 6, October. San Francisco: Institute for Food and Development Policy.

Frischtak, Claudio. 1986. "Brazil." In *National Policies for Developing High Technology Industries*, ed. Francis W. Rushing and Carole Ganz Brown. Boulder: Westview Press.

———. 1989. "Specialisation, Technical Change and Competitiveness of the Brazilian Electronics Industry." Report prepared for the OECD Development Centre Research Project on Technological Change and the Electronics Sector: Perspectives and Policy Options For Newly-Industrialising Economics.

———. 1991. "Banking Automation And Productivity Change: The Brazilian Experience." Industry and Energy Department, Industry Series Paper no. 46, July. Washington, D.C.: World Bank .

———. 1992. "The International Market and the Competitive Potential of National Producers of Equipment and Systems." In *High Technology and Third World Industrialization: Brazilian Computer Policy in Comparative Perspective*, ed. Peter Evans, Claudio Frischtak, and Paulo Tigre. Research Series no. 85. Berkeley: International and Area Studies.

Frischtak, Leila, 1992. "Antinomies of Development? Governance Capacity and Adjustment Responses." Draft Ms. Industry Development Division, World Bank.

Furtado, Celso. 1965. *The Economic Growth of Brazil*. Berkeley and Los Angeles: University of California Press.

Gadacz, Oles. 1987. "South Korea's Supermini Strategy." *Datamation* 1, 2 (June 1): 68.

Gaio, Fatima. 1992. "Software Strategies for Developing Countries: Lessons from the International and Brazilian Experience." In *Hi-Tech for Industrial Development*, ed. Hubert Schmitz and José Cassiolato. London: Routledge.

Gargan, Edward. 1993. "A Students Prayer: Let Me Join the Ruling Class." *New York Times* (December 6): A4.

Geddes, Barbara. 1986. "Economic Development as a Collective Action Problem: Individual Interests and Innovation in Brazil." Ph.D. diss., Department of Political Science, University of California, Berkeley.

Gereffi, Gary, ed. 1991. *Manufacturing Miracles: Paths of Industrialization in Latin America and East Asia*. Princeton: Princeton University Press.

Gereffi, Gary, and Miguel Korzeniewicz. 1990. "Commodity Chains and Footwear Exports in the Semiperiphery." In *Semiperipheral States in the World-Economy*, ed. William Martin. Westport, Conn.: Greenwood Press.

──────. 1993. ed. *Commodity Chains and Global Capitalism*. Westport, Conn.: Praeger.

Gerschenkron, Alexander. 1962. *Economic Backwardness in Historical Perspective*. Cambridge, Mass.: Belknap.

Giddens, Anthony. 1987. *The Nation State and Violence*. Berkeley and Los Angeles: University of California Press.

Gilpin, Robert. 1987. *The Political Economy of International Relations*. Princeton: Princeton University Press.

Gold, Tom. 1981."Dependent Development in Taiwan." Ph.D. diss., Department of Sociology, Harvard University.

──────. 1986. *State and Society in the Taiwan Miracle*. Armonk, N.Y.: M. E. Sharpe.

Goldar, B. N. 1986. *Productivity Growth in Indian Industry*. New Delhi: Allied Publishers.

Goldstar Group (Kumsung). 1987. *The Will to Be #1 in the Field of Consumer and Industrial Electronics*. Seoul: Goldstar.

Gould, David. 1979. "The Administration of Underdevelopment." In *Zaire: The Political Economy of Underdevelopment*, ed. Guy Gran. New York: Praeger.

Gourevitch, Peter. 1986. *Politics in Hard Times*. Ithaca, N.Y.: Cornell University Press.

Gouveia, Raul de. 1988. "Brazilian Exports of Arms: The Catalytic Role of the Government." Paper presented at Multinational Culture: Social Impacts of a Global Economy, March 23–25. Hofstra University.

Government of India. 1988. *Software India '88: Market Backgrounder*. New Delhi: GOI

Gramsci, Antonio. 1971 (1989). *Selections from the Prison Notebooks*. New York: International Publishers.

Granovetter, Mark. 1985. "Economic Action and Social Structure: The Problem of Embeddedness." *American Journal of Sociology* 91, 3 (November): 481–510.

Grieco, Joseph. 1984. *Between Dependency and Autonomy: India's Experience with the International Computer Industry.* Berkeley and Los Angeles: University of California Press.

Grindle, Merilee. 1977. *Bureaucrats, Politicians and Peasants in Mexico: A Case Study in Public Policy.* Berkeley and Los Angeles: University of California Press.

Haggard, Stephan. 1990. *Pathways from the Periphery: The Politics of Growth in Newly Industrializing Countries.* Ithaca, N.Y.: Cornell University Press.

Haggard, Stephan, and Robert Kaufman, 1992. "Institutions and Economic Adjustment." In *The Politics of Economic Adjustment: International Constraints, Distributive Politics, and the State*, ed. Stephan Haggard and Robert Kaufman. Princeton: Princeton University Press.

Hagopian, Francis. 1986. "The Politics of Oligarchy: The Persistence of Traditional Elites in Contemporary Brazil." Ph.D. diss., Department of Political Science, MIT.

———. 1994. "Traditional Politics against State Transformation in Brazil." In *State Power and Social Forces: Domination and Transformation*, ed. Joel Migdal, Atul Kohli and Vivienne Shue. Cambridge: Cambridge University Press.

Hall, Peter. 1986. *Governing the Economy: The Politics of State Intervention in Britain and France.* New York: Oxford University Press.

Hamilton, Alexander. 1817. *The Soundness of the Policy of Protecting Domestic Manufactures* Philadelphia: J.R.A. Skerett.

Hamilton, Nora. 1982. *The Limits of State Autonomy: Post-Revolutionary Mexico.* Princeton: Princeton University Press.

Hamilton, Gary, and Nicole W. Biggart. 1988. "Market, Culture, and Authority: A Comparative Analysis of Management and Organization in the Far East." *American Journal of Sociology* 94 (supplement): S52–S94.

Hanson, A. H. 1966. *The Process of Planning: a Study of India's Five Year Plans 1950–64.* London: Oxford University Press.

Hazari, R.K. 1986. *Essays on Industrial Policy.* New Delhi: Concept Publishing Co.

Helena, Silvia. 1980. "A Indústria De Computadores: Evolução Das Decisões Governamentais." *Revista De Administração Pública* 14, 4 (October–December): 73–109.

———. 1984. *Rastro De Cobra.* 1984. Rio de Janeiro: Caio Domingues & Assocs.

Heller, Patrick. 1991. "The Politics of the State and the Politics of Society." Ms., Department of Sociology, University of California, Berkeley.

———. 1994. "The Politics of Redistributive Development: State and Class in Kerala, India." Ph.D. diss., Department of Sociology, University of California, Berkeley.

Herring, Ronald J. 1991. *Contesting the "Great Transformation": Land and Labor in South India.* Ms., Department of Political Science, Cornell University.

Hewitt, T. 1986. *Internalising the Social Benefits of Electronics: Case Studies in the Brazilian Informatics and Consumer Electronics Industry.* Brasilia: Projeto PNUD/OIT/CNRH.

Hirschman, Albert. 1958. *The Strategy of Economic Development.* New Haven: Yale University Press.

———. 1967. *Development Projects Observed.* Washington, D.C.: The Brookings Institution.

———. 1973. *Journeys Toward Progress: Studies of Economic Policy Making in Latin America.* New York: W. W. Norton.

———. 1977. "A Generalized Linkage Approach to Development, with Special Reference to Staples." *Economic Development and Cultural Change* 25 (supplement): 67–98.

———. 1981. *Essays in Trespassing: Economic to Politics and Beyond.* Cambridge: Cambridge University Press.

———. 1982. "Rival Interpretations of Market Society: Civilizing, Destructive, or Feeble?" *The Journal of Economic Literature* 20, 4 (December): 1463–84.

———. 1989. "Reactionary Rhetoric." *The Atlantic Monthly* (May): 63–70.

Hobday, Michael. 1984. *The Brazilian Telecommunications Industry: Accumulation of Microelectronic Technology in the Manufacturing and Service Sectors.* Textos para Discussão, no. 47. Rio de Janeiro: IEI/UFRJ.

Hong, Sung Gul. 1992. "State and Society in East Asian Development: Industrial Leapfrogging for Semiconductors in Taiwan and South Korea." Ph.D. diss., Department of Political Science, Northwestern University.

Hopkins, Terence, and Immanuel Wallerstein. 1986. *Processes of the World-System.* Beverly Hills: Sage Publications.

Huber, Evelyne, 1993a. "Assessments of State Strength in Comparative Perspective." Paper prepared for conference on Comparative Approaches to Latin America: Issues and Methods, July 29–31. Quito, Ecuador.

———. 1993b. "The Changing Role of the State in Latin America." Paper presented for the conference on Rethinking Development Theory, March. Chapel Hill, N.C.

Hull, Galen. 1979. "Zaire in the World System: In Search of Sovereignty." In *Zaire: the Political Economy of Underdevelopment,* ed. Guy Gran. New York: Praeger.

Itautec. 1987. *Relatório Anual—1986.* São Paulo: Itautec.

International Trade Administration, U.S. Department of Commerce (ITA). 1981. "Computers and Peripheral Equipment: Korea." Country Market Survey (March). Washington, D.C.: Government Printing Office.

Johnson, Chalmers. 1982. *MITI and the Japanese Miracle: The Growth of Industrial Policy, 1925–1975.* Stanford: Stanford University Press.

Johnson, William A. 1966. *The Steel Industry of India.* Cambridge: Harvard University Press.

Jones, Leroy P., and Il Sakong. 1980. *Government, Business and Entrepreneurship in Economic Development: The Korean Case. Studies in Modernization of the Korean Republic, 1945–75.* Cambridge: Harvard University Press.

Jones, Leroy P., and Edward S. Mason. 1982. "Role of Economic Factors in Determining the Size and Structure of the Public-Enterprise Sector in Less-Developed Countries with Mixed Economies." In *Public Enterprise in Less-Developed Countries,* ed. Leroy Jones. New York: Cambridge University Press.

Joseph, K. J. 1989. "Growth Performance of Indian Electronics under Liberalization." *Economic and Political Weekly* 24, 19 (August): 1915–20.

Jun, Sang-In. 1991. "State Making in South Korea: The U.S. Occupation and Korean Development." Ph.D. diss., Department of Sociology, Brown University.

Kabwit, Ghislain. 1979. "Zaire: The Roots of the Continuing Crisis" *Journal of Modern African Studies* 17, 3:381–407.

Kahler, Miles. 1990. "Orthodoxy and Its Alternatives: Explaining Approaches to Stabilization and Adjustment." In *Economic Crisis and Policy Choice: The Politics of Adjustment in the Third World*, ed. Joan M. Nelson. Princeton: Princeton University Press.

Kang, Mungu. 1989. "The Military Seizure of Power in 1979–80 in South Korea." Ph.D. diss., Department of Political Science, University of New Mexico.

Karl, Terry (forthcoming). *The Paradox of Plenty: Oil Booms and Petrostates.* Berkeley and Los Angeles: University of California Press.

Katzenstein, Peter J. 1984. *Corporatism and Change: Austria, Switzerland, and the Politics of Industry.* Ithaca, N.Y.: Cornell University Press.

———. 1985. "Small Nations in an Open International Economy: The Converging Balance of State and Society in Switzerland and Austria." In *Bringing the State Back In*, ed. Peter Evans, Dietrich Rueschemeyer, and Theda Skocpol. Cambridge: Cambridge University Press.

———, ed. 1978. *Between Power and Plenty.* Madison: University of Wisconsin Press.

Kelkar, Vijay. 1990. "India's Industrial Economy: Policies, Performance, and Reforms." Mimeo. New Delhi, India.

Kelkar, Vijay, and S. N. Kaul. 1989. "Identifying the Role of the Electronics Industry in India's Growth Strategy." Paper presented for OECD Development Centre Research Project—Perspectives and Policy Options for Newly-Industrializing Economies, June. Paris: OECD.

Kelkar, Vijay, and K. V. Varadarajan. 1989. "India's Computer Industry: Perspectives and Options for Latecomer Strategies." Paper presented for OECD Development Centre Research Project—Perspectives and Policy Options for Newly-Industrializing Economies, June. Paris: OECD.

Khanna, Sushil. n.d. "Transnational Corporations and Technology Transfer: Contours of Dependence in the Indian Petrochemical Industry." Calcutta: Indian Institute of Management.

Killick, Tony. 1986. "Twenty-five Years in Development: The Rise and Impending Decline of Market Solutions." *Development Policy Review* 4:99–116.

Kim, Byung Kook. 1987. "Bringing and Managing Socioeconomic Change: The State in Korea and Mexico." Ph.D. diss., Department of Government, Harvard University.

Kim, Eun Mee. 1987. "From Dominance to Symbiosis: State and Chaebol in the Korean Economy, 1960–1985." Ph.D. diss., Department of Sociology, Brown University.

———. 1992. "Contradictions and Limits of a Developmental State: With Illustrations from the South Korean Case." Ms., Department of Sociology, University of Southern California.

Kim, Jong-Whan. 1988. "Kukmin Yongum Jonsan Chori Iroke Dalajinda" (New computer processing of national pension). *Kukmin Yongum* (September): 37–43.

Kim, Kwang Woong. 1987. "The Role of the State Bureaucracy in Development Policies: Cases of Selected Countries in Asia." *Papers of the ASEAN and Japan Project*, no. 21. Nihon University, Tokyo.

Kim, Linsu. 1991. "National System of Industrial Innovation: Dynamics of Capability Building in Korea." Paper presented at the National Technical System Project, Columbia University.

Kim, M. S. 1987. "The Making of Korean Society: The Role of the State in the Republic of Korea (1948–79)." Ph.D. diss., Department of Sociology, Brown University.

Kim, Y. H. n.d.. "The Role of Technical Higher Education in the Industrialization of Korea." Ms., Korean Educational Developmental Institute, Seoul.

Kim, Young-Kon, and Chang Bun Yoon. "Country Strategy for Developing the Information/Communication Technology and Its Infrastructure in Korea." *Jeonbo Sahoi Yongu* (Information Society research). (Summer): 140–88.

Kohli, Atul. 1989. "Politics of Economic Liberalization in India." *World Development* 17, 3 (March): 305–28.

———. 1990. *Democracy and Discontent: India's Growing Crisis of Governability.* New York: Cambridge University Press.

———. (forthcoming). "Where do High Growth Political Economies Come From: The Japanese Lineage of Korea's 'Developmental State.'" *World Development.*

Koo, Hagen. 1987. "The Interplay of State, Social Class, and World System in East Asian Development: The Cases of South Korea and Taiwan." In *The Political Economy of the New Asian Industrialism*, ed. Frederic Deyo. Ithaca, N.Y.: Cornell University Press.

Korean Electrotechnology and Telecommunications Research Institute (KETRI). 1984. *1984 Research Activities Review.* Chung Nam, Korea: KETRI.

Korean Information Industry Association (KIIA). 1987. *ASCIO (Asian-Oceanian Computing Industry Organization) Country Report on the Current Status and Policy of Information Industry.* Seoul: KIIA.

Krasner, Stephen. 1979. *Defending the National Interest.* Princeton: Princeton University Press.

———. 1985. *Structural Conflict: The Third World Against Global Liberalism.* Berkeley and Los Angeles: University of California Press.

Kravis, Irving B. 1970. "Trade as a Handmaiden of Growth: Similarities Between the Nineteenth and Twentieth Centuries." *Economic Journal* 80, 320 (December): 850–72.

Krauss, Ellis. 1993. "US-Japan Trade Negotiations on Construction and Semiconductors 1985–1988: Building Friction and Relation-chips." In *Double-Edged Diplomacy: International Bargaining and Domestic Politics*, ed. Peter Evans, Harold Jacobson, and Robert Putnam. Berkeley and Los Angeles: University of California Press.

Krueger, Anne O. 1974. "The Political Economy of the Rent-Seeking Society." *American Economic Review* 64, 3 (June): 291–303.

Krugman Paul. 1987. "Strategic Sectors and International Competition." In *U.S.*

Trade Policies in a Changing World Economy, ed. Robert M. Stern. Cambridge: MIT Press.

Kurth, James R. 1979. "Industrial Change and Political Change: A European Perspective." In *The New Authoritarianism in Latin America*, ed. David Collier. Princeton: Princeton University Press.

Laitin, David D. 1985. "Hegemony and Religious Conflict: British Imperial Control and Political Cleavages in Yorubaland." In *Bringing the State Back In*, ed. Peter Evans, Dietrich Rueschmeyer, and Theda Skocpol. Cambridge: Cambridge University Press.

Lal, Deepak. 1988. *The Hindu Equilibrium*. Vol. 1: *Cultural Stability and Economic Stagnation, India c.1500 B.C.–A.D. 1980*. Oxford: Clarendon Press.

Lall, Sanjaya. 1987. *Learning to Industrialize: The Acquisition of Technological Capability by India*. London: Macmillan.

Langer, Eric. 1989. "Generations of Scientists and Engineers: Origins of the Computer Industry in Brazil." *Latin American Research Review* 24, 2:95–111.

Lee, Eung-Hyo. 1987. "Modernization Program of the Rural Telephone Network in Korea." Mimeo. Seoul: KTA.

Lee, Myung Jae. 1988. "Outline of the Development Project of Main Computer for the National Administrative Computer Network." Report presented at the Board of Science and Technology, March 25. Seoul: ETRI, Korean Information Science Association, Computer Science Study Association.

Lee, Su-Hoon. 1988. *State-Building in the Contemporary Third World*. Boulder: Westview Press.

Leipziger, Daniel, ed. 1988a. "Korea: Transition to Maturity." *World Development* 16, 1 (January).

———. 1988b. "Industrial Restructuring in Korea." *World Development* 16, 1 (January): 121–35.

Lemarchand, Rene. 1979. "The Politics of Penury in Rural Zaire: The View from Bandundu." In *Zaire: the Political Economy of Underdevelopment*, ed. Guy Gran. New York: Praeger.

Levi, Margaret. 1981. "A Theory of Predatory Rule." *Politics and Society* 10, 4:431–65.

———. 1988. *Of Rule and Revenue*. Berkeley and Los Angeles: University of California Press.

Levy, Brian. 1988. "The State-owned Enterprise as an Entrepreneurial Substitute in Developing Countries: The Case of Nitrogent Fertilizer." *World Development* 16, 10 (October): 1199–1211.

Lew, Seok-Jin. 1992. "Bringing Capital Back In: A Case Study of the South Korean Automobile Industrialization." Ph.D. Diss., Department of Political Science, Yale University.

Lieten, Georges Kristoffel. 1982. *The First Communist Ministry in Kerala 1957–9*. Calcutta: K. P. Bagchi & Company.

Lim, Linda Y. C. 1993. "Technology Policy and Export Development: The Case of the Electronics Industry in Singapore and Malaysia." Paper presented at the First INTECH Research Conference, June 21–23, Maastricht, The Netherlands.

Lipton, Michael. 1991. "Market Relaxation and Agricultural Development." In *States or Markets?: Neo-liberalism and the Development Policy Debate*, ed. Christoper Colclough and James Manor. Oxford: Clarendon Press.

List, Friedrich. 1885 (1966). *The National System of Political Economy*. New York: Augustus M. Kelley.

Luedde-Neurath, Richard. 1986. *Import Controls and Export-Oriented Development: A Reassessment of the South Korean Case*. Boulder: Westview.

Mahalingam, Sudha. 1989. "Computer Industry in India: Strategies for Late Comer Entry." *Economic and Political Weekly* 24, 42 (October 21): 2375–84.

Mann, Michael. 1984. "The Autonomous Power of the State: Its Origins, Mechanisms and Results." *Archives Européennes de Sociologie* 25:185–213.

———. 1986. *The Sources of Social Power*, vol. 1: *A History from the Beginning to A.D. 1760*. Cambridge: Cambridge University Press.

———. 1993. *The Sources of Social Power*, vol. 2: *The Rise of Classes and Nation States, 1760–1914*. Cambridge: Cambridge University Press.

Marathe, Sharad S. 1989. *Regulation and Development: India's Policy Experience of Controls over Industry*. New Delhi: Sage Publications.

March, James G., and Johan P. Olsen. 1984. "The New Institutionalism: Organizational Factors in Political Life." *American Political Science Review* 78: 734–49.

Martins, Luciano. 1977. "A Expansão Recente Do Estado No Brasil: Seus Problemas E Seus Atores." Research report to FINEP, Rio de Janeiro.

———. 1985. *Estado Capitalista E Burocracia No Brasil Pos64*. Rio de Janeiro: Paz e Terra.

Mathur, Kuldeep, ed. 1986. *A Survey of Research in Public Administration 1970–1979*. Project sponsored by Indian Council of Social Science Research. New Delhi: Concept Publishing Company.

Mencher, Joan. 1980. "The Lessons and Non-Lessons of Kerala." *Economic and Political Weekly* 15, 41–43:1781–1802.

Meyer-Stamer, Jorg. 1989. "From Import Substitution to International Competitiveness—Brazil's Informatics Industry at the Crossroads." Berlin: German Development Institute (GDI).

———. 1992. "The End of Brazil's Informatics Policy." *Science and Public Policy* 19, 2 (April): 99–110.

Migdal, Joel. 1988. *Strong Societies and Weak States: State-Society Relations and State Capabilities in the Third World*. Princeton: Princeton University Press.

———. 1994. "The State in Society: An Approach to Struggles for Domination." In *State Power and Social Forces: Domination and Transformation*, ed. Joel Migdal, Atul Kohli, and Vivienne Shue. Cambridge: Cambridge University Press.

Ministry of Communications, Republic of Korea (MOC). 1987. *Tele-Korea Today*. Seoul: Ministry of Communications.

Ministry of Government Administration, Republic of Korea (MGA). 1986. "Wages in Public Service and Private Companies." Seoul: Ministry of Government Administration.

Ministry of Science and Technology, Republic of Korea (MOST). 1987. *Introduc-*

tion to Science and Technology, Republic of Korea. Seoul: Ministry of Science and Technology.

Mody, Ashoka. 1986. "Korea's Computer Strategy." Harvard Business School Case no. 0-686-070. Boston: HBS Case Services.

———. 1987a. "Planning for Electronics Development." *Economic and Political Weekly* 22, 26–27 (June): 1041–45.

———. 1987b. "Growth of Firms under Uncertainty: Three Essays." Ph.D. diss., Department of Economics, Boston University.

———. 1989. "Institutions and Dynamic Comparative Advantage: Electronics Industry in South Korea and Taiwan." World Bank Industry and Energy Department, Industry and Energy Department Working Paper. Industry Series Paper no. 9 (June).

Moe, Terry. 1987. "Interests, Institutions, and Positive Theory: The Politics of the NLRB." *Studies in American Political Development* 2:236–39.

Moore, Barrington. 1967. *Social Origins of Dictatorship and Democracy.* Boston: Beacon Press.

Moore, Jeffrey, and Bart Narter. 1988. "Senior Executive Computer Use in the Americas: A Study of the U.S., Mexico and Brazil." Paper presented at the International Symposium on Technology Policy in the Americas, December, Stanford University.

Moorthy, K. Krishna. 1984. *Engineering Change: India's Iron and Steel Industry.* Madras: Technology Books.

Moran, Theodore H. 1974. *Multinational Corporations and the Politics of Dependence: Copper in Chile.* Princeton: Princeton University Press.

Murilo de Carvalho, José. 1974. "Elite and State-building in Brazil." Ph.D. diss., Department of Political Science, Stanford University.

National Association of Software and Service Companies (NASSCOM). 1989. "Indian Software Industry, 1990–95." Background document presented at National Software Conference '89. July 14–15, New Delhi.

National Computerization Coordination Committee. 1988. *Comprehensive Collection of Documents on National Computerization.* Seoul: NCCC.

National Informatics Centre, Government of India (NIC). 1987. *Profile of Services.* New Delhi: NIC/GOI.

———. n.d. *District Information System of the National Informatics Centre (DISNET).* New Delhi: NIC/GOI.

Nelson, Richard R., and Sidney Winter. 1982. *An Evolutionary Theory of Economic Change.* Cambridge: Harvard University Press.

Newfarmer, Richard. 1980. *Transnational Conglomerates and the Economics of Dependent Development: A Case Study of the International Electrical Oligopoly and Brazil's Electrical Industry.* Greenwich, Conn.: JAI Press.

Niskanen, William A. 1971. *Bureaucracy and Representative Government.* Chicago: Aldine-Atherton.

Noble, Gregory. 1988. "Between Cooperation and Competition: Collective Action in the Industrial Policy of Japan and Taiwan." Ph.D. diss., Department of Government, Harvard University.

North, Douglass C. 1981. *Structure and Change in Economic History.* New York: Norton.

———. 1986. "The New Institutional Economics." *Journal of Institutional and Theoretical Economics* 142:230–37.

———. 1990. *Institutions, Institutional Change and Economic Performance.* Cambridge: Cambridge University Press.

North, Douglass C., and Robert Thomas. 1973. *The Rise of the Western World: A New Economic History.* New York: Cambridge University Press.

Nunes, Edson de Oliveira, and Barbara Geddes. 1987. "Dilemmas of State-led Modernization in Brazil." In *State and Society in Brazil: Continuity and Change*, ed. John D.Wirth, Edson Nunes, and Thomas E. Bogenschild. Boulder: Westview Press.

Okimoto, Daniel I. 1989. *Between MITI and the Market: Japanese Industrial Policy for High Technology.* Stanford: Stanford University Press.

Olson, Mancur. 1965. *The Logic of Collective Action.* Cambridge: Harvard University Press.

———. 1982. *The Rise and Decline of Nations.* New Haven: Yale University Press.

Öniş, Ziya. 1991. "The Logic of the Developmental State." *Comparative Politics* 24, 1 (October): 109–26.

Overseas Economic Cooperation Fund. 1991. "Issues Related to the World Bank's Approach to Structural Adjustment—A Proposal from a Major Partner." OECF Occasional Paper no. 1 (October). Mimeo.

Paige, Jeffrey. 1987. "Coffee and Politics in Central America." In *Crises in the Caribbean Basin*, ed. Richard Tardanico. Beverly Hills: Sage.

Pang, Chien Kuo. 1987. "The State and Economic Transformation: The Taiwan Case." Ph.D. diss., Department of Sociology, Brown University.

Pani, Narendar. 1987. "A Demographic and Economic Profile of Bangalore." Paper prepared for seminar on Bangalore 2000—Some Imperatives for Action Now. Bangalore: Times Research Foundation.

Park, Mi-young. 1991. "Kukmin Yongumei Kwalli Unyong Chegee Daihan Bunsok" (An analysis of the management of the national pension system). M.A. thesis, Korea University.

Parthasarathi, Ashok. 1987. "Informatics for Development: The Indian Experience." Paper prepared for the North-South Roundtable of the Society for International Development, Tokyo.

Pessini, J. E. 1986. *A Indústria Brasileira De Telecomunicações: Uma Tentativa De Interpretação Das Mundanças Recentes.* Disertação de Mestrado. Campinas: Instituto de Economia/UNICAMP.

Petri, Peter A. 1988. "Korea's Export Niche: Origins and Prospects." *World Development* 16, 1 (January): 35–63.

Piore, Michael J., and Charles F. Sable. 1984. *The Second Industrial Divide.* New York: Basic Books.

Piragibe, Clelia. 1983. "A Indústria de Computadores: Intervenção do Estado e Padrão de Competição." Master's thesis, Universidade Federal do Rio de Janeiro.

———. 1988. "Electronics Industry in Brazil: Current Status, Perspectives and Policy Options." Report to OECD Project on NICs and the Global Electronics Industry.

Polanyi, Karl. 1957 [1944]. *The Great Transformation*. Boston: Beacon Press.

Pontusson, Johan. 1992. *The Limits of Social Democracy: Investment Politics in Sweden*. Ithaca, N.Y.: Cornell University Press.

Porter, Michael E. 1990. *The Competitive Advantage of Nations*. New York: Free Press.

Poulantzas, Nicos. 1973. *Political Power and Social Classes*. London: NLB and Sheed and Ward.

Powell, Walter W., and Paul DiMaggio, eds. 1991. *The New Institutionalism in Organizational Analysis*. Chicago: University of Chicago Press.

Prebisch, Raul. 1950. *The Economic Development of Latin America and Its Principal Problems*. New York: United Nations.

Prestowicz, Clyde. 1988. *Trading Places: How We Allowed Japan to Take the Lead*. New York: Basic Books.

Rao, K. K. 1987. "Public Sector in Bangalore's Metropolitan Economy: The 2000 A.D. Perspective." Paper prepared for seminar on Bangalore 2000—Some Imperatives for Action Now. Bangalore: Times Research Foundation.

Ramamurti, Ravi. 1987. *State-Owned Enterprises in High Technology Industries: Studies in India and Brazil*. New York: Praeger.

Raw, Silvia. 1985. "The Political Economy of Brazilian State-Owned Enterprises." Ph.D. diss., Department of Economics, University of Massachusetts.

Reich, Robert B. 1992. *The Work of Nations*. New York: Vintage Books.

Ripper, Mario Dias. 1988. "The Structure of the Computing Industry—Opportunities for Developing Countries." Paper presented at the International Symposium on Technology Policy in the Americas, December, Stanford University.

Rodrik, Dani. 1994. "King Kong Meets Godzilla: The World Bank and *The East Asian Miracle*." Ms. prepared for the Overseas Development Council.

Rudolph, Lloyd I., and Susanne Hoeber Rudolph. 1987. *In Pursuit of Lakshmi: The Political Economy of the Indian State*. Chicago: University of Chicago Press.

Rueschemeyer, Dietrich, and Peter Evans. 1985. "The State and Economic Transformation: Toward an Analysis of the Conditions Underlying Effective Intervention." In *Bringing the State Back In*, ed. Peter Evans, Dietrich Reuschemeyer, and Theda Skocpol. Cambridge: Cambridge University Press.

Ryavec, Carole. 1987. "South Korea—A Growing Force in the World's Electronics Markets." New York: Salomon Brothers.

Samsung. 1987. *The Samsung Group Annual Report—1986*. Seoul: Samsung.

Samsung Electronics. 1985. "Samsung Electronics Today." Seoul: Samsung Electronics.

Samuels, Richard J. 1987. *The Business of the Japanese State: Energy Markets in Comparative and Historical Perspective*. Ithaca, N.Y.: Cornell University Press.

Schmitter, Philippe. 1971. *Interest Conflict and Political Change in Brazil*. Stanford: Stanford University Press.

———. 1990. "Sectors in Modern Capitalism: Modes of Governance and Variations in Performance." In *Labor Relations and Economic Performance*, ed. R. Brunetta and C. Dell'Aringa. New York: Macmillan.

Schmitz, Hubert, and José Cassiolato, eds. 1992. *Hi-Tech for Industrial Development: Lessons from the Brazilian Experience in Electronics and Automation.* London: Routledge.

Schmitz, Hubert, and Tom Hewitt. 1991. "Learning to Raise Infants: A Case-Study in Industrial Policy." In *States or Markets?: Neo-liberalism and the Development Policy Debate,* ed. Christopher Colclough and James Manor. Oxford: Clarendon Press.

———. 1992. "An Assessment of the Market Reserve for the Brazilian Computer Industry." In *Hi-Tech for Industrial Development,* ed. Hubert Schmitz and José Cassiolato. London: Routledge.

Schneider, Ben R. 1987a. "Politics within the State: Elite Bureaucrats and Industrial Policy in Authoritarian Brazil." Ph.D. diss., Department of Political Science, University of California, Berkeley.

———. 1987b. "Framing the State: Economic Policy and Political Representation in Post Authoritarian Brazil." In *State and Society in Brazil: Continuity and Change,* ed. John D. Wirth, Edson de Oliveira Nunes, and Thomas E. Bogenschild. Boulder: Westview Press.

———. 1991. "Brazil under Collor: Anatomy of a Crisis." *World Policy Journal* (Spring): 321–47.

———. 1991. *Politics within the State: Elite Bureaucrats and Industrial Policy in Authoritarian Brazil.* Pittsburgh: University of Pittsburgh Press.

Schware, Robert. 1992a. "Software Industry Entry Strategies for Developing Countries: A 'Walking on Two Legs' Proposition." *World Development* 20, 2 (February): 143–64.

———. 1992b. "Can Brazil's Software Industry Walk on Two Legs? Trends, Opportunities and Issues for the 1990s." In *High Technology and Third World Industrialization: Brazilian Computer Policy in Comparative Perspective,* ed. Peter Evans, Claudio Frischtak, and Paulo Tigre. Research Series no. 85. Berkeley: International and Area Studies.

Secretaria Especial de Informática (SEI). 1983. "Parque Instalado." *Boletim Informativo* 3, 11:1–44.

———. 1985. "Parque Computational Instalado." *Boletim Informativo* 5, 14:1–59.

———. 1987. "Panorama Do Setor De Informática." *Boletim Informativo* 7, 16:1–192.

Secretaria of Science and Technology, Government of Brazil (SCT). 1990. *A Política Brasileira de Ciência e Tecnologia: 1990/95.* Brasília: Government of Brazil.

Seidman, Gay. 1994. *Manufacturing Militance: Workers' Movements in Brazil and South Africa, 1970–1985.* Berkeley and Los Angeles: University of California Press.

Senghaas, Dieter. 1985. *The European Experience: A Historical Critique of Developmental Theory.* Translated from the German by K. H. Kimmig. Leamington Spa, Dover, N.H.: Berg Publishers.

Sengupta, Ramprasad. 1984. "Technical Change in the Public Sector Steel Industry." *Economic and Political Weekly* 19, 5 (February 4): 206–15.

Seo, Jung-jin. 1990. "Kukmin Yongum Josanmangukchuk Odikajioana" (Present situation of computer network of national pension). *Kukmin Yongam* (newsletter published by the Kukmin Yongum Kwalli Kongdan) (Summer): 38–41

Shafer, D. Michael. 1983. "Capturing the Mineral Multinationals: Advantage or Disadvantage?" *International Organization* 37, 1 (Winter): 93–119.

———. 1990. "Sectors, States, and Social Forces: Korea and Zambia Confront Economic Restructuring." *Comparative Politics* (January): 127–50.

———. 1994. *Winner and Losers: How Sectors Shape the Developmental Prospects of States.* Ithaca, N.Y.: Cornell University Press.

Shaiken, Harley. 1989. *Mexico in the Global Economy: High Technology and Work Organization in Export Industries.* San Diego: Center for U.S.-Mexican Studies.

Shapiro, Helen. 1988. "State Intervention and Industrialization: The Origins of the Brazilian Automotive Industry." Ph.D. diss., Department of Economics, Yale University.

———. 1994. *Engines of Growth: The State and Transnational Auto Companies in Brazil.* New York: Cambridge University Press.

Shepsle, Kenneth. 1987. "The Institutional Foundations of Committee Power." *American Political Review* 81: 85–104.

Shivdasani, Prem. 1990. "Information Technology: Heading for a Dead-end?" *The Economic Times,* July 11: 11. New Delhi.

Sikkink, Kathryn. 1991. *Ideas and Institutions: Developmentalism in Brazil and Argentina.* Ithaca, N.Y.: Cornell University Press.

Singhal, Arvind, and Everett M. Rogers. 1989. *India's Information Revolution.* New Delhi: Sage Publication.

Skocpol, Theda. 1985. "Bringing the State Back In: Strategies of Analysis in Current Research." In *Bringing the State Back In,* ed. Peter Evans, Dietrich Rueschemeyer, and Theda Skocpol. Cambridge: Cambridge University Press.

Smith, Peter H. 1979. *Labyrinths of Power: Political Recruitment in 20th Century Mexico.* Princeton: Princeton University Press.

de Soto, Hernando. 1989. *The Other Path: The Invisible Revolution in the Third World.* New York: Harper and Row.

Sridharan, Eswaran. 1989. "The Political Economy of Industrial Strategy for Competitiveness in the Third World: The Electronics Industry in Korea, Brazil and India." Ph.D. diss., Department of Political Science, University of Pennsylvania.

Srinivasan, T. N. 1985. "Neoclassical Political Economy, the State and Economic Development." *Asian Development Review* 3, 2: 38–58.

Stallings, Barbara. 1992. "The Role of Foreign Capital in Economic Growth." In *Manufacturing Miracles,* ed. G. Gereffi and D. Wyman. Princeton: Princeton University Press.

Stepan, Alfred. 1971. *The Military in Politics: Changing Patterns in Brazil.* Princeton: Princeton University Press.

———. 1985. "State Power and the Strength of Civil Society in the Southern

Cone of Latin America." In *Bringing the State Back In*, ed. Peter Evans, Dietrich Rueschemeyer, and Theda Skocpol. Cambridge: Cambridge University Press.

Stephens, Evelyne Huber. 1987. "Minerals Strategies and Development: International Political Economy, State, Class and the Role of the Bauxite/Aluminum and Copper Industries in Jamaica and Peru." *Studies in Comparative International Development* 22, 3:60–102.

Stephens, Evelyne Huber, and John Stephens. 1986. *Democratic Socialism in Jamaica: The Political Movement and Social Transformation in Dependent Capitalism*. Princeton: Princeton University Press.

Streeck, Wolfgang, and Philippe C. Schmitter. 1991. "From National Corporatism to Transnational Pluralism: Organized Interests in the Single European Market." *Politics and Society* 19, 2 (February): 133–64.

Suarez, Marcus Alban. 1986. *Petroquímica e Tecnoburocracia: Capítulos do desenvolvimento capitalista no Brasil*. São Paulo: Editora Hucitec.

Subramanian, C. R. 1989. "India and the Computer: A Compendium of Policies, Plans, Progress and Views." Ms., Bangalore.

Supple, Barry. 1959. *Commercial Crisis and Change in England, 1600–42*. Cambridge: Cambridge University Press.

Taub, Richard P. 1969. *Bureaucrats under Stress: Administrators and Administration in an Indian State*. Berkeley and Los Angeles: University of California Press.

Tendler, Judith. 1968. *Electric Power in Brazil: Entrepreneurship in the Public Sector*. Cambridge: Harvard University Press.

Tigre, Paulo Bastos. 1983. *Technology and Competition in the Brazilian Computer Industry*. New York: St. Martin's Press.

———. 1984. *Computadores Brasileiros: Indústria, Tecnologia, E Dependência*. Rio de Janeiro: Campus/IMPES/IPEA.

———. 1987. *Industria Brasileira De Computadores: Perspectivas Ate Os Anos 90*. Rio de Janeiro: Campus/IMPES/IPEA.

———. 1988. "Brasil: Para Onde Vai a Informática." *Ciencia Hoje* 8, 43 (June): 60–66.

———. 1993. "Liberalização e capacitação tecnológico: O caso da informática pós-reserva de mercado no Brasil." Paper prepared for the Project on the Current State and Future Role of Science and Technology in Brazil.

Tilly, Charles. 1985. "War Making and State Making as Organized Crime." In *Bringing the State Back In*, ed. Peter Evans, Dietrich Rueschemeyer, and Theda Skocpol. Cambridge: Cambridge University Press.

Todaro, Michael. 1977. *Economic Development in the Third World: An Introduction to Problems and Policies in a Global Perspective*. London: Longman.

Topik, Steven. 1980. "State Enterprise in a Liberal Regime: The Banco do Brasil, 1905–1930." *Journal of InterAmerican Studies and World Affairs* 22, 4 (November): 401–22.

———. 1987. *The Political Economy of the Brazilian State, 1889–1930*. Austin: University of Texas Press.

Toye, John. 1991a. *Dilemmas of Development*. Oxford: Basil Blackwell.

————. 1991b. "Is There a New Political Economy of Development?" In *States or Markets?: Neo-liberalism and the Development Policy Debate*, ed. Christopher Colclough and James Manor. Oxford: Clarendon Press.

Trebat, Thomas. 1983. *Brazil's State-Owned Enterprises: A Case Study of the State as Entrepreneur*. Cambridge: Cambridge University Press.

Tugwell, Franklin. 1975. *The Politics of Oil in Venezuela*. Stanford: Stanford University Press.

UNESCO. 1991. *Statistical Yearbook, 1990*. New York: United Nations.

United Nations. Department of International Economic and Social Affairs, Statistical Office. 1986, 1987. *International Trade Statistics Yearbook*. New York: United Nations.

————. 1990. *UN International Trade Statistics Handbook, Vol. 1*. New York: United Nations.

Uricoechea, Fernando. 1980. *The Patrimonial Foundations of the Brazilian Bureaucratic State*. Berkeley and Los Angeles: University of California Press.

Venkataramani, Raja. 1990. *Japan Enters Indian Industry: The Maruti/Suzuki Joint Venture*. New Delhi: Radiant Publishers.

Vernon, Raymond. 1966. "International Investment and International Trade in the Product Cycle." *Quarterly Journal of Economics* 80:190–207.

Vernon, Raymond, and Brian Levy. 1982. "State-Owned Enterprise in the World Economy: The Case of Iron Ore." In *Public Enterprise in Less-Developed Countries*, ed. Leroy P. Jones. Cambridge: Cambridge University Press.

Wade, Robert. 1982. *Irrigation and Agricultural Politics in South Korea*. Boulder: Westview Press.

————. 1985. "The Market for Public Office: Why the Indian State is Not Better at Development." *World Development* 13, 4 (April): 467–97.

————. 1990. *Governing the Market: Economic Theory and the Role of Government in East Asian Industrialization*. Princeton: Princeton University Press.

Wallerstein, Immanuel. 1974a. *The Modern World-System*, vol. 1: *Capitalist Agriculture and the Origins of the European World-Economy in the Sixteenth Century*. New York: Academic Press.

————. 1974b. "The Rise and Future Demise of the Capitalist World System." *Comparative Studies in Society and History* 16, 4 (September): 387–415.

Waltz, Kenneth. 1979. *Theory of International Politics*. Reading, Mass.: Addison-Wesley.

Waterbury, John. 1992. "The Heart of the Matter? Public Enterprise and the Adjustment Process." In *The Politics of Economic Adjustment: International Constraints, Distributive Conflicts, and the State*, ed. Stephan Haggard and Robert R. Kaufman. Princeton: Princeton University Press.

————. 1993. *Exposed to Innumerable Delusions: Public Enterprise and State Power in Egypt, India, Mexico, and Turkey*. New York: Cambridge University Press.

Weber, Max. 1968 [1904–1911]. *Economy and Society*, ed. Guenter Roth and Claus Wittich. New York: Bedminster Press.

Wells Louis T. 1972. *The Product Life Cycle and International Trade*. Boston: Graduate School of Business Administration, Harvard University.

White, Gordon, and Robert Wade. 1984. "Developmental States in East Asia."

IDS Research Report #16. London: Gatsby Charitable Foundation.
———. 1988. "Developmental States and Markets in East Asia: An Introduction." In *Developmental States in East Asia*, ed. Gordon White. London: Macmillan.
White, Gordon, ed. 1988. *Developmental States in East Asia.* London: Macmillan.
Williamson, John, 1993. "The Emergent Development Policy Consensus." Paper presented at the Global Studies Research Program Conference on Sustainable Development with Equity in the 1990s, May 13–16, Madison, Wisconsin.
Williamson, Oliver E. 1975. *Markets and Hierarchies: Analysis and Antitrust Implications.* New York: Free Press.
Willis, Eliza J. 1986. "The State as Banker: The Expansion of the Public Sector in Brazil." Ph.D. diss., University of Texas, Austin.
Wirth, John. 1970. *The Politics of Brazilian Development.* Stanford: Stanford University Press.
Woo, Jung-eun. 1991. *Race to the Swift: State and Finance in Korean Industrialization.* New York: Columbia University Press.
World Bank (IBRD). 1987a. *Korea: Managing the Industrial Transition.* A World Bank country study. Washington, D.C.: World Bank.
———. 1987b. *Vol. I, India: An Industrializing Economy.* Report no. 6633-IN. Washington, D.C.: World Bank.
———. 1991. *World Development Report, 1991.* New York: Oxford University Press.
———. 1993 *The East Asian Miracle: Economic Growth and Public Policy.* A World Bank Policy Research Report. New York: Oxford University Press.
Yun, Young-min. 1994. "Economic Development and Social Fluidity: Capitalist Developmental State and Class Mobility in Japan, South Korea and Taiwan." Ph.D. diss., Department of Sociology, University of California, Berkely.
Yun, Young-Min, and Brian Folk. 1990. "Intellectuals and Working-Class Formation: A South Korean Case in the 1980s." Prepared for annual meeting of the American Political Science Association, San Francisco.
Zeitlin, Maurice. 1984. *The Civil Wars in Chile, or the Bourgeois Revolutions that Never Were.* Princeton: Princeton University Press.
Zeitlin, Maurice, and Richard Ratcliff. 1988. *Landlords and Capitalists: The Dominant Class of Chile.* Princeton: Princeton University Press.
Zysman, John. 1993. "Thinking about Institutions: Institutions and Economic Development in the Advanced Countries." Ms.

Newspapers and Periodicals

B. K. Electronics (Korea)
Business India (India)
Business Korea (Korea)
Business Latin America
Chungang Ilbo (Korea)
Computers Today (India)
Computerworld (Brazil)

Datamation (United States)
Datanews (Brazil)
Dataquest (India)
Economic Times (India)
Electronic Engineering Times (United States)
Electronics Korea (Korea)
Financial Express (India)
Financial Times (London)
Gin Donga (Korea)
Hanguk Kyongje Sinmun (Korea)
Korea Herald (Korea)
Kookmin Ilbo (Korea)
Kyongongkwa Computer (Korea)
Meltron Newsletter (India)
New York Times (United States)
Pioneer (India)
San Francisco Chronicle (United States)
Sematech Update (United States)
SIPA News (Silicon Valley Indian Professional Associations Newsletter)
The Times of India (India)
Wall Street Journal (United States)
Wolgan Computer (Korea)

Index

Acatel (U.S.), 272n.57
Acominas (B), 262n.35
Adler, Emanuel, 266nn.21 and 28
Africa, 34, 36–38. *See also* Zaire; Zambia
Amakudari (Japan), 50
American Telephone and Telegraph (AT&T) (U.S.), 128, 170, 272nn.48, 50 and 57; joint ventures with, 194, 200, 217, 279n.9. *See also* UNIX
Amsden, Alice, 18, 22, 38–41, 44, 89–111, 215, 234, 253n.31, 254–55n.23
Amstrad (Britain), 264–65n.1
Anchordoguy, Marie, 265n.11
APPD (Association of Data Processing Professionals) (B), 118
Apricot Computers (Britain), 264–65n.1
Argentina, 255n.4
Association of Data Processing Professionals (APPD) (B), 118
Atlantic Computers (Britain), 264–65n.1
Auster, Richard D., 253n.4
Austria, 17, 240–42, 246–47
Automobile industry, 83, 91–94, 263nn.48–50, 264nn.51–56; in Brazil, 65, 91–92; in Korea, 87, 91–93
Autonomy, state, 45, 57–58, 72–73, 248. *See also* Embedded autonomy; *individual countries*

Baer, Werner, 258n.43, 261n.28
Banco Itaú (B), 155, 163, 275n.1. *See also* Itautec
Bangalore (I), 130, 151, 194, 266n.27
Bara Hindu Rao mill (I), 75–76, 89, 90
Barbudinhos (B), 107–9, 118, 155, 165–66, 187, 188, 204, 214–16, 221, 223, 232. *See also* Brazil, IT industry in
BARC. *See* Bhabha Atomic Research Center (I)
Bardhan, Pranab, 18, 66, 68, 253n.31
Bates, Robert H., 18, 34–35, 38, 253n.31, 254nn.15 and 21
Batsu (J), 51
BEL. *See* Bharat Electronics Ltd. (BEL) (I)
Belgo Mineira (B), 86–87

Bell Laboratories (U.S.), 194
Bennett, Douglas C., 263n.50
Bhabha, Homi J., 266n.18
Bhabha Atomic Research Center (I), 106, 113, 131, 221, 232
Bhabha Committee (I), 105–6, 113, 214
Bharat Electronics Ltd. (BEL) (I), 130–31, 151
Biggart, Nicole Woolsey, 254n.22
Birlas (I), 68, 157
Blue Chip (U.S.), 282–83n.51
Blue House Group (K), 110, 143–44, 214, 221, 232
Blue House (K), 110 125
BNDE. *See* National Economic Development Bank (BNDE) (B)
"Bodyshopping," 195, 204
Bombay (I), 269n.19
Bradesco (B), 163, 187, 189, 207
Brazil, 8, 12–13, 60–66; auto industry in, 65, 91–92, 263n.48; banks in, 155, 163, 166, 257n.33; bureaucracy in (*see* Brazilian state); comparative advantage of, 215; domestic market in, 137, 165, 276n.15, 277n.36; electronics in, 158, 163–64; engineers in, 15, 215; exports from, 65, 87–88, 167, 183–85; fiscal problems in, 153, 167, 188, 213, 258n.43; "greenhouse" in, 16, 111–12, 116, 120–21, 153, 165, 266n.30; imports to, 117, 182–83; industrial transformation in, 44, 107, 266n.30; IT industry in, 15, 116–24, 127–29, 155–56, 160–68, 185–90, 207–8, 212–14, 267nn.35–43, 276n.12; local entrepreneurs in, 154, 158–59, 179, 183, 187–88 (*see also* Brazilian state, relations of with industry); market reserve in (*see* Market reserve [Brazil]); military in, 62–63, 108, 118, 136, 258n.40; research and development in, 148–50, 188, 274n.81; SOEs in, 14, 129, 136–39; and steel industry, 86–89, 261n.28, 261–62n.29, 262nn.30, 35 and 36; telecommunications system in, 272n.56; textile

Brazil (cont.)
   industry in, 91, TNCs in, 11, 63, 107–9,
   111–12, 158, 164–65, 213
Brazilian Computation Society (SBC), 118
Brazilian state, 60–66, 71, 222, 259n.54;
   autonomy of, 209; corruption in, 64,
   65; embeddedness of, 62, 72–73; Foreign Trade Council (CONCEX) in, 117;
   husbandry by, 150, 190, 219, 222–23;
   "law of similars" of, 266–67n.30; midwifery by, 14–16, 116, 124, 164, 187,
   212; National Intelligence Service (SNI)
   in, 118; protectionism by, 111–12, 123,
   272n.50 (see also Brazil, "greenhouse"
   in); regulations by, 14, 210, 213 (see
   also Market reserve [B]); relations of
   with industry, 63–64, 98, 104–5, 107–9,
   163, 208–9, 219
Brenner, Robert, 9
Britain, 8; computer industry in, 99–100,
   214, 264–65n.1, 265n.4
Buchanan, James, 23 25, 253n.4
Bull International, 181, 191–92
Bureaucracy, 29–30, 40. See also State
   bureaucracy
Burroughs (U.S.): in Brazil, 108, 158, 161;
   in India, 169; in Korea, 159

C-DOT. See Center for the Development
   of Telematics (C-DOT) (I)
Calder, Kent, 256n.12; 265n.14
California Steel Industries (U.S.), 262–
   63n.37
Callaghy, Thomas, 45–46, 253n.7
Capital, 6, 79. See also Local private capi-
   tal; State bureaucracy, as entrepreneur;
   Transnational capital
Capitalism and bureaucracy, 29–30
CAPRE. See Commission for the Coordina-
   tion of Electronic Processing Activities
   (CAPRE) (B)
Cardoso, F. H., 18, 63
Castells, Manuel, 257n.29
Castro, Edson de, 271n.42
Center for the Development of Telematics
   (C-DOT) (I), 134–35, 139, 151, 211,
   270nn.23, 26, 27 and 28, 271n.34
Center for Research and Development
   (CPqD) (B), 149–50
Centro Technológica para Informática
   (CTI) (B), 149

Chaebol (K), 53, 92, 110, 143, 214, 231–
   32, 252n.25; international alliances of,
   185, 199–201; and state, 125–26, 159,
   174, 209, 219–20
Chemical industry, 263n.39
Cheng, Tun-jen, 256n.16
Chile, 84, 258n.49
China, 54
China Steel (Taiwan), 56, 261n.27
Chips. See Semiconductors
Choi, Byung Sun, 51, 256n.15
Chun Doo Hwan, 125
Chung Hong Sik, 110
Citibank, 193
Citicorp Overseas Software Ltd. (COSL)
   (I), 194
Civil service, American, 243. See also Bra-
   zilian state; Indian state; Korean state;
   State bureaucracy
Civil service exams: in India, 66–67;
   in Japan, 48, 256n.10; in Korea, 51–
   52
Clientelism, 61, 63, 72, 90, 220, 235
Cline, William, 8, 9, 165
Clones. See Personal computers
CMC. See Computer Maintenance Corpo-
   ration (CMC) (I)
COBRA. See Computadores e Sistemas
   Brasilieiros SA (COBRA) (B)
Colclough, Christopher, 26
Collander, David, 24
Collor, Fernando, 64–65, 73, 153, 167,
   185, 259n.54
Commission for the Coordination of Elec-
   tronic Processing Activities (CAPRE) (B),
   116–20, 123–24, 154, 207, 221–22;
   267n.41, 271n.37
Commodities: defined, 268n.2, 271n.36,
   278n.50; returns on, 218; services as,
   95; and state firms, 139
Commodity chains, 251–52n.16
Communism, 245; in Kerala, 237
Compania Siderurgica Nacional (CSN) (B),
   86–87
Comparative advantage: in Britain, 99; construction of, 8–10, 82–83; in India, 134–
   35, 171, 215; state action and, 9–10,
   102–3; of TNCs, 158
Comparative institutional approach, 18–
   20, 28–34, 37, 39–42, 97, 220–21,
   254nn.19 and 22

Competition, 101. *See also* "Greenhouses"; Protectionism

Computadores e Sistemas Brasileiros SA (COBRA) (B), 128–29, 136–39, 146, 149, 162, 185, 211, 213, 221–22; hardware from, 148, 163, 170, 266n.29; software from, 128, 166–67, 272n.48, 276n.18

Computer Maintenance Corporation (CMC) (I), 132–34, 139, 168–69, 173, 196, 211, 269n.17, 268–70n.20

Computers: components of, 184–85; mainframe, 103–4, 119, 266n.17; micro (*see* Personal computers); mini, 103, 160, 267nn. 31, 37 and 39, 268nn.10 and 11; personal (*see* Personal computers); production of (*see* Information technology industry); supermini, 103–5, 155, 163, 185, 187, 212, 267nn.37 and 38. *See also* Information technology industry

CONCEX (Foreign Trade Council) (B), 117

Consumer electronics, 109, 110, 125–26, 157, 163–64; in India, 168; in Korea, 174–78

Contraband IT products, 276nn.16–18

Control Data Corporation (U.S.), 268n.12

Costa Marques, Ivan da, xiii, 107, 128, 138

CPqD. *See* Center for Research and Development (CPqD) (B)

CTI. *See* Centro Technológica para Informática (CTI) (B)

Cumings, Bruce, 254n.22

Custodian role, 13–14, 78, 80; in Brazil, 14, 112, 116–24, 152–53; in India, 14, 112–16, 152–53, 157; in IT industry, 97; in Korea, 124; in textile industry, 83, 89–91

DACOM (K), 144–46

Daeduk Science Town (K), 147, 148

Daewoo (K), 110, 145, 175, 273n.60, 282n.48; international alliances of, 93, 200–202, 264n.55, 278n.50; and state, 92. *See also* Chaebol (K)

Data General (DG) (U.S.), 137, 267n.39, 271nn.42 and 43

Data processing, 95, 104, 105

Datamatics (I), 173, 193–95, 277n.35

DCM. *See* Delhi Cloth Mills

de Soto, Hernando, 253n.3

DEC. *See* Digital Equipment Corporation (DEC) (U.S.)

Defense. *See* Security

Delhi Cloth Mills (DCM) (I), 75–76, 157, 168–69, 277n.34

Demiurge role, 13–14, 77–80, 83–91, 93, 252n.23; in Brazil, 86–87, 152; in India, 87, 90–91, 152; in IT industry, 97, 129–39, 205, 210; in Korea, 87–88; in mineral extraction, 83–86, 260n.17; in steel industry, 86–89, 261n.27; in Taiwan, 261n.27. *See also* State-owned enterprises

Department of Electronics (DOE) (I), 112–16, 131–32, 151, 210, 221, 269–70n.20, 275n.89, 277–78n.38

Department of Public Administration (DASP) (B), 61–62

Department of Telecommunications (I), 271n.34

Desai, Anita, 3

Despande, Vinay, 151, 172, 281n.30

Developing countries. *See* Newly industrializing countries (NICs)

Development, 7–8, 31, 235. *See also* Industrial transformation; *individual industries*

Developmental state, 12, 47–59, 248, 255n.1, 257n.28; autonomy of, 59, 232; challenges to, 223–34, 245; embedded autonomy in, 50, 72, 77; Japan as, 47–50; 58, 245; Korea as, 51–54, 229–34; reconstruction of, 243; Taiwan as, 54–58

DG. *See* Data General (U.S.)

Digilab (B), 163, 187, 189

Digital Equipment Corporation (DEC) (U.S.), 103, 122, 195, 217, 267n.39, 268n.10; in Brazil, 185–86, 188, 207–8; in India, 132–33, 181, 269n.14, 281n.27

DiMaggio, Paul, 253n.30

DISNET (I), 275n.88

Division of labor, international. *See* International division of labor

DOE. *See* Department of Electronics (DOE) (I)

Doner, Richard F., 264n.52

Dongyang (K), 273n.60

DoT. *See* Department of Telecommunications (I)
DRAM chips, 272n.54, 274n.75, 278n.42. *See also* Four-Megabit DRAM Project; Semiconductors
Durkheim, Emile, 26, 49
Dutkiewicz, Piotr, 255n.1
Dytz, Edison, 120–21, 155, 161–63

East Asian countries, 22, 44; bureaucracies in, 58–59; state reconstruction in, 243–45. *See also* Japan; Korea; Taiwan
ECIL. *See* Electronic Corporation of India (ECIL) (I)
Economic Planning Board (EPB) (K), 51, 52, 110, 229, 256n.16
Education, technical, 147–48, 151, 170, 172. *See also* Research and development
Egypt, 36–38, 226
Elebra (B), 162–65, 185–86, 188, 207, 276n.15
Electronic Corporation of India (ECIL) (I), 113–14, 131–32, 139, 168, 169, 171, 173, 196, 211, 221–23; 268nn.10–12, 268–69n.13
Electronic Data Systems (U.S.), 200
Electronic switching systems (ESS), 134–35, 141–43, 150, 270nn.24 and 28, 272n.57, 273nn.59 and 64
Electronics, consumer. *See* Consumer electronics
Electronics and Telecommunications Research Institute (ETRI) (K), 141–43, 145, 146, 148, 151, 209, 211, 272n.55, 278nn.58, 59 and 68, 273–74n.69
Embedded autonomy, 12–13, 50, 70, 144; in Kerala, 240; in Korea, 12–13, 17, 124, 126–27, 146, 209; and social structure, 17, 72; and state efficacy, 77, 210, 248, 249; variations of, 72–73, 243
Embeddedness, 32, 57–59, 72–73, 210, 248; in Austria, 242; in Brazil, 62, 72–73; in India, 69, 209; in Japan, 50; in Kerala, 238; in Korea, 53; in new internationalization, 205–6
Engineers: in India, 170–73, 85, 195–96, 215; in Brazil, 15, 215
England. *See* Britain
Entrepreneurs. *See* Private local capita; State bureaucracy, as entrepreneur; Transnational capital

EPB. *See* Economic Planning Board (EPB (K)
Epson (U.S.), 171, 192, 278n.52
Ericson, L. M., 142, 272n.57, 273n.59
Ernst, Dieter, 143, 197, 266nn.16 and 17, 277n.37, 283n.52
ESPRIT (Europe), 96, 264n.58
ESS. *See* Electronic switching systems (ESS)
ETRI. *See* Electronics and Telecommunications Research Institute (ETRI) (K)
Europe, 242; Eastern, 9, 280n.18; IT in, 96, 264n.58; market in, 186, 189. *See also* Austria
Evans, Peter, 63, 252–53n.28
Exports, low-return, 197, 204. *See also* Brazil, exports from; India, exports from; Korea, exports from

Fairchild Semiconductor Korea Ltd., 159, 196–97
Fang, Isu, 260n.14
Federation of Korean Trade Unions (FKTU), 227
FERA. *See* Foreign Exchange Regulation Act (FERA) (I)
Ferranti, 264–65n.1, 271n.40
Financial automation in Brazil, 15, 163, 166, 179, 186, 189, 215
Flamm, Kenneth, 96, 99, 100, 209, 265–66n.15
Folk, Brian, 230
Foreign capital. *See* Transnational capital
Foreign Exchange Regulation Act (FERA) (I), 191, 266n.23
Foreign subsidiaries. *See* Subsidiaries
Foreign technology. *See* Technology
Formation (U.S.), 121, 155, 267–68n.43
Four-Megabit DRAM Project, 141, 146, 148, 174, 272n.54
Fregni, Edson. *See* SCOPUS
Frischtak, Claudio, xiii, 166, 188–89
Fujitsu (Japan), 99, 214, 264–65n.1, 279n.9; and Daewoo (K), 201
Furnas (B), 258n.44

Gandhi, Indira, 91
Gandhi, Rajiv, 114–15
Geddes, Barbara, 60–61
Geisel, General Ernesto, 107, 110, 118
General Electric (U.S.), 200, 265n.7
General Motors (U.S.), 93

Gennari, Octavio, 119
Germany, 189
Gerschenkron, Alexander, 18, 22, 30–32, 36–38, 41, 44, 48, 221, 254–55n.23
Gil, Antonio Carlos Rego, 186
Gilpin, Robert, 5, 10
Gold, Tom, 18, 54
Goldstar (K), 145, 198, 274n.75, 275–76n.10; and computers, 175, 282n.46; and electronics, 110; international alliances of, 200–202, 217; and semiconductors, 141, 273n.60, 278n.41. *See also* Chaebol
Gomes, Severo, 119
Gould, David, 46, 255–56n.5
Gramsci, Antonio, 59, 231n.5
Granovetter, Mark, 26
"Greenhouses," 13, 15, 78, 80; and auto industry, 91–91; in Brazil, 126, 153–54, 185; in India, 16, 126, 168, 170, 212; and internationalization, 183–84, 217; in IT industry, 97, 111, 126, 153–54, 160, 168, 170, 178–80, 183–84; in Korea, 89, 126; results of, 139–40, 183; in textile industry, 89–91. *See also* Midwife role; Protectionism; Tariffs
Guaranys, José, 118, 271n.37

Haggard, Stephan, 254n.22
Hagopian, Francis, 63, 64
Hamilton, Alexander, 7, 18, 111, 231n.11, 254n.22
Hardware. *See* Information technology
HCL. *See* Hindustan Computers Ltd. (HCL) (I)
HCL American, 190–91, 202
Herring, Ronald J., 237, 239
Hewlett-Packard (U.S.), 195; in India, 132, 181, 191, 217, 281n.27; in Korea, 200
Hindustan Computers Ltd. (HCL) (I), 157, 168–71, 173, 190–91, 218, 267n.39, 269n.14, 281nn.24 and 27; international alliances with, 185, 190–91, 202, 217, 279–80n.10, 281n.22
Hindustan Reprographics (I) 170–71
Hirschman, Albert, 22, 252n.19, 254–55n.23, 259n.78, 260n.13; on international division of labor, 7; on midwife role, 80, 211, 224; on state action, 31–32, 36–38, 41, 44, 48, 57, 221
Hitachi (Japan), 190, 200, 282n.46

Honeywell (U.S.), 200, 265n.7
Honeywell-Bull (U.S.), 267n.39, 268n.11, 279–80n.10
Hong Sung Won, 110
HP. *See* Hewlett-Packard (U.S.)
Husbandry role, 13–14, 78, 81, 205, 210; in Brazil, 91, 150, 190, 219, 222–23; in India, 150–52, 205–219; in IT industry, 97, 140–52, 212, 218; in Korea, 89, 140–49, 205, 219–20; in textile industry, 89–91
Hyundai Electronics America, 202
Hyundai (K), in automobiles, 91–93, 264nn.55 and 56, 274n.75, 282–83n.51; in electronics, 110, 145, 175, 177, 200–201, 275–76n.10; international alliances of, 200–202

IAS. *See* Indian Administrative Service (IAS)
IBM. *See* International Business Machines (IBM) (U.S.)
ICL. *See* International Computers Ltd. (ICL) (Britain)
ICS. *See* Indian Civil Service (ICS)
ICs. *See* Integrated circuits
IDB. *See* Industrial Development Bureau (IDB) (Taiwan)
IDM. *See* International Data Management (IDM) (I)
Import quotas, 100, 263n.41. *See also* "Greenhouses"; Protectionism
Incentives, state, for new industry, 80. *See also* Midwife role
India, 11, 44, 60; auto industry in, 92; comparative advantage of, 215; education in, 151, 170, 172, 275n.87; engineers in, 170–73, 185, 195–96, 215, 268n.6, 270n.27; exports from, 168–69, 184, 194–96, 204–209, 214, 280n.18; fiscal problems in, 153; "greenhouse" in, 16, 168, 170, 212; imports to, 182–83; IT industry in, 15, 104–6, 113–16, 152–53, 160, 168–73, 190–96, 268n.6, 277–78n.38; landowners in, 68; military in, 106; PC market in, 193; private capital in, 68–69, 91, 112–14; research and development in, 148, 150–52; SOEs in, 69–70, 130–35, 213, 259n.52; software in, 147, 168–73, 190–96, 204, 209, 214, 277nn.36 and 37; and steel

India (*cont.*)
  industry, 86–88, 261nn.24 and 28,
  262nn.30–33; telecommunications system in, 270n.23, 272n.56; textile industry in, 8, 75–76, 90–91; TNCs in, 168,
  212 (*see also* IBM in India); wars involving, 106. *See also* Indian state
Indian Administrative Service (IAS), 66
Indian Civil Service (ICS), 66
Indian Institutes of Technology (IIT), 151,
  275n.87
Indian state, 12–15, 66–70, 71; autonomy
  of, 237; corruption of, 67, as custodian,
  14, 112–16, 157; as demiurge, 112,
  114–15; embeddedness of, 69, 209; husbandry by, 150–52, 205, 219, 281n.30;
  members of, 66–67, 259n.51, 266nn.24
  and 25; midwifery by, 16, 116, 134–35,
  154, 212; protectionism by, 112, 223;
  regulations by, 14, 210; relations of,
  with industry, 68–70, 73, 98, 104–6,
  127–152–53; relations of, with society,
  67–68, 130 208–9, 236
Industrial automation, 189
Industrial Development Bureau (IDB) (Taiwan), 55, 56, 139, 257n.25
Industrial transformation, and society, 38,
  227–234; states and, 4–6, 9–17, 22, 39,
  77–84, 93–94, 255. *See also individual
  industries and states*
Industries. *See* Automobile industry; Industrial transformation; IT industry; Sectors, industrial; Steel industry; Textile industry
Informatics. *See* Information technology
  (IT) industry
Informatics Law (B), 185, 279n.5
Information technology (IT) industry, 11,
  94–98, 102–6; in Brazil (*see* Brazil, IT industry in); changing structure of, 95,
  184–85, 278n.50; in India (*see* India, IT
  industry in); in Korea (*see* Korea, IT industry in); in Japan (*see* Japan, IT industry in); state roles in, 83, 102, 152–54,
  207–26, 232–34; in the 1970s, 94–95,
  117, 126; in the 1980s, 94–95, 26, 185,
  213; in the 1990s, 185–88
Infrastructure, 4; electric power, 65; state
  provision of, 132; telecommunications,
  100, 134–35, 142, 146, 213, 270n.23,
  272n.56

Institutional analysis. *See* Comparative institutional approach
Integrated circuits, 103–4, 160. *See also*
  DRAM chips; Semiconductors
INTEL, 168, 171
Intermediate states, 45, 60–70, 77, 246;
  state reconstruction in, 143–44. *See also*
  Brazil; India
International Business Machines (IBM)
  (U.S.), 99, 100, 102–4, 166, 207–8,
  283n.1; in Brazil, 108–9, 158, 161–62,
  165, 182–83, 187, 204, 217, 223,
  276n.14, 279n.7, 280n.13; in India, 16,
  106, 114, 170, 171, 181–82, 212,
  266n.23, 279n.1; in Japan, 100; joint
  ventures with, 184–85, 200–201,
  283n.52
International Computers Ltd. (ICL) (Britain), 99, 169, 214
International Data Management (IDM) (I),
  171, 277n.28
International division of labor, 6–10, 82–
  83, 95, 102, 214, 216, 252n.20
International markets. *See* Markets, international
Internationalization, 180; "new" (*see* New
  internationalization); "old," 182–84,
  187, 197, 217–18
Iochpe group, 279–80n.10
IT. *See* Information technology (IT) industry
Itaú group (B), 121–22
Itautec (B), 155, 162–64, 185–86, 218,
  275n.1, 280n.13; and IBM, 182, 186,
  188, 204, 217, 279n.7

Jamaica, 84
Japan: bureaucracy in, 49, 256nn.10, 11,
  13, 14 and 15; as developmental state;
  47–50, 58, 245; IT industry in, 96, 99–
  104, 148, 176, 278nn.44 and 53; Lib-
  eral Democratic Party in, 234–35, 243
Japan Development Bank (JDB), 101
Japan Electronic Computer Corporation
  (JECC), 101, 265n.10
Japanese technology, licensed, 178
JDB. *See* Japan Development Bank (JDB)
JECC. *See* Japan Electronic Computer Cor-
  poration (JECC)
Johnson, Chalmers, 18, 47–49, 58,
  253n.31, 256nn.9 and 10, 259n.6

Joint projects (state-private) 38, 41–42, 60
Joint ventures (international), 184; in Brazil, 65, 122, 262n.37, 267n.32, 279nn.4 and 5, 280n.13, in Japan, 100 257n.25, 262–263n.37, 265n.7; in Korea, 75, 282n.42; in Taiwan, 257n.25. *See also* International Business Machines (IBM) (U.S.)
Jones, Leroy, P., 82, 83, 93, 259n.52

Kahler, Miles, 27
Kang Mungu, 256n.13
Kanodia, L. S., 173, 193
Karaosmanoglu, Atilla, 21, 28, 39, 244
Karl, Terry, 85, 252n.19, 260n.13
Katzenstein, Peter, 240–42, 254n.19, 285n.22
Kawasaki Steel, 262–63n.37
Kenya, 34–35
Kerala (I), 17, 235–0, 246–47, 284nn.13–17, 284–85n.18; land reform in, 236–238; state-society relations in, 238, 246
Killick, Tony, 253n.6
Kim, Linsu, 202
Kim Byung Kook, 51–52
Kim Jae-Ik, 231, 232
Kim Sung Jin, 110
KIST. *See* Korean Institute of Science and Technology (KIST)
KIT. *See* Korea Institute of Technology (KIT)
KMT regime. *See* Taiwan
Korea, 11; auto industry in, 91–92, 263n.48, 264nn.52, 54, 55 and 56; comparative advantage of, 215; domestic market in, 126, 159, 163, 165, 197; education in, 147–48, 274n.79; exports from, 74–75, 87–88, 91–92, 143, 160, 173–76, 179, 184, 196–204, 278n.44; "greenhouse" in, 16, 111–12, 212, imports to, 182–82, 197–98, 262n.30, 276n.15, 278n.53; industry in, 11, 74–75, 143 (*see also* Chaebol [K]); IT development in, 104, 109–12, 124–27, 143, 214, 222–23, 275n.4, 276nn.16 and 17, 278n.47, 282n.42; military in, 10; research and development in, 147–48, 212–13; and semiconductors, 160; SOEs in, 74–75, 141–46, 259n.52; software in, 274n.71, 277nn.36 and 37; steel industry in, 74–75, 86, 87, 261–62n.29;

textile industry in, 74, 89–90, 283–84n.2; TNCs in, 110–11, 149–198–99; trade unions in, 227–28, 230, 282n.2, 283–84n.2. *See also* Korean state
Korea Institute of Technology (KIT), 147
Korean Institute of Science and Technology (KIST), 274n.78
Korean state: challenges to, 229–30; as custodian, 124; as developmental state, 51–54, 71, 105, 109–12, 222–23, 228–30, 244, 245, 285n.25; embedded autonomy of, 12–13, 17, 124, 126–27, 146, 209; embeddedness of, 53; husbandry by, 140–49, 205, 219; members of, 51, midwifery by, 14–16, 198, 212; political repression by, 230–31, 245; regulations by, 127; relations of, with industry, 14, 53–54, 146, 159; relations of, with society, 126, 140, 230–31, 245
Korean Telecommunications Authority (KTA), 142, 272n.56
KTA. *See* Korean Telecommunications Authority
Kubitschek, Juscelino, 61
Kuomintang (KMT) regime. *See* Taiwan
Kuwait, 193
Kwangyang Bay (K), 74, 262n.35

LABO (B), 162, 266n.29, 279–80n.10
Labor: in Austria, 241–42; developmental success and, 227–32; engineering, 15, 171–73, 195–96, 214; low-cost, 157, 159, 196–97, 215–16, 284–85n.18; political role of, 229–31, 241; skilled, 162, 166, 267n.35; unions of, 227–28, 230, 241
Lal, Deepak, 66, 69
Lall, Sanjaya, 26n.24
Landowners, 37, 62–63, 258n.49; in India, 68
Lange, Ove, 192
LDP (Liberal Democratic Party, Japan), 234–35, 243; model, 235, 243
Leading Edge (U.S.), 201, 278n.52
Lee Byung Chul, 141, 176
Levi, Margaret, 255n.3
Lew, Seok-Jin, 264n.55
Licensed technology, 117, 121–22, 171, 178, 184, 189, 192, 265n.7, 266n.29, 267n.41, 268n.12
Linsu Kim, 274n.79

Lipton, Michael, 27
List, Friedrich, 7, 111, 231n.12
Local private capital: in Brazil (*see* Brazil, local entrepreneurs in); in India 68–69, 91, 112–14; in Korea, 53–54, 146, 159 (*see also* Chaebol); as political constituency, 205, 208, 219, 224, 235; and states, 16–17, 57–58, 79–81, 93, 223, 268n.5; in Taiwan, 56–57; and transnational capital, 15–16

Machines Bull (France), 279n.56
Machline group (B), 186
Maharastra (I), 133–34
Malabar. *See* Kerala (I)
Malaysia, 275n.4
Malhotra, Arjun, 157
Manaus free zone (B), 122–23, 158
Mann, Michael, 45
March, James G., 253n.30
Market reserve (B), 117, 150, 165, 183, 187, 267n.31, 276n.14; effects of, 120–21, 161, 271n.42; exploitation of, 120–21, 209, 211
Markets: domestic, 89–90, 143, 157, 159; international, 8, 85, 89, 94, 153, 183, 216, 231, 245–46; for IT products, 100–101, 157; in neo-utilitarian theory, 23, 25–27, 33; and society, 26–27, 29; and state, 21, 27, 29–30, 39, 57–58, 74–76, 82, 101; for textiles, 57–58, 89–90
Martins, Luciano, 252n.23
marx, Karl, 24, 229, 234
Marxism, 5, 45, 252n.19, 260n.13
Masan free export zone (K), 282n.42
Mason, Edward S., 82, 83, 93, 259n.52
Mathias Machline (B), 163
Meltron (I), 133–34, 139, 270n.22
Memory chips. *See* Semiconductors
Menon, M.G.K., 266n.22
Mentor Graphics (U.S.), 190, 281n.21
Mexico, 237, 263n.50
Meyer-Stamer, Jorg, 124
Microcomp (I), 168–69
Microcomputers. *See* Personal computers
Microtec (B), 161, 162
Midwife role, 13–16, 80–81, 93- 126, 210–12, 224; in Brazil, 14–16, 116, 124, 164, 187, 212; and husbandry, 78, 81, 97, 140; in India, 16, 116, 134–35, 154, 212; and internationalization, 16,

83, 184, 204, 217; and IT industry, 97, 111, 126, 153–54, 160, 168, 170, 178–80, 183–84; in Japan, 100–101; in Korea, 14–16, 89,198, 212. *See also* "Greenhouses"
Migdal, Joel, 36–38, 40–41, 45, 47, 254nn.20 and 21
Military. *See* Brazil, military in; Security and IT industry
Minas Gerais (B), 63
Mineral extraction, 83–86, 260–61n.20
Minicom. *See* Ministry of Telecommunications (B)
Minicomputers. *See* Computers, mini
Ministry of Communications (MOC) (K), 110–12, 141–42, 144, 146, 209, 221–22, 272n.56
Ministry of International Trade and Industry (MITI) (Japan), 48, 50, 100, 101, 111, 139, 256n.9
Ministry of Science and Technology (MOST) (K), 112, 146–47
Ministry of Telecommunications (Minicom) (B), 122
Ministry of Trade and Industry (MTI) (K), 112, 125
MITI. *See* Ministry of International Trade and Industry (MITI) (Japan)
Mitsubishi (Japan), 93, 264n.56, 264–65n.1
Mobutu Sese Seko, Joseph, 43–47, 255–56n.5
MOC. *See* Ministry of Communications (K)
Modi group (I), 193
Moe, Terry, 33
Moorthy, K. Krishna, 88
MOST. *See* Ministry of Science and Technology (K)
Motorola (U.S.), 159, 168; in Korea, 201, 227–28
MS-DOS, 167
MTI. *See* Ministry of Trade and Industry (K)
Murilo de Carvalho, José, 62

Nadar, Shiv, 157, 170–71
NAIS. *See* National Administrative Systems (K)
Nakane, Chie, 49
Narasimhan, Ashok, 171
Nasser, Gamal Abdel, 36–38, 226

National Administrative Information System (NAIS) (K), 143–46, 281n.22
National Advanced Systems (NAS), 190
National Computerization Coordinating Committee (K), 110, 112
National Economic Development Bank (BNDE) (B), 61, 118, 128–29, 271n.37
National Informatics Centre (NIC) (I), 152
National Institute of Information Technology (NIIT) (I), 170
National Intelligence Service (SNI) (B), 118
National Resources Commission (NRC) (Taiwan), 55
Nationalism, 216, 217, 219
NCCC. See National Computerization Coordinating Committee (K)
NEC (Japan), 187, 200, 265n.7, 279n.56, 280n.11
Neoclassical economics, 23–24
Neoliberalism, 21, 27–28, 229–30, 245, 252–53n.28
Neo-utilitarian theory, 21–29, 32–34, 36, 40, 45–46, 71, 95, 220–25, 232, 244, 246, 248, 253n.4
New internationalization, 15–16, 180–82, 184, 189, 192–93, 203, 204, 216–18, 281n.27; and India, 16, 194–95; state involvement in, 204–6, 224–25
New Projects Division (I), 133–34
Newly industrializing countries (NICs), 4, 11, 253n.6, 261n.21, 261–62n.29
NIC. See National Informatics Centre (I)
NICnet, 152
NICs. See Newly industrializing countries
Nippon Steel, 74, 262–63n.37
Nippon Telephone and Telegraph (NTT) (Japan), 101
Niskanen, William A., 253n.4
Norsk Data (Norway), 268n.12, 268–69n.13
North, Douglass C., 33–34
NTT. See Nippon Telephone and Telegraph (NTT) (Japan)

O'Connor, David, 143, 197, 266nn.16 and 17, 277n.37, 283n.52
OEM. See Original Equipment Manufacture (OEM)
Ohlin, 9
Okimoto, Daniel I., 49–50, 58
Olivetti, 136, 193, 200

Olsen, Johan P., 253n.30
Olsen, Kenneth, 208
Olson, Mancur, 254n.15
Open economies, 246
Oriental Precision Co. (K), 175
Original Equipment Manufacture (OEM), 178, 278n.52

Park Chung Hee, 52–53, 74, 76, 110, 125, 264n.55, 283n.2, 283–84n.2
Pelúcio, José, 271nn.37 and 38
Pereira Nunes, Artur, 267n.33
Personal computers (PCs), 266n.17; in Brazil, 126, 138, 160–61, 165; clones of, 177–78, 215; in India, 131, 170–72; in Korea, 140, 165, 173–78
Pertech Computers Ltd. (I), 131, 169, 172, 280n.18
Peru, 84–85
Petrobras (B), 65, 274n.81
Petrochemical industry, 85, 256n.9, 271n.38; in Brazil, 65, 267n.32
Phillips, 167
Pitroda, S. R. "Sam," 270n.23, 271n.34
Pohang Institute of Technology (POSTEC) (K), 147
Pohang Iron and Steel Company (POSCO) (K), 74–76, 87, 261n.26, 263n.38
Polanyi, Karl, 18, 22, 29
Pontusson, Johan, 242
Porter, Michael E., 9
POSCO. See Pohang Iron and Steel Company (POSCO) (K)
POSTEC. See Pohang Institute of Technology (K)
Prebisch, Raul, 7, 231n.13
Predatory state, 12, 50, 58, 72, 77, 248, 255n.3; Zaire as, 43–47
Premji, Azim, 171
Prices, IT, 165, 177–78, 276n.12 and 13, 277n.23
Prime Computers, 190
Private capital. See Local private capital; Transnational corporations
Privatization, 89, 263n.38
PROCOMP (B), 189
Prológica (B), 161
Protectionism, 78, 101, 111–12, 223. See also "Greenhouses"
PSI Data Systems (I), 151, 172, 185, 191
Pyrethrum, 254n.15

Quotas, import, 100, 263n.410. *See also* "Greenhouses"; Protectionism

Rao, A. S., 266n.22
Ratcliff, Richard, 257–58n.38, 258n.49
Ravindran, V. K., 172
RAX (Rural Automatic Exchange) (I), 135
RCA (U.S.), 265n.7
Regulations, 13, 77–78, 83, 89, 90–91, 164, 210. *See also* custodian role of state; Midwife role of state
Reliance group (U.S.), 189, 263n.44
Rent-seeking, 24, 46, 179, 223. *See also* Neo-utilitarian theory
Research and development, 143, 147–52; in Brazil, 148–50, 188; in India, 148, 150–52; in Korea, 147–48, 212–13
Revealed institutional advantage, 260n.17
Rhee Syngman, 51–52
Rima (B), 189
Ripper, Mario Dias, xiii, 107, 207, 265–66n.15
Rogers, Everett M., 268n.6, 270nn.27 and 32, 272n.56
Roh Tae Woo, 227
Rudolph, Lloyd J. and Susanne Hoeber Rudolph, 66, 67, 259n.54
Rueschemeyer, Dietrich, 49, 254nn.18, 19
Rural elites. *See* Landowners
Russia, 253n.10

SAILNET (I), 269n.19
Samsung (K), 110, 141, 145, 175, 176, 214, 164n.55, 273n.60, 274n.75, 275–76n.10, 282n.45; and IBM, 182, 202, 283n.52; subsidiaries of, 200–202. *See also* Chaebol
Samsung Semiconductor Inc. (U.S.), 202
Samuels, Richard J., 50, 63
Sarabhai, Vikram, 106
Sarney, José, 167
Saur, Ricardo, 107, 136, 164, 271n.37
SBC. *See* Brazilian Computation Society
Schmitter, Philippe, 242, 260n.12
Schneider, Ben R., 61, 63, 64, 257n.37, 258n.44, 262n.34
Schumpeterian, 90, 223; anti-Schumpeterian bargain, 68, 130, 235, 268n.5 (defined)
Schvartzman, Simón R., xiii, 155, 163
Schware, Robert, 195, 204, 277n.36

SCL. *See* Semiconductor Complex Ltd. (I)
SCOPUS (B), 161, 162, 166–67, 187, 267n.41, 276n.18, 280n.11
SECOMU. *See* Seminars on Computation at the University (SECOMU) (B)
Secretaria Especial de Informática (SEI) (B), 112, 153–54, 161, 207, 209–11, 213, 221–22, 267n.33, 276n.18
Sectors, industrial, 77, 81–94
Security and IT industry, 100, 106, 108, 118, 125, 131
SEI. *See* Secretaria Especial de Informática (B)
Seidman, Gay, 18, 229
Sekhar, P. S., 134
Sematech (U.S.), 96, 264n.58
Semiconductor Complex Ltd. (SCL) (I), 277–78n.38
Semiconductor industry, 103, 159–60, 167, 188, 214, 215, 272n.54, 278n.46; in Brazil, in India, 277–78n.38; in Korea, 141, 173–77, 197, 215; and memory chips, 174, 176, 179; in Taiwan, 272n.52
Semiconductors, 103–4, 141, 168
Seminars on Computation at the University (SECOMU) (B), 118
Seghaas, Dieter, 9
Sengupta, Ramprasad, 262n.32
Seoul (K), 227–28, 274n.71
Seshagiri, N., 115, 152
Shafer, D. Michael, 82, 85, 260n.13
Shapiro, Helen, 65, 263n.49
Sharp (Japan), 163–64
Sharpe, Kenneth, 263n.50
Shepsle, Kenneth, 33
Shigeru, Sabashi, 265n.2
Shipbuilding in Korea, 87
Shivdasani, Prem, 279n.1
SID Informatica (B), 162–64, 185–88, 266n.29, 279n.9
SIDERBRÁS (B), 262n.36
Signetics, 159
Silicon Valley (U.S.), 201–2
Silver, Morris, 253n.4
Singapore, 59, 190, 257n.26, 281n.20
Singhal, Arvind, 268n.6, 270nn.27 and 32, 272n.56
Sinjin (K), 264n.55
SISNE (B), 167
Sistema (B), 189, 204

Skocpol, Theda, 251n.2, 254n.18
Smith, Adam, 26, 71
SNI. *See* Brazil, National Intelligence Service in
Social classes, 72, 97, 107, 236–39, 241, 252n.18. *See also* State-society relations
Socialist party in Austria, 241
SOD, 137
SOEs. *See* State-owned enterprises
Software: in Brazil, 166–67; custom, 194–95; design of, 134–35, 137–38, 145, 177, 215; in India, 157, 168–73, 190–96, 204, 209, 214, 277nn.36 and 37; and internationalization, 184–85; in Korea, 173; packaged, 277n.36, 281n.34, 282nn.35 and 39
Somalia, 59
SOX, 128, 137–38
Sperry (U.S.), 159
Sridharan, Eswarhan, 106
Srinivasan, T. N., 23, 26
Ssangyong (K), 264n.55
State, 18; and class structure, 238–39; constituencies of, 204, 208, 219, 224, 235, 246; as entrepreneur, 13, 31–33, 48, 75, 128–54, 213, 221–22, 248, 260–61n.20 (*see also* Demiurge role of state; State-owned enterprises); and industrial transformation, 4–6, 9–17, 22, 39, 77–84, 93–94, 98, 255; and IT industry, 95–97, 208–9, 218, 220–21, 232; and local private capital, 14, 31, 94, 146–49, 211, 224–26, 228–32, 234–35, 240–42, 245 (*see also individual countries*); roles of, 5, 13–15, 93–94, 77–84 (*see also* Custodian role; Demiurge role; Husbandry role; Midwife role)
State bureaucracy, 29–30, 40, 71, 246, 250; capacity of, 71, 85, 210, 222–23, 236–37, 244; and development, 23, 34–35, 40–41, 203–6, 208, 250, 268n.5; members of, 58–59, 61, 233, 238, 244; "pockets of efficiency" in, 61, 65, 73; selectivity by, 58, 71, 244
State-owned enterprises (SOEs), 14, 79–82, 129–54; in Brazil, 14, 129, 136–39; in India 69–70, 130–35, 168–69; in Korea, 74–75, 141–46, 259n.52; in mineral extraction, 83–86; in Taiwan, 55–56. *See also* Demiurge role
State-society relations, 18, 22–24, 28, 35–

38, 59, 208, 226, 228, 234, 244, 248, 249; in Brazil, 63; and development, 41–42, 246; in East Asia, 38; in India, 67–68, 130, 208–9; in Japan, 49–50; in Taiwan, 56; in Zaire, 47. *See also* Embeddedness
Statism, 22
Steel industry, 8, 74–75, 83, 86–89, 261–63; in India, 86–88, 261n.28, 262nn.30–33; in Korea, 74–75
Stephens, Evelyne Huber, 18, 253n.32, 260n.18, 260–61n.20
Stephens, John, 18, 252–53n.28
Sterling Computers Ltd. (Britain), 131, 169, 172
Streeck, Wolfgang, 242
Subramanian, C. R., 268–69n.13
Subsidiaries, foreign, 187, 203, 282n.37; in Brazil, 112, 161–62, 165; in India, 116, 190; in Korea, 159, 197–99
Subsidies, state: for new industry, 80; in textile industry, 89–90. *See also* Midwife role
SUFRAMA. *See* Superindencia for Amazonia (B)
Sun Microsystems (U.S.), 104, 192, 201
Sun Yat-sen, 55
Superintendencia for Amazonia (SUFRAMA) (B), 122
Supermini computers. *See* Computers, supermini
Sybase (U.S.), 281n.24
Sycor (U.S.), 136
Systems integration, 177, 204, 268–69n.13, 278n.51

Taiwan: bureaucracy in, 55, 256n.20; demiurge role of state in, 256n.23, 261n.27; industrial transformation in, 51, 54–59, 245, 278n.46; SOEs in, 55–56, 256n.21, 272n.52, 283n.53; state-industry relations in, 39, 56–58; state-society relations in, 56; textile industry in, 57, 63, 80
Tamil Nadu (I), 269n.19, 284n.13
Tandem (U.S.), 192, 269–70n.20
Tariffs, 13, 80, 100–101, 265n.16. *See also* "Greenhouses"
Tata Consultancy Systems (TCS) (I), 157, 168–69, 173, 193, 195, 266n.66, 269–70n.20

Tata group (I), 68, 157
Tata Information Systems Ltd. (TISL) (I), 181–82; and IBM, 184, 193
Tata Iron and Steel (I), 261n.24
Tata Unisys Ltd. (TUL) (I), 168–69, 266n.26
Taub, Richard P., 258n.47
Tavares, Christina, 119
TCS. See Tata Consultancy Systems Ltd. (I)
TDX (K), 143, 146
Technology, global standards of, 120, 145, 160, 182; Japanese, 178; licensing of, 100, 130, 178, 185, 266n.29, 267n.39
Tecnicos, 179, 252n.24
Telebras (B), 149–50, 274n.81
Telecommunications networks, 134–35, 142, 146, 273n.62; in Japan, 100. See also Electronic swtiching systems
Tendler, Judith, 61, 65
Texas Instruments (U.S.), 116, 167, 194, 201, 266n.27, 282n.37
Textile industry, 8, 83, 89–91, 263nn.41–47, 264n.57; in India, 75–76, 90–91; in Korea, 74, 89–90; in Taiwan, 57
Third World countries: bureaucracy in, 24, 40; development in, 31; and global economy, 94–95; and IT industry, 96; and mineral extraction, 84–86; and steel industry, 86
TICOM, 145, 273n.68
Tilly, Charles, 5
TNCs. See Transnational capital
Tokyo Law School, 256n.11
Tolerant (U.S.), 145, 273n.68, 274n.73, 281n.22
Tollison, Robert D., 24, 253n.4
Toye, John, 254n.16
Trade. See Markets
Trade theory, 7–8
Trade unions: in Austria, 241; in Korea, 227, 230, 283n.2, 283–84n.6
Transnational capital (TNCs), 79, 94; and automobile industry, 91–93; in Brazil, 63, 107–9, 111–12, 158, 188–89, 210–11; and high technology, 83; in India, 106, 116, 168, 190, 212; and Korea, 110–11, 159, 198–201, 283n.52; and local firms, 182–84, 216–17, 219, 224; and oil, 85; and SOEs, 81; and steel industry, 87, 88. See also individual companies
Tri-pé (B), 118, 136, 263n.48, 267n.32, 271n.38
Trigem (K), 177
Tubarão (B), 262–63n.37
TUL. See Tata Unisys Ltd. (I)
Tullock, Gordon, 25
Turing, Alan, 99

U.S. Steel, 75
Unisoft (U.S.), 128
UNISYS (U.S.), 181; in Brazil, 162, 183, 187; in India, 193, 278n.53
United States, 259n.6, 278n.53, 280n.18; and Brazil, 64, 122, 138, 183, 189, 276n.18, 279n.9; Indian engineers in, 151; IT industry in, 96, 148, 149, 264n.58; market in, 177, 201, 254n.14, 278n.44; subsidiaries in, 202
UNIX, 128, 137–38, 168, 170, 181m, 194, 268n.1, 272nn.48 and 50, 273–74n.69, 277n.25, 279n.9. See also AT&T
UPTRON (I), 276n.22
Uricoechea, Fernando, 62
Usiminas (B), 262–63n.37
Uttar Pradesh (I), 276n.22

Vargas, Getúlio, 61–62, 87
Vernon, Raymond, 7
Very Large Scale Integration (VLSI) project (Japan), 101, 265n.12
Vijayaker, S. R., 115, 266nn.24 and 25

Wade, Robert, 18, 22, 38–41, 44, 57, 67, 234, 253n.31, 256nn.20 and 22, 257n.25
Wafer fabrication, 174, 176–77, 215, 272n.52, 275n.4, 278n.41
Wallerstein, Immanuel, 231nn.8 and 14
Wang (Japan), 193–94
Waterbury, John, 27, 79
Weber, Max, 5, 18, 21–22, 29–30, 39–42, 33–39, 71, 72. See also State bureaucracy, Weberian ideal of
Welfare, 6; in Kerala, 235–37
Wells, Louis T., 7
Western Design Center, 201
Williams, Gavin, 255n.1

Williamson, Oliver E., 26

Willis, Eliza J., 257n.33

WIPRO (I), 157, 169, 171–72, 191, 266n.26, 281n.32, 282n.35

Working class, 239; in Austria, 241. *See also* Labor; Social classes; Trade Unions

World Bank: and bureaucracy, 21, 28, 39, 40, 58, 255n.25; and Korea, 74, 231, 261n.26; and Japan, 50; and Taiwan, 56

World War II, effects of, 245

World-system theory, 251n.14, 252nn.18 and 20

Yin, K. Y., 54, 57, 63, 80, 89, 256n.18

Yun, Young-min, 230, 283nn.1 and 5

Zaire, 43–47, 71, 85, 229, 248, 255–56n.5, 260n.19

Zambia, 85, 260n.19

Zeitlin, Maurice, 9, 18, 257–58n.38, 258n.49

Zenith (U.S.), 172

ZFM. *See* Manaus Free Zone

Zymos (U.S.), 201, 282n.48